Appalachia on Our Mind

Appalachia
on Our Mind

The Southern Mountains and
Mountaineers in the American
Consciousness, 1870–1920

by Henry D. Shapiro

The University of North Carolina Press
Chapel Hill

© 1978 by The University of North Carolina Press
All rights reserved
Manufactured in the United States of America
ISBN 0-8078-1293-5
Library of Congress Catalog Card Number 77-2301
First printing, April 1978
Second printing, September 1979
Third printing, May 1986

Library of Congress Cataloging in Publication Data
Shapiro, Henry D.
  Appalachia on our mind.

  Bibliography: p.
  Includes index.
  1. Appalachian Mountains, Southern. I. Title
F217.A65S52   301.29'74   77-2301
ISBN 0-8078-1293-5
ISBN 0-8078-4158-7 (pbk.)

For my great teachers,
Joseph Shapiro and Harry Wolfson

Contents

Preface

This is not a history of Appalachia. It is a history of the idea of Appalachia, and hence of the invention of Appalachia. It attempts to examine the origins and consequences of the idea that the mountainous portions of eight or nine southern states form a coherent region inhabited by an homogeneous population possessing a uniform culture. It argues that the emergence of this idea, between 1870 and 1900, involved an attempt to understand reality, or more precisely reality perceived in a particular way from a particular point of view, and it seeks to explicate the manner in which the idea of Appalachia came to be used as a way of dealing with the "strange land and peculiar people" of the southern mountains. It is thus a history of America and of the American consciousness, for its concern is with the attempts of Americans to understand the nature and meaning of their civilization, and to develop modes of action which to them seem consonant with this understanding. And as such it is itself an attempt to understand the nature and meaning of American civilization, and hence part of a larger work in which Americans have been engaged for some two hundred years.

At another level, the concern of this book is with the taxonomy of reality, the process by which experience is defined, ordered, organized into coherent and actionable schemes, the process by which a new reality or reality newly perceived is integrated into existing knowledge, the process by which taxonomic schemes are rearranged to make space for new knowledge, the process by which knowledge becomes the basis for public action. Because this is an essay in intellectual history, it begins with the assumption that the way people view the world determines how they will act in it. It attempts, however, to go beyond conventional studies of the history of ideas and of the history of "influences" by recognizing that the pattern of relationships between ideas and action is significantly more complex than the cause-and-effect model we often use in talking about the role of ideas in human life or as explanations for human behavior. This essay does not assume that men and women are "motivated" by desires or needs, but that desires and needs—and especially the desire and need to understand the world—function in a problem-solving situation to direct problem solving along particular kinds of lines. It also assumes that men and women periodically, like Henry Adams, find that history hits them on the head, that reality seems incomprehensible, disorderly, confusing. How they get that feeling is not the business of this book. What they do once they have it is what I am after here.

In this case, the history that hit them on the head was the perception of the "otherness" of the southern mountains and mountaineers. Between 1870 and 1900, it became clear to a number of persons that the existence of a strange land and peculiar people in the southern mountains could not be understood in terms of contemporary conceptions of America as a unified and homogeneous national entity; and that conventional modes of resolving the dilemma posed by the perception of "deviance" from the American norm by a region or a people—ascription of geographic, chronological, or ethnic distance which made such "deviance" seem natural and normal—could not be utilized to explain the "deviance" of white, Anglo-Saxon, Protestant, native-born Americans living in the present and within miles of the older centers of American civilization.

Between 1870 and 1900, as a consequence, a number of persons acknowledged this dilemma explicitly or, more often, implicitly by attempting to deal with it. Especially after the mid-1880s, a number of persons attempted to construct "explanations" for Appalachian otherness, and a number of persons—sometimes the same—proposed or actually engaged in remedial, philanthropic, benevolent, or uplifting activity designed to alter the reality of mountain life, so that the region and its people might be integrated more fully into the nation. That process, discussed in the first chapters which follow, yielded in the end the explanation that Appalachian otherness was "natural" because Appalachia was a legitimately discrete region of the nation. The second half of this book is an attempt to examine the consequences of the notion of Appalachian regionalism and its corollary

—that the mountaineers form a legitimately distinct people—for thought and action in America during the first decades of the twentieth century.

Most phenomena of discovery involve the perception of a new reality, the "fact" of which—the "fact" of America after 1492, for example—must be integrated into existing notions about the nature of the world. Sometimes the result of such discovery is the abandonment of old notions and the erection of new schemes for the organization and description of reality. Sometimes the result is a reinterpretation of the newly discovered "fact," so that it can be understood in terms of the old notions, catalogued in terms of the old schema. In either case, as in all the cases between these extremes, the "cause" of the process of reconceptualization is the accident of discovery itself.

The "discovery" of Appalachia after 1870 was not a phenomenon of this sort, for it did not involve the perception of a new reality. Rather it followed from the recognition that the well-known realities of southern mountain life were not consonant with new notions about the nature of America and American civilization which gained currency during this period: that America was, or was becoming, or ought to become a unified and homogeneous national entity, and that what characterized such an entity was a coherent and uniform national culture. Where these notions came from and how they became a convention of the American consciousness after the Civil War is the subject of a different book than this one. It was only in the context of such new notions about the nature of America, however, that the southern mountains and mountaineers became Appalachia, a "strange land and peculiar people" whose existence engaged the attention of Americans after 1870 as it does again in the 1970s. It was only in the context of such new notions about America, that is, that what had earlier seemed normal or at least explicable came after 1870 to seem nonnormal and inexplicable. And it is only in the context of other new notions about the nature of America and American civilization that Appalachia in our own time will ever cease to seem an "other" America.

At least from the second quarter of the nineteenth century, the "peculiarities" of life and landscape in the southern mountains were well known to Americans. The mountains themselves stood as natural curiosities to the first generation of American geologists, who were prevented by the difficulty of obtaining access to the region from engaging in the kind of systematic exploration which made the mountains of New York instead the basis for an "American system" in geology. The botany and to a lesser degree the zoology of the southern mountains also stood outside the experience of naturalists increasingly familiar with the flora and fauna of the more accessible coastal and midwestern sections of the country. Most important, the inhabitants of the southern Appalachians, as backwoodsmen par excellence, seemed as strange to the residents of the seaboard or inland cities of the new nation as did Leatherstocking to the residents of James Fenimore Cooper's fictional Otsego.[1]

The peculiarities of Appalachian geology, botany, and zoology during the first half of the nineteenth century were only "apparent" peculiarities, resulting from the unfamiliarity of the scientific community with the natural history of an as-yet unexplored territory, while the peculiarities of the mountain people were easily understood as temporary and as the product of a natural distance separating the backwoods from civilization. The inevitable progress of civilization would make the natural history of the region familiar to those who cared to know about it just as it would eliminate the disparity between mountain life and the life of the more densely settled portions of the nation. Although a Herman Melville, writing of the prototypical "handsome sailor" whom Ishmael saw at the Spouter Inn and easily identified as a Virginian by his speech and a mountain man by his lankiness, tended to see the mountaineers as romantic figures, while a George Washington Harris, writing of the adventures of Sut Lovingood as the archetypical bumpkin, tended to see the mountaineers in a less flattering manner, in neither case was the existence of a disparate pattern of culture in the rural mountain region of the South in itself a fact worthy of comment.

This early nineteenth century interest in Appalachia possessed two characteristics which distinguish it from the later phenomenon which is our principal concern. First, Appalachia as terra incognita was not seen to differ in this respect from other unexplored or undeveloped areas of the nation, at a time when much of the continent was at the very beginning of European settlement and such commonplace features of the American landscape as waterfalls and prairies could elicit considerable scientific and popular discussion. Second, a conception of Appalachia as a distinct region of the nation did not exist except in physiographic terms, and then only insofar as physiography had human consequences, as on the process of westward migration, for example; the identification of Appalachia as a thing-in-itself was the product of a later consciousness.

By the 1870s, however, the progress of civilization in America, and Americans' self-consciousness of their progress, was such that the apparent persistence of pioneer conditions among the mountain people made Appalachia seem a strange land inhabited by a peculiar people. The existence of a vast, unexplored territory within miles of Cincinnati or Lexington, and as easily accessible by rail from Boston or Indianapolis, moreover, offered opportunities for a new generation of writers in search of exotic "little corners" of the nation suitable for description in the travel sketches and short stories which emerged as important literary forms in this period. The idea that Appalachia was a strange land inhabited by a peculiar people, and hence an exception to what the local colorists saw as the new rule of national unity and homogeneity, received its articulation in the context of the conventions of local color writing as a literary mode.

The same characteristics which appeared to make Appalachia "interesting" to readers and writers of local color sketches also made Appalachia seem available as a suitable area for home-missionary activity beginning in the 1880s. Just as the local colorists persuaded themselves that Appalachia was "unknown" because they had never been there, the home missionaries persuaded themselves that Appalachia was "unchurched" because their own denominations were not represented there. As an "unchurched" area in this special sense, Appalachia was by definition "needy," but what it needed was not only the good news of the Gospels but also the good news of the emergence of a national culture. Upon the local colorists' vision of

Appalachian otherness, the home missionaries imposed a secondary vision of Appalachia as an area in need of assistance from outside agencies. Because of its traditional separation from the slavocrat South, manifested by its reluctance to join the Confederacy, moreover, Appalachia appeared worthy of northern aid.

Both the local-color writers and the Protestant home missionaries had a practical stake in promulgating their respective visions of Appalachia, for the validity of their efforts depended upon public acceptance of assertions that Appalachia was indeed a strange land inhabited by a peculiar people, a discrete region, in but not of America. It should thus come as no surprise that they insisted vigorously on the accuracy of their vision of Appalachian otherness, or that their assertions were made more often in New York and Boston and Philadelphia than in Asheville or Knoxville. And it should come as no surprise either, that their discussions of the nature and meaning of Appalachian otherness were rarely made with reference to the real conditions of mountain life or the normal complexity of social and economic conditions which prevailed in the mountains as in every other section of the nation.

The local colorists and the Protestant home missionaries claimed a monopoly on knowledge about the "true" conditions in Appalachia, and dominated public discussion of the nature of mountain life between 1870 and 1890. Dissenting voices, including those of the mountain people themselves, went largely unheard and the idea that Appalachia was a discrete region of the nation became a convention of the American consciousness by 1890. After this date, as a consequence, two patterns of response to the "fact" of Appalachian otherness developed. Explanation sought to integrate the fact of Appalachian otherness into the conceptual schemes by which American civilization was defined. Systematic social action sought to integrate the mountain region and the mountaineers into modern American life. Both followed from the perception that the existence of Appalachia as a discrete region posed a problem, in that it challenged dominant conceptions of America as a unified and homogeneous nation. Both explanation and systematic social action thus may be said to have functioned as responses to the conceptual dilemma which the existence of Appalachia posed, rather than to the "reality" of Appalachian otherness, as the "idea" of Appalachia became not only a conventional literary image but the basis for public action.

At first glance, this identity of function between explanation and systematic benevolence is hidden from view. It is easy to say that the attempts of "intellectuals"—who are so defined only by the fact of their making the attempt—to solve an abstract problem are "responses" to a conceptual dilemma. Our own sympathy for the plight of people living in underdeveloped areas or participating in underdeveloped cultures predisposes us to assume that late nineteenth-century efforts to meliorate the conditions of mountain life must have been a natural response to a genuine need on the part of an emerging philanthropic sensibility. There was nothing at all natural about the inauguration of benevolent work in the southern mountains after the mid-1880s, however. Indeed even those most active in the mountain field acknowledged that the "need" for benevolent work among the mountaineers lay more in the anomaly of Appalachia's existence as a discrete region of the nation than in the particular conditions which prevailed in the southern mountains, about which they knew very little.

Neediness, after all, does not inhere in the objects of systematic benevolence, but is a characteristic attributed to them as a result of their deviance from particular social or cultural norms. By 1890, the southern mountain region was by definition an area characterized by such deviance, and hence an appropriate field for systematic benevolence. While different agencies entered the mountain field at different times and for different reasons, and attempted to carry out different kinds of programs, the particular manifestations of the mountaineers' alleged deviance from the social and cultural norms of American civilization were less important to the conduct of benevolent work than the structural deviance which followed from the fact of Appalachian otherness. For the first decades of benevolent work in Appalachia, indeed, the short stories of Mary Noailles Murfree's *In the Tennessee Mountains* (1884) remained the principal text used to understand the peculiarities of mountain life. Not until after the establishment of the Southern Highland Division of the Russell Sage

Foundation in 1912 was any thought given to whether the mountaineers were in fact "needy," or any attempt made to design programs to meet their needs.[2]

What is significant about this situation is not the doubt thus cast upon the motives of those who initiated benevolent work in Appalachia because of an a priori definition of the mountaineers as "needy" rather than out of a simple humanitarian concern for their welfare, but the relationship it suggests between explanation and social action as responses to the dilemma generated by the perception of Appalachian otherness. Both patterns of action depended upon a definition of the southern mountain region as a strange land inhabited by a peculiar people. Both developed from a point of view in which America appeared as a unified and homogeneous national entity, and Appalachian otherness as an undesirable exception to this rule. Both sought to integrate Appalachia into America—the one literally, by making Appalachia like America, the other figuratively, by explaining Appalachia's deviance from the American norm as only an apparent deviance, or as a deviance which did not threaten the viability of the norm as a statement of American reality. Thus both may be seen as attempts to deal with the dissonance generated by the fact of Appalachian otherness, rather than directly with the reality of Appalachian otherness.

"Cognitive dissonance" is the name of that situation familiar to us both privately and professionally, as students of history, in which a particular conception of reality and reality as perceived do not seem to agree.[3] With reference to any situation of dissonance, we may hypothesize the availability of four modes of action which will provide ways of dealing with the apparent disparity between conceptions and perceptions. All of them, as it turned out, occurred as responses to the perception that Appalachia was a strange land inhabited by a peculiar people.

(1) Dissonance may be contained by the use of metaphor, as when the mountaineers were called "our contemporary ancestors" by William Goodell Frost or "our Southern Highlanders" by John C. Campbell.

(2) Dissonance may be resolved by explanatory statements, as

when the alleged "peculiarites" of mountain life were described as the products of the region's isolation from the rest of the nation or the particular ethnic or cultural heritage of the region's original settlers.

(3) Dissonance may be eliminated through overt action directed at altering the reality perceived as dissonant, in such a way as to make it consonant with conceptions of how reality ought to be, as when the agents of systematic benevolence and the agents of economic modernization for different purposes but in similar ways sought to integrate the mountains and the mountaineers into the mainstream of "modern" American life.

(4) Dissonance may be destroyed by an act of reconceptualization. The reality perceived as dissonant may be redefined as not dissonant, as when in recent years some few observers of Appalachian life have suggested that neither a strange land nor a peculiar people are to be found in the southern mountains. Alternatively, and more frequently, those conceptions about reality which form the assumptions in terms of which a particular aspect of reality is perceived as dissonant may be altered, as when the first halting steps toward redefinition of American civilization as regionalist and pluralist, rather than nationalist in its nature, were taken by those who accepted a vision of Appalachia as a legitimately discrete region and of the mountaineers as a legitimately distinct people, and who subsequently identified the "peculiarities" of mountain life as appropriate aspects of "Appalachian culture."

The utility of such a model in a history of American responses to the "fact" of Appalachian otherness or a history of American "attitudes" toward Appalachia—and this essay assumes that they are the same—lies in its ability to fill the gaps in an otherwise incomplete sequence, to make the connections between apparently distinct phenomena. In this case, as in other "problems" in intellectual history, we have at the start only the "cause" and the "effect," and nothing in between. We have the identification of Appalachia as a strange land inhabited by a peculiar people. We have the phenomena of explanation and systematic social action which utilized this notion. We can either attempt to understand what connects them or we can waste our time arguing with the past, asserting that its vision of reality was incorrect, that Appalachia was not a strange land nor the mountaineers a peculiar people. If the past can't answer, neither does it care.

Our job as historians is not to argue with the past but to understand it, and in attempting to understand we must take great pains to remember that what "actually happened" need not have happened in the way it did; but that "what" actually happened and "how" it actually happened is what we are after. The discovery of Appalachia, we must remember, did not in itself pose a problem which required solution or create a dilemma which demanded resolution. And although the dilemma which the existence of a strange land and peculiar people in the southern mountains posed occurred in the realm of ideas rather than action, it was not for this reason any less a dilemma, nor were the "real-life" responses of railroad promoters or home missionaries for this reason inappropriate.

By talking about cognitive dissonance, we insist that ideas are not natural emanations from objective reality but are the creation of men, and stand between consciousness and reality; and that insofar as ideas become the surrogates for experience and representations of reality, they become also the subjects of discourse and the objects of action. It was not reality that concerned those who saw Appalachia's existence as a bothersome fact to be explained or altered, but reality defined in a particular way. They defined Appalachia as a discrete region and the mountaineers as a distinct people, and responded to the abstract dilemma which this "fact" seemed to pose without asking whether it was a "true" fact, or indeed whether it was *still* a true fact in 1920 as it might have been in 1900 or 1870. Our own judgments about the accuracy of these definitions can have nothing to do with our judgments about their utility in the past.

The present, however, is another matter. We have now the opportunity to reassess the accuracy of that fundamental assumption about Appalachian otherness as it has persisted into the present. We have now the opportunity to acknowledge that it has been this assumption which has generated, during the past decade, a new series of attempts to explain the "deviance" of the mountaineers and of mountain life from the American norm, to integrate the region and its people into "modern" American life, and to legitimize Appalachian otherness by reasserting the existence of an indigenous mountain culture which, if revived among the mountaineers and acknowledged by outsiders, will provide the "Appalachians" with the desirable status of a distinct population in the pluralist American nation. And we have now the opportunity to ask under what circumstances a definition of Appalachia as a strange land inhabited by a peculiar people proves useful in the present, and how, and to whom. This book, indeed, is intended in part to raise such questions for the present as it seeks to answer them with reference to the past.

Each time I have had occasion to work over this manuscript, I have learned new things about the relationship of ideas and action in the history of American responses to the existence of Appalachia. My attempts to share that new knowledge have made this a longer book than I had originally expected it to be, and have delayed its publication far beyond the date I had originally projected for its appearance. I can only beg sincerely the forgiveness of those who have waited, sometimes patiently but always graciously, for the final version of this study, and of those who will now read a book which is both long and detailed, yet not so detailed as to be more than a beginning.

The debts I have incurred during the years when this book was in preparation are predictably numerous. It is my hope that those to friends and colleagues can be repaid in kind, by support and companionship as we help each other try to make sense out of our world, and that those to teachers can be repaid at least indirectly, by passing on not only the content of their teaching but its real substance—the conviction that understanding is possible, and liberating. Those to institutions, however, can only be acknowledged, but they are no less debts for this reason, and no less sincerely felt.

During the past years I have enjoyed the use of library facilities at the University of Cincinnati Library, the New York Public Library, the Ohio State University Library, and the Harvard College Library, and also at the Library of Congress, the Hutchinson Library of Berea College, the University of Kentucky Library, and the Public Library of Cincinnati and Hamilton County, without which this book would not be. Permission to consult and/or quote from manuscripts collections has been graciously granted by the Russell Sage Foundation, the Berea College Archives, the Harvard College Archives, the Houghton Library, the Manuscript Division of the New York Public Library, the Minnesota Historical Society, and the Southern Historical Collection of the University of North Carolina Library.

In 1971–72, I held appointment as Visiting Research Fellow at the Charles Warren Center for Studies in American History at Harvard University, where the preliminary draft of this book was written. I wish to acknowledge my sincere appreciation for the great gift of time provided during that year by the President and Fellows of Harvard University and the President and Board of Directors of the University of Cincinnati, and for the personal and practical support afforded me in Cambridge by the Charles Warren Center, its advisory board and staff, and its familiars in that year and since, especially Oscar Handlin, the late Mary Flugg Handlin, Donald Fleming, Frank Freidel, Bernard Bailyn, the late Merle Fainsod, Barry D. Karl, Stephen Saunders Webb, Stuart Blumin, Willi Paul Adams, Irene Hecht, and Angela Meurer Adams. At the University of Cincinnati, before and since that year, I have enjoyed and profited from my relationship with a group of colleagues and students who have helped me clarify my sense of the historian's task and have been welcome companions in our collective attempt to lead the life of the mind in America. Two of these in particular, Zane L. Miller and Saul Benison, have shared my agonies and joys, and have provided practical advice and material support during the time this book was in composition. They deserve special mention here. They have already my special thanks.

I would also acknowledge at this time my gratitude for the support and companionship afforded by other colleagues, teachers, and friends, who have helped at one time or another, in one way or another, by making it possible for me to understand what this book was about and what I was up to, including first of all Warren I. Susman, who opened more doors than I knew existed and offered more answers than I knew there were questions, but also and hardly less, Richard Maxwell Brown, Hamilton Cravens, David B. Davis, Sanford Elwitt, Paul Wallace Gates, Ronald J. Grele, William H. Harbaugh, David W. Levy, Janet Smith Miller, Barbara Ramusak, Barbara

Gutman Rosenkrantz, Nancy K. Shapiro, Samuel Tate Suratt, and Mary E. Young. In recent years I have enjoyed correspondence and sometimes also conversation with a number of persons interested in the southern mountains and mountaineers, whose encouragement and in a few cases whose practical efforts facilitated the transformation of manuscript into book. For their support I am particularly grateful to Richard B. Drake, Ronald Eller, Malcolm MacDonald, George B. Tindall, and David Walls, and to Anna Mayans and John Patton who graciously shared with me their knowledge of the extent and contents of the John C. and Olive Dame Campbell papers in the Southern Historical Collection.

A grant from the Charles Phelps Taft Memorial Fund of the University of Cincinnati to cover the cost of typing a portion of the manuscript, and a separate and generous grant in aid of publication, are gratefully acknowledged.

Cincinnati, Ohio
5 April 1977

Appalachia on Our Mind

1. The Local-Color Movement and the "Discovery" of Appalachia

In the autumn of 1869, Will Wallace Harney had occasion to journey in the Cumberland Mountains. Who he was and where he was going is of little interest now, and his trip would be forgotten had he not written of his experiences for *Lippincott's Magazine*. Published in 1873 as "A Strange Land and Peculiar People," Harney's account contains anecdotes of the hardships of travel and little stories of Civil War days in the mountains, but hardly a word to justify so striking a title. Yet throughout, one senses Harney's sense of great adventure in a land of "geological and botanical curiosities" where unfamiliar customs prevailed among an unfamiliar population.

> The natives of this region are characterized by marked peculiarities of the anatomical frame. The elongation of the bones, the contour of the facial angle, the relative proportion or disproportion of the extremities, the loose muscular attachment of the ligatures, and the harsh features were exemplified in the notable instance of the late President Lincoln. A like individuality appears in their idiom . . . [which] is peculiar to the mountains, as well on the Wabash and Allegheny, I am told, as in Tennessee.[1]

Harney had been trained as a physician,[2] and may well have been familiar with the sketches of travel published in American medical journals during the first half of the nineteenth century as contributions to an understanding of the climate, geology, and human ecology of the nation, and as raw data from which conclusions concerning the etiology of endemic and epidemic diseases might be drawn.[3] His piece on the southern mountains shows the marks of this tradition, in the distinction drawn between his ostensibly objective observations as a man of science and the more sentimental responses of his female traveling companion toward the picturesque aspects of mountain life, for example; but it is with the newer forms characteristic of the local-color movement in American literature that the sketch must be identified. Its emphasis, like the literary efforts of other physicians of Harney's generation who found science increasingly a monopoly of professionals at a time when literature was opening its doors to amateurs, was on the peculiarities of life in a little-known corner of the nation. Its object was to entertain rather than to inform, by describing a region which seemed interesting because it was so different from the familiar world in which the author and his readers lived. It was composed of splashes of local color, offering a glimpse of a life which was literally exotic.

Harney's sense of the "otherness" of Appalachia must not be seen as a naturally appropriate response to some objective reality, however. It involved the selection of certain aspects of reality for consideration instead of others, and an attempt to order the aspects of reality thus perceived. Most important, his sketch took as its subject not the conditions of the region, by which its otherness was defined, but the fact of otherness. In this "A Strange Land and Peculiar People" is an entirely characteristic, if somewhat early example of local-color writing. But this is as it should be, for the rise of the local-color movement cannot be divorced from the economic, social, and cultural conditions which made literary careers like Harney's possible, and the "discovery" of Appalachia, which rested on a perception of the otherness of mountain life, cannot be divorced from the local-color movement. By an act which was itself conditioned by the demands of his literary medium, Harney made the southern mountains and mountaineers available as subjects for literary treatment. It is an accident of fate that he is remembered (if at all) as a minor figure in the literary exploitation of Florida, where more skillful writers worked, rather than in connection with the literary gold mine of Appalachia which, having discovered, he promptly abandoned for a more congenial setting.

In a real sense it was Harney and the editors of *Lippincott's* who "discovered" Appalachia, for they were the first to assert that "otherness" which made of the mountainous portions of eight southern states a discrete region, in but not of America, and which, after 1890, would seem to place Appalachia and America in radical opposition. The emergence of a tension between Appalachia and America, however, was the result of a twenty-year long process which began with the exploitation of Harney's sense of "otherness" by writers who would use it to justify extensive descriptions of "figures suggestive of the Homeric age" leading lives "as unfamiliar to us as the dweller in a wheeled house on the Scythian steppes,"[4] and to provide ready-made the aesthetic distance which makes such description possible.

The cumulative effect of the publication of the numerous descriptive sketches and short stories of local color which took Appalachia as a subject was the establishment of a conventional view of the mountain region as an area untouched by the progressive and unifying forces that seemed to be at work elsewhere in the United States. In Appalachia, it was said, a style of life and a mode of social organization once common to all areas of the country seemed to persist unchanged after a hundred or more years. Harney's perception of the "otherness" of the mountain region thus became transformed by its reiteration into a conception of Appalachia as a discrete region. From here it was but a short step soon taken to the perception that the characteristics which set the mountain section of the South apart as a strange land inhabited by a peculiar people made Appalachia the opposite of America.

By 1890 the sense of wonder which characterized the local colorists' sketches of Appalachia as terra incognita had begun to disappear. In its place, especially in the "uplift" literature which dates from the last decade of the century, was a new note of distress at the discrepancy between what contemporaries had begun to call the "promise" of American life, on the one hand, and an apparent reality of degradation and degeneracy in the mountain region, on the other; and, more generally, a new note of concern at the anomaly of Appalachia's existence within an otherwise homogeneous and unified America. It is from this time that one may speak of the emergence of a tension between Appalachia and America, and recognize as efforts at resolution of this tension those attempts at explanation which begin to intrude upon the narrative and descriptive sketches published after that date.

The "discovery" of Appalachia with which we are immediately concerned, however, took place in the new middle-class magazines that flourished in the years following the Civil War, in the context of an emerging literature of local color. Although this discovery occurred simultaneously with the first systematic development of the natural resources of the region, it was the strangeness of the strange land rather than the economic opportunities which it offered that made Appalachia seem interesting and hence a suitable field for literary exploitation. This is not to say that the growth of industry did not direct the attention of Americans toward this little-known land, just as the development of resort areas, especially around Asheville, North Carolina, brought outsiders—including home missionaries on vacation and the writers E. A. Pollard, Charles Dudley Warner, Frances Hodgson Burnett, Constance Fenimore Woolson, and Rebecca Harding Davis—into the area; but simply that what Americans saw in the mountains was not the usual but the unusual, not progress but its opposite: a strange land and peculiar people.

The history of American literature between 1870 and 1890 is very much the history of the new magazines—*Lippincott's*, *Scribner's*, *The Century*, *Appleton's*, *The Living Age*, *The American Review of Reviews*, and the prototype of these genteel magazines designed for a mass, middle-class audience, *Harper's New Monthly Magazine*. Established in 1850 by the already prominent publishing firm of J. Harper and Brothers to service a developing market for occasional literature, *Harper's* was for the family, designed to entertain, illustrated, not so much serious as sincere. It was with some pride, indeed, that J. Henry Harper acknowledged that the magazine had never been directed at "a limited class of highly cultivated readers," but rather was "addressed to all readers of average intelligence." Its purpose was "their entertainment and illumination, meeting in a general way the varied claims of their human intellect and sensibility, and in this accommodation following the lines of their aspiration."[5] The brothers Harper, in other words, wished to sell magazines, and perceived—correctly—that they could do so by telling their middle-class audience what it wished to hear: that it was the center of the universe and the true bearer of American culture.

Their successes with this new venture yielded the establishment in 1857 of *The Atlantic Monthly*, the halfway covenant of New England

Brahminism, and by the proliferation of magazines on the Harpers' model in the years following the Civil War. Although each of these differed slightly from the others and from their common prototype, no single magazine catered to a single, self-conscious clientele, and all faced the problem of competing for the same, essentially fickle, readership. The solution to this problem seems to have been implicit in the Harpers' formula which utilized the vogue of the interesting and the mode of pictorial representation. In the context of post-Civil War cultural nationalism, these combined to form the local-color movement.[6]

Much of the confusion which has attended the use of the phrase "local color" to describe the work of a generation of writers whose dialect tales and sketches describing little-known or forgotten aspects of American life dominated literary production in the United States during the 1870s and 1880s seems to be a direct result of the paucity of aesthetic merit which this work possessed. The local-color "movement" has, as a consequence, more often been regarded as a bridge (or hiatus) between the romanticism of the 1830s and 1840s and the realism of the 1890s than as a literary phenomenon worthy of study for its own sake.[7] In the absence of serious modern attempts to understand the nature and function of the local-color movement, moreover, we have inevitably carried on the arguments of earlier generations of critics and historians, whose vision of their more recent literary past was a function of their own present. What we think we know about the theory and practice of local-color writing in America, for example, we have taken from those critics of the 1890s and early twentieth century, especially William Dean Howells and the young Hamlin Garland, who saw Frank Norris, Theodore Dreiser, Edward Kirkland and Edgar W. Howe as rightful heirs to the mantle of genteel acceptability once worn by Bret Harte, G. W. Cable, Mary Murfree, and Thomas Nelson Page. What we think we know about the meaning of the local-color movement in American literary history, on the other hand, we have taken from Fred Lewis Pattee and that first generation of critics interested in the role of literature in the development of American culture, who, beginning about 1910, found in the work of the local colorists a vision of nationalism and

patriotism which seemed to provide a needed corrective to the fragmented vision of their own time, a protopluralism that acknowledged the diversity of American life while asserting its essential
unity.[8]

If we refuse to ride the ideological hobby horses of the Garlands
or the Pattees, or to choose between their competing attempts to
create usable pasts, then the local-color movement may be viewed as
a thing in itself and in terms of its own time. As a thing in itself, its
nature is not difficult to perceive nor is its occurrence unimportant. It
was, first of all, not a movement in the conventional sense of that
word, for it lacked the coherence which might have been provided by
the social interaction of its participants and it lacked the direction
which might have been provided by an articulated set of goals or
principles. In this it differed significantly from the self-conscious literary movement of the earlier nineteenth century which bore the
same name. Its very existence as a literary phenomenon was acknowledged only long after the fact, moreover; contemporary critics
failed to distinguish between local color and other kinds of writing,
so intent were they on preaching a set of principles which would
encourage the production of a mature and coherent American literature. Their emphasis was on structure rather than content.[9]

This is not to say that the local-color "movement" did not possess characteristics which set it off from other literary modes. It was
descriptive rather than analytical. It was short rather than long. It
was enormously popular. It aided in the sale of the literary magazines
in which it appeared, bolstered the fortunes of those publishing
houses which brought out volumes of collected stories and sketches,
and established the literary reputations of innumerable young and
middle-aged writers. It was popular also in the sense that it was
consciously not directed at a limited readership of sophisticates
and/or aesthetes. These very characteristics point to the central fact
about local-color literature—it emerged as a response to the existence
of a substantial market for descriptive pieces which the readers of the
new middle-class monthlies would find interesting.

Long after local-color writing had gone out of vogue, Hamlin
Garland noted that "authors write for publication," and that "the

conditions which govern the distribution and sale of books and magazines have more to do with determining the form and spirit of a nation's literature than most historians are willing to admit," and acknowledged, perhaps ruefully, that "authorship as an art may be free of such limitations, but in so far as it approaches a trade it must conform."[10] Few historians have been willing to accept so empirical an understanding of the process of literary creation, and few modern authors are free of that sense of the late nineteenth century as a golden age in literature which prohibits them from generalizing from their own experience in the present to understand the local colorists as practitioners of a craft. Yet the writers, editors, and publishers of the 1870s and 1880s knew quite well what local-color writing was about, and one at least remembered very clearly the practical circumstances of publishing in those days. "The fact that English fiction in serial form was . . . of such eminence as to command the preference of readers, and therefore a larger space in the pages of the Magazine, caused special stress to be laid upon the short stories of American writers."[11] And while we may doubt the ascription of intentional support for American letters suggested by this remark, its tone is surely correct. This the published and unpublished correspondence of contemporary authors bears out. The editors had space to fill, and they chose to fill it with material which their readers would find "interesting." But what was interesting? Or, more precisely, what were the characteristics of local-color writing which made it interesting, and to whom?

As literature, the work of the American local colorists is most closely tied to the travel sketches and descriptions of scenery written by the naturalists and physicians of the first quarter of the nineteenth century, who sought to make knowledge of the climate, geology, resources, and natural history of America available to the scientific community.[12] To them and to their readers, the newness of the new world, and the possibilities inherent in systematic observation and careful description for the achievement of scientific understanding, made all areas of the nation interesting. The literary form of the travel sketch which emerged out of this tradition during the second quarter of the century differed from it in tone, purpose, and focus, however.

It was explicitly bellestristic. It was personal rather than objective. And it was intended to entertain, to give pleasure through its artful reportage of the experiences of a particular person. Not the object of observation, nor the naked act of observation, but "sensibility," that nexus between observer and observed, was what made such material interesting. "I sought," one writer said, "to give a clear and vivid daguerrotype of the districts I traversed and the incidents which came under my observation," and he begged the indulgence of a "sympathetic circle" of readers for such inartful qualities as his sketches possessed.[13] The use of visual metaphors in discussions of the genre by its practitioners was both conventional and crucial, moreover, for whether they offered "daguerrotypes," or "pictures," or "sketches," or—neologism of neologisms—"hurrygraphs," their manner was that of the artist, and it was manner rather than matter that was to be judged. The favorable judgment of such a "sympathetic circle" as might be found among the readers of a journal with local or regional circulation in an age of personal literature was one thing. The favorable judgment of the entire magazine-reading public, which became the travel sketch's audience after the mid-century, however, was something more difficult to obtain, and the travel sketch was forced to change its focus accordingly.

The reading public of the 1870s and 1880s had been raised on the vivid descriptions of places and events characteristic of the journalism of the Civil War years, and had experienced the revolution wrought by the illustrated weekly and the "special correspondent." To them the perceptions of a particular man of sensibility were of no more inherent interest than those of any "ordinary" man. Indeed, they demanded to know about places and events as they might see them, as anyone might see them. In this context, when personality could no longer be counted on to sell magazines, then subject matter became a crucial commodity. During these decades only the most obviously or grossly "interesting" subjects were acceptable to the editors: Europe, conceived of not as the mother continent but as a quaint and picturesque land, and those truly picturesque lands of Africa and Asia; historic sites in America, especially those associated with that central unifying event in the heritage of a recently divided nation, the Revolutionary War; resort areas, primarily on the Atlantic Coast but on the Great Lakes and in the Appalachian Mountains as well, where readers might, or might aspire to spend a summer; the South, America's newest territorial acquisition; and those picturesque "little corners" of the nation, not yet assimilated into the middle-class, nationally oriented culture which seemed dominant in America.

What was true of the travel sketch was true of the short story as well during these decades. Indeed, the line between journalism and fiction became more and more tenuous as authors and aspiring authors scrambled to find "interesting" subjects on which to build a literary reputation. Writers with a firsthand knowledge, however slight, of some exotic or picturesque place were urged by the editors to turn that knowledge into literature. Those without such knowledge were sent, or went on journeys in search of local color, and characteristically wrote first travel sketches and then short stories set in the locale visited.[14] The literary career of Miss Constance Fenimore Woolson offers a case in point.

At the age of twenty-nine, following the death of her father, Constance Woolson began a new life as artist. Her literary aspirations at this time appear to have extended no farther than the desire to find "something to do" in a period of familial disorganization, preferably something that would provide a degree of freedom from the personal and financial dependence on aunts and uncles which would otherwise have been her lot.[15] Her first published sketch, and apparently the first effort of her nascent literary career, appeared in *Harper's New Monthly Magazine* for July 1870 as "The Happy Valley," an account of a visit to the Zoarite community in the Tuscarawas Valley of Ohio.[16] How extensively Woolson had studied current periodical literature in order to master the conventions of the travel sketch is uncertain. But she had mastered them, and thereby laid the groundwork for her success as a writer.

"The Happy Valley" is a nearly perfect example of the new style of travel sketch which appeared during the 1870s. It pretends to be the narrative of a journey undertaken for pleasure or out of curiosity, and thereby locates its point of view in the personae of the travelers.

Its travelers are themselves irrelevant to the purpose of the sketch, however, which is not the revelation of character or the relationship between point of view and "reality," but rather description of the locality visited as *anyone* (anyone accepting as valid the point of view of the travelers/author) might perceive it. The sketch itself begins, moreover, by pointing to the physical, social, and cultural distance separating the locality to be described and the more familiar world which the travelers must leave in order to begin their journey, but in which their consciousness continues to reside. "In this practical century, with its railroad insulting the venerable majesty of Mount Washington, its suspension bridge spanning the tremendous chasm of foaming Niagara, and its telegraph penetrating the sacred mysteries of the deep sea, there were yet found three souls who dared to start on a pilgrimage to the Happy Valley that lies hidden away from the world among the mountains through which winds the Tuscarawas River, in Ohio."[17]

The aesthetic distance thus established is essential to the success of the travel sketch, for it permits the author to maintain at arm's length the implication of those very peculiarities which make a locality seem interesting. The utopian communism of the Zoarite experiment, for example, is allowed to pose no challenge to the social and economic patterns of the "normal" world of author and reader, and Woolson can freely acknowledge the differences between "our ways" and "thy ways." Her concluding question, "who can say that thou hast not chosen the better part," is only politeness since aesthetic distance has made the question rhetorical. Aesthetic distance is thus functional: the city on a hill need not be razed if it can be transformed into a resort.[18]

Woolson's second sketch, "Fairy Island," a description of the history and life of Mackinac Island, also appeared in July 1870, in *Putnam's Magazine*, the first of a series which John Dwight Kern calls her "lake country writings."[19] Written in 1872–73, these include "American Cities: Detroit," in *Appleton's Journal*, "Round by Propeller," a semifictional account of a steamer voyage from Buffalo to Chicago, in *Harper's Magazine*, "Mackinac Island," in *Appleton's Journal*, "The Wine Islands of Lake Erie," in *Harper's*, and "Lakeshore

Relics," an historical sketch published in *Lippincott's Magazine*. At the same time she was at work on a number of short stories which used the lake country as background, and which derived their merit primarily from their detailed description of an unfamiliar locality. The best of these were collected and published by J. R. Osgood as *Castle Nowhere: Lake Country Sketches*, in 1875.

Of the relationship between these travel sketches and short stories of the lake country one might say either that Woolson wrote of what she knew, her own "little corner" of experience, and did no more than mine the field once she discovered that her local-color pieces met with a more favorable reception than the precious essays and sentimental stories she had offered the editors between 1870 and 1872; or that in reworking the travel sketch into the short story of local color, she was following a course which led her to an increased understanding of the complexities of situation and action. The first proposition tends to make her seem a hack; the second, an artist. In fact, both propositions and both conclusions may be held adequately to describe Woolson and her work, for the process of developing the short story out of the travel sketch was repeated after 1873 with Florida and then with western North Carolina as background.[20] Woolson as hack knew a good field when she saw one, and proceeded to extract as much "literary material" as she was able. At the same time, Woolson as artist was developing her ability to deal with background in the travel sketch apprenticeship before proceeding to the more difficult forms of short story and novel. The real issue, however, is not Woolson's literary reputation but the existence in general of an empirical continuity between the travel sketch and the short story of local color.

It was upon the presumptive use of real landscapes as background in the local-color sketches of the 1870s and 1880s that later critics would base their assertions of the innate realism of the genre. Not realism but the conditions of the literary marketplace determined its shape in an age when literary merit came increasingly to be defined as a quality inhering in the subject of a sketch rather than in a writer's craft. "Even the best writers shun delineations of the higher emotions or of delicate shades of character, and prefer to describe unfamiliar aspects of nature as travellers, or dramatic incidents and peculiar people moulded by phases of experience foreign to their readers," Caroline Kirkland complained in 1877. "To this end they climb mountains and swim rivers, descend into craters and penetrate pathless deserts, [while] with the naive ingratitude of a child the spoilt public turns away to welcome some newer sensation."[21] As professional writers, the local colorists required subjects which, by attracting the interest of editors and the reading public, would permit them to write professionally. That such subjects permitted them, or some of them, to develop their craft while they built their reputations was fortuitous and ultimately irrelevant to their central concern, and it is presumptuous of us to explain their systematic exploitation of "interesting" subjects as mere apprentice-work or as temporary and unfortunate lapses from a commitment to "art." As critics and historians, rather, we must acknowledge that subject was their central concern, and make it our own.

At the heart of local-color writing is comparison, a perception of alternative modes of life, a confrontation between the "we" readers and the "them" read about. It was this which made "local color" seem a useful weapon to such as Théophile Gautier and Prosper Mérimée in their attack on what they regarded as the dullness of early nineteenth-century France. Against the bourgeois reality of the familiar, they sought to counterpose the "exotisme" of Turkey or Corsica, taking the one as a measure of the other's failure.[22] In America during a later period, however, "local color" may be said to have functioned in a different and indeed opposite way. The very "exotisme" of Creoles and Cajuns, of Southern mountaineers singing old English ballads, of preindustrial New England seen from the point of view of the present was proof of the victory of nationalizing and homogenizing tendencies over the resistance of regionalism and diversity. The American local colorists embraced the present and articulated for the nation a vision in which the past was merely quaint, the exotic merely picturesque. Comparison functioned not to point up failure but to acknowledge success.[23]

What provided the focus for the sketches of the American local colorists was never a contrast between alternative social or cultural systems, but rather a perception of the peculiarity of life in the "little corners" of America that they described. At most those areas "in the country and in those sections which have been least affected by the progress of a growing national unity" represented exceptions that proved the rule of the dominance of a national culture. More generally, however, those "little corners" were separated from the bourgeois, urban present by an ethnic or chronological distance which transformed the potential challenge to the idea of a dominant national culture implicit in the fact of their existence, into additional evidence for the reality of such a national culture.[24] The peculiarities which the local-color sketches described were those to be expected among Majorcans in Florida, Creoles in New Orleans, Negroes in Georgia, or among the people of "olden times." The lessons taught were two: the monolithic character of modern, middle-class American culture, and the pastness of the past.

The bulk of local-color fiction in fact concerned "olden times" in America, before the Civil War, before industrialization, before the homogenization effected by the railroad, the national magazine, the stereoscope, and a national administrative system made union a fact rather than an issue. As account of the seedtime of the Republic, as reminiscence, as description of a golden age, most local-color writing treated the past as interesting because it was different from the present. "I would endeavor to show you New England in its seed-bed," Mrs. Stowe remarked in the preface to *Oldtown Folks*, "before the hot suns of modern progress had developed its sprouting germs into the great trees of today."[25]

Not only the New England tales of Harriet Beecher Stowe and Sarah Orne Jewett but the stories of Virginia by Thomas Nelson Page, of Georgia by Joel Chandler Harris, of Louisiana by George Washington Cable and Grace Chopin, of Indiana by Edward Eggleston, of Illinois by Edward Kirkland and Edgar Howe, of Kentucky by James Lane Allen and John Fox, Jr., of Tennessee by Mary Noailles Murfree, of the Michigan Lake Country by Constance F. Woolson, of the "middle border" of the Dakotas by Hamlin Garland were set in a past viewed quite consciously from a reference point in the present. Although the Mountain West described by Bret Harte, Owen Wister,

Theodore Roosevelt, and Hamlin Garland (after he had exhausted his "middle border" material) was contemporaneous with the publication of the sketches and tales which took it as a subject, it was also of the past viewed from the point of view of the present in that it represented a recapitulation of the history of the East at an earlier period. Indeed, Harte, Wister, and the rest were conscious chroniclers of the passing away of the last remnants of an earlier stage in American history, giving way to progress and the modern age.[26]

To the local color writers, the contemporary South was also regarded as being in a transitional state, as a "new" South rose phoenixlike from the ashes of war. Here was no earlier stage of development giving way naturally to a later (and presumably preferable) stage, but a happy departure from the normal historical process which would have yielded a Cavalier alternative to the Yankee present of the rest of the nation.[27] Of no less interest during these years, although for different reasons, were descriptions of the South as America. Designed to present useful information about the region to potential immigrants and investors from the North, and to satisfy the curiosity of the nation about its newest territorial acquisition, southern sketches which took this point of view facilitated the conceptualization of America as a unified and homogeneous nation by denying the reality of sectional division and the relevance of the Confederate past to the southern present.[28]

Although "negligible as art,"[29] the work of American local colorists was widely published and, so far as one can tell, widely read during the 1870s and 1880s. So effectively did the conventions of local-color writing condition the manner in which American authors dealt with American materials, moreover, and so satisfactory was the local-color formula in meeting the need for a literature which would reinforce dominant conceptions of the nature of American civilization, that a generation of Americans came to accept an essentially literary vision of life and society in the United States. At the hands of the local colorists, the unfamiliar became merely quaint and picturesque, and the familiar became normative.[30]

Unlike most of the areas described by the local colorists, Appalachia was not in fact separated from America by ethnic, geographic, or chronological distance. The mountaineers were native-born, white, Anglo-Saxon, Protestant. The mountain region was not only in America, but in that part of America which had been settled by the first generation of frontiersmen, hence where the rude conditions of the frontier ought long ago to have given way to the more sophisticated and "civilized" conditions of modern life. It was indeed the perception of the "otherness" of Appalachia despite this similarity and proximity which had seemed most intriguing to the first group of writers who followed Harney's lead in using the southern mountains as subject or setting for literature. Their sketches and stories tend as a consequence to express a note of wonder quite uncharacteristic of the local-color mode more generally. The protagonist of John Eston Cooke's "Owlet," for example, felt as if he had "stumbled upon another world and another race of human beings."

Nothing could have surprised me more than to meet these people in this hut of the Blue Ridge Mountains in Virginia, in the nineteenth century. Twenty miles from them railway trains were speeding along freighted with well-dressed passengers reading the latest telegraphic news in the day's paper, and here were two beings who, as I soon found, could neither read nor write, and were destitute of all ideas beyond the wants of the human animal in the state of nature.[31]

A sense of wonder can provide only the flimsiest structure from which to hang a story or on which to base a sketch, but "wonder" in any case became an inappropriate response to the otherness of Appalachia once this otherness had become a familiar fact, if only to the editors. The successful literary exploitation of the southern mountain region depended rather on the possibility of conceptualizing the otherness of Appalachia as a fact independent of its perception. If the otherness of Appalachia were "real," it would form an appropriate subject for description and explication, or the donnée of fiction. It should come as no surprise, then, that the sense of wonder which characterized the earliest sketches of Appalachia rapidly gave way before assertions that the southern mountain region really was a strange land inhabited by a peculiar people. Indeed, the first writer to take for granted the fact of Appalachian otherness, Mary Noailles Murfree, has generally (albeit incorrectly) been credited with the literary "discovery" of the mountains.[32]

At issue is not simply the history of "Appalachian fiction," but the history of the idea of Appalachia itself, for it was through literature that the otherness of the southern mountain region was introduced as a fact in the American consciousness. The sketches and stories of the local-color movement, like all literature perhaps, claimed attention as renderings, reflections, or abstractions from real life. The scenes and events they described were presented as typical of scenes and events which anyone visiting the area might observe, the persons typical of those whom anyone might meet. Although a function of the literary form in which it occurred, the vision of reality thus offered had consequences beyond the pages of the magazine in which a sketch or story appeared, to the degree that it became the basis for private or public action. And this is what happened to the local colorists' vision of Appalachia as a strange land inhabited by a peculiar people. Reiterated in some 90 sketches and more than 125 short stories published between 1870 and 1890,[33] it established Appalachia in the public consciousness as a discrete region, in but not of America. After this time travelers, writers, missionaries, economists, geographers, sociologists, teachers, geologists, land developers, and industrialists all tended to approach the southern mountains from this point of view. They began with the assumption that it really was a strange land inhabited by a peculiar people, and responded in what to them seemed the appropriate way. In practice this involved a variety of modes of action, but what characterized them all was the assumption that the mountainous portions of eight or nine southern states composed a distinct region of the nation, with physical, social, and cultural characteristics that made it fundamentally different from the rest of America.

The process of reification, by which the perception of Appalachian otherness became transformed into a conception of Appalachia as a thing in itself, occurred within the context of the conventions of local-color writing, and in particular of the claims of that genre to verisimilitude. It occurred when it did, however, largely as a result of the work of Mary Noailles Murfree, whose gothic tales of unrequited love, tragic misunderstanding, and fatal accident, set in the Tennessee mountains, enjoyed a considerable vogue during the early 1880s. Where the first local-color sketches describing the southern mountain region had emphasized the disparity between Appalachia and America and used the exotic mountain scenery as a neutral background against which dramatic incidents might be played out, Murfree's stories took the fact of Appalachian otherness as their donnée and sought to describe aspects of life "among an interesting primitive and little known people in a wild and secluded region."[34] Especially in the sketches later collected as *In the Tennessee Mountains*, Murfree created a mood peculiar to the mountain region, and described a population whose expression of "settled melancholy" reflected that mood—"the indefinable tinge of sadness that rests upon the Allegheny wilds, that hovers about the purpling mountain-tops, that broods over the silent woods, that sounds in the voice of the singing waters."[35] She thus provided the mountain region with the simulacrum of an existence independent of its observation from a train window or a hotel's veranda, and established a vision of the strange land and peculiar people to which the perception of Appalachian otherness might subsequently be tied. In the process, the fact that her tales also were set in the "olden times" before the Civil War was largely overlooked, and she emerged as the chronicler of Appalachia in the present.

It is perhaps ironic that Murfree, whose literary reputation rested primarily upon that "apparent fidelity in the rendering of mountain life" which seemed to make her an American Thomas Hardy,[36] in fact knew very little about Appalachia. Her own observations of the region and its people were limited to girlhood summers spent at Beersheba Springs, a favorite watering place of the Tennessee gentry, and to a brief journey in search of local color during the summer of 1886, after the publication of *In the Tennessee Mountains*. This fact goes far to explain the impressionistic character of her sketches, however, and suggests that her essentially romantic vision resulted from an attempt to replicate in prose the feelings of a youthful sensibility. Indeed, her entire experience in the mountains, as a civilized lowlander of good family confronting "the gloomy primeval magnificence of nature," predisposed her to see Appalachia as a strange land, while the mountaineers appeared a peculiar people if only for their willingness so to live in a wilderness "broken by no field or clearing." That they also refused to acknowledge those distinctions based on education and social class which were so important to the summer visitors gave precision to her perceptions, even as it provided a ready theme for her stories.[37]

Ultimately, the popularity of Murfree's sketches did not depend on the validity of her private experience so much as on her ability to establish the otherness of Appalachia as a matter of fact rather than of mere unfamiliarity, to offer an insider's view which validated the impressions of outsiders. By providing her generation with a clear conception of Appalachia as an essentially alien land, her work facilitated the emergence of Appalachia as a viable field for fiction, and her own success encouraged other authors to take the region as their subject.

The period of Murfree's greatest popularity, from 1878 until about 1886, marks the completion of the first phase of the literary exploitation of the southern mountains, the period of "discovery." After this time American writers, like their readers, having read their own work as accurate representations of reality, came to see Appalachia as a distinct region of the nation and took the otherness of Appalachia as part of the donnée, rather than as the direct subject of their stories and sketches. Led by James Lane Allen and John Fox, Jr., they turned from mere exploitation of the fact of the region's strangeness to an examination of the relationship of Appalachia and America, and particularly of the opposition which seemed to lie at the heart of Appalachia's otherness. Because they were writers, they used this opposition to provide dramatic tension in confrontations between characters emblematic of the two cultures—feudists and lawmen, moonshiners and revenue officers, dirt-farmers and mining engineers, plain folks and politicians, mountain girls and city boys—and found their resolution, when they found it at all, not in action but in explanation.

It has often been said that the local colorists manipulated setting while keeping plot, characterization, and other elements of the short story constant.[38] Such conventional critical wisdom does not fit the case of the first fiction set in Appalachia, however, in which the southern mountains served as a neutral ground, a practical blank stage upon which the drama of social relationships might be played out, or a simplified version of that contemporary literary fascination, the moral confrontation with the self, might be examined. In the sketches and stories of the 1870s and 1880s it was the remoteness of Appalachia rather than any specified characteristics of the region itself which interested the local-color writers, and which made it available as an alternative to the conventional deserted island of romantic fiction, where human passion could be seen unclothed and unfettered by the constraints of society and history.

As the locale of a story, Appalachia thus seemed both convenient and useful. It met the needs of those who wished to neutralize setting in order to focus on characterization, and, alternatively, of those who wished to pass off hackneyed and melodramatic incidents as new and fresh subjects for literary treatment. The conventional acceptance of a link between the travel sketch and the short story of local color, and the contemporary experience of tourism to which both forms spoke, moreover, made unnecessary any elaborate explanations of how sophisticates worthy of an author's interest might be found in so strange a land among so peculiar a people. Everyone understood that they had come by train.

The utilization of Appalachian otherness as an element in the donnée of a story or novel was a later development, and characterized the mountain fiction of the 1890s and later decades. It could occur at all, however, only after Appalachia had been defined as a thing in itself, and as a thing, moreover, which was in one way or another fundamentally different than America. In fiction, this sense of difference was characteristically expressed through opposition, in the form of conflict between insiders and outsiders, or through opposition's mirror-image, love between a mountain girl and a boy from the lowlands. Stories of conflict are rare in the corpus of Appalachian fiction, but stories of love abound, and if only for this reason deserve serious examination. It was in the context of their attempts to write of love, however, that American writers were forced to take those first steps toward the articulation of a clear vision of the differences between Appalachia and America, and ultimately of Appalachia as a thing in itself, for in their love stories the perception of Appalachian otherness became transformed into opposition.[39]

The classic love story of Appalachia is surely Mary Noailles Murfree's "The Star in the Valley," which established as a convention in mountain fiction that the participants in a love relationship should function also as emblems of the two cultures, Appalachian and American, and that their love should ultimately fail because of allegedly fundamental differences, characteristically expressed as opposition, between those cultures. Yet Murfree was not the first to attempt such a tale, at least if date of publication is an index to priority. The earlier stories describing love affairs between city men and mountain girls utilized the mountain setting as neutral ground, however, and hence point up the particular contribution which Murfree made in facilitating the emergence of the idea of Appalachia. Three of these were published within fourteen months of "The Star in the Valley," moreover, and as a group stand as evidence of the more general tendency of the late 1870s, to acknowledge the "reality" of Appalachian otherness when viewed from the perspective of contemporary American civilization.

"Lodusky," by Frances Hodgson Burnett, is the story of a young-man artist on vacation in the North Carolina mountains in the company of his young-lady friend, a writer, and her aunt as chaperone. The young man meets and becomes fascinated with a handsome mountain girl named Lodusky, whose own interest in the young man derives largely from her hope that he will save her from the tedium of rural life by taking her along (as wife of course) when he returns to his home. Lodusky's love is thus tainted and the young man's love for Lodusky thus inappropriate. In explanation, we are told that she has been to Asheville and hankers after city ways, and it is this which has "spoiled" her for continued life in the mountains even as it has transformed the natural affection of woman for man into pride and avarice. It is this also which "spoils" Lodusky as an emblem of Appalachia, and which makes the mountain setting into neutral ground. Indeed, the issue upon which the story turns is not the confrontation between Appalachia and America but the young man's own confrontation with himself and his art, impulse and responsibility, dalliance and hard work. Precipitated by his abortive love-affair with Lodusky and his subsequent flight from its mountain setting, this confrontation in the end leaves him healthy, wealthy (the experience liberated his creative genius), and married to the young-lady writer.

Julia Schayer's "Molly" offers a variant on the familiar traveling salesman-farmer's daughter motif in a well-written, fast-paced melodrama set in the West Virginia hills. Molly had gone to Richmond to make her fortune but instead had come to grief at the hands of the hardened Dick Staples. She has returned to the mountains of her childhood, married Sandy King, slow-witted but a prince of a fellow, and has settled down to be wife and mother when her seducer shows up, on a walking tour of the mountains. Molly agrees to meet Staples in the woods where she rejects his advances, repents of her past indiscretions, and (in a struggle to protect her virtue, such as it is) pushes him off a cliff. Sandy finds the body, Molly dies of grief and shame, and her little boy learns to call King "Dad-dy."

John Esten Cooke's "Owlet" is at once the most contrived and the most interesting of these three stories, since it involves a potential decision on the validity of the principle of "all for love," and its first person narrative articulates a sense of the strangeness of the mountain world seen from the point of view of a young lawyer from Richmond. The narrator first sees Owlet, as the girl is called by her white-bearded octogenarian guardian, swinging from a thick grape-vine near the path along which he is riding. Unkempt and in tatters, rude, unlettered, she nonetheless possesses a kind of natural grace and womanly modesty, but whether such civilized qualities are endemic to the (noble) savage which she seems to be or a consequence of heredity is not clear. As things turn out, Owlet is the only daughter of an English gentleman, the late Henry Austin, Esq., of Fernhall, whose solicitors in London have on hand some £70,000 for his heirs if any there be. The young lawyer and Owlet, now the charming and literate and wealthy Miss Pauline Austin, are married after some stagey renunciations of supposed-unrequited love, and live happily ever after.

Even without Cooke's solicitor-ex-machina, and in spite of his tentative protestations to the contrary, no real tension between Appalachia and America might have emerged from this story since Owlet's relationship with the Blue Ridge Mountains was one of residence only. She is not a mountain girl; she is a not-yet-city girl, as the easy transition she makes, even before her true identity is known, from the primitive hut to the genteel circumstances of life at "The Glades" (the estate of the narrator's aunt) demonstrates. Nor does the characterization of her mountaineer-guardian offer any possibility for such a confrontation, even were he more than a piece of stage-property. He bears no relationship to the "peculiar people" who inhabit the "strange land" of the mountains in the later fiction of Appalachia, but is a trapper and hunter living in a trapper's cabin— a kindly hermit, leatherstocking in Virginia. It remained to Mary Noailles Murfree, the best known and most prolific writer about the Southern Appalachians, and the only one who wrote of that region exclusively, to articulate the tension between Appalachia and America in "The Star in The Valley"—the awkward, stumbling, often forced, but still engaging story of the gulf which separated Reginald Chevis from his mountain sweetheart.[40]

Reginald Chevis is, almost predictably, a vacationer in the southern mountains. With his friend, Ned Varney, a prosaic man-of-affairs, and a native guide, he spends his days in genteel sportsmanship, hunting deer with horn and hounds, birds with a well-trained dog, now and then a bear with the yelping pack. Yet Chevis's poetic sensibilities are not satisfied by the banalities and brutalities of such activities. Often at night, after dinner in the well-appointed tent home, he wanders alone on the mountain-side, gazing upward at the stars and then down at that answering star in the valley, the lamp-lit cabin home of Shaw the blacksmith and his beautiful daughter.

Chevis has seen the girl on the wooded paths along which he followed the hunt. He has noted with appreciation a "graceful poise acquired by the prosaic habit of carrying weights upon the head and

[a] lithe, swaying beauty," but of course he has had no occasion to speak with her. At last his horse Strathspey providentially casts a shoe near the smithy's home, and Chevis goes there to ask the father for help, and a cup of water on the chance that the girl will serve him. Shaw does send Chevis to the spring with the girl—a sign of the father's essential coarseness—and they are alone at last, with an opportunity to converse. She gives him a cup of water. He thanks her. "Ye're welcome," she says.

Chevis would have liked to hear her speak again, but the gulf between his station and hers—so undreamed of by her (for the differences of caste are absolutely unknown to the independent mountaineers), so patent to him—could be bridged by few ideas. They had so little in common that for a moment he could think of nothing to say. His cogitation suggested only the inquiry, "Do you live here?" indicating the little house on the other side of the road. "Yes," she chanted in the same monotone, "I lives hyar."[41]

If we may believe Miss Murfree (for it is she who tells us, not the story), Chevis and the girl have fallen in love, though their love remains undeclared and, ultimately, impossible. The high and low of the mountain camp and the cabin in the valley are but symbols of their occupants' respective stations in life, and the physical distance separating them symbolic of the social distance between civilization and the "peculiar and primitive state of society" in which the mountaineers live. Even after Chevis learns of the girl's extraordinary heroism and nobility of soul (she has walked fifteen miles, barefoot, over snowy ground, to warn the Peel family of an impending attack from a group of drunken mountaineers, including her father), he recognizes that real love—love followed by marriage—for her is impossible, and leaves the mountains.

In the immediate context of the story, neither love nor conflict is fully realized, nor fully explained. Whether the impossibility of union between Appalachia and America inheres in the fact of a social difference amounting to caste, or is a consequence of Chevis's own weakness, an inability or unwillingness to transcend this difference in the name of love, is unclear. Again, whether such ambiguity is intended or is a consequence of Murfree's weakness as a writer, is unclear. Throughout her stories and novels, however, the gulf between the

two worlds remains unbridged, and we may presume that the formula of "The Star in the Valley" was consciously repeated as a viable
way of dealing with the fact of difference between Appalachia and
America.[42] Had Murfree eliminated all ambiguity in such situations,
she would thereby have eliminated that tension which made her
stories interesting and publishable. Even more important perhaps,
had she eliminated all ambiguity she would have had to choose between the alternatives which the existence of Appalachia within
America seemed to pose, and thus been untrue to her own feelings. A
Murfree of Murfreesboro, she stood midway between the Old and
the New South, a member of that generation which tried to look both
ways.

James Lane Allen was not, strictly speaking, a local-color writer.
Early in 1885, however, at the age of thirty-six, after a relatively unsuccessful career as scholar, teacher, and Kentucky gentleman, he
determined to try his hand at writing for a living and traveled to New
York as to the mecca of the new mass literature. There Henry Mills
Alden of *Harper's* told him that he lacked "a definite field" and encouraged him to write of the bluegrass region of Kentucky, with
which he as a resident of Lexington was presumably familiar. From
the editor of the New York *Evening Post* he received in addition a
commission for two descriptive sketches of the Kentucky mountain
region, then of potential interest because of the recent publication of
In the Tennessee Mountains. With this assurance that Kentucky was a
field suitable for literary exploitation, and the understanding that a
literary career in the 1880s might most easily be begun as a local-color
writer, Allen returned to Lexington and began to gather material,
began to familiarize himself with his "field." His plan was to publish a
descriptive sketch, then rework the sketch as background for a short
story, thus guaranteeing the "realism" of his stories while utilizing
his material most efficiently. Allen was in a hurry, but his plan had
been proven successful by a dozen other writers during the previous
decade.[43]

In general, Allen's plan worked. Between 1885 and 1890 he published more than a dozen stories and sketches of Kentucky life,

thereby establishing his reputation as a writer and providing himself with the experience necessary for a venture away from local color and toward the larger themes appropriate to the larger format of the novel. In one respect, however, his plan did not work. His observations of life in the Kentucky mountains yielded no material suitable for transformation into fiction, and the mountain region itself appeared as a bothersome anomaly in his vision of Kentucky as an epitome of the best in the American tradition, where past and present, stability and growth, gentility and vigor were happily combined.

"Through Cumberland Gap on Horseback," Allen's first Kentucky mountain sketch, was the yield from a journey in search of local color undertaken during the early summer of 1885, and was published in *Harper's* for June 1886, just four months after his first essay on "The Bluegrass Region of Kentucky." As a companion piece to and continuation of the earlier article, it was clearly intended to establish Allen's priority in claiming all of Kentucky as his literary field. Its theme, however, was the fact of "two Kentuckys."

It can never be too clearly understood by those who are wont to speak of "the Kentuckians" that this State has within its boundaries two entirely distinct elements of population—elements distinct in England before they came hither, distinct during more than a century of residence here, and distinct now in all that goes to constitute a separate community—occupations, manners and customs, dress, views of life, civilization.[44]

Because the mountain region of Kentucky was as much an unfamiliar land to a resident of Lexington or Louisville as to a resident of Boston or New York during the 1880s, Allen approached the "great Appalachian uplift on the south-eastern border" of his state possessed of no special insights or understanding derived from physical proximity or nativity. Indeed, his attitude toward the mountain region was a function of his complete acceptance of the local colorists' vision of Appalachia as a strange land inhabited by a peculiar people, and hence a viable subject for literary exploitation. His descriptions of mountain life and scenery differ in no significant way from those of any other local-color writer familiar with the conventions of the genre. In his emphasis on romantic scenery, the hardships of horseback and muleback travel in rough country, and the primitive state of social and economic organization among the mountaineers, who seemed to be "utterly exempt from all the obligations and other phenomena of time" and to lack all "sense of accumulation," moreover, one hears echoes of other writers' work. Indeed, it is not unlikely that Allen adopted consciously the tone and point of view of Charles Dudley Warner, whose account of a similar journey in a "wilderness of corn pone and rusty bacon" appeared in the *Atlantic* during the months when Allen was writing his piece for *Harper's*.[45]

If Allen's reiteration of the fact of Appalachian otherness was no innovation, however, his response to that fact was. Because of the distinctness of his vision of Kentucky, perhaps, or because of his sense of the obligations of the essayist,[46] he saw that the existence of an other and alien Kentucky within the borders of the Commonwealth posed a problem which required solution, generated a tension which demanded resolution. This Allen sought to provide in a variety of ways, all of which foreshadowed the techniques utilized after 1890 for dealing with the analogous dilemma of the relationship of Appalachia and America; all of which identified Appalachian otherness as "natural" while offering some explanation for its peculiarities; and all of which had their origins in the conventions of the local-color movement.

The crucial act in this process was the transformation of simile and metaphor into statement of fact. The result was the assertion of the existence of ethnic, geographic, or chronological distance separating the strange land and peculiar people of Appalachia from the more ordinary world with which Allen and his readers were familiar. "This state has within its borders two entirely distinct elements of population," Allen said. "It is but a short distance from the blue-grass country to the eastern mountains, but in traversing it you detach yourself from all that you have ever experienced," he added. In entering the mountains you "take up the history of English speaking men and women at the point it had reached a hundred or a hundred and fifty years ago," he concluded.[47] By asserting that the mountaineers were ethnically distinct from the population of the bluegrass, that they lived in an area geographically distinct from the bluegrass, that they acted out the life habits of a different era, Allen created the emotional distance necessary to the success of any local-color article. At the same time, however, he offered explanations for the peculiarities to be found among a white, Anglo-Saxon, native-born population living in the present and in close proximity to the centers of modern civilization, and hence for the dilemma posed by the existence of "two Kentuckys."

Allen's explanations were offered in passing, in the interstices between passages of description. He attempted no systematic analysis. He was not concerned with the contradictions necessarily resulting from the combination of explanatory statements he offered, and he chose to ignore the problems which his explanatory statements themselves raised. In this also Allen's work foreshadowed the subsequent discussion of the relationship of Appalachia and America which, even in its most analytical forms, displayed a literary quality and a literary intent which made a well-turned evocative phrase more to be desired than clear and unambiguous statement.

The resolution of a dilemma does not alter the reality which created it and which it reflects. It only provides a way of dealing with this reality, however it may be conceived. By pointing to ethnic, geographic, or chronological distance in terms of which the peculiarities of Appalachia might be explained, Allen made possible the maintenance of the southern mountain region as a viable area for literary exploitation while casting the qualities which made it "interesting" in a form that did not challenge his and his readers' notions about the nature of America or of American civilization—notions in terms of which the otherness of Appalachia was defined to begin with. James Lane Allen was thus the first to bring into sharp focus the implications of Appalachian otherness, to articulate (in terms of the dilemma of the "two Kentuckys") the tension which the existence of the mountain region as a strange land inhabited by a peculiar people created, and to attempt resolution of this tension by explanation.

Allen's role in the history of the American dialogue on the meaning of Appalachia's existence was not limited to the mere fact of priority, however. His assertion of the existence of "two Kentuckys" and his manner of dealing with this anomolous situation provided

John Fox, Jr., with both the subject matter and point of view utilized in a series of enormously popular novels and stories of Kentucky mountain life, including *A Mountain Europa*, *The Kentuckians*, *The Trail of the Lonesome Pine*, and *The Little Shepherd of Kingdom Come*. Fox, who freely acknowledged his intellectual debt to Allen and who took personal inspiration from Allen's successful exploitation of Kentucky themes, was to become one of America's best-known authors by the turn of the century. Through him, Allen's ideas reached a significantly larger audience than the publication of two brief sketches in *Harper's Magazine* could have provided and may consequently be credited with a greater influence on the development of American attitudes toward Appalachia than would otherwise have been the case.

Influence is an evanescent thing, however. Whatever the effect of Fox's popularity on the acceptance of Allen's ideas about the relationship of the bluegrass and mountain sections of Kentucky, or by extension about the relationship of America and Appalachia, Allen's statement of the problem and his mode of dealing with it were entirely appropriate to the state of the dialogue on Appalachia during the late 1880s and early 1890s. Given the proposition that Appalachia was a strange land inhabited by a peculiar people, Allen's recognition of the dilemma which this implied and his attempt to resolve it through explanation may be seen as a "natural" development, entirely consistent with the conventions of the local-color mode which had provided the immediate context for his ratiocinations. He took the next step beyond description at a time when descriptive sketches of a mountain region now familiar to editors and readers alike, had lost their attraction, and hence their market value. Indeed, by 1890, when Allen's second mountain sketch was published, others had identified the dilemma in the same terms and had begun to attempt its resolution by means of the same techniques that Allen had used. His work must thus be seen as symptomatic of the emergence of a new phase in the history of the literary exploitation of Appalachia, and of the emergence of a new phase in the history of American responses to the existence of that region. James Lane Allen thus became the means by which a dilemma inherent in the initial description of Appalachia as a strange land inhabited by a peculiar people became manifest, and emerged as a problem not simply in the logistics of literary composition but also in contemporary consideration of the nature of America and of American civilization.

No one said that the existence of Appalachia posed a problem of this magnitude, with implications for an understanding of the nature of American civilization and for the viability of conceptions of America as a unified and homogeneous national entity. Where contemporaries were silent, however, their actions spoke loudly. In writing about the southern mountains and mountaineers, and in dealing with Appalachia "practically," they developed patterns of action which functioned as responses to the fact of Appalachian otherness, and which served in one way or another to integrate the perception of a reality of Appalachian otherness into dominant conceptions of the nature of American civilization. One such pattern of action consisted of self-conscious attempts to explain the causes of Appalachian otherness. Another consisted of equally self-conscious attempts to alter the reality of Appalachian otherness through systematic social action.

By integrating the fact of Appalachian otherness into the cognitive schemes by which the nature of American civilization was otherwise understood, explanation functioned to maintain the possibility of conceptualizing America as a unified and homogeneous national entity, and modern American civilization as the "natural" product of inevitable processes of historical development—processes which operated in and on Appalachia also, albeit with different results. By "Americanizing" the native-born Americans of Appalachia, or by replicating in the southern mountains the social, economic, and cultural patterns which prevailed elsewhere in the nation and which served as the norms against which Appalachian otherness was measured, on the other hand, social action promised to eliminate the disparity between Appalachia and America. It thereby functioned also as an attempt to maintain the possibility of perceiving America as unified and homogeneous. In either case, the "realities" of mountain life were of less interest and less importance than ideas about the nature and characteristics of mountain life—ideas which were developed in the context of notions about the nature of America and of American civilization.

2. Protestant Home Missions  and the Institutionalization of Appalachian Otherness

The local-color writers saw Appalachia as an "unknown" land because they had never been there. In the same way, the home missionaries of the northern Protestant churches saw Appalachia as an "unchurched" land because their denominations were not represented there. The same kind of assumption concerning the otherness of Appalachia, which made the region seem an appropriate field for literary exploitation, thus made it seem a suitable field of action for home missionary endeavor. This was especially true, however, for those denominations which, after the Civil War, began to define their own mission as the establishment of a unified and homogeneous Christian nation through the integration of unassimilated populations into the mainstream of American life. Indeed, it was only with reference to a vision of national community that the "otherness" of Appalachia seemed a problem. Those denominations which did not claim a national mission, including most southern churches, lacked interest in the "plight" of the mountaineers, at least until their own claims to the mountain sections of the South as a field for evangelical work were challenged by their northern brethren.

This is not to say that there were no churches in the southern mountains before the Presbyterians and the Congregationalists and the Episcopalians began to send missionaries into the region during the mid-1880s. It was only when these and other denominations sought to serve the mountain people as a people, rather than as individuals, however, that the churches became involved with Appalachia as a region, and hence only then that their activities form part of the story which this book seeks to tell. Before, during, and after the movement of northern missionaries into the South there were local churches in Appalachia, and it is only an accident of fate and of the politics of denominational competition that the national churches sent missionaries to Appalachia instead of the other way around.

Crucial to the emergence of home-missionary activity in Appalachia was a sense that the mountaineers were in some way or other isolated from the currents of modern American life, and that in their isolation they lacked what the denominations were best able to provide—schools and churches, those critical institutions for the socialization of individuals and, by extension, groups of individuals. The alleged absence of schools and churches in the mountains, moreover, constituted at once a clear indicator of the nature of Appalachian otherness and an adequate explanation for why the mountaineers seemed so "behind the times." If that which was missing could be provided, however, the mountaineers could take their place alongside other Americans in the new national civilization which the churches hoped to create.

Need alone was insufficient to attract the attention of the northern denominations to the plight of the southern mountaineers. The existence of a disparity between the life habits of the rich and the poor, the educated and the uneducated, the urbanite and the resident of the country, the northerner and the southerner was no news, at least to the rich, the educated, the city dweller, the northerner. Only as the efforts of local-color writers to establish the objective reality of Appalachian otherness yielded a conception of the southern mountain region as a thing in itself, and only as the "peculiarities" of mountain life came to be seen as transcending that sense of otherness which resulted from a confrontation with the unfamiliar, could the mountaineers' "need" be placed in context. By the mid-1880s, that need had become an essential aspect of the disparity between Appalachia and America.

Benevolent work in the southern mountains did not begin immediately upon the perception of Appalachian otherness, however, or even upon that special definition of Appalachian otherness which the churches promulgated. It grew naturally, albeit through a series of transformations, out of an earlier program of missionary work in the South and elsewhere in the nation among the "exceptional populations" of America, and had its origins in the somewhat vaguely defined campaign of the northern churches to enter the southern field in the years immediately following the Civil War.[1]

That the renovation of the South on northern principles was seen by many supporters of the Union cause as the purpose both of the Civil War and of the Reconstruction cannot be doubted. In 1863, for example, the New York Times recommended that loyal citizens who were risking their lives to defeat the slavocracy be given an opportunity to purchase small tracts of land in the South from the plantations confiscated by government agents. The trend, according to current reports, seemed to be to leave these plantations intact, and the Times feared lest a new oligarchy be built, as the old had been, on the basis of large holdings of land. If this be the case, the Times warned, "we may bid adieu to the idea of securing the presence of a class throughout the South which, by its freedom and intelligence, will be a protection against further rebellions to overthrow free institutions. Our Northern people are of no better blood than those whom they will displace. Put them in the same circumstances, surround them with the same influence, and they will not be materially different from their predecessors."[2]

There were few who advocated the kind of structural alteration of the South's economy which this newspaper saw as a sine qua non of genuine reconstruction, however. More frequently, "an infusion of the Northern element throughout the South," as the Reverend Horace James suggested, was felt to be sufficient to effect change in the post-war South. The heritage of New England would leaven the southern loaf and thereby "aid in the restoration of the Union upon the basis of freedom, industry, education and Christian morality."[3]

By the concluding years of the war, most of those northern churches with southern counterparts had determined to implement a policy of "disintegration and absorption" toward the southern churches, whose ministers, having supported the Confederate cause, were held to be unfit teachers for the people. As early as 1862, ministers' meetings and annual conferences offered resolutions urging the missionary societies of their denominations to take possession of the South as if it were a missionary field, and after 1863 such societies regularly received authority from the Secretary of War to occupy churches in areas held by Federal forces.[4] Although such occupation did not result in the hoped-for restoration of northern denominational supremacy in the South, but rather increased sectional tensions within American Protestantism, it did make many in the North aware of both the need for and the possibility of rescuing the South from "utter barbarism" by "the infusion of a purer, a liberty-loving Christianity."[5] It also laid the groundwork for denominational work in the South, first among blacks and then, beginning in the 1880s, among whites. In this effort, those denominations which had not been split along sectional lines by the controversies of the antebellum period—especially the Congregational and Episcopal churches and the Society of Friends—also participated.

During the war years, benevolent work in the South was carried on principally among blacks, and particularly by the numerous non-denominational "voluntary" societies created for this purpose and known generically as freedmen's aid societies. By May 1866, when the American Freedmen's Union Commission was established to coordinate the often overlapping and sometimes conflicting efforts of these societies, they numbered in excess of 830, but the end of the war also brought an end to voluntarism in freedman's aid work. In the next years, the independent societies either collapsed or were absorbed by sectarian organizations founded within the several Protestant churches to complement the work of their home-missionary and church extension societies among southern blacks.[6] By 1869 sectarian boards or societies had virtually replaced the nondenominational societies in the South. Within a decade, however, these began to find their work among the freedmen a liability and a burden, and began looking for new work to do, new mission fields to serve, new areas in which to extend their denomination's influence, thereby legitimizing their own continued existence. One place they looked was to the southern mountains.

As early as the spring of 1862, the American Baptist Home Mis-

sionary Society had determined "to inaugurate a system of operations for carrying the Gospel alike to free and bond throughout the
whole Southern section of our country." To no small degree, this
programme was intended to counter the efforts of the nondenominational societies which, they said, were "laboring constantly and by
every means in their power to turn away the colored Baptists from
Baptist communion, and if possible break up their churches."[7] The
Baptists during the mid-century had never been greatly interested in
cooperative Christian work, however, and their rejection of nondenominationalism in this case was no surprise. Their delegation of
freedman's aid work to sectarian societies within their church, in the
name of sectarian interests, and their choice of the Baptist Home
Missionary and Publication societies to carry out this work, however,
foreshadowed developments in other denominations, which also
came to talk of sectarian interests and evangelical efficiency as the
principal purpose for missionary action.

In 1864, the General Assembly of the Presbyterian church (Old
School) also abandoned nondenominationalism, and established
two committees for the education of freedmen, the eastern to solicit
contributions and coordinate work east of the Alleghenies from
headquarters in Philadelphia, the western to do the same in the west
from headquarters in Indianapolis. In the following year, these two
were merged into a single Committee on Freedmen, which in turn
merged with the Committee of Home Missions for Freedmen of the
New School Presbyterian General Assembly in 1869, at the time of
the reunion. Out of this merger came the Presbyterian Committee of
Missions for Freedmen. In the process, the nature of Presbyterian
work among southern blacks also changed, as education to meet the
"pressing need" gave way before efforts to extend northern Presbyterian influence in the South.[8]

In their address to the quadrennial General Conference of 1864,
the bishops of the Methodist Episcopal church took the same line and
reminded the denomination that the progress of northern arms had
thrown open to loyal churches new fields for Christian enterprise and
labor in the South. Denying the legitimacy of the Plan of Separation
by which northern Methodists had been excluded from the southern

field since the establishment in 1845 of the Methodist Episcopal Church, South, the bishops urged that the church enter the South as if it were an "unchurched" area, and appointed David W. Clark to supervise the extension of northern Methodist influence in that section. Although Bishop Clark and others did make gestures in the direction of establishing northern Methodism among southern whites, and achieved some success in this endeavor in the immediate postwar years, a much greater effort was made to win the allegiance of the potentially more sympathetic freedmen.[9]

In August 1866, Bishop Clark called a meeting of persons interested in establishing a freedmen's aid society within the Methodist Episcopal church, including many Methodists who were prominent in the nondenominational societies. The advantages of such an organization along sectarian lines were many, the conferees agreed. First, they said, experience had demonstrated to missionaries working among the freedmen the need for schools to develop the highest usefulness of the colored people; second, the nondenominational commissions could not or would not respond favorably to requests for funds to support Methodist schools in the South, although the need was becoming more imperative with the growth of Methodist missionary effort among the freedmen; third, several leading denominations which had previously supported the nondenominational societies had recently established sectarian boards to coordinate sectarian work among black southerners as an adjunct to their own missionary endeavors, with the result that the support of the nondenominational societies was drawn very largely from among members of the Methodist Episcopal church; fourth, the Missionary and Church Extension societies of the Methodist church had their own special tasks to perform and were unable as a consequence to meet the peculiar educational needs of the colored people; fifth, the money which Methodists would ordinarily contribute to a lay society for work among the freedmen would accomplish more through a sectarian agency and in connection with the church's overall missionary program in the South. A year after its organization, the society reported that its initial efforts had met with great success. "The schools have met a great want which no military or political organization could supply, and without which it would be impossible for peace and harmony to be restored."[10]

The establishment of sectarian freedmen's aid societies had an importance in the history of American Protestantism and in the history of Protestant philanthropy at least as great as their importance in the history of postwar efforts to integrate the South into the American nation. Their establishment provided the northern churches with a first experience of continuous and systematic effort at evangelism and benevolence directed at Americanizing a portion of the American population in a way later advocated by proponents of the social gospel, and may be said to have laid the administrative groundwork for later work in the cities of America. And while one may argue whether the origins of the institutional church and its independent counterpart, the Christian settlement, lay in the efforts of those first teachers at Port Royal or in a later perception of unfulfilled needs among urban populations, in fact the later work possessed little that the earlier lacked, except a more sophisticated organization and a more systematic theoretical and theological base. As agents of home-missionary societies working in the rural South during the early twentieth century pointed out in their own defense, missionaries, not social workers, had been the first to "settle" among those they wished to aid, and their mission stations had been prototypes of the later "institutional" church, which sought to provide educational and social services to the needy as well as the good news of the Gospels.[11]

Denominational work among the freedmen in the South after the Civil War thus represents an initial venture into a new kind of activity which was to characterize Protestant home missionary efforts during later decades. This freedmen's aid work was a precedent for the social uplift activities of denominational agencies later in the century rather than the circumstance which precipitated a new conceptualization of the churches' role in American society, however. Its primary focus was on evangelism conceived as the central process in the establishment of a national community, in the context of an emerging tendency toward denominational competition. Denominational work among the freedmen created this context of competition, moreover, and thus may be said to have provided the impetus for that

extraordinary organizational revolution which the churches under-
went in the name of evangelical efficiency.

Unlike the home-missionary work of the antebellum period,
which sought to support "fledgling churches" among persons composing a "natural" church population—primarily through contributions to a newly-organized congregation's building fund and to the
salary of its minister—the new work was frankly evangelical and
frankly competitive, looking to the extension of denominational influence among the "churched" as well as the "unchurched."[12] In
pursuing this course, however, the churches did not sow their seed
broadcast but sought out those fields of missionary endeavor which
would bear the richest harvest of converts, and hence of influence. As
it became clear that the northern denominations would not be permitted to assume permanent control over the property and church-
organizations of the southern denominations after the Civil War, as
had at first been hoped, for example, they turned their attention to
work among the freedmen. In the same way, as it became apparent
that their efforts on behalf of the freedmen were compromising their
efficiency in evangelism among white southerners, they cast their
eyes upon the large population of "poor whites" whose presumed
alienation from the South of the Confederacy and the slavocracy
made them potentially sympathetic to ministrations from the North.
Among these were the mountain people of Appalachia. At the same
time, however, the churches were looking more broadly to the so-
called "exceptional populations" of the nation as groups available for
missionary work. The Mexicans and Mormons in the Southwest,
Indians in Oklahoma and on the Great Plains, the Esquimaux in
Alaska, as well as newly arrived immigrants in eastern cities and
those same mountaineers of Appalachia, had been "overlooked" by
the normal activities of church extension, and appeared to be in
"need" of home-missionary activity. In addition, their alleged "isolation" from the main currents of American life created "need" of a
different and more compelling kind, for as "exceptional populations"
their existence threatened by definition the possibilities of achieving
national unity and homogeneity. It was this threat which ultimately

provided an immediate rationalization in terms of which the appeal for funds and workers might be made.[13]

In a real sense, this shift in the definition of home-missionary activity marked a total transformation of the churches' conception of their role in American life. No longer could the national entities function as coordinating agencies for the activities of affiliated ministers and congregations. Between 1865 and 1885, as a consequence, each of the Protestant denominations effected some degree of organizational restructuring in the name of evangelical efficiency, thereby transforming themselves from the loose associations characteristic of the period of sectarian division and theological flux before the Civil War, into highly structured, national organizations composed of church members owing a primary allegiance to the denomination and its affiliated societies, and only afterward a loyalty to Christianity or benevolence in general. What came first in this process is not clear. By the mid-1880s, however, virtually all the Protestant denominations had established centralized agencies for the direction and control of the affairs of these new national churches and for the extension of influence and membership throughout the nation.[14]

One result of this reorganization was the institutionalization of what Leonard Woolsey Bacon called "the spirit of sect" through the articulation of distinctions based less on debatable issues of theology or church polity than on an essentially arbitrary allegiance of church members to one denomination and its affiliated benevolent societies rather than to another. Another result was the facilitation of sectarian competition in missionary and benevolent work by the abandonment of nondenominational societies and the rationalization of the structure of denominational boards and societies.

We have already noted the establishment of sectarian freedmen's aid societies to engage in a work which previously had been nondenominational. In the same way, the Congregational churches, for example, agreed in 1865 to adopt three previously nondenominational societies—the American Missionary Association, the American Home Missionary Society, and the American Board of Commissioners for Foreign Missions—as agencies of the denomination for the work of evangelism. The societies in turn agreed to bring an end to the traditional competition among them, and subsequently effected a division of mission fields by which the A.M.A. transferred its stations in India to the American Board, the American Board transferred its stations in Alaska and among the Indians on the Great Plains to the A.M.A., and so forth. By 1882, all Congregational work in the western states and territories (among whites) was under the supervision of the American Home Missionary Society, all work among "colored" populations—blacks and Indians—under the supervision of the American Missionary Society, and all work in foreign lands under the supervision of the American Board of Commissioners for Foreign Missions.[15]

Other denominations adopted different schemes for the division of missionary, and then educational work. Some utilized geography as a principle in allocating responsibility, others utilized race or nativity of the client population, others "degree of American-ness." Others sought to distinguish among the kinds of work carried on in particular areas or at particular mission stations. Centralization of denominational control over the denomination's societies and hence over the church's resources was also an issue fought out in the context of denominational politics from time to time, as was the relationship among local, regional, and national boards and societies—most notably within the Presbyterian church.[16] In contrast, the Methodist Episcopal church kept their administrative chart simple by containing all such work within a single agency. In 1864 the quadrennial General Conference of the denomination merely revised the constitution of the Methodist Missionary Society to enable it to engage in the new work. After that date, the society's efforts were divided into three classes: Foreign Missions, Domestic Missions, and Domestic Foreign Missions.[17]

It was in this context of denominational competition and the search for unexploited mission fields that benevolent work among the "mountain whites" of Appalachia had its origin. Essentially ameliorative, this work emphasized the need for education in Christian and American values, and in the ways of modern life, as the basic method by which the mountaineers, like other "exceptional populations" of the nation might be equipped for full participation in the life of the nation. Its principal fruits were two: the establishment of several hundred denominational and some dozen "independent" schools in the southern mountains; and the consequent institutionalization of Appalachian otherness through the implicit insistence that the mountaineers did in fact compose a distinct element in the American population.

The problem of the specific process by which denominational uplift work in the mountains began is one which remains complex, though not so complex as the problem of describing the nature and extent of this work. Elizabeth R. Hooker, whose *Religion in the Highlands* (1933) remains the best single study of denominational activity in the region, provides extensive information about current work, but passes over the period before 1900 with a series of generalizations. One of these, eminently logical but, as it turns out, not entirely correct, suggests that denominational interest in Appalachia involved a natural extension of work already under way at the time, among the freedmen.[18] Other secondary sources are even less helpful. The numerous denominational histories written during the late nineteenth and early twentieth centuries view mountain white work as of the present, and hence familiar to all readers, and mention it only as additional proof of the particular denomination's national mission to all in need of Christian education. More recent studies, imbued with the spirit of ecumenism and Christian cooperation in benevolent work taught in the liberal theological seminaries and by the example of the interdenominational agencies which grew up in the teens, tend entirely to ignore that phase in the history of Christian philanthropy in which the churches competed frankly and openly in the mission fields.

Contemporary sources are only slightly more useful. The first mission-study texts describing work in Appalachia only appeared in the early twentieth century, and tend to treat the recent past as a time of heroic endeavor. The published reports of the numerous agencies active in Appalachia are of only dubious value, since they were consciously designed to convince parent boards or the national denomination of the "pressing need" for more money and more personnel.

They fail in any case to discriminate between southern work and southern mountain work.

That very fact, of a tendency to confuse southern work with southern mountain work, however, provides the essential clue to an understanding of the origins of denominational activity in Appalachia. It was not a natural extension of work already begun among the freedmen. It was not the result of a new perception of the "needs" of the mountaineers. The several northern churches began to send missionaries to Appalachia in the 1880s during a renewed campaign directed at the evangelization and Americanization of the South. Given the reiterated declarations of respect and Christian fellowship toward "our sister congregations" to the South made at the periodic meetings of the national denominations, it was a campaign of doubtful propriety. Given the hostility with which many white southerners regarded the northern churches, it was a campaign of dubious potential for success. And given the obstacle to white evangelism which the continued commitment of the northern churches to work among the freedmen presented, it was a campaign which had to be described in official publications only with the utmost delicacy. The evangelization of the South was what everyone wanted, however, and the churches did what they could. The first thing was to clear out the race issue.

It was the "anti-caste" commitment of the northern Protestant churches which had created the greatest hostility between northern and southern denominations, and which made the missionaries of the northern churches suspect in the eyes of southern whites. In their desire to extend their influence to the South and thereby reestablish their national character, the northern denominations turned themselves into segregated entities, in the process abandoning the greater part of their work on behalf of southern blacks. Neither simple racial antipathy nor disillusionment with the results of freedmen's aid work can account for this turnabout. Indeed, there is considerable evidence that freedmen's aid work had been enormously successful. As the record sometimes shows, it was rather the expressed desire of the northern churches to win converts in the South which led to their abandonment of the Negro after 1876.

In 1880, for example, at the quadrennial General Conference of the northern Methodist church, it was noted that the refusal of that denomination's South Carolina Conference to segregate itself along racial lines had caused "the utter failure [of Methodism] to secure a hearing among the white people of the country." In this, it was added, the South Carolinians were unique. Racial segregation had been approved in principle by the General Conference of 1876 and had been carried out under its mandate by all other southern conferences of the denomination, including the Kentucky, Tennessee, Holston, North Carolina, Georgia, Alabama, and West Texas conferences. To remedy this situation, it was felt, the bishops of the church had to act despite the resistence of local ministers and congregants, and in 1882 they simply transferred the two white circuits in the South Carolina Conference to the all-white Blue Ridge Conference. After this time, segregation in the name of evangelical efficiency was made an integral part of Methodist church polity and was reflected in Methodist church organization. And the Methodists were by no means unique in this.[19]

Among Methodists, this generalized desire to enter the southern field during the 1880s yielded vertical conflict between entities representing a divergence between local and national policy, and involved a confrontation over the locus of power within the denomination. Among Congregationalists, on the other hand, it generated horizontal conflict between the American Missionary Association and the American Home Missionary Society, each of which claimed to represent the historic obligations and contemporary concerns of the church, and involved direct political confrontation between the two over the nature of their respective responsibilities. In 1883, for example, the annual meeting of the American Missionary Association addressed itself in part to the possibility that their monopoly on Congregational work in the South was being challenged by the desire of the A.H.M.S. to enter the southern field. The Association's work was among the freedmen. The Home Missionary Society claimed to represent their denomination's "deep, unmistakable interest in those long-neglected whites" of the South, whose needs in any case would not fall under the purview of the Association's charter as Congregationalism's agency for work among blacks and Indians. To the members of the American Missionary Association, the prospect of increased Congregational activity in the South thus raised political as well as moral and tactical problems. How were they to turn their parent church's "unmistakable interest . . . into channels that shall benefit these people without on the one hand neglecting the work already undertaken among the freedmen or on the other giving some suspicion of countenancing a color line and perhaps bringing a clashing of interests between sister societies?"[20] And if the Congregationalists abandoned their commitment to freedmen's aid work, what would become of the freedmen, and what would become of the American Missionary Association?

It was in response to this immediate dilemma that Charles Fairchild of Berea College phrased his remarks on the need for increasing work among the "mountain whites" of the South. Indeed, Fairchild noted, missions to the mountaineers would satisfy the demands of those who wished Congregationalism to compete more actively with other northern denominations in the southern field without compromising their traditional "anti-caste" position. The very history of Berea College and the Berea community, he pointed out, stood witness to the possibility of retaining a commitment to racial equality while engaging in missionary and educational work among southern whites. "Certainly there will arise in your minds no suspicion of waning interest in the colored people or sympathy with caste on the part of those who have heretofore been closely connected with this mountain work at Berea College and the surrounding regions." But mountain work sought to achieve the end of racial equality indirectly, by attempting to leaven the South. It was a complementary work, but not unimportant. "It is [our] unanimous conviction that work undertaken for these mountain people . . . will assist in unfurling upon a higher masthead the broad motto borne on the seal of Berea College for twenty-five years past: 'God hath made of one blood all nations of men.'"[21]

Fairchild's own concerns lay principally with the future of Berea, and especially its recognition by the American Missionary Association as a suitable agency of Congregational benevolence and an appropriate recipient of funds and support. He cast his appeal in more general terms, however, of need and possibility, and of the appropriateness of mountain white work by agencies of northern benevolence. He thereby spoke also to the immediate dilemma which the American Missionary Association faced, for in arguing the availability of the southern mountaineers as objects of home missionary endeavor it was their availability which he stressed. They were southern. They were white. They were unchurched. They were sympathetic to the ministrations of northern missionaries. In the immediate context of the American Missionary Association's dilemma they had particular usefulness. Although Fairchild did not say so explicitly, everyone must have known that the old connection between the A.M.A. and Berea, dating back to the itinerant ministry of John G. Fee before the Civil War, might be offered as proof of the Association's longtime presence in southern white work, and hence a persuasive claim to the southern field as a whole.[22]

As to the mountain country itself, Fairchild noted that it was considerably larger than most persons in the North realized, an area rich in undeveloped natural resources and capable of supporting an agricultural population many times greater than its present two thousand inhabitants. The mountain people themselves, he added, were "of the same stock and lineage that furnished from more favored sections the Clays and Breckinridges, that gave to this country Abraham Lincoln," and as a result the mountain region was "a country with different social and political characteristics" than those which prevailed elsewhere in the South. "If the North cares to dignify physical labor in the South, if it feels the need of a class that has a natural love for free, republican institutions, if it cares to have the common-school system take rooting in this soil, if it desires a class of whites that shall be the wise, consistent friends of the colored people, perhaps it may find that this large body of whites rejected by slavery will prove the effective agency under the divine planning for this purpose. The stone which the builders rejected may become the head of the corner."[23]

To some, of course, neither the needs of the mountain people for

Christian education nor their availability to northern missionary effort was relevant to the real issue at hand. "When our zeal for the propagation of Congregationalism leads us to slur over the everlasting verities of Christ's kingdom, it is leading us in doubtful ways," Washington Gladden reminded the members of the American Missionary Association. It was true that the association's work among southern blacks had caused many white southerners to turn a deaf ear to Congregationalism's message. It was true that the association's domination of the southern field was being threatened by the efforts of the American Home Missionary Society. To compromise principle in the name of evangelical efficiency, to retain institutional control over a mission field by abandoning its mission was unthinkable, however.

The disability under which this Association labors is its glory. And I do not believe that it will prove to be a permanent impediment in its work. No; that cannot be. I believe in the victorious might of Christian principles. . . . It is the one power that is irresistible. The barriers of caste will go down before it, and the color line will no longer stain the threshold of the Christian Church.[24]

Washington Gladden's cry of "no compromise" went largely unheard during the 1880s, for compromise was the rule of the day as Americans began their retreat from an earlier commitment to the integration of the freedman into the life of the nation. Ironically, the very success which had attended the churches' first efforts in the South during and immediately after the Civil War, and which had yielded substantial black membership for the northern Protestant denominations, may be said to have precipitated the events of the 1880s. As black membership in the denominations became a liability in evangelical effort among white southerners, black membership was the "problem" to be solved. In order to achieve their goal of national integration, that is, the northern denominations were forced to redefine the status of blacks so that they became one among the unassimilable populations of the nation. Thus they justified the establishment of separate-but-equal congregations, synods, assemblies, or conventions. And thus they justified the maintenance of black colleges and seminaries in a mission status, as in the case of similar institutions among other groups considered alien and unassimilable. As additional obstacles to racial integration were erected, moreover, it began to seem clear that the integration of the freedman into American life would indeed take a long time. Under such circumstances what could the churches do but turn their eyes toward different fields with a more desirable crop?

In 1880, in their formal address to the quadrennial General Conference of their church, the Methodist Episcopal Bishops asked that, along with increased evangelical work in the South, "educational work among the poorer white people of the South should be in some way developed through the general benevolence of the Church," and suggested that "the sphere of the Freedmen's Aid Society might be enlarged, so that it would work in the same lines in this field also." This matter was referred to the Standing Committee on Freedmen's Aid and Southern Work, which informed the General Conference that the phrase "and others" in the society's constitution made such an extension of the field possible. Upon the recommendation of this committee, the conference instructed the board of managers of the Freedmen's Aid Society "to give such aid" to white schools in the South "as can be done without embarrassment to the schools among the freedmen." This mandate was renewed by the General Conferences of 1884 and 1888, and in the latter year the society's name was changed to accord more with the nature of its work, so that it became the Freedmen's Aid and Southern Educational Society of the Methodist Episcopal Church. Its board of managers preferred the more ambiguous name, "Southern Education Society."[25]

By the mid-1880s, all the northern Protestant churches had determined to extend their missionary activities among southern whites. The road south, the Presbyterians were told in 1884, for example, was marked by "a wide open door" which gave access to "a ripe field . . . much neglected in the past."[26] As things turned out, however, the door was not quite so open, the field not quite so ripe, and not at all so neglected as at first seemed to be the case. Thus while the rhetoric of home missions continued to focus on the "Americanization" of the South through the end of the century, in practice the southern campaigns of the northern churches yielded instead the establishment of preaching station and mission schools in the southern mountains.

In the churches' experience with freedmen's aid work during the 1860s, perception of need came first, before formulation of a program to meet that need, establishment of agencies to carry out the program, or articulation of a rationale to justify both. The northern denominations entered the southern mountains during the 1880s, however, already equipped with program, agencies, and rationale. Indeed, to the degree that southern work at the end of the nineteenth century resulted from a search for "new worlds to conquer" rather than from the identification of special needs among southern whites, the dominant motif of this effort must inevitably have become a process of accommodation by which an institutionalized program, established agencies, and a conventional rationale were utilized for purposes other than those for which they had been created. In practice this meant that sometimes program, agencies, and rationale would be altered to fit southern conditions, and sometimes southern conditions would be defined in such a way as to make the use of available techniques seem appropriate. In either case, however, at the heart of home-missionary work during the 1880s stood the school, the crucial institution of that epoch as the church had been the crucial institution of an earlier effort.

Until the 1870s, denominational agencies rarely engaged in educational work below the seminary level, except among the freedmen in the South. The extension of home-missionary efforts in the American West among the newly discovered "exceptional populations" of the nation, however, was accompanied by the inauguration of educational work by agencies previously concerned with evangelism or sustentation exclusively. It was this new work, of course, which precipitated the transformation of home-missionary activity more generally, but it also initiated a period of inter-agency competition as the several freedmen's aid societies found their monopoly on educational work within a denomination challenged by the new work of the home missionaries. In 1877, for example, the Presbyterian Board of Home Missions informed the General Assembly that although school work was entirely new to its operations, "now we have reached a point where something of the kind must be done."

We must begin work among the Indians, the Mexicans, and the Mormons, very much as we would in Persia or India; very much as foreign missionaries begin their work in foreign lands. Finding no material ready to our hand from which to organize churches, we must begin among the children . . . and through these expect to reach parents and the adult population, and with this new material at length build up Christian congregations, and prosecute the work of evangelization among the people.[27]

Objections to this extension of the home mission board's mandate beyond support of fledgling churches in established presbyteries persisted, however, and in its annual report of 1878, the board reminded the General Assembly that educational work was a necessary part of its total effort on behalf of Presbyterianism. Such work could not properly be limited to a single geographic area, moreover, although the board agreed that it would be conducted "only among populations that cannot be reached as yet by churches," and then stipulated that "this condition shall be understood as referring to Mormons, Mexicans, Aztecs, Indians, Chinese, and natives of Alaska. No school shall be established or supported by this Board, in States or Territories which have already, or are likely soon to have school-laws, unless there shall appear to be strong and special reasons for making a temporary exception to this rule." Lest suspicion be aroused that this new work would compromise the old, the board noted that "so far as may be practical," support for the schools "shall be committed to the women of our Church as their special trust, out of whose contributions, without drawing upon our regular Home Missionary Fund, shall be taken what . . . may be needed for this work."[28]

Despite such disclaimers by the managers of the several home-missionary agencies, it was clear both that the new work marked a significant departure from traditional denominational activity and that its effect would be to elevate in importance the home-missionary agencies at the expense of other boards and societies. For these reasons, because change is often painful and because many had much to lose, the inauguration of educational work by the northern Protestant denominations was accompanied by the emergence of a new vocabulary in which change was not change and loss was gain. From the mid-1870s, as a consequence, the institutionalization of educational work as a normal aspect of home-missionary activity was represented as a temporary effort capable of achieving its goals in a short time, directed exclusively at those "exceptional populations" who, like the freedmen during Reconstruction, would otherwise turn their proverbial deaf ear to the good news of the Gospels.

The consequences of this situation for the conduct of northern denominational work in the South during the 1880s were considerable. It was virtually required that all educational work be conceived of as a temporary expedient rather than a long-term commitment, and that the churches' goal of the Americanization and Christianization of the nation be viewed as realizable within one generation. It virtually required that any population to be served by denominational schools be identifiable, and be identified, as "exceptional." And it virtually required that established educational institutions—including the numerous schools and colleges founded by the freedmen's aid societies—be maintained in (or in some cases restored to) the dependency of mission status.

Unlike the Mormons, the Mexicans, the Chinese, unlike the freedmen, increasingly identified in the 1880s as "African" and hence explicitly as alien, southern whites were at least ostensibly as "American" as northern whites, members already by congressional fiat if not by culture and historical experience of the American national community. To the degree that the churches' earlier work among exceptional populations of the nation provided a model for the conduct of this new southern white work, however, the latter tended to focus on those groups within the southern population which might be identified as "exceptional," and whose alienation from modern American life seemed to present obstacles to the creation of a unified and homogeneous nation: the "poor whites" and the "mountain whites."[29] Because of the northern churches' desire to avoid conflict with their sister denominations to the south, however, "southern white work" tended in practice to mean work among the mountaineers of Appalachia, and this in turn tended increasingly to mean the identification of the mountaineers as one among the "exceptional populations" of the nation.

By 1886, virtually all the northern Protestant denominations had initiated evangelical and educational work in the southern Appalachian mountains, or, more precisely, had initiated work which they designated as serving the needs of the mountain whites of the South. Prior to the twentieth century, of course, neither the boundaries of Appalachia nor the definition of "mountain whites" was drawn with any precision, but the essential casualness of contemporary usage was not without function. For the agents of the northern churches, there were significant advantages to be gained from an identification of their client population as mountain whites. For one thing, it cast the work clearly within the context of southern white work, as part of a highly advertised but often unspecified effort to extend northern values and northern influence among southerners. At the same time it pointed to the traditional isolation of the mountaineers from the rest of the southern population—an isolation which was the result of geography and perhaps also of ethnicity, but which in any case had preserved them from the taint of slavery and prevented their full complicity with the slavocracy, and thus made them at once more deserving of and more amenable to the ministrations of the northern agencies of benevolence. "Mountain whites" not only identified the residents of Appalachia as composing a distinct element of the southern population, however. It also made an implicit comparison between the mountaineers and the so-called "poor whites" of the South, with whom they had in common a condition of ignorance and poverty and hence the status of an "exceptional population," but whose situation of degradation they did not share. Like the "poor whites," that is, the mountaineers were needy, but unlike the "poor whites," their condition was not hopeless. The inauguration of evangelical and educational work could be expected to yield satisfactory results from a small investment.

There was one other advantage as well, of course. The "mountain whites" were the same people whose ignorance, whose poverty, and especially whose apparent isolation from the main currents of modern American life had made them available as subjects for literary treatment, which in turn had effected a definition of them as a peculiar people in a strange land. As such, they fit easily into the churches' notions of what made an "exceptional population" exceptional, even while their treatment at the hands of the local-color writers cast about them a romantic haze. They were, as a consequence, "exceptional" in a very special and not particularly troublesome way. By the mid-eighties, moreover, they were familiar.

During the late 1880s and the 1890s, evangelical and educational work both in the mountains and near the mountains tended to be identified as "mountain white work," without real regard to what we would now consider the crucial relationship of location and the character of the population such work was intended to serve, and hence without real regard to what we would consider the "needs" of the community. Preaching stations and churches, day schools, boarding schools, academies and normal schools were established as convenience dictated, and tended for obvious reasons to cluster around the larger centers of population. One result of this, as we shall see, was an increasing tendency for the agents of the northern churches to define the mountaineers' "need" in terms of the absence of community rather than in terms of the absence of schools and churches, as their own experience in Appalachia suggested that schools and churches were symbols of community and the agents of its creation, rather than discrete institutions for the "uplift" of individuals. In this early period, when denominational activities in the southern mountains were viewed primarily as an aspect of southern white work, the very vagueness of contemporary notions of who were "mountain whites" and where they might be found facilitated the inauguration of programs for "their" benefit. It made possible, that is, the justification of a wide variety of activities as serving the needs of the "mountain whites." After 1900 this same vagueness drew those agencies which had justified the extension of their own work into the South on the basis of the "needs" of the mountaineers into a genuine confrontation with the problem of what those "needs" were, and into a genuine commitment to meet them.

The vagueness of contemporary notions of who were "mountain whites" and where they were to be found makes it particularly difficult to assess the extent and even the nature of denominational work in Appalachia during the 1880s and 1890s. No consolidated data exist for the period prior to John and Olive Dame Campbell's surveys of southern mountain work, begun in 1908 under the aegis of the Russell Sage Foundation as an initial attempt to understand a complicated and rapidly changing situation, while later studies necessarily treat the development of mountain work as a prelude to that present with which they are primarily concerned. Nonetheless, two general tendencies may be said to have characterized the development of benevolent work in Appalachia: first, the rapid emergence and escalation of mountain white work as a distinct category of home-missionary activity after about 1886; second, a corresponding tendency to identify work already begun in the South outside of Appalachia, as serving the needs of the mountaineers, in an effort to justify the new work as something old and hence no innovation, and also in an effort to indicate the viability of the new work on the basis of past successes.

To the Presbyterian church goes the honor of having been the first to institute educational work for the benefit of the "mountain whites." In the mid-1870s, Reverend L. M. Pease, his health impaired by many years of labor at the Five Points Mission in New York City, either moved to or visited Asheville, North Carolina, well-known as a resort town since the 1850s. There he became interested in the plight of the little mountaineer girls and informed Reverend Thomas Lawrence, then on the faculty of Biddle Memorial University, a Presbyterian college for blacks located in Charlotte, North Carolina, of his desire to found a school for their benefit. Specifically, he offered to deed to the church a thirty-three acre farm and a furnished boarding house near Asheville as a site for the school, but neither Pease nor Lawrence seems to have initiated any action to bring the school into existence.

In 1877, however, when the Presbyterian Board of Home Missions was searching for a school site, Lawrence informed them of Pease's offer, which was then accepted. The Home Industrial School for Girls was opened on 4 October 1877 by the Board of Home Missions, which subsequently established the Asheville Farm School for boys in 1886–87. Both schools later came under the supervision of the Woman's Executive Board of Home Missions of the Presbyterian church, which had been created in the mid-1870s to administer all school work under the Presbyterian Board of Home Missions. In 1892, Lawrence himself moved to Asheville to become superintendent of a third school, the Asheville Normal and Collegiate Institute.[30]

The first school in the mountains founded directly by the women of the Presbyterian church, and much loved in consequence by the editors of *Home Mission Monthly*, the organ of the Woman's Executive Board, was Whitehall Seminary in Concord, North Carolina. Whitehall was the creation of the New York Woman's Home Missionary Society, and opened in June 1879. Frances E. Ufford of Bloomfield, New Jersey, who had served an apprenticeship in the mountains at the Home Industrial School, was in charge. After a fire destroyed the school building in the winter of 1890–91, Ufford raised over $10,000 from Presbyterian women to continue the work. A new building was completed in 1897, and the school was renamed after Laura Sutherland.[31]

The origin of the Dorland Institute at Hot Springs, North Carolina, was similar to that of the Home Industrial School. In 1879 the Reverend Luke Dorland and his wife visited Hot Springs to recoup their health. There "the low and degraded condition of the mountaineers appealed to them," and they determined to open a school for girls modeled after Scotia Seminary, a Presbyterian school for black girls in Concord, North Carolina, which he had helped found in 1872. The school was taken over by the Presbyterian Board of Home Missions in 1883 and administered by the Woman's Executive Board.[32]

Between 1885 and 1895 the Presbyterians organized thirty-one schools in the mountains, and in the following decade, an additional thirty-four. In 1885, however, the work was just beginning. It was only in that year, for example, that the home missions board mentioned its work among the mountaineers specifically in its annual report to the General Assembly, and even then only in the context of efforts on behalf of southern whites more generally. (During the later 1880s, on the other hand, "Southern white work" in the board's reports was to be understood as a metaphor for "mountain white work," while "schools among southern whites" came to mean schools in or near the mountain region, serving the mountaineers as one of "the exceptional populations of our land.")[33] In 1886 the board could point to the existence of only two Presbyterian schools in Appalachia, however, as compared to eighty-five in other parts of the country. Yet the need was apparent.

Among Presbyterians, religion and knowledge go hand in hand; churches and schools supplement and assist each other. . . . The Presbyterian Church does not prosper in ignorance or illiteracy. In pushing our missionary work into the South, we have struck another great mass of illiteracy, this time among the whites. . . . The census tells the story. . . . These hardy mountaineers are eager for schools. . . . The first expressed want is an academy— and perhaps they are quite right, for if universal education is to be introduced in their States, as the common school system is in some other States, the first want is the education of their sons and daughters that they may become teachers.[34]

From these Presbyterian beginnings, directed at alleviating a situation of poverty, illiteracy, and degradation consequent to the mountaineers' isolation from American life and their long "neglect" by the churches, denominational uplift work in the southern mountain region developed. In 1884 the American Missionary Association began a campaign to raise funds for the establishment of schools and particularly colleges in the mountains, to serve Appalachia and the South as their institutions among the freedmen had served the South and the nation after the Civil War. In 1882, Dr. Edward O. Guerrant, a Southern Presbyterian layman, was appointed "Mountain Evangelist" by the Kentucky Synod of the Southern Presbyterian church and became the first full-time worker of that denomination in the mountain region. Between 1890, when he founded the "Soul-Winner's Society," and his retirement in 1912, he organized thirteen schools in the mountains, and by the end of the period was recognized as the Southern General Assembly's agent for mountain white work. The Southern Baptist and Southern Methodist churches began sending evangelists into the mountains in the mid-eighties and subsequently began school work also. The Protestant Episcopal church began work among the mountaineers in 1889. The women's societies of the Methodist Episcopal church organized their first school in Appalachia in 1892.[35]

In general, the denominational agencies which worked in the southern mountain region were content to see the discrepancy between Appalachia and America as a "social problem," the result of the mountaineers' isolation from those two pillars of American culture, the church and the school. If these were provided, then the mountaineer could literally be "uplifted" into modern American life, and that danger to American homogeneity and unity implicit in the very existence of "exceptional populations," be eliminated. This phase of the uplift movement in the mountains may be called "ameliorative" since it sought simply to provide that which was lacking as an isolated act of benevolence, without serious consideration of the nature, the extent, or the origins of the needs it sought to meet.[36]

It was no accident that the northern churches began work in the southern Appalachian mountains at a time when the popularity of Murfree was at its height, or that *In The Tennessee Mountains* was used as a first mission-study text for those who wished to understand conditions in the region. The interest in Appalachia generated by the descriptions of the local-color writers was consciously used by the agents of denominational work in the region to support their claim to attention from the churches' boards and societies, and to financial support from their membership, while the very existence of a substantial body of literature describing a strange land and peculiar people in the southern mountains lent credence to their assertions of Appalachian otherness. That the churches' discovery of Appalachia occurred at this time and in this context was not without consequences, moreover, for it meant that the Appalachia they discovered would be the Appalachia of the local colorists, not merely another region in need of home missionaries.

The churches discovered Appalachia quite independently of the local colorists, and saw the region in terms of their own experiences and in terms of their own needs. But because they shared with the local colorists certain notions about the nature of American civilization and about the exceptional quality of cultural diversity in America, they found an essentially literary vision of Appalachia as a discrete entity, in but not of America, not simply the most readily available but an entirely acceptable picture of the reality with which they were to deal. As a result, like the local-color writers, it was to this vision of reality, and to the dilemma which Appalachia's existence as a discrete entity seemed to pose—rather than to the reality of Southern mountain life—that their response was made.

3. Solving the "Problem" of  Appalachian Otherness: The Role of History and Environment

Because the basic unit of church membership was the individual communicant, the focus of denominational benevolence in Appalachia as among the so-called exceptional populations of America generally, was on the individual. When those engaged in benevolent work spoke about the mountaineers as a group, a class, or a population they meant an undefined number of individuals conceived of as individuals, and incidentally located in a single geographic region. They did not mean a distinct population composing a discrete social or cultural unit, an entity which might be regarded as existing independent of the particular individuals of which it was composed. It was only the convenience of the collective noun, and the desirability of asserting a reality of need by emphasizing its widespread occurrence among numerous individuals that led them to speak of the mountaineers as a group, a class, or a population at all. Yet having once begun, the impulse to continue was irresistible. It was thus almost inevitable that their collective nouns should be taken in a corporate sense, and the existence of a "degenerate" class in Appalachia, for example, or an "as-yet unregenerate" class, be discussed in terms of the implications of its existence for American civilization and the American social order.

Since mountain white work was generally conducted by those denominational agencies which already had responsibility for home-missionary work done among the exceptional populations of America, there was a certain logic in the classification of the mountaineers as one among these populations. Despite obvious differences between the respective situations of the mountain people of Appalachia and the Catholic Mexican-Americans of the Southwest, for example, it enabled the churches to justify their new southern work in the same terms as this other. They were thus able to identify the inauguration of mountain white work as meeting a more broadly conceived need than the situation of the mountaineers themselves might have suggested, and to pass over the use they sought to make of this work, as providing an ingress to the southern field.

Discussion of the mountaineers as a group, a class, or a population had an additional advantage for the agents of denominational benevolence, in that it identified the objects of their concern with those "peculiar people" described by the local-color writers, and hence made possible not only easy reference to conventional images derived from the work of a Mary Noailles Murfree or a John Fox, Jr., but also a capitalization on the general interest in Appalachia which this literature had generated. While the churches' programs for the integration of the mountaineers into modern American life focused on work with individuals, moreover, their general conception of the problem of the meaning of Appalachia's existence was conditioned by their utilization of an essentially literary vision, in terms of which individuals were merely emblems, the representatives of a group, a class, or a population, and by the demands of the literary medium in which their own appeals for financial assistance and continued denominational support were presented.

At the outset, the agents of denominational uplift merely carried over into their own work the sense of otherness which was the burden of the local colorists' sketches of the strange land and peculiar people. It was this "otherness" which made the mountaineers available for definition as an "exceptional population" of the nation and hence as legitimate objects of home missionary endeavor. But where the local colorists had been content to see mountain life as quaint and picturesque, and for this reason inherently interesting, the agents of denominational benevolence necessarily saw Appalachian otherness as an undesirable condition and viewed the "peculiarities" of mountain life as social problems in need of remedial action. And where the local-color writers had been content to utilize the fact of Appalachian otherness as the basis for sketches and stories set in the region, the agents of denominational uplift found otherness acceptable as the basis for a perception of the need for action, but of no help whatsoever in designing a program for action.

Help was available, however. The agents of denominational uplift had only to choose from among the numerous details of life in the southern mountains provided by the local-color writers, those which best suited the churches' needs and intentions in initiating work among the mountain whites. In choosing, however, they necessarily selected those characteristics which suggested that the conditions of mountain life were undesirable per se, and, more to the point, undesirable because of the threat they posed to the maintenance or establishment of a unified and homogeneous American nation. In choosing, moreover, they necessarily committed themselves to a particular view of Appalachian otherness and to a particular view of the characteristics by which this otherness was defined, without regard to the realities of mountain life, the changes which time and their own efforts had wrought, or the complex patterns of social and economic diversity within the region itself. Like the local colorists, who had to insist on the reality of Appalachian otherness lest their work lose its validity and its appeal, the agents of denominational benevolence had to insist on the reality of the mountaineers' need lest their work lose its purpose. And they had to insist on the reality of this need even as they insisted on the success of their own efforts to meet it.

The inauguration of denominational work in the southern mountains thus had enormous consequences for Americans' understanding of the nature and implications of Appalachian otherness. It meant the institutionalization of a peculiar ambiguity, inherent in the work of the local colorists, by which the mountaineers became at once like us and not like us and the characteristics of mountain life came to seem at once permanent, descriptors of a reality of Appalachian otherness, and temporary, remediable conditions which would yield to systematic social action. It also meant the institutionalization of a particular definition of mountain life as squalid and degenerate, of the mountaineers as those who lived in squalor and degeneracy, and of Appalachian otherness as a social problem. The abandonment of the local colorists' vision of mountain life as quaint and picturesque and of Appalachia as an unknown "little corner" of the nation thus meant the institutionalization of Appalachian otherness as a dilemma, to be dealt with as such, and quite independently of programs for dealing with the needs of the mountaineers.

What had been no more than an abstract issue emerging out of the work of the local-color writers now assumed a reality and an immediacy it had not had. As the agents of denominational benevolence sought to describe the conditions of mountain life in periodicals, mission-study texts, and reports to their parent boards or societies, and as they sought to define the special quality of mountain white work which distinguished it from southern work and from work among the exceptional populations of the nation more generally, moreover, they asked a new question, about the "meaning" of Appalachia. And as mountain white work became a regular and continuing aspect of denominational benevolence in America, their vision of Appalachia as an anomaly within an otherwise homogeneous and unified nation and of the mountaineers as "needy" emerged as the unchallenged assumptions upon which an entire institutional structure rested. If those assumptions should prove to be incorrect, that structure would fall, and with it would fall those whose work was directed at improving the quality of mountain life. There were few indeed who viewed that possibility without distress.

The agents of denominational benevolence had not only a stake in a continuing vision of Appalachia as a strange land inhabited by a peculiar people, but also an apparently legitimate claim to special knowledge concerning the nature of mountain life. Theirs was not the knowledge of casual observation from a train window or a hotel's veranda but was derived from actual residence in the region, and an intimacy with the people themselves. When the home missionaries spoke of mountain life as squalid and degenerate, on the one hand, and of the mountaineers as ethnically and religiously identical with the dominant groups in the American population, on the other hand, they spoke with the voice of authority. Indeed, after 1890 they became the experts on mountain life which the local colorists had been in earlier decades, so that their particular vision of mountain life, rather than the more generalized sense of otherness which the local color writers had advanced, came to dominate, not only the literature of uplift but also fiction and belleslettres and the literature of the new social sciences.

After 1890, as a consequence, it becomes impossible to draw clear distinctions based on conceptions of the nature of Appalachian otherness, or indeed on content generally, between the literature of the later local colorists and their successors, like John Fox, Jr., and the literature of systematic benevolence. Not only did the authors of mountain fiction accept as authoritative the descriptions of mountain life as squalid and degenerate propounded by the agents of denominational uplift, and follow their logic by echoing their call for remedial social action, but they also turned increasingly to the schools and mission stations in Appalachia as centers from which to observe mountain life. Just as the hotel owners in the developing resort areas of the southern mountains appear to have encouraged local-color writers to stop for a visit, expecting that the delights of mountain scenery as viewed from a particular hotel's veranda would appear as an element in some story or sketch and hence encourage business, so also in the 1890s the teachers and preachers in Appalachia encouraged writers to pay a call. It was a different view of mountain life which was thus to be obtained, however. Not scenery but human need formed the focus of the new stories and sketches which this generation of writers produced. No longer were tourists the protagonists of their literary efforts—artists, writers, sportsmen on vacation —but teachers, social workers, engineers, the agents of social and economic modernization. If Appalachia was needy, then what was interesting now became the causes of that need, and the attempts to meet it.

In the literature of Appalachia published after 1890, then, the mountains were no longer presented simply as a strange land inhabited by a peculiar people. The existence of Appalachia itself now appeared as a problem to be solved, and the apparent disparity between mountain life and the "normal" life of Americans elsewhere in the nation as a "social problem" to be remedied through systematic benevolence. Along with description and anecdote, the new literature of the southern mountains characteristically included explanations for the "causes" of Appalachian otherness, at least a passing remark on the "pressing need" for remedial social action, and often a description of the activities of those currently engaged in attempts to modernize mountain life and thereby to integrate the region and its people into the life of the nation.

It is a warrant of the essential ambiguity with which Americans confronted the fact of Appalachian otherness during these years that this should have been so, for the function of explanation was conservative in that it argued for the "normality" of Appalachian otherness, while the thrust of the calls for social action obviously looked to the elimination of otherness. The transformation of Appalachian otherness from an "interesting" fact to a bothersome reality in either case was the critical phenomenon of the 1890s, however. And while the "dilemma" of Appalachian otherness was implicit in the work of the local colorists, it emerged when it did, and in the form it did, as a direct result of the efforts of home missionaries and secular reformers to explain to themselves, to their parent boards or societies, and to the general public what they were up to and why. In this effort, they all began with the same assumption: that Appalachia was a strange land inhabited by a peculiar people, that Appalachian otherness—defined by contrast with an unspecified but clearly conceived notion of what American civilization was or ought to be—was a reality.

To the local-color writers of the 1870s and 1880s, Appalachia seemed to be interesting intrinsically. As an unknown region of the nation, and as an exception which proved the rule of American progress and of American unity and homogeneity, its availability as a subject of literature derived from the fact of its existence. To the agents of Protestant home-missionary work during the 1870s and 1880s, Appalachia also seemed intrinsically interesting. As an unchurched area, and as a potential portal of entry into the South for northern denominational activity, its availability as a mission field derived from the fact of its existence in just the same way. The institutionalization of Appalachian otherness, which was the legacy of twenty years' activity by writers and home missionaries, altered this situation. By 1890, widespread acceptance of Appalachian otherness as a fact of American life made the southern mountains region less interesting in and of itself. By casting Appalachia in the role of America's opposite, however, the institutionalization of Appalachian otherness gave this strange land and peculiar people an extrinsic interest much greater than the intrinsic interest it had possessed for an earlier generation.

What made Appalachia interesting after 1890 were the implications which the fact of its existence held for an understanding of America itself. As America's opposite, as the past persisting into the present, or simply as a discrete region, in but not of America, Appalachia appeared no longer as the exception which proved but as the exception which challenged the rule of progress and of national unity and homogeneity. Discussion of Appalachian otherness after this date, as a consequence, was concerned less with the peculiarities of mountain life and more with the meaning of Appalachia's existence and the relationship of Appalachia and America. American interest in the southern mountains, indeed, became part of a larger dialogue on the nature of America, its history, its current situation, and its future.

In this context, the attitude one struck towards Appalachia had less to do with one's perception of the reality of mountain life than with one's conception of what America was or ought to be. Those who approved of American civilization as it was at the end of the century, or as it was becoming, necessarily disapproved of the characteristics of mountain life. Those who were ambiguous in their judgment about American civilization, on the other hand, characteristically saw in Appalachia an alternative pattern of culture from which Americans might learn to recognize their own faults. Those who regarded American civilization as the product of inevitable processes of historical development were at pains to explain how one region of the nation had been excepted from the operation of these transforming processes. Those who regarded American civilization as the product of historical processes the outcome of which was uncertain, on the other hand, saw Appalachia as the product of the same historical processes operating in a different environment and/or among a different people. For all, however, the existence of Appalachia had become a "problem."[1]

No one said that the existence of Appalachia posed a problem. After 1890, however, writers found Appalachian otherness less quaint than bothersome, and sought to provide some explanation for it in their stories and sketches. After 1890, the Protestant home missionaries found the otherness of Appalachia less an index of the mountaineers' "need" than an undesirable situation, and sought to find some explanation for it which could guide them in meliorating the conditions of mountain life and integrating the region into the nation. And after 1890 also, practitioners of the new social science disciplines turned increasingly to Appalachia as a test case, through which they might develop their own understanding of the relationship of culture, environment, and population in American history. In the fact of answers offered we may find evidence of a question understood if never asked. In the fact of solutions proffered we may find evidence of a problem understood if never clearly stated. That we must be at some pains to recognize what was going on does not mean that contemporaries found it equally difficult.

In one sense it was inevitable that the existence of Appalachia should emerge as a "problem" around 1890. The question "how came men so ancient in their type, so indifferent to progress or 'style' to exist in the heart of the nineteenth century, in the United States at that?"[2] was, after all, inherent both in the local colorists' discovery and in the definition of Appalachia as an appropriate field for missionary endeavor. In addition, the institutionalization of Appalachian otherness functioned not only to validate the claims of writers and home missionaries to be dealing with reality rather than with notions about reality, but also to create a situation which could sustain a continuing interest in the southern mountains as an area of literary or benevolent activity after the period of discovery. It was then but a logical next step to transform the rhetorical question of the local colorists' surprise into a real question to be answered.

Logical or not, this next step need not have been taken. Mary Noailles Murfree, for example, did not take it, but continued writing

stories and sketches emphasizing the quaint and picturesque qualities of mountain life through the last decades of the century. It is
significant, however, that few of her efforts of this later period were
acceptable to the editors of the middle-class monthlies who had
sought her stories in the late seventies and eighties. Her work had
come to seem "old-fashioned," and only the new children's magazines that appeared at the end of the century welcomed those long
passages of description and the melodramatic incidents which had
always characterized her work. James Lane Allen also did not take
the next step, but instead backed off from the dilemma posed by
Appalachia's existence once he saw it clearly, and turned his attention to "larger themes" which were by their very nature easier to
handle. Only with the emergence of a new generation of writers, who
sought both to build on the work of their predecessors and to do them
one better, and who, most important, approached Appalachian otherness as an already established fact, was the problem of Appalachia
articulated in literature. In the history of benevolent work among the
mountaineers, the same pattern is apparent. Only with the emergence of new agencies or of new persons to take charge of old agencies did "mountain white work" begin to achieve a distinct status
within home-missionary work, or did the "problem" of Appalachia's
existence as a discrete region of the nation begin to seem the central
fact with which benevolent workers had to deal.

The occurrence of explanation always points to the existence of
something which needs to be explained. The surest sign that the
existence of Appalachia had become a "problem" was the emergence
of a convention that required explanation for the fact of Appalachian
otherness or the disparity between Appalachia and America in even
the briefest and least analytical sketches of mountain life published
after 1890. We may ourselves "explain" the occurrence of such explanatory passages as the result of trends or fashions in nonnarra-
tive American prose as it developed at the end of the nineteenth
century, or of trends or fashions within the genre of writing about
Appalachian literature. The very fact that explanation had become a
necessary or expected element in such literature suggests that acknowledgment of the "problem" of Appalachia had also become

conventional. And that is all we need to say, for it was from the widespread acknowledgment that the existence of Appalachia did pose a problem that subsequent patterns emerged.

Explanation was indeed itself one such pattern, and involved not only the passing attempts at explanation alluded to above, but also the development of a substantial literature dealing more directly with the "causes" of Appalachian otherness and with the implications of Appalachian otherness for an understanding of American civilization more generally. As such, explanation functioned to resolve the dilemma generated by the fact of Appalachian otherness by transforming it into an abstract issue of concern only to philosophers and social scientists or by identifying the disparity between Appalachia and America as the "natural" consequence of the special characteristics of the region, its people, and its unique history. In addition, explanation provided the concepts and defined the problems in terms of which other kinds of responses to the existence of the strange land and peculiar people of the southern mountains occurred, and hence must be seen as central to an understanding of American interest in Appalachia after 1890.

At its simplest level, explanation involved nothing more than naming. The designation of the mountainous portions of eight southern states as "Appalachian America," a discrete and natural unit of the nation, "one of God's grand divisions" of the continent, as William Goodell Frost put it, functioned as explanation to the degree that it implied that the perceived otherness of Appalachia was normal, for example.[3] In the same way, the designation of the region as "the Southern Highlands" by John Campbell and others in the early twentieth century not only recognized the independent existence of the region (and hence the normality of Appalachian otherness), but suggested that the disparity between mountain life and life in the rest of America was merely another instance of the normal disparity between life among highlanders and lowlanders so familiar to the readers of Walter Scott.[4] Because Appalachia possessed no reality independent of its conceptualization as a discrete entity, however, naming was also an act of creation, and explaining was also an act of naming. Appalachia was what it was named, and it was to the reality contained in the name or explanation, rather than to the reality of mountain life itself, that response occurred.[5]

The manner in which explanation functioned to resolve the tension between Appalachia and America can be seen most easily in fiction, for the demands of the literary medium tended to prohibit an author from leaving this tension, characteristically expressed in the relationship between emblematic characters, unresolved. Explanation was not the only available technique by which such resolution might be achieved, of course. Death and departure were significantly easier, and certainly more final ways of disposing of the bothersome emblems of opposing cultures. In Mary Noailles Murfree's "The Star in the Valley," as we have already noted, the disparity between Appalachia and America is symbolized by the physical, social, and personal gulf which separated Reginald Chevis, a gentleman sportsman vacation in the southern mountains, and the winsome daughter of a local blacksmith. When Chevis finds himself falling in love with the girl, he determines to beat a hasty retreat to the safety of his more familiar New York. Shortly thereafter, the girl herself dies in an incident concocted by Murfree to tie up all the loose ends of the story.

For Murfree and many of her contemporaries during the 1870s and 1880s, the disparity between Appalachia and America was more a matter of difference in social class than in culture, or more precisely it was a matter of class difference which amounted to cultural difference. Chevis's camp on the hilltop and the girl's cabin in the valley stood for the high and low of their respective stations in life, although like all Murfree's mountaineers neither the girl nor her father acknowledge this difference, in this way displaying further evidence of their low station. From Murfree's point of view on the hilltop, the girl is never seen as even a potentially acceptable mate for Chevis, although he persists in his infatuation so long that the author must arbitrarily remove him from the environs to prevent any further development of the relationship. "He had not even a subacute idea," Murfree explains "that he looked upon these people and their inner life only as picturesque bits of the mental and moral landscape; that it was an aesthetic and theoretical pleasure their contemplation afforded him; that he was as far as ever from the basis of common humanity."[6]

The reification of the local colorists' vision of Appalachia as a strange land inhabited by a peculiar people, which occurred in part as a result of Murfree's own work, and the consequent identification of the mountainous portions of eight states as a discrete unit of the nation, worked a transformation in the nature of the perceived opposition of Appalachia and America. Though still important, class distinctions could no longer be seen as the sum of this opposition. The emergence of a new series of problems consequent to Appalachia's new status as an entity in but not of America further complicated the matter, moreover, as John Fox's reworking of "The Star in the Valley" into "A Mountain Europa" demonstrates.

"A Mountain Europa" was Fox's first mountain story, begun in 1888, under the immediate influence both of Murfree's work, then recently collected as *In the Tennessee Mountains*, and of James Lane Allen's sketch, "Through Cumberland Gap on Horseback." Allen provided the title for the story by his remark that in the Kentucky mountains one may see women "going to mill with their scant sacks of grain, riding on a jack, a jennet, or a bridled ox. But this is not so bad as in North Carolina, where, Europa-like, they ride on bulls."[7] The story itself, however, is pure Murfree.

Like Chevis, Fox's Clayton first sees the girl of the story on the sylvan paths near his camp and is attracted by her lithe, swaying beauty. The fact that she is astride a bull seems incidental to this attraction. Where for Chevis the girl and her fellow mountaineers, and the mountains themselves are ultimately no more than inert bits of local color, background to his vacation experience, however, Fox's hero is directly involved with the physical and social reality of the mountain environment in which he finds himself.

Like John Fox himself, who entered the mountains on family business, Clayton is a young mining engineer who has been called back from student days in Germany to develop the mineral lands in the South which his father had purchased shortly after the Civil War and which remained as the only resource left to a family whose fortune had been wiped out by economic depression. Coming to the mountains "was like beginning a new life with a new identity" for him, so striking was the transition from his life in New York to this one in the mountains. Then he had been heir to all of modern civilization; now he was its agent. "There was nothing in the pretty glen, when he came, but a mountaineer's cabin and a few gnarled old apple trees, the roots of which checked the musical flow of a little stream. Then the air was filled with the tense ring of hammer and saw, the mellow echoes of axes, and the shouts of ox-drivers from the forest . . . and suddenly a little town sprang up before his eyes, and cars of shining coal wound slowly about the mountain side."

Clayton's town and its inhabitants, like Clayton himself, although in the mountains were nonetheless not of the mountains. The mines were worked by "simple, good-natured darkies . . . magnificent in physique and picturesque with rags," and by immigrants newly arrived from Castle Garden "with the hope of the New World still in their faces." The mountaineer could be seen only on the sidelines, observing the scene with wonder and confusion and not a little hostility, "stalking awkwardly in the rear of this march toward civilization."

Gradually it dawned upon [Clayton] that this last, silent figure, traced through Virginia, was closely linked by blood and speech with the common people of England, . . . that now it was the most distinctively national remnant on American soil, and symbolized the development of the continent; and that with it must go the last suggestion of the pioneers, with their hardy physiques, their speech, their manners and customs, their simple architecture and simple mode of life. It was soon plain to him too, that a change was being wrought at last—the change of destruction.[8]

Knowing this, that he was himself the representative of those forces of destruction, Clayton nevertheless found himself drawn more and more deeply into the life of the mountains. "He discarded coat and waistcoat, wore a slouched hat, and went unshaven for weeks. He avoided all conventionalities, and was as simple in manner and speech as possible," Fox tells us, "and he soon fell into many of the quaint expressions of the mountaineers and their odd, slow way of speech."

Unlike Chevis or Murfree, on vacation in search of local color, Clayton had come to the mountains for an indeterminate length of time. He had ample opportunity, as a consequence, to confront the otherness of Appalachia, even as he was forced to grapple with the realities of the mountain environment in connection with his mining activities. Murfree was not incapable of providing her protagonists with the opportunities offered by long residence, as in "The Romance of Sunrise Rock," where Reginald Chevis becomes John Clever, but opportunities proffered are not the same as opportunities taken. While the differences between Chevis's response to the fact of Appalachian otherness and Clayton's reflect the disparate personal experiences of Murfree and Fox in the mountain region, they also reflect different conceptions of the nature of Appalachia itself. Fox's work depended on a definition of Appalachia which Murfree's work made possible, but he was the first major literary figure to utilize this definition and examine its consequences. Thus while Chevis's relationship with Miss Shaw is ultimately doomed because he is unable to transcend class differences and build upon their common humanity, Clayton's relationship with his mountain sweetheart is doomed despite the fact that he transcends class differences and builds upon their common humanity. It is doomed because Appalachia is conceived not merely as a strange land inhabited by a peculiar people but as a discrete entity. Clayton may "go native," but he cannot become a mountaineer any more than Easter Hicks can stop being a mountaineer.

Clayton's interest in the girl at the start is purely philanthropic, for he sees in her the capacity for improvement. Although he worries about lifting her "above her own people, and of creating a spirit of discontent that might embitter her whole life"—had he read "Lodusky"?—his attempt to educate her in the ways of modern America involved little more than providing her with the glove of civilization which he in his newly acquired slouch hat was in the process of removing along with his waistcoat. As philanthropy turns to self-interest, however, Clayton has a vision of his life with Easter. They would marry and make their home in the mountains, in a cottage at the outskirts of the town that would grow up around the mining camp. Thus joined together, they would stand literally between the old civilization and the new, "understanding both, and protecting the native strength of the one from the vices of the other, and training it after more breadth and refinement."

The penetration of Appalachia by America which their marriage would symbolize could become union only if each were to give up his essential self, however. Both in the context of the story, and in the context of the larger issue of the existence of Appalachia as a discrete entity, this was impossible. Fox lets the wedding ceremony take place, but before the marriage can be consummated he brings Easter's father, a moonshiner and feudist, onto the scene. A quarrel erupts, old man Hicks threatens to shoot "thet furriner," Easter intervenes and receives a bullet in the breast for her trouble. Clayton, probably as relieved as we are, leaves Appalachia to return to the civilized America with which he is familiar and to which he belongs.

Resolution of the tension generated by the existence of Appalachia was impossible by the use of normal literary techniques. Individuals representative of the two disparate cultures could not become what they were not and remain consistent with themselves or with their roles as emblematic figures, yet these roles could not be discarded or altered so long as the opposition of Appalachia and America was the donnée of the story and functioned to provide an essential tension to the work. Only through some extraliterary device by which explanation was offered for the discrepancy between life in the mountains and life elsewhere in the nation could this tension be resolved. Because Fox provided no such explanation in "A Mountain Europa," consistency and the logic of his argument required him to kill off his heroine. He learned his lesson, however. Subsequent stories and novels included some comment explaining the nature of the relationship of Appalachia and America, either directly from the author or from some minor character. Thereby was the unnecessary slaughter of perfectly good characters avoided.

Boone Stallard, Fox's protagonist in *The Kentuckians*, for example, is Easter Hicks after the education from which death kept her. "He's half a savage," remarked Anne Bruce, the governor's beautiful daughter, upon first meeting Stallard at one of her father's receptions for state legislators. Stallard was indeed half a savage, but only half. He had come under the tutelege of a country newspaper editor who had trained him in the ways of "the settlemints," and had then spent four years in that great American institution for the civilization of savages, the state university. In Fox's novel, the fact of Appalachian otherness is no less intensely realized in Stallard because of this veneer of civilization, however, any more than the disparity between Appalachia and America is blunted by the fact that Anne and Stallard's opposite, the young Randolph Marshall, represent bluegrass aristocracy rather than New York "society." The theme of the novel indeed is James Lane Allen's perception of the existence of two Kentuckys, and the ambiguity which follows from that perception in the context of Allen's identification of Kentucky as America. Of this Fox reminds us at the outset in a paraphrase of Allen's own observation that "the men of the mountains and the people of the blue-grass know as little and have as little care of one another as though a sea were between them."[9] Not only does Stallard's education not unfit him as an emblem of Appalachian otherness in the context of the novel (he is in fact literally a representative of the region in the Kentucky legislature), but it makes him "an easy peer" to Marshall both in political affairs and in affairs of the heart. Fox thus provides himself the luxury of a situation in which Anne has at least the appearance of an option in her choice of suitors, and in which the choice between Appalachia and America is apparently real.

As in "A Mountain Europa," the emblematic function of Fox's characters prohibits simple personal resolution of their relationships. At the same time, given the "easy peerage" of Stallard and Marshall, any choice on Anne's part would have seemed arbitrary, or personal in such a way as to deny the relevance of the larger tension generated by the fact of Appalachian otherness, which provided the dynamic of the story. Even death or departure would not have satisfied, and Fox wisely leaves the issue unclear at the end. He is able to do this, however, only because he has provided resolution for the tension at an earlier stage in the novel, by explaining Appalachian otherness as "natural" and thereby transforming the tension between Appalachia and America into stage scenery. Anne's dilemma is thus transmuted into a personal choice, which may legitimately be left unresolved.

At a dinner party in the governor's mansion attended by all the principals of the novel, conversation turns inevitably to the central theme of the book, the disparity between Appalachia and America. A northern newspaperman is haranguing Reynolds of the "geological corps": " 'The accepted theory of the origins of the Mountaineer, particularly of the Kentucky mountaineer, is that he is the descendant of exported paupers and convicts, indents, and "pore white trash," ' he said, quietly and quite impersonally." Reynolds, whose scientific work has made him familiar with mountain conditions despite his own aristocratic bluegrass background, replies sharply.

"That is a very foolish theory. Some of them are the descendants of these people, of course. There are more of them in the mountains than in the bluegrass, naturally; but the chief difference between them and us comes from the fact that they have been shut off from the world absolutely for more than a hundred years. Take out the cavalier element, and, in rank and file, we were originally the same people. Until a man has lived a year at a time in the mountains he doesn't know what a thin veneer civilization is. It goes on and off like a glove, especially off. Put twenty *average* blue-grass families down in the mountains half a dozen miles from one another, take away their books, keep them there, with no schools and no churches, for a hundred years, and they will be as ignorant and lawless as the mountaineer . . . and, with similar causes, fighting one another just the same."[10]

By identifying the differences between the mountaineers and the residents of the bluegrass as the result of nurture rather than of nature, Fox is able through Reynolds to establish the reasonableness of his characterization of Stallard as Marshall's equal, and hence of Stallard's candidacy for Anne's hand. Equality does not make them identical, however, any more than the equality of the regions they represent, implicit in Fox-Reynolds's explanation of the disparity between them as the result of processes operating on both regions, and explicit in the egalitarianism of legislative representation, makes these regions identical. Indeed, by establishing the disparity between the mountains and the bluegrass as a matter of scientific fact rather than of sensibility, Fox insists on the reality of Appalachian otherness even while identifying this otherness as natural. By locating the disparate realities of Appalachia and America in the context of acceptable or conventional modes of understanding, explanation thus functions to facilitate the maintenance of the tension generated by their opposition, in that it makes their coexistence conceptually possible without denying the appropriateness of choice between them. Although culture is like a suit of clothes, to extend Fox's metaphor, without which we would be all equally naked, nice tailoring is still preferable to an ill-fashioned garment.

Fox's emphasis on environment as a determinant of culture, and on culture as the critical difference between the mountaineers and the residents of the bluegrass, was one of the two major modes of explanation which characterized the attempt to understand the nature of and causes for Appalachian otherness, and by extension the relationship of Appalachia and America. The other was the argument advanced by that unnamed newspaperman at the governor's dinner party: that the mountaineers were the descendants of exported paupers and convicts, indents, and "pore white trash," and hence that the characteristics of the mountain population, rather than of the mountain region, accounted for the peculiarities of mountain life. While each argument had a distinct history, and functioned in different contexts to resolve the tension generated by the apparent existence of Appalachia as a discrete entity, the thrust of explanation in general was to establish a degree of ethnic, chronological, or geographic distance between Appalachia and America, and thereby to make the otherness of Appalachia seem normal.

Because this was ultimately the (unstated) goal of explanation, the manner in which it was achieved was of less importance than the achievement itself, for explanation was required by the demands of logic or completeness in an essay or story, or by the need to maintain at once the disparity between mountain life and the life of the rest of America and the remediability of this situation of disparity in the literature of the social uplift movement. As a result, the explanatory arguments in the literature on Appalachia published after 1890, taken as a whole, present no meaningful chronological or developmental pattern. The explanations came in rush, tumbling over each other, often contradicting each other, but always emphasizing the reality of Appalachian otherness and the naturalness of Appalachia's existence as a discrete region of the nation.

What this otherness consisted in was itself not always clear, however. The voluminous literature on Appalachia published after 1890, while unified by the presence of explanatory argument, lacks as a consequence the coherence normally ascribed to a body of material dealing with a single problem. Explanation was a response to the fact of Appalachian otherness, and to the tension generated by the perception of this otherness in the context of a conception of American as a unified and homogeneous nation. Because explanation did not follow from observation of the particular set of characteristics by which this otherness was defined, moreover, each argument of explanation involved also the identification of a particular set of characteristics which set Appalachia off from America, and was thus an act of creation. Even at this level, however, it is not always clear whether an author's conception of Appalachian otherness preceded explanation, or whether a particular explanatory argument itself generated a process of definition by which certain characteristics were offered as the crucial ones that separated the strange land and peculiar people from the nation of which they were nominally a part.

It is in a sense tautological to say that the isolation of Appalachia from the currents of modern American life was the principal characteristic by which Appalachian otherness was defined. From 1870 until the present, however, isolation has been the single characteristic which all descriptions of the region note, and about which all commentators upon the nature and implications of Appalachian otherness have had something to say. The fact of isolation has never been offered as a purely descriptive characteristic, however. By isolation has been meant a state of mind, an undesirable provincialism resulting from the lack of contact between the mountaineers and outsiders. The anonymous author of one of the first attempts at systematic description of the quality of life in the region, in 1882, noted that during a two-month visit to the mountains he (or she) was "so shut off from the nineteenth century that it was like a dream to think that out beyond the mountain barrier, existed a contemporaneous world, full of ideas, projects, motion. And now, how like a dream it is, to think that in the heart of *this* world exists that other, of men who have never heard the shriek of an engine, the click of the telegraph, the whirr of machinery."[11] It was this isolation which was the principal focus of the early local colorists' sense of wonder, and it was the fact of the region's isolation which became the principal element in subsequent definitions of Appalachia as a discrete entity.

With the emergence of the idea of Appalachia as a discrete entity, isolation became not only an essential aspect of the definition of the region as a region, but also a phenomenon to be explained. At the same time, it became itself an explanation for the occurrence of other characteristics which seemed to set Appalachia off from America. In the process, the perceived otherness of Appalachia was given focus in a manner which did not in any way contradict dominant notions about the nature of American civilization. When the isolation of the region was the essence of Appalachian otherness and the cause for the peculiarities of mountain life, the disparity between Appalachia and America became a matter of the absence of certain characteristics rather than of the presence of other contradictory characteristics.

Although William Perry Brown noted as early as 1888 in the *Overland Monthly* that the persistence of traditional patterns of culture among the mountaineers represented an "unconscious . . . protest against the enervative influences of our civilization," for example, neither he nor any other commentator of the late nineteenth or early twentieth centuries felt that mountain life was to be valued or emulated for this reason alone, and few expressed Brown's own ambiguity toward the civilization of modern America. Instead the mountaineers seemed simply to be behind the times in their indifference to "the spirit of modern innovation," while the aggressive localism which resulted from their isolation stood in striking contrast to "that general homogeneousness of custom and taste that is one of the most pleasing results of our national life."[12] Indeed, being isolated and being "behind the times" seemed essentially the same. "Ease of communication is so important a factor in modern social development," the geographer C. Willard Hayes explained in 1895, "that regions abundantly supplied with railroads advance far beyond those still dependent on less rapid transit," while those remote from railroads "are relatively more isolated than they were when the only means of travel between the different parts of the country were on horseback or by stage." Because many of the mountain people "have been scarcely at all affected by the modern industrial and social revolutions which have been going on around them," their isolation was more intense and their backwardness more striking.[13]

The same theme appears in almost all the discussions of Appalachian otherness published at the turn of the century. Grace Ryan, writing in *The Outlook* for February 1898, remarked that "one who has never visited this land of spinning-wheels, patchwork quilts, feather beds, and fireplaces might wonder why the inhabitants should be so far behind the times. But when once he had traveled over the mountain roads . . . he might easily understand the reason. They are so shut in!" Taking a slightly larger view of the mountaineers' situation in the context of American historical development, but arriving at the same conclusion, the Chicago sociologist George E. Vincent suggested that the mountain region represented "a retarded frontier" and that the anomaly of its existence might best be understood in terms of the normal processes of westward migration. "Following physiographic lines of least resistance," he said, the rushing tide of progress "left quiet pools in the mountains of Virginia, North Carolina, Kentucky and Tennessee [where] the frontier has survived in practical isolation until this very day. Only recently have we fully realized this fact made vivid by the stories of Miss Murfree, Mr. John Fox, Jr., and other writers." In the same terms, and with an unacknowledged nod in Vincent's direction, William Goodell Frost explained the "Rip Van Winkle sleep" of the mountain people by noting that they "unconsciously stepped aside from the great avenues of commerce and thought" into a region where they were subsequently "beleaguered by nature." It was this isolation which made them "our contemporary ancestors" by permitting the life habits and personal characteristics of the American frontiersman to persist unchanged into the present. "In this vast inland and upland realm" might thus be found a survival "of that pioneer life which has been such a striking feature of American history."[14]

Although their own impatience with "those who are 'behind the times'" led Frost and others to engage in efforts to direct mountain culture into more modern and more desirable patterns, the existence of a disparate culture in Appalachia, thus defined as a survival from an earlier stage of historical development, ceased to be a matter of concern in and of itself. As the natural result of the operation of natural processes, it posed no challenge to conceptions of America as a unified and homogeneous national entity, nor even to notions of the normality of progress elsewhere in the United States. Appalachian otherness was simply the result of an historical accident, by no means unique to the American situation. In a long essay published in *Scribner's Magazine* in 1901, John Fox, Jr., made this point quite explicit. The cultural conservatism of isolated mountain peoples was not peculiar to the residents of Appalachia, he said. "Arcadia held primitive the primitive inhabitants of Greece who fled to its rough hills after the Dorian invasion . . . just as the Rocky Mountains protect the American indian in primitive barbarism." It was then no wonder that "the Cumberland range keeps the Southern mountaineer to the backwoods civilization of the revolution." Because the mountain dweller in general lives thus isolated from the world, he has no incentive to change, no experience of alternatives to the patterns of life with which he is familiar. "An arrest of development follows; so that once imprisoned, a civilization, with its dress, speech, religion, customs, ideas, may be caught like the shapes of lower life in stone, and may tell the human story of a century as the rocks tell the story of an age."[15]

It was not only the "civilization" of the eighteenth century which isolation thus preserved intact in the southern mountains according to this line of argument, however. The "ethnic type" was also kept pure. "It is a law of biology that an isolating environment operates for the preservation of a type by excluding all intermixture which would obliterate distinguishing characteristics," Ellen Churchill Semple noted in "The Anglo-Saxons of the Kentucky Mountains: A Study in Anthropogeography" (1901). "In these isolated communities, therefore, we find the purest Anglo-Saxon stock in all the United States. They are the direct descendants of the early Virginia and North Carolina immigrants, and bear about them in their speech and ideas the marks of their ancestry as plainly as if they had disembarked from their 18th-century vessel but yesterday. . . . The stock has been kept free from the tide of foreign immigrants which has been pouring in recent years into the States."[16]

Most writers tended to hedge on the question of the relationship between the ethnic composition of the mountain population and the characteristics of mountain life, being content to use its "pure" Anglo-Saxon character as further evidence for the historical quality of mountain civilization. There were those, as we shall see, who argued that at least particular aspects of the peculiar culture of Appalachia were a direct result of who the mountaineers were, or more precisely, of who their ancestors had been. Even these, however, agreed that isolation was the primary "cause" of Appalachian otherness. In the same way, although spokesmen for the agencies of denominational uplift which were entering the mountain field during the 1890s often argued that "neglect" had combined with physiography to cause the isolation of Appalachia, such disagreements of emphasis as did occur in discussions of the nature of Appalachian isolation, as being either natural or artificial (the result of neglect), were never serious. They neither involved questions about the reality of Appalachia as a discrete entity, nor denied the importance of isolation as an element in the definition of Appalachia as such an entity, and the issue of historical responsibility for this isolation was moot in any case. Those who talked of "neglect" were less concerned with the past than with the future, when through the assistance of outside agencies of benevolence the isolation of the region might be overcome, and the mountains and mountaineers integrated into the mainstream of American life.[17]

If there was thus fundamental agreement on the importance of isolation as a cause of Appalachia's existence as a discrete region and as the principal characteristic by which Appalachian otherness was defined, there was no real agreement on the manner in which isolation affected the quality of mountain life. To a significant degree, this was because there was no clear notion of what mountain life was actually like, and hence no possible agreement on what was to be explained. In the sketches and stories of the local-color writers, assertion of the otherness of Appalachia was more critical than close description of its characteristics. In the literature on the southern mountains generated by the agencies of systematic benevolence, assertion of the mountaineer's "need" was more critical than close description of that need, or of the conditions which created it. Given the absence of hard information about the characteristics of mountain life, writers on Appalachia even at the turn of the century were thus free to offer metaphor instead of statement of fact, to speculate on the consequences of isolation on Appalachian otherness, to propose programs for the melioration of mountain conditions appropriate to their speculations, and to generalize broadly on the "meaning" of Appalachia's existence for an understanding of American history. At a time of intellectual and professional turmoil within the young disciplines of the social sciences, moreover, there was no check either to metaphoric statement or to speculation, and little impetus to collect hard data upon which more precise generalization might be built. If anything, indeed, the chaotic state of the social sciences reinforced this tendency to speculation as academic social scientists themselves sought to take advantage of contemporary interest in Appalachia, by preparing speculative articles for the popular press and by utilizing Appalachia as a "test case" for one or another hypothesis of their own.[18]

Discussion of the consequences of isolation on the characteristics of mountain life rarely took the form of abstract debate, however. Not only did such "objective" social-scientist commentators as Hayes and Vincent often have both professional and personal axes to grind, but even they recognized that the choice of one explanatory argument over another had practical implications for the conduct of benevolent work in Appalachia, and more generally for one's conception of the nature of American civilization. More was always at issue than the efficacy of a particular explanation for the peculiarities of Appalachia, that is, but *what* was at issue was always something extraneous to the matter at hand. As a result, juxtaposition of a variety of alternative explanations for Appalachian otherness was more characteristic of the literature on the southern mountains than was systematic argument for one position over another. Because any explanation functioned to resolve the dilemma created by the fact of Appalachian otherness, and because the resolution of this dilemma was the first task of explanation, moreover, the addition of extra explanations in a single essay or story could only be to the good. Indeed, consistency had its positive disadvantages, both theoretical and practical.

If simple cultural isolation, the result of an historical accident, had "caused" the mountaineers' Rip Van Winkle sleep, as Hayes and Vincent had argued and as most spokesmen for the home-missionary agencies agreed, for example, an end to isolation would work to break down the fact of Appalachian otherness and hence facilitate the integration or reintegration of the region and the nation. It would also remove the special status which the mountaineers possessed as one of the exceptional populations of America, however, and therefore eliminate them as potential clients of the benevolence establishment and even as appropriate subjects for literary examination. If, on the other hand, the physical characteristics of the region—which necessarily set it off from the rest of the nation—amounted to a special environment as well as an isolating factor, as Ellen Churchill Semple suggested, then the disparity between Appalachia and America was not at all the result of an historical accident. Isolation was rather an element of the physiographic reality in terms of which a separate mountain culture had developed, and this culture would resist all outside attempts to change it until the physiographic characteristics of Appalachia itself were changed. For this to happen it was not enough that the mountains be penetrated by railroads, or that schools and churches be established. Acceptance of an environmentalist explanation for Appalachian otherness did not make the peculiarities of mountain life seem any more desirable because they were the result of normal processes in any case, and even Semple retained her commitment to the melioration of mountain conditions through traditional forms of benevolent work. In addition, this environmentalist explanation raised the spectre of a role for environment in the creation of culture generally which ran counter to contemporary notions about the inevitability of progress as a characteristic of American civilization, and about the possibility of achieving cultural unity and homogeneity in the United States in the face of physiographic diversity through "will" and institutional reorganization.

With the aid of hindsight, we can see that disagreements about the manner in which isolation affected mountain life were in fact disagreements about the nature of what we call culture, as being a coherent body of custom, tradition, or values, transmissible as such from generation to generation, on the one hand; or a set of conventional ways of dealing with reality as it presented itself, necessarily changing with a changing reality, on the other. In terms of the first position, the impact of isolation on Appalachia was seen to result in the preservation among the mountaineers of the ethnic characteristics, the songs, the patterns of economic and social organization, the dress, the architecture of a vaguely defined but nonetheless distinct historical past, the time of "our pioneer ancestors" in the era of first settlement. In terms of the second position, the impact of isolation on Appalachia was seen to result in the development of a culture appropriate to the characteristics of the mountain environment, including the characteristic of isolation, the similarities of which to the culture of "our pioneer ancestors" was the result of the persistence of a similar environment rather than of the absence of any impetus to change. In their attempt to explain the peculiarities of Appalachia as the result of isolation in either way, however, Americans of the late nineteenth and early twentieth centuries were forced to confront the broader issues of the nature of progress, and the extent to which progress, as distinct from historical change, was a characteristic of American life.

4. Solving the "Problem" of Appalachian Otherness: The Role of Ethnicity and Culture

For the local-color writers and the agents of denominational benevolence working in Appalachia during the late 1870s and 1880s, the identity of the mountaineers was not an issue distinct from the more general problem raised by the fact of Appalachian otherness. It was the disparity between the life patterns of native-born, white, Anglo-Saxon, Protestant Americans in the southern mountains and the life patterns of native-born, white, Anglo-Saxon Americans elsewhere in the nation, both North and South, which made the mountaineers a peculiar people and hence interesting, and which made them appear as appropriate objects of northern home-missionary work. Their neediness followed from their apparent nonparticipation in the civilization of modern America. Their availability as the objects of home-missionary endeavor followed from the apparent genetic continuity which linked the isolated mountain people and their brethren in other parts of the United States, and which indeed made mountain work seem more certain of success than analogous work among other "exceptional" populations of the nation.

During the 1890s, however, the emergence of mountain benevolence as a distinct aspect of denominational activity, and an increasing secular interest in the mountain field as an area for the exercise of systematic "scientific" philanthropy, tended to alter this situation. The institutionalization of "mountain white" work virtually required that the mountain people themselves be identified a priori as a "needy" and "client" population rather than simply as an aggregate of individuals defined by residence and a peculiar (undesirable) culture. At the same time, the emergence of a corps of benevolent workers whose personal and professional interests depended upon a definition of the mountain field as a viable area for philanthropic work yielded an inevitable tendency to objectify their mountaineer clients as a distinct people with distinct characteristics, and to write about them in such terms. An emerging popular interest in the possibility of classifying populations on the basis of phenotypical rather than cultural characteristics, in an effort to establish cognitive schemes for the organization of contemporary perceptions of the patterns of diversity which prevailed in late nineteenth-century America, provided the crucial context in which this definition of the mountaineers as a distinct people occurred.

It was thus almost inevitable that the language and concepts of "social Darwinism" and popular genetic theory should be utilized in discussions of the mountaineers defined as a discrete group within the American population, and that the contemporary fascination with ethnic or racial distinctions should play a role in the redefinition of the mountaineers as a distinct people. By the 1890s in any case, consideration of the characteristics of the mountain population, as distinct from the characteristics of mountain life, had become an essential element in discussions of Appalachian otherness, and seemed to provide an effective mode of explaining the fact of Appalachian otherness. On the question of the identity of the mountaineers, moreover, turned both the issue of the responsibility of northern benevolence for the melioration of mountain conditions and the issue of the remediability of mountain conditions.

So long as the mountaineers were identified as one among the numerous "exceptional populations" of the nation deserving the care and concern of northern Protestants, denominational workers in the mountain field were forced to compete for funds and for the attention of their parent boards or societies with workers in other fields. In addition, their efforts were always subject to challenge by supporters of the claims of foreign missions, ministerial sustentation (denominational support for ministerial salaries in impoverished congregations), Sunday school work, and other "normal" denominational activities, who could assert that the churches' first obligations were to their own congregants and to their traditional commitments in the foreign fields. Work among essentially alien groups in America—including former Confederates or simply southerners—seemed of dubious merit, and seemed to require pouring money and effort into a bottomless pit. From the very outset, as a consequence, benevolent work in Appalachia was discussed in contradictory terms. On the one hand, the initiation of work among the mountaineers was justified on the grounds that it constituted nothing more than a necessary extension among a newly discovered "needy" population, of established programs for the integration of the exceptional populations of the nation into the American community. The possibility that work in the mountain field would also provide northern denominations with a way of entering the South without antagonizing their sister churches of that section was incidental to the general thrust of the argument, which emphasized the conservative nature of the new home-missionary efforts in Appalachia. At the same time, however, efforts were regularly made to distinguish mountain white work from work among the other exceptional populations of the nation and from southern white work more generally, in order to emphasize the special claims of the mountaineers on the benevolence of northern Protestantism.

As early as 1883, as we have noted, Charles Fairchild of Berea College reminded the Congregational American Missionary Association of the mountaineers' traditional sympathy with northern principles and northern Protestantism. True or not, this had in fact been the assumption upon which Berea's founders had acted in projecting the establishment of an "Oberlin in Kentucky" as a base of operations for moral and political evangelism in the antebellum South. It remained also the fundamental assumption in terms of which the college's commitment to the co-education of southern blacks and whites was carried out in the years after the Civil War, and a continuing theme in its promotional literature through the presidency of William Goodell Frost. In the late 1880s and early 1890s, however, such generalized assertions were given precise focus in a series of books and articles which identified the contemporary mountaineer as the legitimate descendant of that "unsung hero" in the winning of the American West, the Scotch-Irish frontiersman, and which called attention to the continuity of patriotism between the activities of the backwoods riflemen at King's Mountain and the Unionists of East Tennessee.

Probably the first of these was Thomas Wilson Humes's *The Loyal Mountaineers of Tennessee* (1888), which became in any case a standard authority for denominational writers wishing to support their contentions concerning the natural sympathy of the mountaineers for northern principles. Humes took as his subject the wondrous fact that "the people of East Tennessee . . . set their faces as a flint against secession," and designed his four-hundred-page rhapsody in part as a "help . . . to some gifted mind that shall in the future attempt a history of the War of 1861–'65 in the spirit of a sound Christian philosophy."[1] Though not itself quite providential history in the grand manner, *The Loyal Mountaineers* provided nonetheless the crucial data for those who would later see the mountain whites as a reserve force for Christ in the coming confrontation with the evils of socialism and Romanism, just as they had been a reserve force in other more mundane battles. Its principal focus, however, was on what a later writer would call "the debt of our country" to the mountain people of Appalachia. "To whatever causes their conduct may be attributed," Humes remarked, "it is certain . . . that the steadfast attachment of East Tennessee to the Union and the efficient aid it gave to its preservation, formed an important factor in the war and contributed in no small degree to its final result. It was the reproduction, upon the same stage, after nearly a vanished century, of the same broad patriotism—to some extent inherited—which sent a thousand riflemen from Sycamore Shoals on the Wautauga River, to win for the American colonies a victory at King's Mountain; and which afterwards triumphed over a spirit of revolutionary separation, in retaining the allegiance of the people of Franklin to the mother state of North Carolina."[2]

In 1891, in an address to the American Missionary Association, Joseph E. Roy used Humes's material to argue that the "instincts" and "habits" of colonial times—which isolation had preserved in the mountains and which made the mountaineers seem so "behind the

times"—were not entirely undesirable, and to support his formulation of the standard contention, that the mountain people "take hold
upon the North by agreements of principle, by traditions of sympathy, and by large contributions to it from the best of their stock by
reason of these affinities." The mountaineers, he said, "retain the
elements of noble character" despite the fact that they have "fallen
behind our standards of enlightenment." Others would later say that
the mountaineers retained the elements of noble character precisely
because they had fallen behind in this way, but Roy's argument was
directed at legitimizing the American Missionary Association's interest in the mountain whites as objects of uplift work. He achieved his
end by pointing to the mountaineers' historical participation in
American life. If they were in fact the descendants of "indents, convicts, and 'poor white trash,'" as Fox's newspaperman suggested,
they were nonetheless "rich in the heredity of patriotism . . . which
animated these loyal mountaineers in our second revolution, when
our country rose up and threw off the yoke of the slaveholders' oligarchy."[3]

The implications of Humes's insistence on the crucial role played
by the "mountaineers" of Knoxville in the preservation of the Union
were spelled out fully in Charles Jackson Ryder's address to the
American Missionary Association in 1892. *The Debt of Our Country to
the American Highlanders during the War* reminded his auditors, and
subsequently his readers, of the continuity of patriotism displayed by
the southern mountain people from the time of King's Mountain
through the struggles in East Tennessee, and concluded that it was
nothing less than the obligation of Christian patriots to redeem their
gifts to the nation with gifts of equal value. "We must invade their
coves and press up the mountain sides with an army of Christian
teachers and preachers," Ryder said, mixing metaphors in a characteristic way, "until the grey old forests that echoed with the shout of
these loyal Highlanders shall echo again . . . with the sound of the
church bell and school bell." Those who took upon themselves "the
larger sacrifice of the war" must know "that we are ready to share
with them the blessed fruits of peace."[4]

Ryder's address did more than merely establish the relationship of the mountaineers and the agencies of northern benevolence on the new ground of obligation for services rendered, rather than of need or availability alone. By introducing into discussions of Appalachian otherness images of the log cabin, a symbol of the heroic age in American history, and of Abraham Lincoln, a symbol of commitment to the cause of national unity, and by designating the mountaineers as "American Highlanders," he focused on the issue of who the mountaineers were in a new way.

In this process, the image of the log cabin was crucial. An established if somewhat shopworn symbol in the American rhetorical vocabulary, it stood for the nobility which seemed to accompany a particular kind of poverty and the dedication to individual freedom which seemed to accompany a particular stage of social development. In Ryder's hands, the log cabin in the southern mountains ceased being a detail of mountain life and a manifestation of the persistence of an outmoded civilization in the region, as it had been for the local-color writers whose focus was on the old-fashioned quality of life in Appalachia. By identifying the log cabin of the contemporary mountaineer with the birthplace of "our noble martyred President," Ryder gave the image new vitality, and he provided in the person of Lincoln the crucial nexus between the heroic past and an apparently degraded present. "The cabin in which [Lincoln] was born and in which he passed the early years of his childhood can be duplicated in the mountain region to-day," Ryder reminded his readers, "and men of just such manly and heroic mold as Abraham Lincoln come from these same mountain cabins."[5] If the mountaineers were to be "our contemporary ancestors," Ryder made certain that there would be no doubt about what that meant. Descended from the pioneers, heirs to their patriotism and simple nobility of character, the mountaineers retained the life habits and, no doubt, the virtues also, of that romantic age.

Ryder's designation of the mountaineers as "American Highlanders" was logically inconsistent with his suggestion that the quintessentially American past of the pioneers had persisted unchanged into the Appalachian present. In a context of "fine writing" and polemics, however, images of the mountaineer as pioneer and the mountaineer as Highlander could coexist with ease. Both were derived from a past long past, in which chronological and even national distinctions were of little importance. Both were contained within a single Anglo-Saxonism, an ethnic (or in nineteenth-century usage, racial) identity in terms of which chronological or national distinctions were meaningless, mere anecdotes manifesting the single philosophical principle of progress. To this notion the fact that the Highlanders of Scotland might not have been Anglo-Saxons presented no obstacle. At the very least their chroniclers, Scott and Stevenson, were major British writers, and that was sufficient connection. The identification of the mountaineers as Highlanders reinforced the sense of them as a romantic people, and located them securely in the heroic past.[6]

In addition, of course, the designation of the mountaineers as Highlanders reinforced the conventional argument that they were owed assistance from the agencies of northern benevolence by ties of blood and lineage, for it contained in a single image the several arguments concerning the ethnic identity of the mountaineers. As Scotch-Irish or Scottish Presbyterians, they were in either case descended from religious dissenters, hence somehow one both with those Protestants whose protestations had made the American Revolution and with those frontiersmen whose discontent with the conservative aristocracy of the seaboard towns had led them into the wilderness in the name of individual freedom and individual profit—the contradictory epic motives of American bourgeois mythology. "Highlanders" explained the relationship of the mountaineers with the lowlanders of the South, their cultural conservatism, their poverty, their ignorance, their anarchic individualism, and made it all seem a matter of choice rather than of necessity, the result of a peculiar but nonetheless admirable stoicism, characteristic of the race.

The advantages of this particular mix of images to Ryder and his contemporaries were far greater than the simple connection it made between the peculiar people of Appalachia and those backwoodsmen who populated Theodore Roosevelt's enormously popular epic historical narrative, *The Winning of the West*, although that alone would have been sufficient and may be presumed to have been the reason for Ryder's argument. The mountaineer-Highlander comparison was largely based upon conventional generalizations about the characteristics of mountain life derived from the work of the local colorists, for one thing, and hence agreed with what was assumed to be reality. More important, however, it identified the peculiarities of mountain life as resulting from who the mountaineers were, rather than in terms of their generalized condition as one among the exceptional populations of the nation. In an age obsessed with the utility of genealogical categories in the definition of a people, moreover, American Highlanders defined the mountaineers in historical terms, and treated their "heritage of patriotism" and their "heritage of individualism" as if history were a genetic characteristic with behavioral consequences. It thereby legitimized benevolent work among the mountain whites by asserting that they were not only worth the trouble but were also, like earlier avatars of the pioneer race, capable of self-improvement and willing participants in the progress of the nation.

The commitment of the agents of denominational benevolence to an explanation for Appalachian otherness as the result of who the mountaineers were, made them peculiarly susceptible to suggestions in the work of historians concerning a degraded origin for that population which settled the mountains originally. Theodore Roosevelt himself, for example, had noted that "the two extremes of society, the strongest, best, and most adventurous, and the weakest, most shiftless, and vicious, are those which seem naturally to drift to the border," and referred his readers to Henry Cabot Lodge's brilliant essay on the triumph of the New England way of life over the slavocracy, *A Short History of the English Colonies in America* (1881), for "an account of these people." "Many of the Southern Crackers or poor whites sprang from this class, which in the backwoods gave birth to generations of violent and hardened criminals," Roosevelt continued, "and to an even greater number of shiftless, lazy, cowardly cumberers of the earth's surface."[7]

Roosevelt's remarks were tempered by the suggestion that in the freedom of the backwoods a man might become what he liked, and genetic incapacity of this sort overcome. Sympathetic to the role of these poor whites as the victims of the slavocrat system in any case, Roosevelt's unflattering comments on the possible origins of the mountaineers were made too early to cause concern among the propagandists for denominational benevolence, whose own commitment to mountain white work was just beginning. It was enough for them that Roosevelt had discovered, or rediscovered, the frontiersman, and that their own mountain folk fit his model well enough for a case to be made on behalf of the principle of ethnic continuity. When John Fiske presented a variety of the Lodge-Roosevelt argument in *Old Virginia and Her Neighbors* ten years later, however, after the agencies of benevolence had made their stand on the principle of ethnic continuity, the issue was joined in such a way as to carry the dialogue on the nature of Appalachian otherness one step further, and to transform it into a dialogue on the nature of American civilization itself.[8]

Fiske's intention in *Old Virginia* was to complete his history of early America, begun in *The Origins of New England*, by demonstrating the relevance of the basic philosophical structure of his earlier work to the history of the southern colonies in the seventeenth century. Of particular importance was the establishment of a uniform origin for all the American colonies as a precondition to the uniform progress of the several American states toward a uniform destiny and national unity. The apparent discrepancy between the forms of institutions in the two great sections, the North and the South, Fiske resolved by describing Virginian local government as an imperfect reversion to the forms of a common Teutonic past, and it remained only to explain the existence of the "mean white" class of the South in such a way as to make tenable an assertion about the uniform origin of the American population.

According to Fiske, the structure of Virginia's society reflected exactly the immigration to that colony from England in the early seventeenth century. Thus the tidewater aristocracy were descended from noble or well-connected settlers, of the same class as emigrated to the northern colonies; the small planter ("yeoman") class from the "thrifty redemptioners and gallant rebels" transported to the colonies as indentured servants to provide cheap labor and to ease economic and political pressures in England, some of whom later rose to positions of wealth and power in Virginia; the "mean white class" from the more degraded among this class. Any suggestion of fundamental differences among Virginia's settlers at the time of their migration to the new world would have invalidated Fiske's proposition of social and cultural homogeneity. All such differences, as a consequence, as between the "yeoman" and "mean white" descendants of the "thrifty redemptioners and gallant rebels," for example, had to be identified as developments occurring in America, the result of conditions peculiar to America, and which precipitated the exodus of dissonant and dissident elements from the symbolic Virginian center of southern civilization.

The fact that manual labor was a badge of servitude, while the white freedmen of degraded type were by nature and experience unfitted to perform any work of a higher sort, was of itself enough to keep them from doing any work at all, unless driven by impending starvation. . . . They were loungers in taverns and at horse-races, earning a precarious livelihood or a violent death by gambling or thieving; or else they withdrew from the haunts of civilization to lead half-savage lives in the backwoods. In these people we may recognize a strain of the English race which has not yet on American soil become extinct or absorbed. There can be little doubt that the white freedmen of degraded type were the progenitors of a considerable portion of what is often called the "white trash" of the South. . . . Concerning the origin of this degraded strain, detailed documentary evidence is not easy to get; but the facts of its distribution furnish data for valid inferences such as the naturalist entertains concerning the origin and migrations of some species of animal or plant.[9]

Although Fiske's own brand of evolutionism, as set forth in the early *Outlines of Cosmic Philosophy*, provided for periods of real or apparent decline or degeneration within an historical experience characterized by progress, it was the *end* of history, not its process, which interested him and which alone, he felt, gave meaning to history. Throughout his career, as a consequence, historical study was "scientific" when it directed attention to the grand design which the process of change made manifest. The writing of history thus consisted of description of the stages of development through which institutions passed in the process of their maturation, the process of the emergence of intended forms, while progress became "the one grand phenomenon, to explain the presence and the absence of which is to explain the phenomena of history."[10]

Fiske's commitment to teleological analysis of the process of historical change led necessarily into ambiguity, especially with regard to the issue of change and continuity in American history. This is clearly evident in his discussion of the origins of the "mean white" class of the South, which developed, according to Fiske, in accordance with the laws of natural selection—laws which described the dynamics of a constantly changing social system in terms of the dynamics of the system itself. Fitness or unfitness were not qualities possessed by the colonists of Virginia except in the context of Virginia life. Those who were least fit for life in Virginia were most fit for life in the ruder circumstances of North Carolina or the Appalachian frontier, and the "mean white" class emerged accordingly. Once such a class *had* emerged, however, historical change gave way to historical continuity, and yielded the persistence of this class in the South throughout the nineteenth century.

John Fiske was not the first to attempt to explore the consequences of the social structure of early America upon American social history in the nineteenth century, or to attempt to explain American social history by reference to the nature of the colonial population. Indeed, the entire pattern of discourse which informs Fiske's multivolume study of early American history may be said to have been developed from the schema utilized by Henry Cabot Lodge in his Harvard lectures, published in 1881 as *A Short History of the English Colonies in America*. It was Lodge, moreover, who appears to have introduced the issue of the origin of the "mean white class" of the South into late nineteenth-century historiography, with particular reference to the relationship of nineteenth-century events and America's eighteenth-century origins.

As Fiske would later, Lodge attempted to explain the origins of the "mean white class" of the South in terms of the consequences of heredity and environment both. The "poor whites" were descended from degraded stock, paupers and criminals, "the scum of the London streets" transported to colonial Virginia. The establishment of the institution of chattel slavery, which made labor seem ignoble and slaveowning the key to social status, provided the circumstances in which a nonslaveholding, laboring population would emerge as a social class or caste, excluded from participation in the social and economic life of the colonial South. Lodge did not take the next step which was Fiske's contribution to the social history of the South, and attempt to trace the migration of this group from Virginia to the Carolinas, thence to the Piedmont, finally to the mountains. Lodge left them instead where he had found them, in or close to the tidewater, a blight upon and a natural consequence of the existence of an aristocratic social system built upon human slavery.[11]

For Lodge, the existence of this class of poor whites, forced into a life of poverty and degradation by the slavocrat system (whether they were of "degenerate" origins or not is irrelevant here, of course), was proof of the fundamental dissimilarity between Puritan New England and Cavalier Virginia. For Lodge it was this dissimilarity, and the conflict between progress and conservatism which it precipitated, that gave shape to American history before the Civil War, and meaning to it afterward.

New England represented democracy and progress; Virginia, aristocracy and conservatism, and they contended for the possession of the middle states, which held the balance of power. These two opposing elements go back to Plymouth and Jamestown. From Plymouth went forth one great column of civilization which controlled the states of the West and North; from Jamestown went out the other column to possess the West and South. . . . The two hostile and advancing columns met far out on the plains of Kansas. There was a moment's pause, and the battle raged along the whole line. After a bloody civil war of four years the democracy of Plymouth triumphed, and the conservative aristocracy of Virginia was broken in pieces, together with the slave system which supported its power. With the close of the war between the states a new era begins.[12]

Lodge's choice of an historical pattern of conflict rather than one detailing a uniform progress from common roots led him to take an ambiguous attitude toward the poor whites in Virginia, "rude, noisy, brawling, drinking fellows, very lazy and sometimes criminal; but with a redeeming dash of generous and hospitable good-nature." If only because they were the victims and outcasts of the detested slavocracy, these poor whites seemed to Lodge to stand closer to New England, democracy, and progress, and to possess a kind of moral status which success in the South would have denied them.

This same ambiguous attitude easily attached to the contemporary mountaineer, defined as the descendant of this outcast class of colonial Virginia. Although poverty and peculiar customs set them off from more successful classes in the South as in the North, their degradation had an honorable character about it. "They would have no complicity with slavery, and hence the slavocracy would have nothing to do with them," Mrs. S. M. Davis argued in 1895. "They were crowded into the mountains. . . . They had no teachers nor preachers, and sank into dense degradation. . . . Yet of this same stock came *heroes* in the time of our civil war."[13] The assertion of antisouthernism from the fact of nonsouthernism was an easy one to make. Lodge's analysis facilitated the identification of Appalachia as an enclave of pronorthern sentiment during the antebellum period and hence as the crucial flaw in the fabric of southern civilization, which permitted its rending during the war of 1861–65, and suggested a certain utility to mountain white work. "Who knows," Mrs. Davis asked, "whether these people be not a reserve force that God will bring out of these mountains, saved by Christ, for the coming crisis of conflict, a stalwart band to stand with us in defense of Protestantism?"[14]

Where Lodge's discussion of the presumptive ancestry of the contemporary mountaineers, reinforced by the authority of its repetition as fact in Theodore Roosevelt's *The Winning of the West*, thus served the purposes of the agents of denominational benevolence, Fiske's later discussion of the same problem, though offered virtually in passing, was seen as an intentional attack on the legitimacy of mountain white work. A caveat concerning the tenuousness of any identification of his "mean whites" and the contemporary mountaineer went unread, as caveats often do, despite the fact that Fiske there indicated his own acceptance of a more conventional explanation for Appalachian otherness: "Prolonged isolation from the currents of thought and feeling . . . will account for almost any extent of igno-

rance and backwardness; and there are few geographical situations
. . . more conducive to isolation than the south-western portion of
the great Appalachian highlands."[15]

One may speculate about whether the agents of denominational
benevolence who argued with Fiske over a position he did not properly take were not attempting to objectify and confront their own
doubts concerning the character of the mountain population and the
legitimacy of their own efforts in this area. Their denials were
phrased as responses to assertions which appear nowhere in Fiske's
writings, but which might well have been made by contemporary
observers of mountain life in their own attempts to explain the otherness of Appalachia, and particularly the apparent prevalence of feuding and moonshining in the region. For whatever reasons, however,
Fiske became the symbolic spokesman for an argument which no one
seems actually to have advanced, but the mere logical possibility of
which appeared as a threat to the viability of mountain benevolence.

It was directly to the allegations of "Fiske and others" concerning the degenerate origins of the mountaineers that William Goodell
Frost sought to respond in his *Atlantic Monthly* article of 1899, for
example, by calling for "a scientific spirit and some historic sense" in
any assessment of the nature and meaning of Appalachian otherness. "The impression has been made that some of the early settlers
. . . were 'convicts,'" Frost explained, and this has led many to the
conclusion that the southern colonies contained a high proportion of
degenerates among its eighteenth-century population. "It must be
remembered that many of them were only convicted of having belonged to Cromwell's army, or of persisting in attending religious
services conducted by dissenters," however, and that behavior which
seems abnormal in one age may well seem normal or indeed merito-
rious in another. The reverse was also true, that behavior which
seemed normal in one age may seem abnormal in another, and this
principle, Frost suggested, could provide guidance in understanding
the situation of the mountaineers. Because isolation from the main
currents of modern life had preserved in the mountains an enclave of
eighteenth-century civilization, the bothersome fact of Appalachian
otherness represented nothing more and nothing less than "a con-

temporary survival of that pioneer life which has been such a striking feature of American history," and the mountaineers themselves might best be regarded as "our contemporary ancestors."[16]

By talking when he did and the way he did, of the mountaineers as "our contemporary ancestors," William Goodell Frost effectively brought to a conclusion one line of discussion concerning the relationship between who the mountaineers were and the peculiarities of mountain life as they were perceived in the present. Although others, including John Campbell of the Russell Sage Foundation, would later take their turn in attempting to define the ethnic characteristics and national origins of the contemporary mountain population, such commentators employed a pluralist rather than a hierarchical model in their discussion of population diversity in the United States. They did not attempt to rank populations on a scale of degeneracy and normality, or on a scale of primitivism or savagery and civilization or progress. Instead, they sought to utilize historical data as one of the sources for an understanding of the function of national origin, ethnic or racial characteristics, environment, and group experience in the development of a particular population with particular physical, mental, and cultural traits. More important, they tended to begin their studies with a sense of the particular traits dominant in a particular population—traits by which that population was defined—rather than with some vague, evolutionary notion concerning the manner in which the past necessarily yielded a particular kind of present. This pattern of analysis also followed from Frost's comments of the 1890s, for, as we have already noted, his designation of the mountainous portions of nine southern states as "one of God's grand divisions" of the continent, "Appalachian America," had the effect of legitimizing Appalachian otherness as the natural consequence of the existence of a discrete region inhabited by a distinct people.

This later interest in the origins and nature of the Appalachian population was a phenomenon of the teens, and especially of the 1920s and 1930s, and hence falls outside the period of our immediate concern.[17] Because it followed from Frost's legitimation of Appalachian otherness during the nineties and earlier twentieth century, however, it deserves mention at least, but in addition, it is noteworthy because its characteristics differ significantly from the working through of Frost's implications after 1900.

In the later period, the nature of the Appalachian population and the characteristics of the distinct, regional culture of the southern mountains appeared as abstract issues, of primary interest to classifiers and model builders among a new generation of social scientists and social psychologists. In the earlier period, the working through of Frost's implications involved a general abandonment of abstract consideration of the nature and meaning of Appalachian otherness and a new focus on practice, and the relationship of theory and practice, especially in the conduct of benevolent work in the southern mountains. If in fact Appalachian otherness was the legitimate product of the existence of a discrete region and a distinct people, were attempts to alter the reality of mountain life appropriate or legitimate? And in what directions and by what means? If simple otherness were no longer a valid justification for attempts to integrate the mountains and the mountaineers into modern American life, and/or if Appalachian otherness no longer could be seen to pose a threat to conceptions of America as a unified and homogeneous national entity, what posture ought Americans in general, and benevolent workers in particular, to take toward the strange land and peculiar people of the southern mountains? "Sentiment may say: Let the mountaineers alone; they are content," Samuel T. Wilson acknowledged in 1906, but he hastily added that "reason and the Spirit of the Master say: Enlist them in service; thus they will be useful: Release these imprisoned powers of body and mind and Spirit; then will these powers be employed in fruitful service for humanity."[18]

Wilson's acknowledgment of the dilemma which followed from the legitimation of Appalachian otherness at the turn of the century was rare, even in so limited a form as it there appears, a rhetorical ploy in a home-mission study text. The evidence that a dilemma did in fact follow from Frost's 1899 explanation of Appalachian otherness consists less of formal statements defending the desirability of mountain work, however, than in the emergence of a dialogue which approached the formality of a debate concerning the direction which mountain work ought to take. In this, moreover, Frost himself was a major participant, as he sought to alter both the nature and function of the educational work carried on at Berea, and Berea's public image, in order to bring both into accord with what appeared to be the real needs of the mountaineers.

In an article of 1900, for example, Frost pointed out that, despite its name, Berea was only a "brevet college," and that it had never sought to fill the role of the traditional southern academy or college, which provided an impractical, "classical" education to an elite few. Instead, Berea was really "a kind of social settlement, Cooper Institution, and extension bureau of civilization" among the mountaineers, "leading them rapidly through the stages of progress which *our* families have already traversed."[19] We shall examine the transformation of benevolent work in Appalachia after 1900 in several contexts below, but it must be noted here that in its general outlines, mountain benevolence did not differ from systematic philanthropy generally in America at and after the turn of the century, when both the nature and the techniques of benevolence were undergoing reconsideration and revision.

In one way, however, the history of mountain benevolence does stand as a special case, even within the "special cases" of rural and southern benevolence. The programmatic and practical problems involved in designing an appropriate scheme for the conduct of work in a legitimately discrete region and among a legitimately distinct population of white, Anglo-Saxon, native-born, American Protestants were so complex, and were viewed with such ambiguity and as having such uncertain consequences for mountain life, that only the institutional conservatism of agencies already committed to systematic benevolence in Appalachia can explain why the work was continued, and indeed appears to have increased in extent after 1900. The course of wisdom, like the advice of sentiment, was indeed to let the mountaineers alone. It was not reason, as Wilson argued, but rather the normal tendency of agencies to continue doing what they have been doing, which explains why mountain white work was not terminated at the beginning of the twentieth century when there was indeed every reason to do so. For it was at the turn of the century that the mountaineers themselves gave new evidence of being "unworthy" of the efforts of systematic benevolence, as a series of family wars or "feuds" erupted and extended outside the mountain region itself to become a factor in state politics, thereby directing the attention of the nation toward Appalachia in quite a new way. When the mountain people of Kentucky came to town with their rifles as they did in 1901, images of the mountaineer as pathetic and romantic gave way before a new set of images of mountaineers as feudists and desperadoes, criminals and social deviants.[20]

As we shall see, it was only by an extraordinary wrench of the imagination that benevolent workers were able to utilize the feuds as the occasion for profitable publicity on behalf of their own efforts, for this involved a fundamental reconceptualization of the nature and causes of Appalachian otherness and of the function of benevolent institutions working in the mountains. Although Frost himself was able to acknowledge that he was "burdened with the weight of his discoveries in this unknown land," few others were similarly outspoken, and even he admitted to distress only as a way of introducing a plea for funds to support the same sort of "educational beginnings" which had made such an impact on the violent society of America's western frontier. Spokesmen for benevolent agencies working in the mountains more characteristically passed over the problems which the feuds might have presented, in their defense of the mountaineers as objects of benevolence. To a commitment to mountain work which had always existed a priori and independent of real observation of mountain needs and conditions, they simply added a commitment to the proposition that "this condition has come about through natural causes, so that we cannot blame the people as negligent or despise them as inferior."[21]

The outbreak of the feuds at the turn of the century did have significant consequences, both for the history of benevolent work in Appalachia and more generally for the history of America's relationship with the strange land and peculiar people of the southern mountains. First in importance if not in order of occurrence, the feuds precipitated a redefinition of Appalachia as a thing in itself rather than an entity defined by reference to characteristics which prevailed in "normal" American culture, and thereby transformed the function of Frost's 1899 suggestions about the "naturalness" of Appalachian otherness from explanation to explication. Second, they precipitated a reassessment of the utility of developmental or historical models for understanding the origins of Appalachian otherness, which yielded in turn a new emphasis on the role of environment not simply as an "isolating factor" but as the critical context in response to which human institutions—social, economic, political, and cultural—functioned. Third, they precipitated a revision of the practice of benevolence in Appalachia, the goal of which now became less to provide "uplift" to individuals and more to provide the mountaineers as a group with a sense of community and with institutions of social interaction and social control, the absence of which appeared as a principal "cause" of the prevalence of feuding in the region. And fourth, they required a reconsideration of generalizations concerning the relationship of who the mountaineers were and the nature of Appalachian otherness, in light of newly perceived patterns of behavior which unfitted the mountaineers for designation as *our* contemporary ancestors.

Feuding, and what came to be seen as the analogous activity of manufacturing blockade or moonshine whiskey, as simple "characteristics" of mountain life alone could not have yielded such consequences. Feuding and moonshining, in the context of contemporary concerns with the need to establish community on a neighborhood as well as a national level in America; with the need to find an alternative model or models for discussion of American civilization to replace the nationalist conception which had been dominant through the nineteenth century but which could not adequately deal with the perceived reality of American social and cultural diversity; with the need for revision of what appeared to be unworkable and inappropriate systems of education; and in the context of the contemporary state of the dialogue on the nature and meaning of Appalachian otherness could and did yield such consequences. The outbreak of feuds at the turn of the century, that is, provided the occasion on which a series of processes came together.

The tendency of mountaineers to engage in feuds, and more specifically the practice of private justice through ambush or "bushwacking," and the tendency of mountaineers to manufacture illegal or untaxed whiskey, had already become a part of the mythology of Appalachian otherness by 1900. As indicators of a disregard for duly constituted authority, feuding and moonshining long had functioned in fiction as overt indicators of the distance which separated Appalachia and America, and hence had the potential to crystallize a sense of Appalachia as a thing in itself. Even during the last years of the nineteenth century, however, feuding and moonshining continued to appear as picturesque customs in an exotic land. As late as 1895, for example, a reviewer of John Fox's fictional account of "a Cumberland vendetta" remarked with a tone reminiscent of the early days of local-color writing, that "a shock falls across the mind to realize that such a community of lawlessness should exist in a country that calls itself civilized." It was not until after the murder of the governor-elect of Kentucky on the steps of the state house in 1903 and the outbreak of feuding in "bloody Breathitt" county, however, that Appalachia itself came to be seen as "a community of lawlessness," a thing unto itself, although even in the early twentieth century writers like Fox continued to exploit the picturesque aspects of feuding and moonshining in novels and short stories.[22]

Conflicts between mountaineers and revenue officers over enforcement of the federal excise tax on whiskey were reported as early as 1867, but it was only in the next two decades, as a general interest in Appalachia developed, that serious attention was paid to moonshining as one of the "peculiarities" of mountain life. By the 1890s, moonshining had become so integral an element in the popular conception of mountain life that discussion of the phenomenon, often coupled with a defense of such illegal activity on historical grounds— by reference to the whiskey rebels of the 1790s for example—became virtually a requirement in descriptive pieces dealing with the region, while an escape from or an attack by "revenooers" similarly became a standard incident in mountain fiction. At worst merely anecdotal, at best such incidents became part of the donnée of a story or novel and thereby worked to transform Appalachian fiction from local-color writing into literature, by suggesting conventional literary images of banditti or outlaws caught in historical processes which they could neither understand nor control. In either case, however, fictional confrontations between moonshiners and "foreigners" representing the legal and social standards of the larger national community functioned to epitomize the tension between Appalachia and America, to reinforce the emerging notion of Appalachia's historical character, and to provide precision and focus to generalizations about the otherness of mountain life.[23]

Feuds in Appalachia received less public attention during the 1870s and 1880s, when private wars and the exercise of private justice in the southern mountains could be dismissed as a natural extension of hostilities engendered by the Civil War, especially in the so-called border states. During these years, moreover, feuding and bushwhacking were in no way restricted to the southern mountains, or even to the South. In the age of Jesse James, mountain violence seemed less exotic rather than more, and it was only during the 1890s that descriptions of feuding in Appalachia began to transcend the anecdotal and came to be tied to conceptions of the nature of mountain life. Like moonshining, however, feuding tended to be viewed as a picturesque if unfortunate practice. Like moonshining also, it tended to be explained in historical terms, as resulting from the persistence of "the frontier" in Appalachia.

The outbreak of a series of extended family wars around the turn of the century, and the eventual extension of private conflict into the area of public affairs, involving local and then state and interstate politics, brought feuding to the attention of the nation in a new way. Like moonshining, this new outbreak of feuds involved the mountaineers in a direct confrontation with the world of more normal American behavior, and in particular with the outsiders' institutions of social control. While the possibility of romanticization existed here also, to the degree that the feuds extended outside the immediate context of mountain life the requirements of the social order for maintaining its viability demanded that this particular aspect of mountain life be defined positively as "lawlessness," even as it demanded that the feudists themselves be convicted as murderers and sentenced to terms in the penitentiary. And this in turn precipitated a redefinition of Appalachia in positive terms, as a land of violence and lawlessness.[24]

In and of itself this new emphasis involved only a more sharply focused conception of the nature of Appalachia's strangeness. A kind of aesthetic distance continued to separate the mountaineers as objects of popular interest from the writers, home missionaries, and social workers who went among them and described their peculiar habits to the rest of America. In the context of a conventional description of the mountaineers as "our contemporary ancestors" and of mountain violence as a survival from an earlier stage of historical development, however, the identification of Appalachia as a lawless land created a dilemma within the American dialogue on the meaning of Appalachia's existence, and raised questions concerning the nature of American civilization as well. Over against an idyllic vision of mountaineers as hard-working pioneers, dependent on their own resources and initiative, was placed what seemed to be a more realistic picture, of pioneer individualism as anarchy and self-help as antisocial behavior. If private justice yielded public chaos, if radical private enterprise involved the rejection of public morality, were our pioneer ancestors, like our contemporary ancestors, merely brawlers and brigands?

The identification of violence and lawlessness in the southern mountains as a survival of the American past, which consistent definition of the mountaineers as our contemporary ancestors demanded, thus created a dilemma. What this meant in practice was that explanation of feuding and moonshining by reference to an historical situation came to be seen as inadequate or, to the degree that it unbalanced the equation of a known present and a presumed past, unsatisfactory. In the early twentieth century, as a consequence, two new emphases appeared in discussions of mountain life, which may be seen as direct responses to the conceptual dilemma which conditions of lawlessness in Appalachia created. The first of these involved identification of the more violent aspects of mountain life as European rather than American in origin, thus permitting continued utilization of the doctrine of survivals while maintaining a traditional conception of the American past as rude but law-abiding. The second involved abandonment of the doctrine of survivals entirely and the development of a new emphasis, in accord with general trends of early twentieth-century social theory, on environment as the determinant of social and cultural patterns. In these terms, Appalachia was seen to be characterized by frontier conditions but was no longer defined as The Frontier.

From the publication in 1878 of Reverend James Craighead's *Scotch and Irish Seeds in American Soil*, the mountaineers of Appalachia were conventionally assumed to be the descendants of Scottish and Scotch-Irish settlers in western North Carolina and Pennsylvania. The outbreak of feuds in the late 1890s gave those old generalizations about the ethnic origins of the mountain population a new utility, however. In his address before the American Missionary Association in 1897, for example, Charles J. Ryder attempted to combine images of the mountaineer as contemporary ancestor and as Scotch-Irish frontiersman in such a way as to explain the occurrence of feuding without compromising assumptions about the inherent nobility of our real pioneer ancestors on the one hand, and without falling in to the trap of Fiskean degeneration theory, on the other.

The mountaineers were "American Highlanders," Ryder asserted, using a term which carried at once the ambiguity of all "hyphenate" designations during these and later years and the explanatory function which such designations also later provided. Where Fiske, for example, had used data concerning the national origins of America's eighteenth-century immigrants only as the basis for commenting upon national origins, Ryder talked the language of contemporary race theory in which Scotch-Irishness became not only a heritage but a designation for particular heritable characteristics. The mountaineers *were* Highlanders. "They have Highland clans with Highland chieftans at the head of them. Highland feuds flame out now and again, often bringing death and ruin. . . . The relationship between the Lowlanders of the South and the Highlanders is also much the same as that which obtained between the same classes in Scotland. . . . In general character and in physical endurance the comparison between the Highlanders of Scotland and America holds good."[25] Feuding and moonshining, and a general proclivity to violent and lawless behavior, could thus be explained as the result of a particular set of ethnic characteristics dominant in the mountain population—rather than as the persistence of an essentially lawless strain in some uniform American national character, which the identification of the mountaineers as "our contemporary ancestors" and of mountain life as "survival" seemed to suggest.

The use of an environmental explanation for the peculiarities of Appalachia functioned in a similar way, as a response to the dilemma which the occurrence of feuds and moonshining presented. Unlike explanation in terms of survivals, however, it did not emerge from within the American dialogue on the meaning of Appalachia as a result of the transformation of metaphor into a statement of reality, but involved the introduction of a new model of social change as a matter of adaptation rather than of development pure and simple. For the environmentalists, as a consequence, while "normal" American culture remained preferable, the legitimacy of a peculiar and indigenous mountain culture was neither denied nor denigrated by its identification with some earlier phase in the evolution of the normal American form. In her seminal essay, "The Anglo-Saxons of the Kentucky Mountains: A Study in Anthropogeography," for example, Ellen Churchill Semple argued in what would become the characteristic way, that the apparent persistence of historical forms in the mountains might be better understood as a matter of adaptation to a particular environment. Utilitarian ethics, an independence of spirit bred by isolation and the necessity for self-reliance, an economy "severely limited in its possibilities" by lack of transportation facilities were the circumstances in which feuding and moonshining developed as appropriate means of obtaining justice and disposing of a corn crop, respectively. "The same conditions which have kept the ethnic type pure have kept the social phenomena primitive," she noted, "with their natural concomitants of primitive ethics and primitive methods of social control."[26]

This new view marked a significant advance over earlier, neo-Lamarckian and/or neo-Positivist models of social evolution, in its acceptance of a Darwinian emphasis on the continuity of the process of selection and on the dynamic character of biotic (and by extension social) systems. It saw environment as the cause of Appalachian otherness no longer simply in the sense that it preserved intact an earlier stage of social development by isolating the mountain region from the rest of the nation and from the tendencies to progress which had affected other areas, but in the sense that it composed the crucial context which determined the appropriateness or inappropriateness of particular forms of behavior. Although the physical isolation of Appalachia from America continued to be regarded as an aspect of Appalachian otherness, it was the isolation of individuals within the region from each other which came to be seen as the fundamental circumstances that caused the peculiarities of mountain life, and a crucial aspect of Appalachian otherness as well.

The utilization of this view to explain the peculiarities of mountain life reflected contemporary interest in the problem of the nature of "community" and in the possibility of achieving it through artificial means, which became indeed a principal object of systematic benevolence in the twentieth century. It was not simply the appropriateness of this mode of explanation in its particular intellectual and historical context that gave this view its popularity, however. It seemed also to make sense. Feuds in Appalachia, for example, might be seen as following naturally from the inadequacy or absence of public agencies to adjudicate disputes between individuals, and/or to provide justice to those who had been wronged; from the necessary reliance on the family as the only effective social unit in frontier conditions; and from the absence of the altruistic spirit of cooperation which the institutions of community both engendered and symbolized. The illicit distillation of alcohol likewise seemed to follow naturally from the inadequacy or complete absence of economic institutions, including roads and railroads, by means of which excess agricultural products might as easily be turned into cash as into "moonshine"; from the necessary dependence on domestic economy in frontier conditions; and from the absence of the spirit of cooperation and community upon which the authority of laws circumscribing individual action rested.

Less undesirable but no less peculiar characteristics of mountain life—the mountaineers' dress, manners, morals, music, and religion —seemed also to follow from the same causes. As a result, the "ancient" quality of mountain life came increasingly to be seen as involving a replication of pioneer life in a similar environment, which happened to be geographically identical, rather than the preservation of an earlier stage of civilization as such. The occurrence of feuds among our "contemporary ancestors" thus implied neither the occurrence of feuds among our pioneer ancestors nor ethnic discontinuity between the heroic pioneer generation and the mountaineers of the present.

Certain problems remained nonetheless. If environmental determinism as explanation made possible the preservation of assumptions about the heroic character of America's pioneer past, in the face of distinctly unheroic behavior on the part of our "contemporary ancestors" in Appalachia, it provided no acceptable explanation for lawless behavior among a population alleged to be uniquely "pure" in its racial or ethnic composition. Were any of the writers on Appalachian otherness even moderately rigorous in their environmentalism, of course, this problem would not have emerged, since one kind of determinism obviously denies the other. Because their intention was essentially literary, in that they sought to provide explanation as a way of resolving a logical and abstract dilemma, and in the case of the agents of systematic benevolence as a way of justifying their efforts among the mountaineers, intellectual rigor was characteristically absent from the literature on the southern mountain region. As a result, environmental and genetic explanations for the peculiarities of mountain life normally stood side by side.

It was in this context that the agents of systematic benevolence in particular, with the greatest stake in maintaining the proposition that the mountaineers were racially pure (that is, not degenerate) as a way of insisting on the remediability of mountain conditions, turned increasingly to an identification of the mountaineer as an American Highlander. Frost's article of 1900, for example, mixed together environmental determinism and ethnic determinism in a characteristic way, while muddling together a whole series of historical images to describe the quality of mountain life and the function of feuding

among the mountaineers. "The fighting propensities of the mountaineers are to be classed with the other survivals of old-world temper
and ideals," reinforced by the conditions of life in the region, he
argued.

It is well to remember that the whole South is still far nearer than the other
parts of the country to the age of chivalry when all gentlemen wore side arms
and felt that the Government was simply to defend them from foreign foes,
while they were to rely upon their own prowess to protect their households
and their honor. . . . Add to this that the mountaineer has the independent
spirit born of solitude. . . . It gives us hope for their future that the frequent
homicides are not committed wantonly nor for purposes of robbery, but in
the spirit of an Homeric chieftain on some "point of honor." . . . Their exag-
gerated individuality is only offset by a spirit of clannishness with which they
gather around a leader in the old feudal way.[27]

By 1916, John M. Moore could remark without the slightest sense that
he was saying anything which was not common knowledge, that
"the peculiarities of an individualistic people have been interpreted
as hideous deficiencies" and that the mountaineer was the pure
Scotch-Irishman. "In manners, beliefs, and speech his lineage can be
traced . . . I found that Scott and Stevenson in their tales of the
Campbells and MacGregors were describing the parties that were
appearing in the later roles of feudists in Kentucky. The heads of
feuds were no ordinary men in Kentucky than in Scotland."[28]

The merits of this "Highlanders" designation as a mode of
explanation for the peculiarities of mountain life, including the apparent proclivity of the mountaineers to engage in feuds and moonshining, is clear. Its widespread use after the turn of the century did
not rest only on its utility in this context, however. When the legitimation of Appalachian otherness seemed to suggest the appropriateness of talking about the regional culture and ethnic characteristics
of the mountaineers, "Highlanders" also suggested the kind of relationship which existed between this people and their culture, as
between the Scottish Highlanders and *their* culture, and thereby provided hints for the construction of programs of benevolence appropriate to this new vision of mountain life. While Frost personally
preferred to identify the mountaineers as "Saxons," for example,[29]
he used the "Highlanders" designation publicly in explanation of the

ways in which Berea College sought to meet the needs of the mountain people, and in advocacy of a new conception of the goal of
benevolent work in the region. We must not seek "to set them in
motion toward the strife of the cities" but must rather "make them
sharers in the essential blessings of civilization in the mountains," he
argued. "We should make them, like the people of Scotland, intelligent without being sophisticated."[30] As Frost was himself learning,
however, the achievement of that goal required both the transformation of benevolent work in the mountains and a transformation in the
conception of Appalachia and of its status as a land in but not of
America. It is to that process that we must next turn our own
attention.

5. Naming as Explaining: William Goodell Frost and the Invention of Appalachia

The division of reality into discrete cognitive units is surely the most ancient act of man's intellectual life. It is as well, of course, the most fundamental, for upon the transformation of perception into conception rests the possibility not only of language and hence of society, but also of the manipulation of reality at secondhand, that is, of understanding. As a form of historical event, however, it is almost invisible, for it possesses a legitimacy and a kind of normalness which permit it to stand within history without itself becoming part of the historical record. At the same time, the conservatism of language and the conservatism of the history of thought conspire to hide new ideas inside old terms, and to disguise new conceptions as new perceptions.

As a result, we have tended to view fundamental acts of conceptualization—including the articulation of a vision of Appalachia as a discrete region inhabited by a distinct population, and of America more generally as a nation characterized by regionalism and pluralism—as nothing more than natural and normal responses to reality. These peculiarly twentieth-century notions, indeed, have been legitimized and historicized as new ways of talking about old ways of thinking, mere translations from the nineteenth century; or even worse, have been accepted as accurate statements of fact, having their origin in the discovery of "truth."[1]

In whatever way we define reality as an abstract or philosophical construct, and in whatever way reality may have been defined in the past, the fact remains that because the way men see the world determines how they act in it, any act of seeing may be said to involve a functional determination of reality. A new way of seeing will thus necessarily involve the creation of a new reality, in terms of which future action will develop. It is with this principle in mind that one must approach the legitimation of Appalachian otherness on regionalist and pluralist grounds, and indeed the more general phenomenon of the emergence of regionalist and pluralist models for the description of the American reality during the early twentieth century. And it is with this principle in mind also, that one must recognize the transformations in thought and action of the early twentieth century as responses to the American reality newly defined in regionalist and pluralist terms.

Seen in these terms, the emergence of regionalism and pluralism, like the "discovery" of Appalachia's regional status, appears as something quite different than the ascription of positive values to previously unarticulated but fully recognized characteristics of American life. Instead, the emergence of regionalism and pluralism, which looked to a redefinition of the nature of America and of American civilization, may be seen to have marked a fundamental transformation in the very nature of America and American civilization. It was of course a transformation which occurred in the world of "ideas" rather than in the "real" world, but it must not for this reason be seen as merely a response to transformations in the real world. It was rather a transformation *of* the real world.

Through the late nineteenth century, "region" meant an area, geographic or other, defined exclusively by its location. It was not until the publication of the incomparable *Oxford English Dictionary* in 1910 that the development of a new meaning for "region," in the context of the new disciplines of zoogeography and climatology and the not yet entirely respectable study of "anthropogeography," was acknowledged formally. In addition to its meaning as an area defined by its location, the *OED* noted that "region" was also used to designate a "more or less defined portion of the earth's surface, now especially as distinguished by certain natural features, climatic conditions, a special fauna or flora, or the like." Even so, no American dictionary of the period included a general definition of "region" as an area characterized by its characteristics or its contents rather than by its location, and it was only with the publication of *Webster's Third New International Dictionary* in 1961 that our modern, regionalist definition of "region" received formal acknowledgment, as "a broad geographical area containing a population whose members possess sufficient historical, cultural, economic, and social homogeneity to distinguish them from others."[2]

Prior to the end of the nineteenth century, the Appalachia which we now know as "a geographic area containing a population whose members possess sufficient historical, cultural, economic, and social homogeneity to distinguish them from others" was defined exclusively by location, as "the central South," or, more frequently, was not defined at all.[3] Composed of the "mountainous backyards" of eight southern states, it was seen to be characterized by the persistence of rude and primitive patterns of social and economic organization more appropriate to the frontier status it once had, than to its current location at the very heart of the oldest and most civilized area of the nation. Appalachia was simply "behind the times," but this very fact, repeated often enough in travel accounts, short stories, and in the literature of social uplift, seemed sufficient basis for the construction of a generalization concerning the coherence of mountain culture and the homogeneity of the mountain population. And it was this which made possible the redefinition of Appalachia as a discrete region of the nation and the redefinition of the mountaineers as a distinct population, and thereby made possible the legitimation of Appalachian otherness. How else, indeed, might Appalachian otherness have been legitimized?

The description of the southern mountain region as composed of the "mountainous backyards" of several states, for example, appears regularly in the essays of William Goodell Frost, initially in his seminal article of 1899 for *Atlantic Monthly*, "Our Contemporary Ancestors in the Southern Mountains." For Frost and others of his generation who repeated his phrases, however, the thrust of this description was ironic, in that the several "backyards"—by their very nature and location separated from the states which claimed jurisdiction over them—in fact composed a distinct region not only of the South but also of the nation, which Frost proposed to call "Appalachian America." Frost thus pointed, albeit in passing, to what within a decade would come to seem a monumental problem in efforts both to understand and to meliorate the conditions of mountain life, that is the division of the "region" into distinct political jurisdictions. His intention, however, was to assert the coherence and homogeneity of conditions within these "mountainous backyards" rather than to acknowledge patterns of real diversity within the region. Except in the work of John C. Campbell after 1912, and particularly his posthumously published *The Southern Highlander and His Homeland* (1921), which argues the noncoherence and nonhomogeneity of mountain life as a preliminary to the articulation of a program for the creation of coherence and homogeneity in Appalachia, after 1900 the mountains and mountaineers were conventionally viewed as a coherent region inhabited by an homogeneous population.

This was not the case in the days of the local colorists' dominance over the southern mountains and mountaineers as objects of American interest. Then the region had been divided up along state lines among the several writers who "specialized" in mountain sketches. Mary Noailles Murfree monopolized Tennessee, Constance Fenimore Woolson monopolized western North Carolina, James Lane Allen and his unacknowledged disciple, John Fox, Jr., monopolized Kentucky, and each found the boundaries of the several states convenient to their division of the mountain region as a field for fiction. Where the local-color writers competed with each other indirectly, by advancing the claims of their respective "little corners" as more interesting, more picturesque, more exotic than the "little corners" claimed by some other writer, however, the home missionaries who entered the southern mountains after the mid-1880s competed directly. They sought to dominate the region as a whole, denying the boundaries of the separate states' jurisdictions even as they denied the jurisdictions of their sister denominations. Their emergence as principal authorities on the nature of mountain life during the 1890s thus had the consequence of establishing the basis for a regional definition for Appalachia, even though their own efforts looked to the legitimation of the "central South" as a mission field and the definition of the mountaineers as an appropriate clientele, on the basis of availability rather than upon any recognition of positive characteristics which defined the region and its people.

These assumptions of coherence and homogeneity, which formed the justification for home-missionary work in Appalachia during the 1890s and which received explicit articulation in the twentieth century, were normally based on very scanty evidence and/or limited observation of the conditions of mountain life. Even so "careful" and "scientific" an observer as the Chicago sociologist, George E. Vincent, for example, based his generalizations upon brief visits to three Kentucky counties. In his important essay of 1898 in the *American Journal of Sociology*, "A Retarded Frontier," Vincent felt qualified nonetheless to discuss the nature and causes of Appalachian otherness and to place the conditions of the region *as a whole* in a general context of American historical development. And Vincent was among those most conscious of the limitations of his own observation of mountain conditions. Few of those who wrote about Appalachia during the 1890s and first decades of the twentieth century cared even to indicate the basis for their comments on the nature and causes of Appalachian otherness, and John C. Campbell alone seems to have been justified in his claims to familiarity with conditions in more than one location and more than one state. Campbell's own insistence on the diversity of conditions within the region carries considerable weight as evidence for this reason. His personal and professional commitment to the creation of a viable Appalachian regionalism made the diversity he found a condition to be altered, however, rather than evidence of the inappropriateness of defining the southern mountains as a region in our modern sense of the word, or the mountaineers as a people.

By the end of the nineteenth century in any case, the "old-fashioned" quality of mountain life seemed to demand explanation, both as an abstract problem and as an aspect of the American dialogue on the nature of American civilization. Appalachia—whether defined as region in the old sense, of a place, or in the sense just emerging, as an area characterized by a distinctive culture and a homogeneous population as well as by a particular topography—seemed an exception to the rule of American unity and homogeneity, and of a uniform pattern of progress. It could only be as the result of a series of accidents that the mountaineers, white, Anglo-Saxon, Protestants, descended presumably from the Revolutionary generation like the "best" of the American population, had been excluded from full participation in the processes of nationalization and modernization, and had thereby "fallen behind" the rest of the nation. That in their isolation from the "main currents" of American life they might have "degenerated" from the hardy, adaptable pioneer stock from which they were descended, or alternatively that they were themselves the children of the less adaptable or less competent among the pioneer generation, did not alter the "accidental" quality emphasized in the explanations for Appalachian otherness offered at the end of the nineteenth century. Neither did it alter the intensity of the problem of Appalachian otherness, at least for those whose institutional, occupational, or intellectual commitments led them to identify the existence of this strange land and peculiar people as a problem.

As we have noted, the explanatory arguments developed during the last decades of the nineteenth century functioned not only to resolve the dilemma of Appalachia's existence in a nation presumed to be unified and homogeneous, but also to provide a rational or ideological basis for programs which would effect the modernization of mountain life and the education of the mountaineers in the cultural and economic values of modern urban, industrial life. That such programs as actually developed were continuous with those designed earlier, for work among different populations in and out of the nation, and that identification of the mountaineers as an "exceptional population" of the nation was continuous with definitions earlier applied to other populations does not alter the ideological function which explanation performed in the history of mountain benevolence. Indeed, explanation functioned as ideology in two senses, as rationalization for what was (or what appeared to be); as plan for action.

During the first years of the twentieth century, the essentially simplistic view that Appalachia, characterized by the apparent persistence of pioneer culture, was therefore a kind of incomplete version of modern America, began to give way before an alternative vision of Appalachia as a legitimately discrete region defined by a particular pattern of culture as well as by its location, and inhabited by a legitimately distinct population, similarly defined by their participation in a particular culture as well as by the mere fact of residence. This shift, which may be seen as symptomatic of the emergence of regionalism and pluralism as acceptable models for the description of American reality during this period more generally, in the context of the history of American responses to Appalachian otherness involved nothing more—and nothing less—than the acceptance of Appalachian otherness.

The architect of this new vision was William Goodell Frost, President of Berea College in Berea, Kentucky, from 1893, who coined the phrase "Appalachian America" in order to give the southern mountain region the name-of-its-own which it deserved as a "natural" region of the nation—and thereby made possible its identification as a cultural region as well—and who, by calling the mountaineers "our contemporary ancestors," thereby gave coherence to impressionistic notions that the population of Appalachia composed an homogeneous people. Frost's contribution to the development of our modern notion of Appalachian regionalism, and indeed to the development of concepts of regionalism and pluralism more generally, was thus seminal. But he was not the first to "discover" Appalachia, as has often been suggested, nor was his contribution merely that of naming a preexistent reality. He attempted, in ways conventional to his own time, to achieve explanation by naming. But in the process, and apparently without any full understanding of the consequences of his actions, he did no less a work than the invention of Appalachia.

In December 1895, at the annual banquet meeting of the Cincinnati Teachers' Club, Frost announced the discovery of a new world. "We are familiar with North America and South America," he said, but "have you ever heard of Appalachian America?" Appalachian America was composed of the mountainous portions of eight southern states, "a body of land as large as all New England," where a hardy race descended from our pioneer ancestors continued to live in the virtual conditions of pioneer days. Lacking adequate transportation facilities, Appalachian America had been isolated from the rest of the nation for so long that it appeared as a world fundamentally different from the world with which the rest of us were familiar. To all intents and purposes it was a separate land, Frost said, and as such deserved a name of its own.[4]

Because Frost's rhetoric resonates with contemporary concerns about the nature and future of American civilization, and involves an inward look at America quite characteristic of the 1890s, it has been tempting to explain his discovery of Appalachia as a symptomatic phenomenon of that troubled last decade of the nineteenth century. Frost indeed helps us to make such a connection, by talking about the strange land and peculiar people of the southern mountains in the language of popular cataclysmic thought, with its concerns about race-suicide, American nervousness, and the closing of the frontier. He pointed to the happy accident that "we have discovered a new pioneer region in the mountains of the central South just as our western frontier has been lost in the Pacific ocean." He noted that the isolation of the mountaineers from modern civilization meant that they had been uncorrupted by the "lackadaisical effeminacy" which seemed to accompany modern civilization. He suggested that the mountaineers, as heirs to the strengths and virtues of our pioneer ancestors, stood ready to enter the American population as a saving remnant, able by their presence "to offset some of the undesirable foreign populations" whose presence in the United States threatened the maintenance of traditional American values and patterns of culture. And in general, while arguing that the mountaineers needed the assistance of institutions like his own Berea College, he insisted that the integration of Appalachia into America would benefit America quite as much as it would benefit the mountain region.[5]

Frost was of necessity a man of his own time, and hence spoke the language of his own time, but the phenomenon of "discovery" is a complex one, and we have yet to see just what it was that Frost discovered. As he well knew, he was not the first to discover the existence of a strange land and a peculiar people in the southern mountains. That discovery took place in the 1870s, in the context of a search for exotic "little corners" of the nation available for literary exploitation by the local-color writers. As Frost also knew, he was not the first to discover that the mere fact of the mountaineers' isolation from the mainstream of American life made them available as appropriate objects of systematic benevolence. That discovery took place in the 1880s, in the context of attempts by home missionaries from northern Protestant denominations to establish a foothold among white southerners. Nor was Frost the first to discover that the existence of a strange land and a peculiar people in the southern mountains was psychologically, or more accurately culturally "uncomfortable,"[6] insofar as it stood as a contradiction to dominant notions concerning the essential unity and homogeneity of American civilization.

By 1895, not only the otherness of Appalachia but the bothersomeness of this otherness had become a convention of the American consciousness. It should thus come as no surprise that William Goodell Frost shared not only his contemporaries' sense that Appalachia was a strange land inhabited by a peculiar people, but also their sense that the very existence of Appalachia so defined posed a dilemma. It was in this context, however, that Frost made the discovery which he correctly claimed as his own: that the dilemma posed by the apparent existence of Appalachia as a discrete region, in but not of America, would disappear if Appalachia should turn out to be in fact a discrete region of the nation, and should be accepted as such. The acceptance of Appalachian otherness as the normal concomitant of Appalachia's existence as a discrete region of the nation, and the legitimation of Appalachia's existence as a discrete region through the act of naming, eliminated the necessity of comparing mountain life with the more "normal" life of the rest of the nation. That "normal life" now became—insofar as discussions of Appalachian otherness was concerned, at least—not so much "normal" as "familiar," and Appalachian America as a thing in itself could be accepted on its own terms.

By describing the mountainous portions of eight southern states as a legitimately discrete region of the nation, Frost did not so much "discover" Appalachia as invent it. He thereby provided his contemporaries with an essential tool—in this case a name—for the manipulation of the perceived reality of Appalachian otherness and for its effective integration into contemporary conceptions of the nature of American civilization. His was an act of technological innovation, and thus marks a conclusion to that critical period during which necessity labored long and hard upon the birth of invention, a period during which the perceived dilemma of Appalachian otherness generated explanations which proved inviable, programs which had to be aborted. But technological innovation not only concludes the period of the past. It also begins a new future. By solving the old problem, Frost made the southern mountain region available in a new way as the object of systematic social action and as the subject of discourse.

Frost's own situation made him almost uniquely able to accept what had previously seemed unacceptable. A newcomer to the southern mountains and to the "problem" of Appalachia, but not a tourist in search of local color or a writer in search of literary opportunities to exploit, Frost may have been able for these reasons alone to take for granted the neediness of the mountaineers and the appropriateness of benevolent work among them. Then, wishing to get on with his work, he may have sought simply to redirect the attention of his coworkers to what he regarded as the more important questions, concerning the kind of work which the conditions of mountain life required. As president of Berea College, however, Frost's immediate commitment was not so much to the redirection of benevolent work in Appalachia as to the preservation of Berea as an economically and educationally viable institution, both for its own sake and for the sake of its potential as a leaven to the South.[7]

In the face of Berea's subsequent successes in mountain education we have tended to forget that its mission during the nineteenth century was not to the mountaineers of Appalachia, but rather to the cause of racial co-education, and that Berea was virtually unique among American colleges in maintaining equal enrollment of blacks and whites from 1870 until segregation was mandated by action of the Kentucky legislature in 1904.[8] For a variety of reasons, however, Berea had come upon hard times in the early 1890s, and her viability as a co-educational college in particular was threatened by significant declines in white enrollment. It was in this context that Frost was called from Oberlin to assume the presidency of the college.

Even before he took office, Frost had developed a strategy to meet Berea's needs. As he outlined it in an address to his faculty early in 1894, this consisted of three related programs of action: recruitment of white students from the North, where racial antipathy appeared less strong than it did in the South during the 1890s; "recovery" of Berea's former clientele of white students from the southern mountains—a clientele which had been less aggressively pursued during the last years of President Fairchild's tenure at Berea than had been the case during early years, immediately after the Civil War; and development of "an enthusiasm and missionary zeal among the students" at the college for the cause of co-education and for the principle of racial equality more generally. The first two would meet Berea's immediate enrollment problem. The third would have long-term effects beneficial both to the South and to the college. Berea's impact as a "leaven" to the South would be assured, and as its mission proved successful, future recruitment of white students from the urban and lowland South would be facilitated.[9]

To these three, in practice Frost added a fourth program of action. In a series of speeches, pamphlets, essays and published addresses beginning in 1895, Frost sought to raise money and to obtain public support for Berea, especially in the northeast and midwest, and thereby to create both a national constituency in support of Berea's mission in the South and a national visibility for the college which would facilitate its future efforts at fund-raising and recruitment of students. In the process, while Frost never denied Berea's primary commitment to the co-education of the races, he characteristically gave this work less emphasis than Berea's potential as an agent for the improvement of mountain conditions and her actual work of educating the mountaineers of Appalachia. One result of this was that he established himself as a principal spokesman for the "misunderstood" mountain people and laid the foundation for the myth of Berea's priority in mountain work. Another result was that he focused public attention on the characteristics of mountain life rather than on the anomaly of Appalachia's existence in a unified and homogeneous nation.

Frost lectured widely during the mid-1890s in his attempt to revitalize Berea's flagging fortunes. In the neediness of the mountaineers he found not only a work to be done, but also a more effective basis on which to build his appeal for northern sympathy and northern financial support than the traditional claims derived from Berea's commitment to co-education of the races, which indeed he appears to have abandoned as a theme in his public addresses following his 1894 appearance at the Hotel Thorndike in Boston.[10] To suggest that Frost in his stress on the neediness of the mountaineers was following the main chance and abandoning Berea's work for racial equality on the basis of such evidence is both incorrect and unconscionable. To suggest that he adapted his rhetoric to necessity, and spoke the language of current social problems in order to be heard at all, is more likely, and accords well with his own recollection that, during those years, he had as his "great advisors President Eliot of Harvard, and the two men who were then leading in the new study called sociology, Josiah Strong and Washington Gladden."[11] Like other writers and lecturers, moreover, having read his own words he came to believe them.[12]

From the time of his successful defense of the legitimacy of Appalachian otherness in "The Last Log Cabin" delivered at Cincinnati in 1895, in any case, Frost sought increasingly to direct public attention first to Berea's mission among the mountaineers and then to the appropriateness of northern support for southern educational institutions, "to efface sectional lines." These two indeed became the principal themes in Berea's active campaign of publicity during the later 1890s, as the college's letterhead stationery, which functioned as advertising handbill as well as writing paper, shows. In 1895, for example, before Berea's "mountain white work" had become the central motif of Frost's campaign, underneath the name of the college appeared as motto the first words of Berea's charter, "In Order to Promote the Cause of Christ." On the left side of the paper, where a logo would later appear, was the following message:

Unique Providential Opening.
Founded Among Anti-Slavery Kentuckians—1855.
A College Settlement.
Unsectarian.

A Body of College Students from Good Kentucky Families,
and from the North, with Normal and Industrial Work,
which Reaches All Classes.
Effacing Sectional Lines—486 Students from 17 States.
A Man is a Man. Berea Welcomes the Worthy Student
Without Regard to Race.
Location and Management Bring a Student's Expenses
Within $100 a Year.

Across the top of the sheet in small italics appeared Berea's acknowledgment of the state of current rhetoric among home missionaries at
work in Appalachia: "Located near Boone's Gap, Berea discovered
the loyal 'Mountain Whites' before the War, and is in best position to
fit this vigorous Protestant population for intelligent American leadership."

By December 1898, phrases drawn from Frost's speeches had
replaced the college motto drawn from its charter. Beneath "Berea
College" was printed "What is the Use of Having a Big Country
Unless we Love the Whole of It?" or "What Does America Need So
Much as Americans?"—the equivalents of "effacing sectional lines"
—but in both cases, on the left of the sheet as a logo now appeared an
outline map of the mountain region of the South. By September 1900,
beneath "Berea College" stood a new motto, "Unrivalled Opportunities for the Young People of the Southern Mountains," and replacing
the map-logo was a line drawing of "Capt. John Wilson and Men of
8th K[entucky] V[olunteer] I[nfantry] Putting First United States Flag
on Lookout Mountain." In 1903 the stationery bore the motto "In
Lincoln's State—For Lincoln's People," and a drawing on the left
purported to show "Abe Lincoln, Studying By the Cabin Fire."[13]

This new emphasis in Berea's publicity and in Frost's speeches
and essays on work among the "mountain whites," did not mean
that the college had abandoned its commitment to racial co-education, nor did it mean that Berea began to serve its potential clientele
among the mountaineers only after 1895. Frost's own commitment to
co-education was sufficiently strong that when the Kentucky legislature declared co-education illegal, Frost urged his trustees to remove
the college to Ohio where co-education remained legal, and he was

troubled both personally and professionally by the compromise measure, which utilized approximately half of Berea's endowment to found a separate black college for the benefit of Berea's former black students.[14] He acknowledged publicly that Berea had drawn students from the hill country nearby throughout its history, moreover, but insisted that the college did not educate blacks as blacks or whites as whites, but sought always to serve the needs of its obvious clientele.[15]

Because Frost's initial interest in the mountaineers was as a clientele whose particular needs Berea had to serve if the larger mission of co-education were to be accomplished, he was forced almost from the outset to accept not only the legitimacy of Appalachian otherness as an abstract issue, but also the legitimacy of those very peculiarities of mountain life of which Appalachian otherness was composed. At the beginning of his tenure at Berea, the mountains and the mountaineers appeared only as an undeveloped but eminently available resource, even as they had to Berea's founders, John Gregg Fee and John A. R. Rogers, during the 1850s and 1860s. During the summer of 1893, soon after his arrival at Berea, for example, Frost wrote to his mother about the prospects of his new situation. He was hopeful. "I have seen the mountains, and am encouraged," he told her. "There is a vast population living in pioneer style—Arcadian simplicity—just ready for education. They followed me from place to place to hear the same lecture."[16]

During the next years, however, Frost came increasingly to see the "peculiarities" of Appalachia not so much as symptoms of the absence of characteristics found in the dominant American culture, but as the particularities by which Appalachian culture itself was defined. Although mountain life bore a striking resemblance to the life of "our pioneer ancestors," as Frost noted, it was not for this reason to be regarded only as an undesirable anachronism. Whatever its origins, mountain life was of the present, and as such had to be recognized as an aspect of the reality with which Berea had to work.

It is in this context that Frost's coinage of 1895 must be understood, for his whole career after 1893 may be seen as a series of attempts to respond to the apparent fact of Appalachian otherness, first through understanding and then through practical programs for the education of young people. At the same time, however, like the chief officer of any independent eleemosynary institution, Frost became involved as a matter of course in efforts at fund raising, and this in turn required that he explain Berea's work to a larger public than the benevolent community which formed the principal audience of most of his colleagues in mountain work at this time. Which came first, the work at home which led ultimately to a redefinition of Appalachia as a legitimately discrete region and to the reconstruction of Berea's educational program, or the work outside which forced Frost to articulate *some* vision of the nature of Appalachian otherness to explain his presence in Cincinnati, or New York, or Boston, or Chicago, is simply not clear.

Most appeals for funds on behalf of "mountain white work" before and after 1895 were initiated by agents of national or paranational institutions, either as direct requests to the governing boards of such institutions or as indirect appeals through the institutions to their constituents. Because Berea College was an independent institution by choice and necessity, Frost was cut off from the normal route of appeal through the benevolent community and was forced to direct his appeal to the larger, unorganized public of potentially sympathetic teachers, social workers, and philanthropists when and as he could, through his lectures and particularly through a series of articles in magazines of national circulation. By 1901, as a result, William Goodell Frost had emerged as the public spokesman for the needs of the mountaineers in a way which persons locked into formal institutional networks never could. In the process, he established as fact the notion that Berea was *the* institution which served the needs of the mountain people. His coworkers in mountain benevolence were often unhappy about this situation.

At the time of his Cincinnati address in 1895, however, Frost sought only to add his own voice to the chorus of already vocal promoters of benevolent work among the mountaineers, in order to make known his own presence and to publicize Berea's involvement in the mountain field. There is no evidence that he regarded his vision of the nature or meaning of Appalachian otherness as unique, or that he saw Berea's educational work as possessing special qualities. On the contrary, he seems quite consciously to have attempted no more than a summary of conventional contemporary wisdom concerning the cause of Appalachian otherness—that physical isolation and the absence of modern transportation facilities had prevented the mountain country from becoming modernized and hence had preserved in Appalachia the conditions of pioneer days—in order to assert the "neediness" of the mountaineers and hence the appropriateness of Berea's work among them. His remarks about the "discovery" of a new world may be taken as no more than the rhetoric of fund raising and institutional boosting.

There was a hidden agenda to his talk, however, and it was to serve this purpose that his designation of the mountainous portions of eight southern states as a "natural" region of the nation, Appalachian America, may have been designed. Especially during the 1890s, in the midst of discussions of degeneration and of genetic inferiority, persons active in benevolent work among the mountaineers were at great pains to insist that the "mountain whites" were not the "inherently" inferior "poor whites" of the South, lest financial support for their efforts among an unredeemable population be cut off. Instead, it was argued, the mountaineers were of the same genetic stock as the dominant white, Anglo-Saxon, native-born Protestant population of the rest of the nation, and with the same potential for progress. By suggesting that in the southern mountains the effects of isolation—the "cause" of Appalachian otherness—were so severe as to make the southern mountains a separate land, Frost sought only to defend in one more way the legitimacy of Berea's work among the mountaineers, by asserting their availability to systematic social action while simultaneously asserting their neediness.

The implications of his coinage were quite different than what he must have anticipated. In his attempt to establish once and for all the legitimacy of benevolent work among the mountaineers, Frost provided the crucial phrase by which the otherness of Appalachia might be seen as a natural fact of American civilization. Especially after the publication of an expanded version of his Cincinnati address in the

Atlantic Monthly in 1899, his metaphor came to be taken as a statement of reality which passed like coin of the realm among those who had noted in any way the dilemma posed by the fact of Appalachian otherness. The solution had been so obvious that it had eluded them. Once provided, however, it was accepted with enthusiasm and appropriate public action.

As a widely accepted statement of reality, Frost's assertion of the legitimacy of Appalachian otherness functioned not only to resolve the dilemma of Appalachian otherness, but also to facilitate the transformation of benevolent work in the southern mountains. By the beginning of the twentieth century, even Frost had been forced to reexamine the appropriateness of attempts to Americanize a mountain population whose peculiarities, never clearly defined in the first place, now seemed less a deviation from accepted norms than the legitimate manifestations of a discrete regional culture. At Berea as elsewhere in the mountains, during the next years the thrust of benevolent work shifted from the Americanization programs of the 1890s toward a series of attempts to establish in Appalachia a viable mountain economy and a viable mountain culture, founded on the indigenous characteristics of the region and the indigenous patterns of culture among the mountaineers.

As early as 1899, in the first of his major articles on the southern mountains and mountaineers, Frost himself argued that the aim of benevolent work in Appalachia should be to make the mountaineers "intelligent without making them sophisticated."

As a matter of both taste and of common sense, we should not try to make them conform to the regulation type of Americans; they should be encouraged to retain all that is characteristic and wholesome in their present life. Let us not set them agog to rush into the competition of the cities, but show them how to get the blessings of culture where they are. Let them not be taught to despise the log cabin, but to adorn it.[17]

By this year also, Frost had begun working to alter the direction of Berea's own program, away from a traditional commitment to the collegiate course as the more important and more prestigious part of the institution's work and toward an increased emphasis on secondary and vocational/industrial education for blacks and whites both. By 1900 he was describing Berea as really "a brevet college." Though it had the name and retained the name of college, Berea was in fact "a kind of social settlement, Cooper Institution, and extension bureau of civilization" set down at the edge of the southern mountain region. In 1901 he reminded his trustees that "We are not here to help the prosperous, the enlightened, and the well-to-do. Our work is not to make nice people still nicer, and dispense gilded accomplishments to those who are able to pay for them. We are to help the poor, to deal with crude material, to lay foundations in character, intelligence, and thrift."[18]

At the beginning of the twentieth century, Frost's conviction of the legitimacy of Appalachian culture rested primarily on the fact that it was there. When he came to attempt a description of it, like others of his generation he fell back upon conventional generalizations concerning the persistence of pioneer conditions in the mountains and the physical isolation of the region from the currents of modernization operative elsewhere in the nation, which had preserved pioneer days in Appalachia. Although from time to time he acknowledged explicitly the appropriateness of pioneer patterns of social and economic organization to the social and economic realities of mountain life, especially in defending "moonshining" as merely a modern version of a traditional aspect of domestic economy, to Frost at this time Appalachian culture was the culture of poverty and ignorance. His pluralism extended no further than an acceptance of the fact of social and economic diversity as a normal phenomenon in American life and indeed a normal phenomenon in Appalachia itself.

Between 1900 and 1915, however, a series of events conspired to force Frost and others to articulate a more positive definition of mountain culture, and thereby transformed their conviction of the legitimacy of Appalachian otherness—framed originally for the purposes of explanation and to legitimize benevolent work among the mountaineers—into a commitment to maintain Appalachia as a discrete region and to assist the mountaineers in becoming in fact a distinct people. One of these events was the discovery at the turn of the century of an indigenous crafts tradition in Appalachia, which

Frost saw first as proof of the "historical" rather than the "degenerate" origins of Appalachian otherness, and then recognized as a means to obtain salable items which could help defray the cost of his students' tuition, but which subsequently became the basis for the organization of the "Fireside Industries" at Berea as an indigenous program of industrial education, and ultimately led to the "crafts revival" in Appalachia more generally.[19] Another was the even more momentous discovery about 1905 of an indigenous folksong tradition in the mountains, which again first provided evidence of the legitimacy of Appalachian otherness by demonstrating the participation of the mountaineers in Anglo-American culture, and subsequently became the basis for the construction of a program of education in the culture of Appalachia itself.[20] We shall examine the consequences of these two "discoveries" in greater detail below, but it must be noted here that they formed the basis for a fundamental reconceptualization of Appalachia and Appalachia's place in America, as a kind of folk-society manqué, an incomplete version of itself rather than an incomplete version of the America of which it was a part.

The identification of these two as fundamental elements in Appalachian culture during the first decades of the twentieth century was symptomatic of a more general tendency to focus on the characteristics of the region itself rather than on the fact of Appalachian otherness, but this tendency was itself made possible only by the legitimation of Appalachian otherness effected by Frost's coinage, and it occurred only in the context of his assertion of the reality of Appalachian regionalism. Particular historical events and general tendencies evident during the early twentieth century contributed to this process, of course—particularly the professionalization of benevolent work in the southern mountains and its concomitant, the attempt of workers in the mountain field to utilize "scientific" techniques for the analysis of mountain problems; the fascination of professional benevolent workers with the possibility of achieving "community" among their client populations, as a necessary first step to achieving social and political equilibrium among the peoples and regions of a nation now conceived increasingly in regionalist and pluralist terms; and the apparent need to reassess the particular characteristics of mountain life precipitated by the outbreak of feuding in Appalachia at the beginning of the century. The process itself, however, depended ultimately on the acceptance of Frost's definition of the southern mountain region as "Appalachian America."

From the beginning of the century, in any case, the idea that Appalachia was or ought to be a discrete region of the nation, and that the mountaineers were or ought to be a distinct subgroup in the American population became the fundamental assumption in terms of which public action in and toward the southern mountains and mountaineers developed. For benevolent workers, this tended to mean that the "peculiarities" of mountain life came to be seen less as the consequence of the mountaineers' isolation from America than as a result of the mountaineers' isolation from each other. The establishment of "community" in Appalachia, rather than the integration of the mountaineers into the larger American community, now became the goal to be achieved, and debate over the techniques by which the one was to be pursued replaced debate over how the other was to be pursued. Ultimately this new concern, and the efforts directed at the establishment of community in Appalachia, resulted in the institutionalization of the idea of Appalachia as a discrete region and the mountaineers as a distinct people, which is our own heritage from the turn of the century.

6.   Region as Community
 and the Transformation
of Mountain Benevolence

To the degree that ideas are historically real, they are manifested in patterns of action or embodied in institutions which come to possess a legitimacy and the simulacrum of a life of their own independent of their root ideas. The substitution of a regionalist for a nationalist model in discussions of America or of Appalachia's relationship with America involved, as a consequence, not only a process in intellectual history proper, but also a process in the history of institutions and patterns of action. This was to cause considerable difficulty during the first decades of the twentieth century, for the legitimation of Appalachian otherness, as we shall see, seemed to require either the abandonment of institutions and patterns of behavior which had become conventional during a quarter-century—traditional forms of uplift work, for example, or the literary exploitation of Appalachian otherness—or else an adjustment, in the case of institutions in the nature and focus of their activities, and in the case of patterns of behavior in the rationale which justified them. Appalachia's new status as a legitimately discrete entity, in but not of America, seemed also to require reassessment of the meaning of Appalachian otherness, both as an independent fact with implications for an understanding of the nature of American civilization and as the reality in terms of which public action was conducted. As a result, the early years of the twentieth century were characterized by a series of not inconsiderable debates, in which the issue was joined on a number of levels.

From these debates, however, emerged the two disparate positions which may be said to have determined the limits of American responses to the fact of Appalachian otherness since that time. The first of these was a tendency to see Appalachia as nothing more than a region in a nation of regions, the peculiarities of which, because they could be explained as the natural consequences of a particular pattern of historical development, a particular environment, or a particular distribution of personality types within the mountain population, seemed to that degree inevitable, and hence not worth worrying about. The second was a tendency to see mountain life as a more American alternative to dominant and by implication discredited or at least unsatisfactory patterns of contemporary American life, an alternative to be preserved as such for its own sake or as a model to be emulated. These two functioned as limits, however, rather than as exclusive alternatives. Most of the particular responses observable in the historical record—and indeed in the patterns of our own re-discovery of Appalachian otherness since 1960—fall somewhere be-tween these, and, as one might expect, participate to some degree in both.

Since the beginning of the twentieth century, then, American attitudes toward Appalachia or the "idea" of Appalachia have been characterized by a pattern of ambiguity largely unknown in the nine-teenth century, when the peculiarities of the region and its people cast the southern mountains and mountaineers in radical opposition to the normal patterns of American life and landscape. It was during the first years of the twentieth century and it was among benevolent workers, that this ambiguity was most keenly felt, however, at a time when the professionalization of social service activities had not yet established helping as a normal activity, and at a time when cultural diversity had not yet been established as a normal aspect of American life. Under such circumstances, Frost's attempt to lay to rest the issue of the appropriateness of benevolent work among a degenerate or an "unregenerate" population by designating Appalachia as one of "God's grand divisions" created a situation in which benevolent work might be seen as a violation of the legitimate peculiarites of mountain life. Was it not also an effort which was doomed to fail, insofar as the peculiarities which benevolence sought to eliminate were of their very nature inevitable and hence unalterable? By resolv-ing the dilemma posed by the fact of Appalachian otherness, moreover, Frost eliminated a principal public motive for the expenditure of time and effort among this "exceptional population" of the nation, so that the work needed new justification as well as new programs.

That such a dilemma existed was widely acknowledged by persons active in mountain work during the early twentieth century, explicitly by their assertions of a need to redirect the conduct of systematic benevolence in the region, and implicitly by their practical transformation of mountain work after 1900. It was a dilemma not at all unique to mountain benevolence during this period, however. As acknowledgement (but not acceptance) of diversity as a characteristic of American life emerged as a necessary response to the overwhelming evidence of observation and then as a central motif in both the ideology and in the programs of twentieth-century benevolence, persons active in widely differing areas of philanthropy faced the same dilemma. Filiation between mountain work and other forms of benevolence should come as no surprise, however, and one need posit no pattern of influence linking "progressivism" with mountain work in order to explain its occurrence. Just as missionary and educational work in the southern mountains during the late nineteenth century was continuous in technique and ideology with the dominant forms of benevolence current in the United States, so also that continuity persisted into the twentieth century. How one viewed America continued to determine how one defined deviance, and how one defined deviance continued to determine how one designed and defended programs to deal with it.[1]

Like their colleagues and coworkers in other fields of benevolence, workers in the mountain field dealt with this dilemma in ways characteristic of early twentieth-century philanthropy, for while their immediate dilemmas emerged directly out of the history of American responses to Appalachian otherness, their perception of this dilemma and its dimensions was itself a symptomatic phenomenon of the transformation of benevolence in America. They met the problem of justification by defining their mountaineer clients as needy without regard to their characteristics, or to the place of Appalachia in American life, and only later sought to define and describe with precision and in operational terms the nature of this neediness, through systematic studies or surveys. They met the problem of the locus of need by defining neediness in new ways, not as a characteristic of individuals but as a characteristic of the aggregate population of which these individuals were members, and they tended to explain the origins of neediness not as inherent in individuals or as the result of individual deprivation but as the result of structural characteristics of the social system of which they were members. They took the absence of standard American life habits and standard American institutions of social control as an index of the absence of community and of the sense of social system necessary to create such institutions and maintain such values. Henceforth they directed their efforts not only at the creation of desirable institutions, but also at the creation of a social system and a sense of community necessary to sustain them without continuing assistance from philanthropy. At least at the outset, they met the problem of the legitimacy of diversity with a dodge, by directing their work at meeting needs which existed at a human rather than a cultural level—the need for education, health services, communications facilities, and especially the need for institutions which would foster community and the possibility of cooperation. In so doing, moreover, they altered the role of the benevolent worker, from missionary teacher or preacher, advocate of individual change, to friendly visitor and community worker, demonstrating by example the availability of alternatives to allegedly deviant patterns of culture, and facilitating the indigenous development of such alternatives in the context of the local "neighborhood" and its possibilities.

During the early years of the twentieth century, discussions of Appalachian otherness originating in the benevolence establishment tended, as a consequence, to attempt systematic definition of the mountaineers' need rather than simply to catalogue those characteristics of mountain life which made Appalachia into a strange land inhabited by a peculiar people. As might be expected, however, definition of the mountaineers' need after 1900 was based on that same set of characteristics which, during the 1880s and 1890s, had seemed simply to set Appalachia off from America, or to make it available as a field for home missionary endeavor. The absence of schools and churches, roads and railroads, the "persistence" of peculiar patterns of speech and dress, an economy based on individual modes of production for use or for sale in a geographically limited market had been the indices of Appalachian otherness at the end of the nineteenth century and were explained as consequences of the region's isolation from the rest of America. Now these came to be seen as symptoms of a situation in Appalachia itself, and as the causes rather than as the consequences of isolation. While the content of the discussions of Appalachian otherness remained the same, then, the thrust of these discussions turned from the problem of Appalachia's existence to the problems of mountain life as a way of life. Appalachian otherness itself was transformed by this process, from a dilemma to be dealt with through rationalization into a situation to be dealt with rationally through social action. Especially in the context of the outbreak of feuds at the turn of the century, moreover, "absence of community" appeared as the principal characteristic by which Appalachian otherness was defined, the central fact of which all others were merely symptoms, and the key also to the mountaineers' need. The task of systematic benevolence became then to provide "community" in Appalachia. How this was to be done, and how the doing was to be reconciled with the traditional emphasis of benevolent work on the uplifting of individuals, was another matter.

The identification of "absence of community" as the principal characteristic by which Appalachian otherness was defined involved a significant shift, away from the conventional focus of nineteenth-century social theory on the role of individuals, either as bearers of culture or as personality types, and toward a new concern with the system into which individuals were integrated and its possibilities. In this new context, moreover—whether called anthropogeography or human ecology or "scientific sociology"—the problem of Appalachian otherness appeared in new terms. The old home-missionary question, whether mountain life as it then existed was "what it should be," ceased to have meaning. The new question concerned the possibility of life "as it should be" in the environment of Appalachia. On the issue of the "habitability" of Appalachia, indeed, turned the issue of the appropriateness of efforts to provide that which was missing from mountain life, as we shall see. During the first decade of the twentieth century, however, the creation of community among the mountaineers seemed worth a try, and it was to this effort that systematic benevolence directed its attention.

In the history of twentieth-century philanthropy, we generally explain the transformations of ideology and practice characteristic of the new age of professional social service as separate phenomena, the results of currents in social theory and currents in individual and professional behavior, respectively, and we tend to stress the importance of example and emulation in spreading both the new doctrines of scientific social work and the new social theory. We sometimes suggest but do not examine the confluence of social theory and social-work practice at the point where an institution, like the Russell Sage Foundation, or an individual, like Franklin H. Giddings, appears on the scene and exercises influence over others in a self-conscious effort to redirect theory or practice. And we always have available the explanation that theory leads to practice of particular kinds, or that practice requires justification, rationalization, and ideology to support it. In explanation of the transformation of benevolent work in Appalachia which followed Frost's coinage of 1895, we may look not only to the impact of "ideas" on "action" and the work of crucial institutions and individuals, especially the Russell Sage Foundation's Southern Highland Division under John C. Campbell, however. The history of Appalachia itself in the twentieth century gives evidence of the occurrence of a transforming phenomenon, which alone was sufficient to precipitate the changes which took place in mountain work after 1900.

That transforming phenomenon was the outbreak of feuds, especially in Kentucky, but also in Tennessee and West Virginia, and their extension out of the mountains into the public arena of state politics and hence public visibility. It was the feuds which focused new attention on Appalachia just at the moment that its existence as a strange land and peculiar people had been normalized by Frost's coinage, and hence made to seem less interesting than it had been before, when its very existence was a matter for concern. It was the feuds which provided a preliminary definition of the southern mountain region as a thing in itself rather than as an incomplete version of America—a land of lawlessness rather than a land without law. It was the feuds which brought new agencies into the mountains and provided the occasion for the redirection of the work of the old agencies, in efforts to meet the apparent need of the mountaineers for an alternative to feud law. And it was the feuds which precipitated the redefinition of Appalachian otherness in terms of the absence of community and the characteristics of group behavior or culture. This outbreak of feuds was not the cause of the transformation of benevolent work, but provided the occasion on which the transformation already under way made itself manifest. And that distinction is important, for the feuds themselves were not at issue. What was at issue was how Americans should respond to them.

In this process the work of Ellen Churchill Semple, especially "The Anglo-Saxons of the Kentucky Mountains: An Essay In Anthropogeography" (1901), was critical.[2] Semple was the most prominent American follower of the great German anthropogeographer, Friedrich Ratzel. It is perhaps no more than an accident that her essay on the southern mountains was at once a first attempt at examination of Appalachia as a thing in itself and an early effort at explaining the prevalence of feuding and moonshining in the region, but it was a happy accident from the historian's point of view. The perception that Appalachia was a land of lawlessness facilitated the widespread acceptance of a regionalist view of the southern mountains after 1900, and the general abandonment of a view of Appalachian otherness as a survival of earlier patterns of American civilization. It was only through the insights of the new social sciences, and especially their acceptance of environment as a determinant of culture, however, that an alternative view of Appalachian otherness could have been framed—a view which did not assume that the particular patterns of culture found in the mountains were survivals, degenerations, or developments from patterns of culture found elsewhere in the nation or elsewhere among the racial stock which made up America's native-born population.

Semple was not the first to point to the relationship of man and land as a central fact in American history, or to that special case of the general process, the role of physical geography in isolating Appalachia from America. It was the conventional understanding of nineteenth-century Americans that American progress depended upon the availability of transportation and communications facilities, by which the "natural" barriers to social, political, and economic intercourse posed by geography might be overcome, but the terms in which Semple and her contemporaries spoke were new. Their interest lay not in the static relationship of man with land conceived of as the inert background to American history, which had been the concern of historians of westward expansion in their attempts to summarize the American experience and the American ideology in the decades since independence. Their interest lay rather in the dynamic relationship of man with land conceived of as an active element in the process of history. That was the interest of the practitioners of the new social sciences, in their attempt to utilize the insights of contemporary evolutionary theory in the study of that higher organism, human society.

The older notion that isolation could preserve either an ethnic type "pure" or a culture intact, although expressed in pseudo-scientific terms, ran counter to the dominant motif of naturalistic social theory, which regarded change as endemic to the human situation. It was to this assumption—often phrased in older terms, as "he who will not progress must regress"—that many writers were implicitly responding in their insistence that mountain culture was not degenerate but as yet unregenerate, a survival of the legitimate culture of an earlier time. There were those, however, especially at the turn of the century when benevolent work among the mountaineers had become established as a legitimate and viable activity and the institutions of benevolence in the area had sufficient strength and inertia to maintain themselves, who sought to examine the peculiarities of mountain life in other terms than as survivals. In an often-quoted article of 1899, for example, J. Stoddard Johnston called attention to the "great law of nature, that man is largely a creature of environment, and that the most important factor in his development and progress lies in the physical character of the country which he inhabits, and its adaptability for promoting his elevation in the scale of moral and intellectual, as well as physical progress."[3]

Johnston went no farther in explicating the impact of environment on the development of a mountain culture. Indeed, he said, the idea that "the environment . . . has an important influence in fixing the status and shaping the lives of men, is too self-evident to need argument." Given his dismissal of any suggestion that the mountaineers were of "different stock" than the rest of the American population or the descendants of degenerates, moreover, he was quite correct. It was the only viable explanation for the peculiarities of mountain life. "They were a thrifty people when they came here," Johnston insisted. "Their deterioration, actual or apparent, is the result of their environment."[4]

Johnston's argument was not new, but it made sense, and had a wider circulation as a result of its publication in *Cosmopolitan* than did, for example, the argument offered by the Reverend Robert F. Campbell in his pamphlet of the same year, *Mission Work among the Mountain Whites of Asheville Presbytery*. To Campbell as to Johnston, the first task was to explain the causes of the mountaineers' "degeneration from the intelligent, thrifty, and virtuous Scotch-Irish type" which had first settled the mountain region, and whose descendants in more favored areas had retained these characteristics. Quoting the Reverend W. S. Plumer Bryan, his predecessor in the Asheville mission, Campbell noted that an environment unfavorable to progress lay at the heart of the mountaineers' degradation. Like Fox's geologist, he added that "anyone who would not degenerate under hard conditions like these would be more than human, and in my opinion these strenuous conditions are quite enough to account for the peculiarities and deficiencies of the class under discussion."[5]

Where the unfavorable environment of Appalachia according to Johnston consisted principally in the isolation of the region from the main currents of modern life, which by preventing progress encouraged its opposite, to Campbell it meant something different. It was not simply the isolation of the mountaineers as a group from the dominant American culture that explained the peculiarities of mountain life. It was the isolation of the mountaineers as individuals or as families from other individuals or families which was to blame. "The settlers in the coves and on the poorer highlands were no doubt less aggressive and vigorous than those who pushed on to better lands and more propitious surroundings," Campbell noted, and "the country was so sparsely settled as to make it almost impossible to perpetuate the inherited institutions, the school and the church," those centers for social intercourse which formed the basis for community in any environment. "A mental and spiritual famine has been the natural sequence, the minds and souls of each successive generation becoming more and more anaemic for lack of nourishment."[6]

From this line of explanation Semple's work marks a significant departure, for her concern was not with the historical development of Appalachian otherness but rather with the adaptive significance of mountain culture and mountain social structure in the context of the mountain environment. In explanation of violence as a characteristic of mountain life, for example, she noted that "the mountains, by reason of their inaccessibility and the sparsity of their population, saw a great prolongation of pioneer days and pioneer organization of society, when every man depended on his own strong arm or rifle to guard his interest and right his wrongs."[7] Where earlier commentators had limited their examination to the impact of physical environment on mountain life, moreover, for Semple culture and social structure were also defined as elements composing the human environment. Unlike topography, however, culture and social structure were essentially malleable elements, and it was this assumption which permitted Semple to avoid the pitfalls of simple-minded geographical determinism. It was this also which laid the basis for the appeal of the anthropogeographical mode of environmentalism to persons active in benevolent work, who found there explanation and a program for action neatly combined.

Although "The Anglo-Saxons of the Kentucky Mountains" was widely quoted, especially after its American republication in 1910, its ultimate significance lay more in what it proposed than in what it accomplished. As a discussion of the nature and causes of Appalachian otherness, it was largely descriptive and, despite its periodic anthropogeographical flashes, heavily dependent upon the concept of survivals. The very fact of its 1901 publication, however, in the midst of the confusion occasioned by the outbreak of the feuds, guaranteed that it would receive a more serious attention than might otherwise have been the case. Its obvious utility as an ideology for the emerging settlement movement in the mountains, which was apparent to workers in the mountain field from Semple's own interest in mountain settlement work if not from a reading of the article itself, moreover, made it appear as something more than an abstract consideration of the nature and causes of Appalachian otherness. As a result, Semple's work may be credited with a crucial role in precipitating a reconsideration of the appropriateness of traditional patterns of benevolent work in Appalachia and the redirection of benevolent work toward attempts to alter the consequences of the mountain environment on mountain life rather than to alter the mountain environment itself.

As early as 1901, the year in which Semple's piece first appeared in the *Geographical Journal* of London, Henderson Daingerfield quoted from "The Anglo-Saxons of the Kentucky Mountains" in a paper on the tent-settlement experiment of 1898 at Hindman, Kentucky, delivered at the annual meeting of the American Social Science Association. Because of the crucial role of environment as a determinant of mountain culture which Semple demonstrated, Daingerfield argued, the first task of benevolent work in Appalachia was to overcome the potent impact of isolation as a fact of mountain life on the personality of the mountaineers. Through settlement and kindergarten work— and Daingerfield, like many of her contemporaries, saw them as identical in spirit if not in practice—the undesirable consequences of physical and cultural isolation, manifested most clearly by the prevalence of feuding, might be overcome. "Think for a moment of the far-reaching benefit of kindergarten teaching on the mountains," she asked. "Froebel's ideal of independence with interdependence, gentleness with strength, loving kindness with truth, would develop the mountaineer in the points wherein he is weak, and strengthen his strength. Much of the feud-feeling comes from the narrowness and isolation that fosters a brooding spirit, and makes a little wrong loom large. True kindergarten work develops mind and body and spirit, encourages all right activities, and puts life in true perspective. It teaches the honor due to law and the beauty and blessedness of an ordered life. The effective settlement applies Froebel's plan to every department; for his was not a system of teaching, but a philosophy of life."[8]

Daingerfield's own confrontation with the otherness of Appalachia was symptomatic of those of the new generation of social workers who entered upon mountain work at the turn of the century. Lacking denominational affiliation, and eschewing indeed an explicit missionary point of view, they presented themselves as friendly visitors, seeking to do a work of helpfulness, rather than as the possessors of salvation, seeking to increase their own sanctification by extending the hand of fellowship along with the good news of the Gospels. Their "clients" were not the "unregenerate" of the missionaries, and their goal was not the accession of converts and the transformation of individual lives but the acquisition of friends and the transformation of community life. They did not overlook, we may be sure, the romance of their own adventures in the backwaters of America or the pathetic and picturesque aspects of life among the primitive people they served, but they approached the mountaineers of Appalachia as their sisters had already approached the immigrant Jews and Slavs of the cities, with an understanding that the peculiar people among whom they worked were bearers of a legitimately discrete culture—however inadequate to modern American life it may have been, and however undesirable as the culture which the social workers themselves might like as their own. In this, moreover, contemporary designations of the mountaineers as members of "hyphenate" groups (Scotch-Irish, Southern-Highlanders) facilitated the objectification of this client population *as* a client population.

It was this new group of social-work oriented settlement workers to whom W. G. Frost's legitimations of Appalachian otherness appealed most strongly as a way of further objectifying the peculiarities of their mountain clientele, and who found Semple's suggestion of the determining role of environment on Appalachian otherness most convincing. They saw with their own eyes that the alienation of the mountaineers from American life could not be the result of recent immigration to America. They readily identified the mountaineers as members of an alien community, however, and hence looked to the characteristics of mountain life itself for clues to the nature of Appalachian otherness. Given both their professional commitments and the assumed legitimacy of Appalachia in terms of which they worked, moreover, they could simply ignore the problem of the relationship of Appalachia and America and approach mountain life for what it was, or at least for itself. Especially in the context of the prevalence of feuding, what they found in Appalachia was not simply an alien community, however, but a community which lacked both the institutions and the spirit of community. It was this indeed which appeared the cause from which all else, including the prevalence of violence in the region, followed. So it was the institutions of community and the spirit of community both, which the settlement movement in Appalachia sought to provide.

The origins of settlement work in Appalachia lay not with the summer tenting and practical kindergarten work conducted at Hindman by the Louisville ladies whose efforts Daingerfield described, but rather in the periodic Sunday school or extension teaching begun in the early nineties under the sponsorship of one or another benevolent agency in the less remote but nonetheless rural sections of the mountains. In 1892, for example, Mrs. John Embree of Cincinnati, daughter of Berea's founder, John G. Fee, and wife of one of Berea's most active trustees, spent part of her summer conducting Sunday school classes at Narrow Gap, Kentucky, a few miles from Berea itself. During the following summer she was joined by a Miss Fox of Berea's Department of Domestic Science, who continued this summer mission in the mountains until she left the staff of Berea in 1896 or 1897. About 1900, Fox was recalled from her home in Toledo, Ohio, probably at Frost's instance, and placed in charge of a permanent settlement at Narrow Gap. In a log cabin built for the purpose on land donated by local residents, she taught day school and Sunday school, provided instruction in home economics, and sought to organize a women's industrial department for the domestic manufacture of salable items.[9]

With the aid of hindsight, the transition from Sunday to day school teaching, and thence to industrial and agricultural education, to the organization of clubs, the encouragement of domestic industry, and instruction in cooking and sanitation seems natural, for that was the route followed not only by Berea's Narrow Gap Settlement but by most agencies working in the mountains at the turn of the century. To authors of institutional histories writing in the 1920s and after, on the other hand, the origins of settlement work in religious education has seemed embarrassing, and they have conventionally represented the Sunday school work of agencies which later embarked on settlement work as mere technique, a way of gaining the confidence of a religious but unlettered and mistrustful people, prior to the inauguration of the more sophisticated work of twentieth-century philanthropy. In fact, however, the transition from Sunday school work to settlement work involved a fundamental transformation rather than a mere process of development. Of this, the very fact that virtually all agencies working in the mountains initiated settlement work at about the same time, roughly between 1899 and 1903, or claimed to have done so by the latter date, while several new agencies with explicit settlement goals were established in this period, should make us aware.

For agencies inaugurating rural extension work of any sort during the nineties, religious education appears to have been an end in itself. When conducted by high-church Protestant affiliates, moreover, it was regularly represented as a defense against the encroachments of low-church Protestant missionaries, Roman Catholics, and especially Mormons whose active proseletyzing in Appalachia during the nineties worried everyone, and whose presence in the mountains seemed a thrust at the very heartland of America and a potent basis upon which to launch an appeal for funds well into the twentieth century.[10] Indeed the very first of the log-cabin social settlements in the southern mountains and the model for all the others, organized at Asheville in 1894 by Susan Chester Lyman, combined religious and social-welfare concerns in a manner which we do not associate with the settlement movement in the cities of America, perhaps

because those in cities were staffed by Protestants but characteristically located among non-Protestant populations, whose religious
preferences were better overlooked than attended to if the success of
the settlements were to be achieved. Lyman was a graduate of Vassar
and a member of the College Settlements Association in 1894 when
she launched her venture, and she intended her log-cabin social settlement "to supplement in every possible way the work of a neighboring [Episcopal] chapel and district school usually open for four
months of the year." In her public announcement of the project, she
noted that she had "made a thorough study of the city settlements
and their methods, and . . . will follow as far as possible the general
plan of the other social settlements. The religious side, however, will
be more strongly emphasized than is necessary where churches are
more common." In an editorial comment, the editors of *The Outlook*
added words of encouragement, noting that "the multiplication of
such settlements would do much to solve the pressing problem of
those regions . . . which are gradually becoming unable to support
religious services because of changes in the populations."[11] Even the
most overtly secular of the city settlements at the turn of the century
retained a missionary character and a Christian if not precisely a
religious spirit, however.[12]

   In this context, Daingerfield's summer tent "settlement" at
Hindman, Kentucky, appears indeed to have been "a new departure
in social settlements," as Ellen Churchill Semple styled it in a report
to the American Academy of Political and Social Science, not only for
its imaginative combination of tenting out and settlement work, but
also for its essential secularism. Where Mrs. Embree and Miss Fox at
Narrow Gap had begun with the assumption that the mountaineers'
first need was for religious instruction and only later learned that
they also needed to learn how to cook and bathe, the Hindman
women offered themselves as exemplars of the possibilities of living
the life of the home beautiful, and of having a nice time in the process.
"The tent was pitched about half a mile from the town," Semple
reported, and was made "as clean and attractive as possible . . . with
flags, Japanese lanterns, and photographs of the best pictures. One
who has seen the dirt, poverty, and desolate lack of beauty in the

interior of a mountain cabin, can realize what a revelation this camp was to all who visited it."[13] No wonder, then, that to this place "children far beyond kindergarten age came for the happy mornings, learning gentleness, handiness, and helpfulness. Grave babies, whose mothers had no time for play, even had they had memories of childish games, learned kindergarten plays and songs. Mothers and fathers watched and learned, and Froebel's sunshine made new light on the mountains."[14] Most important, however, as Semple noted and Daingerfield implied, the Hindman experiment "reached the ideal of the social settlement" in that "during the seven weeks it was in operation none of the natives suspected its philanthropic purpose."[15]

The number of log-cabin settlements in Appalachia was never large. As late as 1906, Caroline Williamson Montgomery of the College Settlements Association knew of only two which met her criteria for inclusion in a list published in W. D. P. Bliss' *Encyclopaedia of Social Reform*—the Hindman Settlement, originated by the Kentucky Federation of Women's Clubs and subsequently sponsored by the Kentucky Women's Christian Temperance Union, and Lyman's "Log Cabin Settlement" outside Asheville.[16] To these must be added the Berea settlement at Narrow Gap, Kentucky, omitted from the published list because of its affiliation with Berea and its mixed status as an agent of educational extension as well as of settlement work per se. These three together, however, seem to compose the total number of settlements located in all rural sections of the country, and consist of fully a third of the settlements in the South.[17]

By the end of the first decade of the twentieth century, many of the private and denominational day schools in the mountains appear to have begun settlement work of one kind or another—industrial classes for children, practical agricultural education through model school-gardens, the encouragement of domestic industry among neighborhood women for the production of salable items, and periodic evening or summer courses of adult education. The mountain colleges and boarding schools also began to extend their work to the community, by transforming commencement and school festival days into occasions for demonstrating agricultural methods and the practice of handicrafts. Although few of these were like Berea in beginning formal extension programs or in sponsoring satellite settlements, the impact of the schools and colleges on the community when the community came to it was felt to be salutary. Visitors were regularly treated to uplifting tours of model gardens, model farms, model kitchens, model laundries, model homes, and, especially after 1910, model privies.[18]

It was not properly until the teens that home-missionary agencies per se took cognizance of the thrust of settlement work as the new wave in philanthropic technique, and then only in the context of the country life movement. As early as 1902, however, Sherman H. Doyle acknowledged the settlement function of home-missionary work in his discussion of Presbyterian home missions. Throughout the first decade of the century moreover, many home missionaries, especially those serving in rural sections of the nation, noted with distress that the new spirit of neighborliness and the new emphasis on real-life education which seemed to characterize the settlement movement was nothing new to them, and that they were being incorrectly regarded as "old-fashioned" in their pattern of benevolent work. Had they not, after all, been the first to "settle" among those they wished to aid, and had they not brought the good news of cash economy and upward social mobility along with the good news of the Gospels?[19]

What set settlement work off from more traditional home-missionary and education work, however, was not the philosophy of the social gospel, which its practitioners offered from time to time as explanation for their individual actions, or the technique of settling among a needy population, but its choice of clientele. Where the missionaries of the individual gospel of salvation and the agents of individual philanthropy necessarily looked to the uplifting of individuals, and especially children, the settlement idea focused on work among adults and on the community. Even kindergarten work, that quintessentially child-oriented pattern of action, was proposed as a means of guaranteeing a population of adults whose personal characteristics and personality traits would suit them for community life and cooperative endeavor. Where the old philanthropy justified the need for benevolence as a way of eliminating deviance and thereby of creating a national community, moreover, the new philanthropy of the settlement movement tended to accept patterns of economic and cultural deviance so long as these could be identified as characteristic of groups of persons residing in defined territories. Such populations in such territories they tended to define as communities, and they talked about them in terms of a nation of communities instead of a national community.

The filiation of the new philanthropy with contemporary efforts of social scientists to settle on an acceptable unit for social analysis, which, whatever its dimension they also tended to designate as "community," is apparent.[20] The consequences of such a focus on "community" for the practice of benevolence in America transcended the realm of theory however. It meant that benevolence tended to emphasize work with the community rather than with aggregates of individuals, and to attempt community improvement rather than individual uplift. It meant that in place of traditional patterns of education, of benefit to the individual as individual, it stressed education in skills necessary to the maintenance of the community—social and psychological skills on the one hand, and economic skills on the other. And it meant that the hinterland of any given social service agency was defined a priori as a neighborhood, and was assumed to possess the social, ethnic, economic, and cultural coherence of "a community." When, as in the southern Appalachians, the neighborhoods displayed none of the characteristics of communities, the teachers and preachers and settlement workers set to, and sought to create community.

By 1910, the isolated and periodic experiences of settlement workers in the southern mountains had been given new meaning and new coherence by the rise of the "country-life movement," which directed public attention to the "absence of community" as a characteristic of rural life in America generally, and thereby further legitimized Appalachian otherness by identifying mountain problems with the social problems of other regions and other groups in the nation.[21] In the context of the country-life movement, moreover, "absence of community" appeared not only as a simple need—analogous to the need for Christian education identified by the home missionaries in the late 1880s and 1890s—but also as a fundamental fact of rural and mountain life, in terms of which benevolent work in Appalachia was to be conducted. In practical terms, what this meant was that the mountaineers lacked not only the institutions of community but also the institutions which created community, especially a public consciousness of the advantages of cooperation and a public conscience which ranked altruism above egoism. And it was this condition, rather than the simple absence of schools and churches, which explained the prevalence of feuding and moonshining in Appalachia, just as it explained tendencies toward other forms of antisocial behavior in other rural regions of the nation. "Where there is no cohesive community life [and] where local agencies are nonexistent and non-local agencies inoperative," John Campbell pointed out in 1909, for example, "an over-developed individualism" was the result, and this in turn created additional obstacles to the creation of community by agencies of benevolence.[22]

For Campbell and Warren H. Wilson of the Presbyterian Department of Church and Country Life, the most outspoken proponents of the "country-life" analysis of Appalachian otherness, kindergarten work, to create a spirit of handiness and helpfulness, and the establishment of settlements, schools, and churches as social centers could remedy part of Appalachia's problem. In their advocacy of such institutional mechanisms for the creation of community in Appalachia, however, they differed fundamentally from an earlier generation of workers who also looked to the creation of kindergartens, settlements, schools, and churches, but who saw the existence of such institutions of community as absolute needs of any population. Just as Campbell and Wilson viewed the "hyper-ruralism" of Appalachia as the fundamental fact of mountain life, where others at the turn of the century were content to utilize the observation that the mountain condition was just "the country condition intensified" in defense of mountain white work, so Campbell and Wilson saw the role of benevolent institutions in strictly functional terms, as convenient agencies for the creation of community.[23]

From this position, Campbell at least moved yet one step farther along the road laid out by the country-life movement, towards personal acceptance of the indigenous rural culture of Appalachia. By 1917 he was prepared to argue that "the most serious mistakes that have been made" in mountain benevolence "have arisen from the assumption that what was good for the city school, or the school in the lowland rural sections . . . was, without change, good for the Highlands." Not so, Campbell insisted. "There is a native culture in the mountains that has been too much ignored, which should be given expression in any educational system intended for the mountains."[24] By creating community in Appalachia, benevolent work might provide the advantages of modern urban life without requiring a rural population to suffer the disadvantages of modern urban life, even while it established a self-supporting and self-renewing system of community and culture which could maintain itself without further assistance from outside the region.

As explanation for the peculiarities of mountain life and as the principal characteristic by which the "neediness" of the mountaineers was defined, "absence of community" yielded not only a reconsideration of the function of institutionalized benevolence in the region, but also a reconsideration of the form which that benevolence ought to take. As early as 1900, as we have noted, Frost had initiated an effort to transform the educational program at Berea, despite the resistance of some of his trustees, in directions which seemed to him more appropriate to the needs of the mountain people for practical rather than "classical" education. For the latter, Frost noted, Berea's students were unprepared by their limited experiences in inadequately funded and inadequately staffed mountain schools, but "book education" was not what they needed in any case. A program of practical education was not only an obvious need of the economically unsuccessful and the technologically backward, but would also allow Berea to perform a useful role in mountain life and to establish its credentials as an essential center to the neighborhood which it sought to serve.[25]

Frost sought not only to respond to changing conditions in Berea's own situation, as its mission as a co-educational, traditional college began to wane in importance before its newly defined mission among the mountaineers (although Berea's black students also needed practical education, Frost argued) and to the implications of his own vision of the legitimacy of Appalachian otherness. He was responding also, consciously or unconsciously, to the enthusiasm for industrial and agricultural education which lay at the heart of the contemporary school campaign led by Charles W. Dabney, Philander P. Claxton, and Edgar Gardner Murphy of the Southern Education Board.[26]

In many ways, Frost's suggestions for Berea's future anticipated the emergence of industrial education as a central theme in the southern school campaign, and thereby led him to anticipate also the need for greater coordination between private and public schools in Appalachia, which became an important motif in discussions of mountain benevolence during the early teens. For Frost, however, as for Dabney, Claxton, and Murphy, industrial or practical education was never merely an abstract need of the mountain people. All saw that it was first a practical need, and one keenly felt by the people themselves. "It is not more nor better high schools and academies, and colleges . . . [but] something within their reach which will give them practical instruction along industrial lines" that the people wanted. All saw the political advantages which would accrue to educational institutions, and to school systems, that could "claim the respect of the people" by demonstrating to parents that their children would profit from formal instruction, that it would be "worth while for what he gains to give up his work on their little hillside patch."[27] And all saw that both industrial education and citizen education were necessary for the maintenance of a viable community. "The schools of a people, the schools of a *real* people, must be, primarily, not the moral gymnasia of reminiscence or the transcendent platforms of future outlook. They must touch this day's earth and this day's men through the truths and the perils of to-day." They must provide education appropriate to real life, and in so doing, they will become "instructors of the contemporary civic conscience and . . . bring to men a profounder . . . reverence for the institutions and the processes of public order."[28]

"Education appropriate to real life" was good propaganda for the Southern Education Board in its attempts to achieve passage of mandatory education laws in the southern states and revision of the tax base for the public schools, just as it was good propaganda in Frost's maneuvering with his trustees and in appeals for support from the philanthropic community. Few of the public, and even fewer of the private or denominational schools in the southern mountains seem to have developed curricula during this period which could actually prepare their students for real, practical life, however. Although Martha Berry has generally been represented as achieving notable success in providing agricultural and rudimentary industrial education to her pupils at the Martha Berry School for Boys outside Rome, Georgia, after 1901, and later at the Martha Berry School for Girls, most school-based agricultural education during the first decade of the century seems to have focused on the cultivation of "school gardens" as vehicles for nature study and as models in community beautification, while industrial education seems to have meant woodcarving and weaving—"practical" skills of no practical use, however gratifying as private aesthetic activities. Even Berry's claims as an innovator in real life education rested less on a coherent program for practical education or even with a formal educational philosophy on the merit of working with the hands than on the practical necessity for use of student labor in the school garden, the school laundry, and the school carpentry shop.[29]

The ideal of modern philanthropy was not to provide outside aid, but to facilitate the efforts of an indigenous population to help itself in establishing and maintaining itself as a viable community. In this context, the encouragement of domestic industry and handicrafts, which was a major element in the work of the mountain settlements during the first decade of the twentieth century, the economic function of both settlement and school as places to sell such domestic manufactures, local attempts at agricultural education in order to improve productivity and provide a surplus crop for exchange or sale, were only temporary expedients designed to assure that the population of a neighborhood had the financial means by which community institutions might be supported. If the absence of an adequate economic base made community institutions and the community spirit which they fostered impossible, however, the absence of adequate transportation facilities made an adequate economic base seem impossible. It was not simply that "lack of good roads has caused an undue isolation, and prevented cooperative activity and the realization of the ideals of a modern community life," as one student of the Appalachian economy noted,[30] but that the exchange of goods and services provided a crucial context for the exchange of fellow-feeling, and the overt public ties which linked a community together. By 1910, as a consequence, the possibility of community in Appalachia seemed to turn on the availability of communication facilities. The old explanation for Appalachian otherness, that the region was isolated because of the lack of communication facilities, now came to have a new meaning. Roads and railroads were not only the ties which bound the region to the nation, but were also the ties which bound up the region itself, and provided thereby the basis for a viable mountain community.

Where the disparity between rural life and urban life in the United States conventionally appeared as a difference of degree, the disparity between Appalachia conceived as a legitimately discrete region and the rest of the nation appeared as a difference of kind. (The hyper-ruralism of the southern mountain region, for example, was a characteristic by which Appalachia might be described but not an essential element in its definition as a discrete region.) Just as the occurrence of feuding and moonshining effectively severed the nexus between Appalachia and America that had depended upon a definition of Appalachia as the frontier, the land of our pioneer ancestors, so the institutionalization of Appalachia as a field for benevolent work and its definition as a discrete region of the nation made impossible, both practically and theoretically, the maintenance of a connection between Appalachia and America in terms of an economic/residential model of cities and countryside. The conduct of systematic benevolence in Appalachia thus raised questions which characteristically did not disturb the conduct of such work in urban or in other rural areas of the nation until the 1920s. Benevolent work in

Appalachia provided systematic philanthropy with its first experience in accepting the peculiarities of a client population as legitimate deviations from the American norm, and hence involved a first confrontation with the implications of regionalism and pluralism and of the acceptance of diversity, not only for the practice of systematic benevolence but also for the understanding of American civilization.

The dimensions of this confrontation became clear only after 1910. By that date, the industrial and economic development of the South had progressed sufficiently toward the norm of contemporary American life to create additional contrasts between the bustling New South and the backwardness of Appalachia, and suggested that the persistence of Appalachian otherness was not only undesirable but unnecessary. More immediately, the existence of the recently established mill- and company-towns, especially in the Piedmont and hence almost within "commuting distance" of Appalachia, seemed to offer the mountaineers a first real opportunity to exchange the isolated life of their coves and hillsides for "the advantages of social intercourse, school, and livelihood that village life affords."[31] Indeed, if environment played a crucial role in human civilization, and the inhospitable environment of Appalachia, rather than the inherent degeneracy of the mountaineers, lay at the heart of Appalachian otherness, might not the course of wisdom be simply to transform Appalachia into a national park and remove the mountaineers to the industrial centers of the New South? Such a course not only followed logically from contemporary assumptions concerning the nature of Appalachian otherness, but also seemed necessary to the rational use of national resources. Removal of the mountaineers from the mountains would facilitate their utilization in the labor force, even while making possible systematic timber-conservation practices which would "set the region to performing the function for which it was clearly intended."[32]

7. Economic Modernization and the Americanization of Appalachia

As early as 1890, in an essay which would remain the standard treatment of the subject for two decades, James Lane Allen called attention to the enormous consequences which the development of the natural resources of eastern Kentucky was having on the life of the commonwealth, and especially on its mountain population. In the inevitable processes which follow from economic growth, "a whole race of people," as he called them, "are being scattered, absorbed, civilized."

Some desert the mountains altogether, and descend to the blue-grass region with a passion for farming. . . . [Some are] absorbed by the civilization that is springing up in the mountains. . . . But the third, and as far as can be learned, the most general movement among them is to retire at the approach of civilization to remoter regions of the mountains, where they may live their dirty, squalid, unambitious, stationary life. But to these retreats they must in time be followed, therefrom dislodged, and again set going.[1]

On the whole Allen welcomed the changes which industrialization and economic modernization would bring. They made a fitting conclusion to the commonwealth's first hundred years of existence, which from the vantage point of 1890 and Allen's well-established literary reputation seemed marked by an undesirable provincialism and isolation—those had of course seemed Kentucky's glory in 1886. For Allen personally, what appeared as the inevitability of change in Appalachia had an added attraction, as he brought to a close the local-color phase of his career. The economic modernization of Kentucky would permit him to remain Kentucky's writer and yet still speak with the authority of personal observation about phenomena "that lie in the domain of the human problem in its deepest phases

. . . town-making in various stages, the massing and distribution of wealth, the movements of populations."[2]

Despite Allen's insistence that it was the human problem which concerned him most, his essay provided little more than description of the activities of various groups of speculators, and simply served as the occasion for him to indicate his final rejection of the romanticism of traditional local-color writing, with its tendency to glorify a past long past. Ironically, in the process Allen merely switched allegiances, to the romanticism of the future and of a revitalized, industrialized South. He sought "to call attention to the way in which the new civilization of the South is expected to work . . . and to point out some of the results which are to follow," and "to illustrate the tremendous power with which the new South, hand in hand with the North, works with brains and capital and science."[3]

Within a decade of Allen's paean to the emerging new South, at the beginning of the twentieth century, industrial development in Appalachia was the present, not of the future, and its consequences were part at least of the social and economic reality which was to be observed in the region. One result of this was that descriptions of Appalachia as a strange land inhabited by a peculiar people, though as regularly cast in the present tense after 1900 as before, came equally regularly to contain within them a sudden shift to the past tense in an acknowledgement that the conditions described existed in the mountains a quarter of a century ago, and have vastly improved since that time. A second result was the emergence of a tendency to view economic development, which had occurred independent of the planning or expectations of persons within the region, as a "natural" solution to a whole range of problems which had been seen as resulting from the isolation of Appalachia and the poverty of the mountaineers, including the absence of "community." A parallel tendency justified the economic exploitation of the natural and human resources of Appalachia because of the benefits which would necessarily accrue to the mountain people from the introduction of roads and railroads, mines, mills, factories, schools, churches, and courts of law.

Although specifically benevolent organizations rarely participated directly in efforts for the economic development of Appalachia, many persons active in uplift work did hail such attempts as offering the promise of a new life for the mountain region. In his mission-study text of 1906, *The Southern Mountaineers*, for example, Samuel Tyndale Wilson of Maryville College was careful to note that the undesirable characteristics of mountain life were the result of isolation and an environment unadapted to human progress, rather than of any inherent disability on the part of the mountaineers. "There is a wide world of difference between the degeneracy that Nordau tells of and the provincial limitations that we find in mountain districts," he insisted. Because even the "lowest class among the mountaineers" could be uplifted in a single generation, the mountain "problem" became one of technique only. "How are we to bring certain belated and submerged Appalachian blood brethren of ours out into the completer enjoyment of twentieth-century civilization and Christianity?" Wilson asked. The answer he said, was simple.

The Appalachian problem is to be solved by means of three agencies—the development of trade, the perfecting of the public school system and the multiplication of the home mission agencies of the various Churches and of other philanthropic organizations. . . . American enterprise may safely be trusted to provide the first . . . that is, the development of trade. The Appalachians are one of Nature's choicest storehouses of treasures. . . . The industrial invasion will introduce much evil, but it will, in part at least, prepare the way for better things. It will break up the isolation. Shiftlessness will disappear if the rewards of labor are forthcoming. The days of no trade and no money are passing away. The mountaineer sees it, dreads it, and will profit by it.[4]

Under such circumstances, the proper function of benevolent agencies was to prepare the mountaineer to take fullest advantage of the opportunities which industrialization would present and to strengthen his resistance against the dangers of modern civilization. In particular, this meant that the denominational and independent schools had to provide training in the principles and practices of Americanism and some form of technical education along with education in the traditional school subjects and the principles of Christian morality. In addition, the schools sought to provide boarding facilities wherever possible, not only for the convenience of students living some distance from the institution but also to make their transition to the ways of modern life easier, by removing them from the influence of a degraded and primitive home environment.

In the smaller day schools where regular boarding facilities were unavailable, a teachers' home would be built as a refuge for the "consecrated, self-denying women" of the staff, "it being impossible for them to live with the people," as the Reverend Sherman Doyle pointed out, "lest they die of 'lonesomeness or dyspepsia.'" This teachers' home was not simply a necessity, however, any more than it was simply a convention of missionary work in both foreign and domestic fields. It was both of these, of course, but in addition, as "a model of house-keeping to the women of the neighborhood" and a place where Christian family life might be taught by example, it was an integral element in the total effort to uplift the mountaineers. With this goal its sometime function as an agent of economic modernization, in providing an outlet for the sale of mountain handicrafts in return for cash or day-school tuition was in no way inconsistent.[5]

For Samuel Tyndale Wilson in 1906, the economic modernization of Appalachia meant something quite different than it would a very few years later, and his generally favorable judgment of its consequences for the mountaineers was based upon a different conception of the nature of Appalachian otherness than would prevail by the end of the first decade of the century. In 1906, economic modernization still meant the construction of roads and railroads and the subsequent establishment of extractive industry. That was a familiar pattern even in the "isolated" southern mountains, where extensive timber-cutting operations had been conducted since the 1870s, and where large-scale coal and iron mining had been attempted from the 1880s. Roads and especially railroads were, moreover, the standard symbols of America's inevitable progress, in 1906 as throughout most of the nineteenth century, and continued to represent the crucial means whereby the barriers of localism might be overcome by the force of nationalism. In this context, such a spokesman for the railway promoters of the New South like J. Stoddard Johnston of Louisville, for example, seemed to have reason on his side and the best interests of the mountaineers at heart. The mountaineers had "stood still or retrograded," he argued, "not from want of capacity but of opportunity." In the same way, "lack of transportation for the products of agriculture and mines has retarded the development of a region possessing great possibilities for the future." Conditions were changing, however. "Help has come to these marooned people. The Cheseapeake and Ohio railroads . . . and the Louisville and Nashville system . . . with the Kentucky Eastern have worked wonders along their routes, as is evidenced by thrifty towns, with churches, institutions of higher education, mills, furnaces, and mines, which may now be seen where formerly all was stagnant."[6]

So long as the isolation of Appalachia from the rest of the nation was viewed both as the primary "cause" of Appalachian otherness and the principal disadvantage of mountain life to be overcome by agencies of systematic benevolence, enthusiasm for the changes which economic modernization would bring remained high. By 1910, however, a reassessment of the "needs" of the mountaineers had begun, in the context of that transformation in the nature of benevolent work which we have already noted. As the function of systematic benevolence came increasingly to be defined as aiding in the establishment of "community," those aspects of economic modernization which seemed disruptive or destructive of community came under attack. In the same way, the new interest in establishing an Appalachian community yielded a growing tendency to replace traditional forms of educational work, designed to uplift individuals one by one into modern life and moral rectitude, with efforts directed at altering the social, cultural, and economic environment of Appalachia. In this context, the establishment of schools, churches, industrial facilities, urban centers, and the agencies of local government appeared not merely as the fulfillment of an obvious "need," but as ways of providing the crucial institutions through which the mountaineers might participate in the "normal" patterns of American life.

It is surely no accident that this shift occurred simultaneously with the general acceptance of a regionalist vision of the nature of Appalachian otherness, for it was upon a conception of the southern mountains as composing a legitimately discrete land inhabited by a homogeneous population possessing a distinct culture, that any notion of "community" in Appalachia had to depend. It is surely no accident either, that this shift occurred simultaneously with the emergence of the movement to restrict child labor in the United States through state and federal legislation, for the debate over child labor centered in part upon the assertions by southern cotton-mill agents, that the economic modernization of the South and of Appalachia would yield social modernization also, only if a fundamental alteration of those patterns of isolation and individualism, which characterized both the South and Appalachia, should take place. This might most conveniently be achieved, they argued, through such artificial mechanisms for the socialization of the southern population as the new cotton-mill towns represented. Removal of the South's rural population from the back-country lowlands and highlands to the economically and socially more viable mill towns could solve the problems generated by the absence of community even while it provided needed labor for the South's new industries.

Of these three—the shift in focus of benevolent work, the legitimation of Appalachian otherness, and the justification of industrial development as a solution to the "mountain problem"—which came first is neither apparent nor important. What is clear is that they played into each other in such a way as to create a clearly defined issue around which all subsequent debate on the nature and meaning of Appalachian otherness would turn, indeed until today.

Although industry was not entirely absent from the South before 1900, it was generally believed that the region as a whole was primarily agricultural. Farming remained the occupation of the majority of persons in the South, even if, as some claimed, it did not provide employment adequate for the support of that population. The South was not only agricultural in the focus of its economic activity, however. As both proponents and critics of the rapid industrialization of the early twentieth century noted, prior to the turn of the century the South was agricultural in spirit as well. Such industry as existed tended to be periodic, seasonal, or occasional, to be highly decentralized, to be dependent upon low capital investments except for raw materials (as land for timbering, mining, and, of course, agriculture), and to require occupational skills which were essentially continuous with those already possessed by an agricultural population. The southern economy before 1900, in contrast to the dominant pattern in the nation at large, was characterized by an absence of factories and manufacturing, an absence of concentrated centers of population serving concentrated economic activity, an absence of concentrated sources of capital, and conversely, a persistence of the work patterns and life habits of an agricultural mode of economic activity.[7]

Perhaps the most important exception to this situation was the existence of a growing cotton-manufacturing industry, especially after 1880. Cotton manufacturing offered an apparently viable alternative to an exclusively agricultural way of life and to what were seen as its unsatisfactory concomitants—isolation, ignorance, poverty, economic dependence manifested in the spread of tenancy and share-cropping, and the uncertainty which came from market fluctuations, weather, and later weevils. Yet even here, a tendency toward decentralization of production units, dependence on local capital, and utilization of a local labor force not completely separated from its agricultural past, and hence accepting of the seasonal patterns of employment which water supply and the vagaries of the cloth market necessitated, meant that the southern cotton industry was peculiarly "southern" in its characteristics, at least before the end of the nineteenth century. It was this very fact, however, which permitted the propagandists of the cotton-mill campaign after 1880 to represent the introduction of cotton manufacturing into the South as philanthropy of the best kind—the philanthropy of self-help. Growing naturally out of the South's relationship with King Cotton, the development of cotton manufacturing appealed also as an indigenous pattern of compromise between the southern past and the necessities of the present.[8]

Between 1880 and 1900, in the midst of a concerted and self-conscious effort at capital accumulation and industrial development, the number of cotton mills in the South increased from 180 to 412. During the same period, rapid construction of roads and railroads tied the South more completely into the national economy, making more feasible the transportation of manufactured goods from inland centers to the major shipping depots of the section and thereby creating additional impetus to the booster spirit which motivated the entrepreneurs of the cotton-mill campaign itself.[9] The experience of successful economic development over two decades, when combined with a vision of unlimited profits in a prospering nation after 1900, yielded an unparalleled optimism concerning the benefits which industrialization would bring to the South and convinced northern investors that there was indeed gold in the hills of the Piedmont. As additional capital resources became available, the rate of cotton mill construction began to increase at a fantastic rate. By the beginning of 1904 there were nine hundred mills in the South, more than twice the number in operation in 1900.[10]

In the context of this dramatic development of a manufacturing capacity in the hitherto agrarian South, a first series of questions began to be asked concerning the impact of factory labor and village life on the patterns of southern civilization, and more immediately on the health and well-being of southern mill operatives. As increasing amounts of northern capital brought increasing control by northern interests, and a northern presence in southern state politics which worked for the repeal of Alabama's pioneering child-labor law of 1887 and blocked passage of a new law in 1901, some southerners began to wonder if the New South was not turning out to be just like the old North.[11] When preliminary tabulations of the twelfth census of 1900 revealed that southern cotton mills employed almost twenty-five thousand operatives under the age of sixteen, who composed nearly 30 percent of the total work force in the mills,[12] all the talk about social and economic improvement began to look like so much justification for the exploitation of labor.

Because children composed a larger percentage of the workforce in southern cotton mills than in any other southern industry or in the northern textile industry, local and national concern combined to focus attention on the status of children in the South, and on the nature of the southern industrial economy more generally, beginning about 1901. In that year, Edgar Gardner Murphy helped establish the Alabama Child Labor Committee in order to publicize the extensive use of child labor in the southern cotton mills and to lobby for passage of child labor legislation in that state. He and his colleagues soon found that a campaign in Alabama alone could never succeed, however, and began to urge the establishment of committees in other southern states, and to appeal for support in the North. By 1903 Murphy had come to see child labor as a national problem and, while he remained convinced that only passage of identical legislation state by state could ever curb the evils of child labor, began to advocate the establishment of a national organization which would oversee and coordinate the activities of state and local reform organizations. From this advocacy, articulated in an address at the annual meeting of the National Conference of Charities and Correction, came the impetus for the National Child Labor Committee.[13]

The National Child Labor Committee was organized in April 1904, and thenceforth functioned as the principal proponent of child-labor legislation in the nation. The committee's first campaign was directed at an inquiry into the extent of child labor in coal mining, and at an effort to see restrictive legislation passed in Pennsylvania, West Virginia, Kentucky, and other mining states. By the end of that year, however, the committee gave notice that the interests of southern reformers had not been forgotten by appointing Alexander J. McKelway of North Carolina as "Southern Secretary" of the national committee and the administrative equal of the organization's first and principal secretary, Owen J. Lovejoy. Thus was the challenge given.[14]

In an article prepared for W. D. P. Bliss's *New Encyclopedia of Social Reform* (1910), Owen J. Lovejoy noted with pride that the efforts of the National Child Labor Committee during its first full year of operation had produced passage of child-labor laws in twenty-two states. Lovejoy did not mention that few of these states were in the South, or that those southern states which did pass child-labor laws characteristically institutionalized what was current employment practice in the cotton-manufacturing industry instead of mandating a change in practice. Lovejoy did not mention either, that the southern activities of the National Child Labor Committee had generated a counter-campaign sponsored by the southern cotton manufacturers, to which the committee in turn responded by establishing a permanent office in Atlanta, in 1906, and then in 1909 a temporary office in the very heart of cotton-mill country, at Charlotte, North Carolina, with funds provided for the purpose by the Russell Sage Foundation.[15] From Lovejoy's point of view, some legislation was better than no legislation, as an acknowledgment of the problem of child labor.

By 1910, all the southern states had in fact passed legislation establishing minimum ages for factory employment. Few of these laws, and none of those passed by the legislatures of the cotton-mill states, met what the National Child Labor Committee regarded as adequate standards, however.[16] In addition, most of these laws allowed certain persons or classes of persons to be exempted from their operation, characteristically orphans and the children of "poor" families which might claim dependence upon a child's wage as part of the total family income. Since wages in the cotton mills were based on the assumption that whole families would work—the young as spinners and doffers or at least "sweepers," and the older as weavers —and since many cotton-mill families included unemployed or unemployable fathers whose children might therefore be designated as "orphans" within the meaning of the law, there were few children whose labor did not fall into the exempted category. And enforcement of these laws was virtually impossible in any case. None of the laws passed by the southern states required documentary proof of age as a condition of factory employment, and all placed the burden of enforcement upon special state agents (who might or might not do their job, and who might or might not be appointed to begin with) rather than upon public school officials, as in the northern states.[17]

Alabama, Georgia, South Carolina, and Virginia set the minimum age for factory employment at twelve years, and North Carolina set the minimum age at thirteen, all with exemptions as already noted. The states of West Virginia, Kentucky, and Tennessee, which had no significant textile industry, accepted the National Child Labor Committee's recommendation of fourteen as the minimum age for factory work, although West Virginia exempted children employed in mining, the major industry in that state employing young children.[18] All the southern states exempted children employed in agriculture as a matter of course, and Texas exempted children who were illiterate, despite the thrust of national and sectional sentiment which defined illiteracy as one of the evils to be eliminated by restricting the employment of school-age children. During this period, only North Carolina among the cotton-mill states had a compulsory school law, and this provided only that children should have attended school for four months during the year preceding employment in a regulated industry. Kentucky and West Virginia required children under fourteen to attend school for five months a year, West Virginia again excepting children employed in mining. Alabama, Georgia, South Carolina, and Virginia had no compulsory school attendance laws whatsoever.

In the face of successes like these, the national committee and the child labor movement generally began its move away from an exclusive focus on state legislative action. As early as the end of 1906, Murphy's original quest for a national cooperative effort on behalf of child labor restriction through the agencies of voluntarism had become largely transformed into an effort to involve the federal government in the needs of children. The nature of this involvement was a matter which seriously divided the national committee itself, some opposing any form of legislative interference with state initiatives in economic and social matters, some recognizing that only the federal government could defend the powerless against the powerful in social and economic matters. When the national committee voted to support Albert J. Beveridge's bill prohibiting interstate commerce in nonagricultural goods produced by the labor of children under the age of fourteen, introduced into the Senate on 5 December 1906, Murphy publicly resigned from the committee.

Burned by the discontent among its members generated by their decision to support federal legislation concerning child labor, of which Murphy's action was only the most obvious indication, and by the resounding defeat of the Beveridge bill in Congress, the National Child Labor Committee sought an alternative route to federal involvement in the advocacy of an investigation of the working conditions of women and children in America. With committee (and presidential) sponsorship, a bill authorizing such an investigation was passed by the Congress in late January 1907. In 1908, apparently in an effort to prevent publication of the results of this report prior to the fall elections and thereby to prevent child labor from becoming an issue in the campaign, Congress extended the authorization for this investigation to include an inquiry into the conditions of employment in rural regions of the nation, including those areas of the South from which the mill operatives were drawn.[19]

The escalating campaign of national publicity organized by the National Child Labor Committee between 1906 and 1916 focused particularly on the primitive and exploitive working conditions in the always separate, always alien South, and put the southern cotton manufacturers on the defensive. Against their claims of offering southern workers opportunities for economic and personal improvement, the propagandists for child-labor restriction noted that the mill owners kept hours long and wages low in order to compete with the better-established textile industry of New England, and pointed to the statistical data gathered by the congressionally sponsored survey of 1907–8 and then to the preliminary returns from the thirteenth census of 1910, which revealed that children did in fact work long hours for low wages in the southern mills. Against the manufacturers' claims of providing opportunities for social advancement and improved living conditions in the towns they had built with their own money, and in the schools, kindergartens, and recreation centers they provided, the child labor restrictionists argued that the transformation of a rural yeomanry into mill operatives involved the creation of a "pauperized" class, dependent upon the will and the wages of others, and that this backward step for the South justified comparison of the mill owners with the plantation slavocrats of antebellum days, since both kept their workers in bondage through a monopoly over all available resources for food, shelter, and employment.

Although the southern cotton manufacturers continued to be able to block passage of effective child labor legislation in the cotton-mill states of the South, the growth of child labor restrictionist sentiment nationally suggested that a changed strategy was needed—to repair the mill owners' public image as philanthropists, to restore their private self-esteem, and to counter the compelling arguments of reform propaganda.[20] After 1907, as a consequence, the cotton manufacturers shifted the focus of their own propaganda, from defense of the mills as a positive benefit to the South, to an attack on the conditions of life prevailing in the rural regions from which the cotton mill work force was drawn. Industrialization thus came to be represented less as an absolute good than as a preferred alternative to the poverty and degradation of country living, and the southern cotton mill owners were able once again to enter the mainstream of contemporary reform thought as spokesmen for that disillusionment with rural life which also followed from the 1907–8 congressional survey, and which manifested itself in the establishment of a Country Life Commission by Theodore Roosevelt in 1908 and in the country-life movement which grew out of its report. Once again the cotton manufacturers appeared as reformers, progressives, philanthropists doing the essential work of modernization in the backward South and thereby offering individuals an alternative to a life of limited opportunity in the southern back-country. In the process, and not incidentally, they involved persons active in the country-life movement, especially Walter Hines Page and Charles Wardell Stiles, in what had previously been a matter of limited and local interest, and thereby precipitated the transformation of the child-labor debate into a confrontation on the consequences of modernization and on the nature and future of American civilization.[21]

The cotton manufacturers' new strategy was not without risk to themselves. In attacking the conditions of rural life in the South, would they alienate that rural population whose support they needed for the election of sympathetic members of state legislatures and representatives to the United States Congress? In earlier years, great pains had been taken to argue that the southern mill operatives were not the "degenerate" poor whites of fiction but were rather a rural yeomanry, impoverished by the unsuitability of the southern uplands to cotton culture in an agricultural economy dominated by a single cash crop, a people hitherto excluded from the social and political life of the South. For them, cotton-mill life offered an important —and exclusive—alternative, it was said. Even Edgar Gardner Murphy had acknowledged the importance of this alternative to the

South's poor but not degenerate rural population: "From their little homes in the 'hill country' of the Piedmont, where for years they have maintained a precarious existence upon a difficult and forbidding soil, thousands of them have been drawn within the precincts of the new industrial life . . . [and have] found under the conditions of manufacture at least the possibility of another world."[22] Between 1907 and 1910, however, the cotton mill defenders found a way out of their dilemma in the suggestion that the operatives had been of a pauperized group among this southern yeomanry, for whom even the most undesirable conditions of labor in towns and factories marked an improvement over the conditions of their life in the hills. That pauperized group rapidly became identifiable as "the mountaineers."

Whether or not an increasing number of mill operatives from the more mountainous sections of the South were in fact entering the southern textile industry after 1907, as defenders of the mills asserted, after this date the defense of the mills as philanthropy began to depend on the assertion that a majority of mill operatives were mountaineers.[23] If this were true then the social and economic possibilities available to them in the mill towns marked a significant improvement over the social and economic possibilities of life in Appalachia. Was this not after all the message of the corpus of philanthropic literature about the causes and nature of Appalachian otherness published after 1900? In the mill towns the mountaineers could find community and its institutions, including schools, churches, recreation facilities, and sanitary conditions which would liberate them from that variety of diseases endemic to rural regions.[24]

Ironically, Alexander J. McKelway, southern secretary of the National Child Labor Committee, may have been the first to introduce the possibility of an attack on Appalachia as a tactic in defense of the mills. In 1906, in an address on "The Physical Evils of Child Labor," McKelway called upon the physicians of North Carolina to protest the continued movement of the state's rural population from the healthful conditions which prevailed in the country to the confining atmosphere of the new mill towns. To make his point more telling,

McKelway pointed out that the mill operatives were no longer drawn only from among the "poor whites" of the lowland South, but also from among those independent mountain people who formed the true southern yeomanry, the pride of North Carolina. Worst of all, McKelway said, they were finding employment in the mill towns of other states.

As early as the late eighteenth century, McKelway said, physicians in England had recognized that the grinding pattern of cotton-mill life stunted the physical and blocked the mental growth of children employed in the industry. More recently, the cumulative effect of the employment of children in factories over generations had manifested itself in the decreased vitality of the English population as a whole. It was this fact indeed which was "the real secret of the disaster of the British army in the South African war," and which had led the British government to establish programs to return its manufacturing population to the rural regions of that nation. The physicians' good advice had finally been heeded, but in America it had not yet been offered. The South as a whole and North Carolina in particular now stood silent as its children entered upon factory labor for the first time. "From one little village, called Clyde's, near Waynesville, during the past year fifteen hundred of our splendidly developed mountain people have gone to the mills of South Carolina . . . tempted from the farm by the prospect of getting wages from every member of the family, from eight to ten years up."[25]

Splendidly developed mountain people? In October 1907 the *North American Review* published Julia Macgruder's refutation of McKelway's charges and of the assertions of such other entrepreneurs of sentimentality as Bessie and Marie Van Vorst, whose accounts of factory conditions had first established the crucial nexus between woman and child labor which made possible the union of these issues in the 1907–8 Bureau of Labor study, and subsequently convinced Senator Albert Beveridge of the need for national legislation to regulate child labor in the United States. Macgruder, herself an author "whose name has long been familiar to readers of the best modern American fiction" according to the editors of the *Review*, dismissed the work of the Van Vorsts out of hand. They probably had never been South at all, she said, and even if they had, their observations were as inaccurate as their transcriptions of southern dialect.

More troublesome were the allegations of McKelway and others of the National Child Labor Committee. They had been in the South, and some of whom were of the South as well. Like the Van Vorsts, however, McKelway played on sentiment, Macgruder said, and quite consciously sought to divert attention from the real issue: that there was no viable alternative to employment in the cotton textile industry for that group in the southern population who had become mill operatives. "As a rule, the class from which the mill hands in the South are drawn is the very lowest." Even under the worst of conditions, as a consequence, their utilization as a labor force in the cotton mills provided positive benefits for them as well as for their section.[26]

In October 1907 also, the Charleston, South Carolina, *News and Courier* began publishing a series of letters from August Kohn of its Columbia bureau, describing conditions in the cotton textile industry and the progress of the industry itself within the state. Unlike an earlier series which Kohn had written for the paper in 1903, during the late stages of the cotton-mill campaign, these 1907 letters were designed explicitly as a defense of the mills against the varied charges leveled against them, and focused particularly on the allegations made by McKelway and others from the National Child Labor Committee. Kohn acknowledged that there were large numbers of children to be seen in the mills, for example, but insisted that the greatest number of these were merely keeping their older brothers and sisters company as the latter worked, or were brought to the mills by mothers who had no other place to leave their young children during the day. If the youngsters did a little "helping," it was more play than work, and it kept them out of mischief. At the same time, it instilled good habits of work and provided them with practical experience against the time when, after the age of twelve, they might themselves be entered on the payroll books of their home-town mill.

And so the argument went. Against McKelway's assertions of the unhealthiness of cotton-mill life and labor, Kohn argued that life in the cotton-mill towns marked an important improvement over conditions in the rural regions from which the mill operatives had come, and quoted Dr. Charles Wardell Stiles, who had demonstrated that hookworm disease, so common in the country, was generally absent from more urbanized areas of the South. Against McKelway's charges that cotton-mill workers spent long hours in closed rooms and that the employment of children deprived them of opportunities to play, Kohn pointed out that adult weavers were allowed to open the windows of the weave rooms in summertime and that children employed as sweepers, spinners, and doffers had outdoor playtime during their twenty-minute lunch break. In any case, the children rarely worked more than fifteen minutes out of every hour. The remainder of the time, during which the spindles filled, was waiting time, and might easily be used for indoor play.[27]

Not only in the area of public health did the migration of the South's rural population to the cotton mills mean practical improvement in their lives, however. A cash income provided an increased and increasing standard of living, and the possibility of saving for future investment. The opportunities for personal improvement, provided by the availability of graded schools, and for recreation, provided by the availability of churches, playgrounds, and swimming pools, also marked a significant advantage over rural life. Kohn described in great detail the character of the "welfare work" of the southern mill towns and acknowledged with pride that this was philanthropy inspired by self-interest, necessary to maintain the loyalty of the mill operatives. The independent, liberty-loving working people of South Carolina would not accept factory employment unless it provided significant advantages over conditions in the countryside. Indeed, Kohn argued, the very progress of cotton manufacturing in South Carolina was a manifestation of the qualities of the state's population. It was the skill of native workers and the business acumen of native entrepreneurs which had made industrial growth possible since most of the cotton mill operatives, most of the owners and managers, and most of the capital of the South Carolina cotton industry came from the state itself.

By 1907, however, not all the mill operatives in South Carolina were natives of that state, Kohn admitted with mixed pride and distress. The growth of the southern cotton industry and its attempt to compete in national and international markets had created an insatiable demand for labor. As the market for manufactured goods outstripped the productive capacity of the South Carolina mills as they were currently operated, new or additional machinery was acquired, efficiencies in operation developed, and new sources of available labor explored. Beginning in 1905 or 1906, Kohn explained, the mill operators had begun sending their agents into the rural regions of neighboring states in an attempt to attract new workers, whole families as well as individuals. As the competition for workers among the South Carolina mills increased, and as an experiment in the employment of foreign weavers proved unsatisfactory, thus cutting off that potential source of labor, the cotton-mill agents went further west, beyond the hills of North Carolina into the Tennessee mountains.[28]

Kohn did not venture to examine the consequences of this pattern of labor recruitment upon the composition and hence the characteristics of the state's cotton-manufacturing class. He did suggest, however, although largely by implication, that these new workers from outside the state were not quite so reliable and not quite so skillful as the South Carolinians, and appeared also to be of a lower social class. Among the many children he interviewed in connection with his study, for example, "about the only ones" who could not write their names and "a little sentence" in his notebook "were those who had come into South Carolina from neighboring States."[29]

Kohn's primary purpose was to defend the mills of South Carolina, and he sought to do so merely by contradicting with the "facts" of personal observation the contentions of outside observers, and to explain such social problems as had to be acknowledged as a consequence of the growth in the mill population of operatives from outside the state. In so doing, however, he offered a model of explanation which other propagandists in defense of the cotton mills might use to good effect. By 1910, indeed, it had become conventional to note that immorality among mill operatives, misuse of sanitary facilities, high rates of absenteeism resulting from laziness or illness, extensive illiteracy, high rates of truancy from school might all be blamed upon the characteristic behavior patterns of a new class of operatives from Appalachia, unfamiliar with the urban patterns of life and the industrial patterns of labor required by the new situation in which they found themselves. In this context, even those disadvantages which cotton mill life possessed over the potentially more idyllic patterns of rural or small-town nonindustrial life were more than offset by the significant improvements in living conditions enjoyed by the mill hands as compared with their degraded life in the mountains.

Kohn was himself among the first to utilize this pattern of explanation in defense of the southern cotton industry, in an essay on "Child Labor in the South" prepared for Samuel C. Mitchell's monumental regionalist polemic, *The South in the Building of the Nation*. Where earlier Kohn had ignored the mountaineers per se as an industrial factor in the southern textile industry, now he began his discussion by noting that "the largest proportion of those working in the Southern cotton mills came from the mountain sections of the two Carolinas, Georgia, Virginia and Tennessee." Where earlier he had avoided any real consideration of the conditions under which the cotton-mill operatives labored in their rural homes, writing now in a new context and in a new phase of the cotton-mill debate he insisted that only through a "before and after" comparison could judgments be made about child labor in the cotton textile industry. "The . . . study should be begun by going to the little mountain cottages, where the largest numbers of the operatives come from, and witnessing the utter poverty and hopelessness of most of these poor mountaineers. Now see these same people in their comfortable homes in the mill communities, with churches and schools near-by and pay-day coming with clock-like regularity."[30] As Kohn may well have known, however, such a "before and after" study had already been carried out in connection with the Bureau of Labor's survey of working conditions in the southern textile industry in 1907–8, by a bureau special agent, Thomas R. Dawley.

In a first-person account of his experiences as a social investigator, published in 1912 as *The Child That Toileth Not: The Story of A Government Investigation*, Dawley explained the circumstances under which he found employment with the bureau and sought to "expose" the hypocrisy of his colleagues in the inquiry and the fundamental dishonesty of the survey itself. His style, not accidentally, parodied that of Bessie and Marie Van Vorst, whose exposé of working conditions for women, published in 1903 as *The Woman Who Toils: Being the Experiences of Two Ladies as Factory Girls*, was instrumental in laying the groundwork for the 1907 survey by attracting Theodore Roosevelt's attention to the consequences of female employment in factories for American family life and hence for the "vitality" of future generations. But Dawley, no less than the Van Vorsts, expected to be taken seriously.

Dawley noted that he was responsible for the "before and after" component of the bureau's survey of conditions in the southern cotton mills. His distress and discontent with the influence of Alexander McKelway and others from the National Child Labor Committee on the conduct of the survey led him to suggest that conditions in the hills be compared with conditions in the mills, and he himself prepared the schedules for this phase of the inquiry and did much of the actual investigation in the field. Dawley also insisted that before his appointment as special agent in the Bureau of Labor and his first ventures into the southern mountains, "I knew absolutely nothing about child-labor in the South, nor did I know anything about the conditions of the people either at the mills or on the farms." It was only the reality of mountain poverty as he observed it first-hand that had convinced him of the social advantages which employment in the cotton mills offered the mountain people, and the important educational consequences of cotton-mill labor for the mountaineers' children, he said. His "objectivity" thus established, Dawley noted that he would have welcomed support from the southern textile manufacturers when he was removed from the Bureau of Labor's payroll because of his unorthodox views as to the desirability of employing children in the cotton mills, but none was forthcoming. He was a freelance, he said, and it was as a freelance that his subsequent career as the principal propagandist in defense of the labor practices of the southern cotton manufacturers developed.[31]

Whatever the truth of Dawley's assertions concerning his lack of personal involvement with special-interest groups and the personal origins of his personal campaign to publicize the advantages of cotton-mill life over life in the southern mountains, the impact of his work on the contemporary debate over child labor legislation was considerable. The impact of his work on the history of American responses to Appalachia was, if anything, even greater, for he was the first to articulate a clear vision of the inviability of mountain life and hence of the uselessness of benevolent work in the region, and the first to represent this vision as a matter independent of the debate over the employment of children in factories or the "real" conditions in the cotton mills.

Late in 1909, Dawley prepared a summary of his observations on mountain life for Walter Hines Page's personal journal of reform, *The World's Work*, where it appeared in March 1910 as "Our Southern Mountaineers: Removal the Remedy for the Evils that Isolation and Poverty Have Brought." Page may well have been responsible for the title, which now appears as a parody of the title of William Goodell Frost's essay of 1900, "The Southern Mountaineer: Our Kindred of the Boone and Lincoln Type." Page knew Frost, at least through correspondence, and knew his work at Berea. He also knew his views on the nature of Appalachian otherness, and indeed, as editor of the *Atlantic Monthly*, had accepted Frost's first important article of 1899, to which he had given the striking title "Our Contemporary Ancestors in the Southern Mountains." Was the title of Dawley's article intended as a warning to Frost about Page's views on "adorning the log cabin"? It was no accident in any case that Dawley's article was presented as yet another contribution to the contemporary discussion of the future of Appalachia, and Page asked explicitly, in a prefatory editorial note, that it be read as such: "Because great sums have been wasted in mistaken missionary work to improve the lives of people in these places where they ought not to stay, *The World's Work* publishes Mr. Dawley's article in order, if possible, to hasten the migration from these really uninhabitable regions."[32]

In May 1910, Dawley presented an expanded version of his *World's Work* article as an address before the annual meeting of the American Cotton Manufacturers Association in Charlotte, North

Carolina, which was published and distributed by the association in pamphlet form under the title *Our Mountain Problem and Its Solution*. Again Dawley's stress was on "our mountain problem," and his title and tone conspired to fool contemporary librarians, at least, who catalogued it as if its subject were the mountain whites rather than child labor in the southern cotton mills. Dawley's tone, indeed, was impeccable as he spoke the language and voiced the concerns of contemporary social science and scientific social work. He noted the absence of community among the mountaineers and explained that because the physical and social environment of the region isolated the mountain people from each other, community could never be created in Appalachia. He stressed his own objectivity and the validity of his data. He had himself been in the field. He had "scheduled" 844 families. His diligence proved the representativeness of his survey sample, his disinterestedness proved the accuracy of his observations, and no one in the first decade of the twentieth century was prepared to question his unspoken assumption concerning the uniformity of social—or even the uniformity of physiographic—conditions throughout Appalachia. Nor was anyone prepared to question his conclusions, concerning the neediness of the mountaineers. Dawley only found them to be a bit more needy than others had said they were. "I have seen the poor people of the mountains in the dead of winter, their hungry, half-clad children hovering over a scanty fire in the fire-place, the snow blown between the unchinked logs of their cabins . . . melting upon their bare hands," he noted. "In a moonshiner's cove we scheduled two families consisting of unmarried mothers and several illegitimate children, not one of whom could articulate complete words."[33]

Dawley's description of mountain poverty and of the degradation, if not the degeneracy (he does not indicate the ages of those speechless children, and the implication of degeneracy was clearly no accident) of the isolated mountain people was no more than an extreme version of the conventional image of the mountaineers as "needy." What is striking about his presentation is not the observations he records, or even the pretense to scientific accuracy transcending personal judgment contained in his use of the jargon of survey research, however, so much as his assertion that the mountaineers' condition was not remediable in the context of the mountain region. Indeed, Dawley told the cotton manufacturers, the only solution to the mountain problem was to be found in the utilization of the mountaineers as a labor force in the cotton mills. "The cotton mill is the one industry that gives employment to children, and work that is suitable for young hands to do. And these people of the mountains must be given work while they are young. If you leave them in their isolated coves and mountain retreats until they are . . . set in their ways with generations of idle habits and lack of thrift behind them, you can do nothing with them in a cotton mill, or any other kind of mill. But if you can get them young enough . . . you can train them to work, to acquire industrious habits, and become excellent workmen and good citizens."[34]

The real triumph of this attack on Appalachia in defense of the mills, and the full emergence of this new view of Appalachia as an uninhabitable land, manifested itself not in such obviously polemical works, however, but in the published report of the 1907–8 congressional survey, which appeared in 1910. There are only hints of how this came about, and who was responsible. In an article prepared for *The South in the Building of the Nation*, for example, the special agent of the bureau of labor in charge of the survey for the southern textile industry, Walter B. Palmer, chose to list Appalachia first among those areas in the South from which cotton mill operatives were drawn, thereby suggesting but not directly stating that many mountaineers worked in the mills.[35] He knew, of course, that the data of the survey itself said otherwise. "For the mills visited during this investigation the percentage of such operatives was very much smaller than the percentage of those who come from the low-land farms surrounding the cotton-mill villages."[36] Even more important, Charles H. Verrill, in drafting the formal report of the survey, included paragraphs apparently prepared by Dawley on the circumstances of mountain life. Whether Verrill thus sought to establish the "objectivity" of the survey or simply to utilize data collected at public expense regardless of its merits, is not clear, but the presence of the Dawley material in the report is puzzling. Verrill may himself have been ambiguous about the relationship of the habitability of Appalachia to proposals for legislative restriction on child labor in the South, but the report as a whole is strongly critical of existing patterns of employment in southern industry. The appearance of the Dawley data as interpreted by Dawley thus stands in marked contrast to the tone of the remainder of the study.

Much extreme poverty and hard conditions of life were found. Living isolated in mountain coves, eking out in many cases a wretched existence from small and barren patches of land, with either no facilities or scant facilities for either the education of their children or anything approaching an opportunity for a normal social development, the comfort of this class and the opportunity for the education of their children could not fail to be improved by their migration to industrial communities.[37]

As defenders of the cotton mills thus launched their attack on the habitability of Appalachia, proponents of child labor legislation found themselves forced into what for many of them must have been an uncomfortable position indeed. Insofar as it appeared necessary to counter such charges with coin of the same value, McKelway and others began to articulate a defense of the "peculiarities" of mountain life as both legitimate and preferable to conditions in the cotton-mill communities, and of the mountaineers as "the most vigorous race of people in America today." Indeed, McKelway told the National Child Labor Committee at its annual meeting in 1910, the attack on Appalachia was "the last stand of the cotton manufacturers against our reform."

First they said that child labor was a good thing in itself; then they shifted to the ground that it was a bad thing, but that there was very little of it left; being driven from that position by the overwhelming array of facts presented, they have said that at least the condition of the people was improved by their transportation from the farms to the mills. . . . A cause grows to be desperate, indeed, that it must make its apology with what amounts to a wholesale slander of the great mass of white people in the South, indiscriminately dubbed "poor whites."[38]

Just as Edgar Gardner Murphy had taken pains to separate the issue of child labor legislation from "the advantages and the blessings of the factory, to the community or to the child," at the beginning of the movement for child labor legislation,[39] so after 1910 the proponents of child labor legislation sought to separate the issue of child labor from the issue of the habitability of Appalachia. In this effort, particular weight was accorded the testimony of experts on mountain life, particularly John C. Campbell of the Southern Highland Division of the Russell Sage Foundation, who entered the foray in 1913. At the annual meeting of the National Child Labor Committee in that year, Campbell sought to summarize the state of the argument made in defense of the mills as it related to conditions in the southern mountains. "On the one hand, I hear and read the claim that the sturdy mountaineer and his children, inured to toil and bowed down by the excess of it in their mountain environment, should be taken to the mills where they may have release from excessive labor and may live in comparative ease with only moderate effort; on the other hand, . . . that these mountain people are so debased, so criminal, so shiftless and indolent, that it is a mercy to take them to the mills to better their morals and to teach them how to labor. In either case, one notices that the mill agent is pictured as an altruist."[40]

Removal of the mountaineers to the Piedmont was not the only mode of dealing with the very real problems which characterized mountain life, Campbell insisted, and there was in any case no evidence that the indolence, the improper health practices, and the immorality or unmorality of the mountain people would not be reinforced rather than eliminated in the mill towns, where "many people of the same social grade are closely grouped together, . . . people who have hitherto known little of organized community life."

Why defend the mills . . . by putting forward the limitations of mountain life when all the mills of the South, if manned entirely by mountain operatives, would affect less than one-third of all the rural mountain population in only five of the eight mountain states, and when in point of fact only a small fraction of the total 250,000 operatives are mountain people? . . . The real question, therefore, is not whether the mountain fraction of operatives is better off in the mills than in the mountain environment [but] . . . are the conditions in the mills all they ought to be.[41]

If the issue of child labor and working conditions in the southern cotton mills more generally could thus easily be considered separately from the issue of the needs of the population providing labor to the mills, so also could the needs of the population providing labor to the mills be isolated from the issue of child labor. Although by the end of 1914 the defensive strategy of the mill operators had shifted away from the attack on the habitability of Appalachia,[42] that issue once raised remained, and took on a life of its own. Indeed, the search for information about living conditions in the rural South, including the southern mountains, which both sides in the cotton mill debate conducted between 1907 and 1914, generated the first body of more or less systematically obtained and apparently objective information about mountain life. Like the data generated by the social surveys of urban sections of the nation, during the same period, this information tended to focus not on the responsibility of individuals for undesirable conditions, but upon undesirable conditions as discrete phenomena in need of improvement. In the case of Appalachia as in the case of Pittsburgh, what resulted was a new concern with the character of daily life, including wages and conditions of employment, nutrition, health standards, the use of leisure, opportunities for cultural improvement, patterns of play. And in the case of Appalachia as in the case of Pittsburgh, the data gathered under such circumstances necessarily proved that there were undesirable conditions in need of improvement.

Although all the published literature of this survey research period was overtly polemical, it possessed the simulacrum of objectivity in the statistical mode of its presentation and in its pretense to systematic and thorough coverage of its field. The consequences of this were of enormous importance, for the mere act of collecting data tended to guarantee with the weight of the new social sciences, the validity of assumptions concerning the legitimacy of the particular unit utilized as the basis for the collection of data. When cities were the survey units, cities came to seem real entities with organic lives rather than mere geographic divisions or population aggregates. When counties were the survey fields, counties came to seem the real units of social life. And when Appalachia, the mountainous portions of eight southern states, composed the survey field, Appalachia also appeared to have an existence of its own.[43] Because the focus of survey research at this period tended to be on the undesirable aspects of life, moreover, this newly "real" Appalachia came to be described and defined in terms of the particular undesirable characteristics which accident discovered in the region—hookworm, trachoma, poor nutrition, individual isolation, poverty, extensive adult illiteracy, and what seemed to be the cause of all this, a land unsuited for subsistence agriculture and for modern patterns of community both.

In this context, the arguments of a Thomas Dawley as to the benefits which would be obtained by removing the mountaineers to the mill towns of the Piedmont seemed compelling indeed. What had traditionally been seen to separate Appalachia and America, after all, was not the presence of a genuinely indigenous, alternative pattern of culture, but rather the absence of industry, the absence of urban centers, the absence of the institutions of community, the absence of a cash economy and a cash nexus as the basis of the social order. If roads and railroads had seemed a panacea for the problems of mountain life because of their ability to permit home missionaries, teachers, and social workers to enter the mountains and to permit the mountaineers to leave, how much to be preferred would be the introduction of that which the missionaries and the social workers were preparing the mountaineers to take advantage of, and which the mountaineers themselves were seeking as they left the region. The establishment of manufacturing centers in the mountain region or on its periphery would integrate the mountaineers fully into the economic, and by extension the social and cultural life of the nation, by providing them with what could never be had at home in their lonely cabins and on their unproductive farms. And what could better meet contemporary demands for "real-life education" than the training for work children would obtain in the cotton mills?

Because the new cotton-mill towns of the Piedmont seemed to offer the mountaineers as a group a viable alternative to the undesirable conditions of poverty and isolation which seemed to characterize life in the mountains, the pretensions of the New South industrializers to benevolence and their efforts to recruit mountaineers as mill operatives precipitated a first real consideration of the nature of mountain life among the mountaineers' "friends." These were now forced to ask whether the self-serving programs of the mill owners for obtaining a source of cheap labor did not in fact amount to benevolence. They were forced to confront for the first time the disparity between their own romantic and self-serving view of the mountaineer as "our contemporary ancestor," happy in his isolated mountain cove, satisfied with his poor health, his ignorance, his political impotence, his poverty, his lack of "opportunity," and what appeared to be a more realistic view of mountain life as a most unpleasant set of circumstances for its participants, however much outsiders might find it quaint and picturesque.

Earlier programs for the economic development of Appalachia's natural resources through the establishment of transportation facilities and/or extractive industry had simply not raised these issues. Their focus had been on the integration of the region, the geographic area of the southern Appalachians, into the economic network of modern America, rather than on the alteration of the conditions of mountain life, and they had looked to the exploitation of natural resources without perceiving the possibility of exploiting the human resources of the region. If mountain life itself was altered by these efforts, it was incidental, and if it was altered along desirable lines it was accidental. During this earlier period, moreover, the economic development of Appalachia depended largely on an imported labor force and generally left the mountaineer alone to play out his traditional role as observer of, rather than participant in modern life, as both James Lane Allen and John Fox, Jr., had pointed out. The utilization of mountaineers as a labor force in the cotton mills of the Piedmont, on the other hand, not only involved the integration of the mountain people into the economic network of modern America, but required their emigration from the region.

Under such circumstances, it was with no little trepidation that the agents of systematic benevolence, for example, faced the possibility of having to lose their client population in order to save them, and it was with no little distress that those who had become convinced of the legitimacy of Appalachia's existence as a discrete region of the nation faced the suggestion that, legitimate or not, mountain life was simply not viable. It was in the attempt to respond to such arguments that many persons active in benevolent work among the mountaineers found themselves drawn increasingly to a defense of the habitability of Appalachia, and to an assertion of the essential viability of mountain life despite its "peculiarities," which had been the basis for assertions of the mountaineers' need since the 1880s. It was in this general context also, that Appalachia came increasingly to be defined in terms of itself as an incomplete version of itself, a folk-society manqué, rather than in terms of America and its values and its standard of living.

Although defense of the habitability of Appalachia and of the viability of mountain life was largely the effort of agents of systematic benevolence to preserve a sense of the viability and utility of their own work in the region, it cannot be dismissed as "merely" the result of self-interest. Self-interest there was without doubt, but genuine issues were also involved. Not the least of these was the choice be-tween what Appalachia might be and what the mill towns of the Piedmont had already become. To the degree that this appeared to be the only real choice, few now would fault the agents of systematic benevolence for articulating a fantasy of rural life in Appalachia and for attempting to realize it, rather than yielding to what appeared to be the horrors of an inevitable industrialized future.

8. The Southern Highland Division and the Institutionalization of Appalachian Regionalism

Definition of Appalachia as a coherent entity inhabited by a homogeneous population was implicit in the local colorists' attempts to objectify as reality their essentially literary vision of mountain life. It was not properly until the second decade of the twentieth century that systematic attempts were made to describe Appalachia as a region and the mountaineers as a people, however, or that a true regionalist definition of Appalachia came to be articulated. Even more important, it was only after 1910 that systematic attempts were made to utilize regionalist conceptions—as distinct from regional names—in discussions of Appalachian otherness and as a basis for dealing with the mountains and mountaineers in practical terms.

In this process, which came first, what caused what, is neither clear nor ultimately important. The utilization of regionalist conceptions in dealing with the otherness of Appalachia and in the collection of information on Appalachia occurred simultaneously. Neither was possible without the other. By 1915, however, the acceptance of regionalist conceptions of mountain life was apparent in the identification of Appalachia as a discrete physiographic and economic unit, of mountain life as a distinct pattern of American culture, and of the mountain people as a distinct "subrace" of the American population; in the construction of programs of action designed to deal with Appalachia as a whole and the mountaineers as a group; and in the emergence of a series of institutions the existence of which depended upon a conception of Appalachia as a discrete region of the nation.

The manifestations of this tendency were various and their interrelationships numerous. Passage of the Weeks Act of 1911, creating the Appalachian National Forest for timber and water conservation and for recreation purposes, for example, not only defined Appalachia as a geographic and economic region and sought to deal with it as a discrete unit, but also institutionalized a vision of the southern mountains as unsuited to traditional patterns of subsistence agriculture and hence reinforced the arguments of those who asserted its essential unhabitability. Republication in 1910 of Ellen Churchill Semple's "The Anglo-Saxons of the Kentucky Mountains: A Study in Anthropogeography" (1901), and the simultaneous and consequent rediscovery of C. Willard Hayes's physiographic description of "The Southern Appalachians" (1895), made available two crucial attempts to deal conceptually with Appalachia as a region. These provided contemporaries with basic information about the physical and physiographic reality of the southern mountains, even as they pointed to the impact of physiography on the genetic and cultural characteristics of the mountain population and the character of mountain life.

Mary E. Verhoeff's model study of the impact of the physiography of Appalachia on its economic development, published in 1911 as *The Kentucky Mountains: Transportation and Commerce, 1750–1911. An Essay on the Economic History of a Coal Field*, took the particular characteristics of Appalachia defined as a discrete unit as the fundamental reality with which one began an analysis of the relationship between life and landscape in America. By 1912, John C. Campbell of the Russell Sage Foundation had begun rearranging materials derived from the 1910 Federal Census in such a way as would provide aggregate data concerning the demographic, economic, educational, and occupational characteristics of the mountain population in the region as a whole as well as in the three distinct "physiographic belts" which, following Hayes, he saw as dividing Appalachia into component parts, each with a set of subcharacteristics of its own. At about the same time, United States Commissioner of Education Philander P. Claxton authorized Norman Frost of Berea College to collect and collate educational statistics derived from the boards of education of the several southern mountain states in a report on public education in Appalachia.[1]

Claxton's acceptance of Appalachia as an appropriate unit for educational and social survey research was significant as a first major acknowledgment by an agency of the federal government of the discrete quality of mountain life, as distinct from the physiographic reality of Appalachian regionalism. The Frost survey, and a later survey of social conditions in the mountains conducted by C. G. Burkitt of the Southern Industrial Education Association for the Bureau of Education, as well as Claxton's personal remarks and activities, thus gave a stamp of approval to the conceptual scheme utilized earlier by private and denominational agencies concerned with mountain life.

From about 1908, benevolent agencies at work in the mountains also began to concern themselves with conditions in Appalachia as a whole and with the mountaineers as a people. In some cases, this concern manifested itself in the creation of new organizational units. Both the Southern Highland Division of the Russell Sage Foundation and the Synod of Appalachia within the Southern Presbyterian church, for example, directed their efforts at the special needs of the mountaineers as distinct from the needs of lowland southerners, and sought to work in such a manner as would cut across those "artificial" boundaries of state or county lines, in terms of which most benevolent and religious activity was organized. In other cases, this concern manifested itself in a new interest in the characteristics of the mountaineers as a people or of the mountain region as a region. While denominational agencies engaged in missionary and educational work in Appalachia continued to collect reports and statistics from their mission stations and schools on an individual basis, for example, by 1910 most had commissioned or authorized the publication of one or more studies of Appalachia as a distinct region and the mountaineers as a distinct people.

Most of these denominational studies of mountain life were directed primarily at the supporting clientele of the sponsoring agency, as an effort to justify work in Appalachia despite the evidence of feuding which suggested the mountaineers' unworthiness of such work, and despite the normalization of Appalachian otherness which followed from ascription of regional status to the southern mountains. A few, however—most notably Samuel Tyndale Wilson's *The Southern Mountaineers*, which went through five editions between 1906 and 1915—were widely read outside the home-missionary community. Indeed, Wilson's book was the most comprehensive work on the southern mountains published up to that date, which may explain its popularity. It stood alone in the period before the great secular studies of mountain life written in the teens were published, Horace Kephart's *Our Southern Highlanders: A Narrative of Adventure in the Southern Appalachians and a Study of Life Among the Mountaineers* (1916), which appeared first in serial form in *Outing Magazine*, and John C. Campbell's posthumously published volume, *The Southern Highlander and His Homeland* (1921).[2]

The importance of Wilson's work lay not merely in its comprehensiveness, however. Like the chapters on southern mountain work published in general studies of denominational benevolence during this period, or such specialized shorter works as Walter Hughson's *The [Protestant Episcopal] Church's Mission to the Mountaineers of the South* (1908) or Samuel Hunter Thompson's *The Highlanders of the South* (1910), *The Southern Mountaineers* offered an alternative to the earlier dependence on purely literary materials for information about mountain life, and hence to the inevitable emphasis upon the picturesque which characterized such materials. Its very claim to comprehensiveness, moreover, stands as a warrant of the felt need for discussion of Appalachia as a region and of the mountaineers as a people among benevolent workers in the twentieth century. The new willingness of agencies of denominational benevolence to consider the needs of mountain life as a special phase of missionary and educational work is itself significant, however. Given the extraordinary growth of southern state activity in areas like education, where denominational agencies had previously exercised a practical monopoly, their willingness to deal with Appalachia on a regional basis may be seen as an attempt to find an alternative to the state-by-state pattern of organization which they had previously utilized and to which the state governments were restricted, and thereby to find continued justification for their own work in Appalachia.[3]

The growing acceptance of Appalachia as a thing in itself, and hence as a special field for benevolent work, to which the publication of these volumes attests, manifested itself also in the decision of the

National Conference of Charities and Correction to schedule a session on needs and opportunities in mountain work for its 1908 annual meeting in Richmond, Virginia. As the first recognition accorded mountain work by the national conference, this session was tantamount to its accreditation as a legitimate field of activity for the practitioners of scientific philanthropy. That such recognition was granted at the Richmond meeting made the session additionally significant, for the choice of Richmond as the site for the meeting was itself a symbolic acknowledgment of the emergence of the South as a major focus for benevolent work in the nation. The separation of Appalachia from the South, which had been the thrust of discussions of Appalachian otherness for two decades or more, in the context of the Richmond meeting thus appears transformed into a principle upon which action was to be based.

The National Conference of Charities and Correction had met in the South before 1908, in Louisville (1883), Nashville (1894), and Atlanta (1903), and it would again after 1908, although with even less frequency. The southern location of these earlier meetings appears less as an index of interest in the South as a field for northern or national benevolence, however, than as part of the attempt of the national conference to establish its national character. By meeting in the South, it sought to encourage the participation of southern agencies in its work and to spread its gospel of professional philanthropy and scientific social work. The choice of a southern city as the site for the 1908 meeting, however, appears as a public acknowledgment of the emergence of the South as a field for benevolence and of the important work being carried on by the Southern Education Board and the National Child Labor Committee in particular.

The choice of Richmond represented also an attempt to bring the National Conference of Charities and Correction into "the field," to see for themselves, even as Robert Ogden had brought selected individuals south on numerous railroad excursions. And the choice of Richmond in particular was designed to facilitate the attendance of workers whose field of service in the South normally prevented them from having close personal contact with their coworkers in southern benevolence, much less with the decision-making staff of the north-

ern agencies with which many were affiliated, so that southern workers were often as isolated as the populations they sought to serve. In
so accessible a city as Richmond, it was hoped, representatives of the
northern agencies might learn from workers in the field about the
needs of the South, while workers in the field might learn from the
agency representatives about new techniques in social service and
the new goal of interagency cooperation.[4]

In accordance with these general intentions, Mary Glenn as
chairman of the section on needy families and their neighborhoods—
which was to devote one of its allotted morning sessions to discussion of benevolent work in Appalachia—sent out a series of letters to
persons active in mountain work, inviting them to come to Richmond
in May as guests of the conference. One who received such a letter
was John C. Campbell of Demorest, Georgia, the forty-two-year-old
former president of Piedmont College. In early 1908 when Mrs.
Glenn's letter arrived, Campbell had just returned from a half-year's
vacation in Europe with his new wife, the former Olive A. Dame of
Medford, Massachusetts, and he must have welcomed the opportunity which attendance at Richmond promised. Although he was no
longer connected with Piedmont College, mountain work was what
he knew, and almost all he knew; he had been a teacher and preacher
in Appalachia almost the whole of his professional life since his
graduation from Andover Theological Seminary in 1895.[5]

Three papers were presented at the conference session on
mountain work. These represented the three points of view which
may be said to have been current in mountain work at the beginning
of the century. First, Katherine R. Pettit of the Women's Christian
Temperance Union Settlement at Hindman, Kentucky, spoke of the
needs of the mountaineers, "50,000 people living and conversing
after the manner of three centuries ago," and stressed the opportunities for individuals which the settlement schools had opened up.
Then Philander P. Claxton, at the time the Professor of Secondary
Education at the University of Tennessee, emphasized the benefits
which could be obtained from a well-financed program of agricultural and industrial education in Appalachia. An annual investment
of $40,000 for fifteen years, Claxton claimed, would yield a return of

$50,000,000 annually "from the great natural resources of this region, now untouched." Last, Reverend Bruce R. Payne, at the time the Professor of Secondary Education at the University of Virginia, spoke of the need for interagency cooperation in mountain benevolence, for the professionalization of social work in Appalachia as elsewhere, and for an approach to the mountain problem which took account of the real conditions in the region rather than one based on the assumptions of benevolent workers as to what was probably wanted.[6]

Payne's paper, "Waste in Mountain Settlement Work," was a temperate and systematic examination of "three distinct defects" in mountain benevolence which, he said, amounted to "wasted energy." First was a "lack of cooperation among workers, resulting from denominational differences and difficulty of communications in the mountains." As a remedy, Payne suggested that periodic conferences of southern mountain workers might coordinate efforts among individuals and agencies working in the field and might also publicize mountain work in the larger benevolent community. Second, was a "lack of correlation" of private and denominational effort, especially in education, with the work of the permanent, state agencies. As a remedy, Payne suggested that some person or persons perform as an intermediary between the missionaries and the state officials. Third was a noticeable lack of expert study of the entire complex of social, industrial, educational, and religious problems to be found among the mountain people in their isolated communities, and a lack of knowledge of the resources available to deal with them. Payne suggested that the universities undertake systematic investigations of the needs of Appalachia and that the settlements themselves designate persons to carry out appropriate surveys of their respective fields of activity. "The trained expert could free this entire question from a sort of sickly sentimentality which too often does the cause more harm than good."[7]

Payne offered his comments and suggestions with hesitation, he said, perhaps because the solutions he offered were obvious. And so they were. Indeed, if the National Conference of Charities and Correction had any single work it wished to accomplish at the beginning of the twentieth century, it was to publicize the need for conferences, for coordination of effort among agencies and between voluntary societies and state agencies, and for surveys of the needs and opportunities for benevolence, in order to make social service scientific and systematic. There was a gap between the intentions of the conference and the intensely separatist commitments of the majority of its members, however, as Payne must have known but soon found out in any case. During the discussion which followed his presentation, most commentators chose to ignore his remarks, and instead to defend the legitimacy of the work of their own agencies, or to assert the more romantic view of the quaintness of the "special needs of rural people" which other speakers at the session had emphasized.

John Campbell was not one whose comments were printed in the published *Proceedings* of the conference, nor was he unenthusiastic about what Payne had said. After the session he approached Mrs. Glenn and indicated that he not only agreed with Payne's analysis of the conditions that prevailed in mountain settlement work but had himself long seen the desirability of just such a systematic survey of the needs of Appalachia and the facilities to meet these needs as Payne had advocated. Since he was currently at liberty, moreover, Campbell said that he would be most interested in conducting such a survey if appropriate funding might be obtained. "It was my purpose, had I been able to carry out the plan myself," he wrote subsequently, "to prepare maps, routes, and gather data during the summer, perhaps to spend a few weeks at the Amherst Agricultural Summer School where they are making a very wise beginning in the study of rural conditions."

With this preliminary work done, I had intended to start in with a conveyance in the mountains of Virginia and work southward visiting schools, and during the brief winter rainy season to settle down in some center such as Asheville, in whose environs are many schools that can be easily reached. Then when spring opened, to continue the journey and during the early summer to visit the Conferences and religious gatherings that are held. . . . It is perhaps needless for me to say that Mrs. Campbell and I would welcome the opportunity of doing this work which we had planned to do ourselves, but which our financial situation forbids at present. We should be glad to do it without any remuneration except the expenses which, as I have indicated, ought not to exceed $2500.[8]

It is not at all clear whether Campbell knew in advance of the session what Payne would say, or that Mary Glenn, who was the wife of the director of the recently established Russell Sage Foundation, would welcome a proposal from someone like Campbell to conduct a survey of mountain conditions under the aegis of the foundation. Campbell surely knew that attendance at the conference would offer him an opportunity to speak with the Glenns, who had long been active in the work of the conference and prominent in social work circles. Whether he went to Richmond merely out of interest and curiosity, or with some hope that an opportunity for employment would present itself, however, is uncertain. In any case, after conversation with Mrs. Glenn immediately following the session, and subsequent conversation with John Glenn as well, it appears, Campbell was invited to submit a formal proposal for consideration by the Trustees of the Russell Sage Foundation.[9]

To a striking degree, Campbell's proposal followed the lines laid down in Payne's address, although in general he tended to take the larger view of what might be accomplished through the intercession of the Russell Sage Foundation into the chaotic field of mountain benevolence. He noted, for example, that "a careful, independent study might result in some plan of cooperation whereby good work already under way might be made more effective, other work begun, and work which is already established, but ineffective, be corrected or allied with other work if there should prove to be any overlapping of effort." He implied that the principal obstacles to increased communication among workers in the mountain field—"the salaries of the workers are so low as not to warrant . . . a conference at the expense of the individual" and the secretaries of denominational boards "are so burdened with duties of administration and money raising that visits to the field are cursory and infrequent"—might be overcome through foundation support for periodic conferences and by the appointment of someone like himself as a "friendly visitor" to the several agencies at work in the mountain field. He pointed out that surveys conducted by denominational boards or other agencies directly interested in mountain work might be suspect as being "colored unconsciously by the denominational preferences of those giving information" and that in any case "the pressing need for money to carry on such work . . . leads to emphasis upon the abnormal picturesque and pathetic phases of mountain life."[10]

Campbell's proposal was transmitted to the trustees of the Russell Sage Foundation by John Glenn on 25 May 1908. Soon thereafter, the board's executive committee made an appropriation to meet the expenses of a survey of the type Campbell had indicated. This appropriation was continued annually until October 1912, when the usefulness of Campbell's work in Appalachia was acknowledged and his relationship with the foundation regularized through the establishment of a Southern Highland Division of the foundation, with Campbell as secretary. In March 1913, headquarters were established at Asheville.[11]

From 1912 until his death in 1919, John C. Campbell and the Southern Highland Division of the Russell Sage Foundation were one and the same. He was himself the central repository of data concerning conditions in the mountains to which workers in the field might turn. He was the disinterested outsider, sympathetic to the needs of the mountaineers and familiar with the personnel and programs of the several benevolent agencies active in the region, who could facilitate the cooperation of diverse organizations to improve the quality of mountain life. He was the impartial observer who might judge with impunity the appropriateness of particular solutions proposed for dealing with the problems of the mountaineers, and who might aid workers to reconcile traditional habits of mind and work with the new ideas and new techniques which were transforming American philanthropy during the early twentieth century. The foundation provided support and encouragement, but it was the force of Campbell's personality which made the operations of the division successful, and when he died it simply ceased to be.[12]

Throughout its existence, the Southern Highland Division functioned to meet the needs of benevolent work in Appalachia as outlined by Payne and then by Campbell in 1908, for increased communication, increased cooperation, and increased information. To these three, however, Campbell added a fourth: the redirection of mountain work away from the programs of Americanization characteristic of the efforts of the denominational home-mission boards and toward new approaches which looked to the creation of a viable mountain culture and the redefinition of Appalachia as an alternative version of, rather than as the opposite of America. The Southern Highland Division of the Russell Sage Foundation thereby became the principal agency through which the implications of Appalachian regionalism were worked out, even as it represented by the mere fact of its existence an acknowledgment that the southern mountains composed a special field of benevolent work, and hence stood as a symbol of the legitimacy of Appalachian otherness. [13]

As part of his effort at fostering a spirit of cooperation among competing agencies at work in the southern mountains, and in an attempt to institutionalize the beneficial experience of face-to-face relationships among workers in a common field, otherwise possible only by the accident of mutual attendance at a professional meeting, in 1913 Campbell helped organize what was to become the Conference of Southern Mountain Workers and, after 1944, the Council of Southern Mountain Workers. Meeting for the first time in Atlanta, Georgia, at the invitation of the Home Mission Board of the Southern Baptist church and the Executive Committee of Home Missions of the Southern Presbyterian church, the first annual conference was attended by only thirty-six persons. "The handful of men and women who answered the call—full of curiosity, and full of enthusiasm over their own particular projects—met as strangers," Mrs. Campbell later remembered. "The field and activities of each of us [were] largely unknown to the other." [14]

This first session brought together representatives of the home-mission boards of the Southern Baptist and Southern Presbyterian churches with persons from the Board of Home Missions and the Department of Church and Country Life of the Northern Presbyterian church, from the American Missionary Association, the Christian church, the Methodist Episcopal church, South, and the Protestant Episcopal church. Almost as a matter of course, Campbell was elected chairman of the conference. His status as a disinterested but passionately involved outsider was thereby acknowledged, and he thereby gained the crucial place of *primus inter pares* in the southern mountain-work community, which greatly facilitated the task he had set for himself as secretary of the Southern Highland Division.

As chairman of the conference, Campbell obtained a personal status in mountain benevolence independent of (although of course not unrelated to) his position as secretary of the Southern Highland Division.[15] Even more important, perhaps, he was put in a position from which he might legitimately make contact with persons active in mountain work without arousing suspicion of wishing to interfere with or infringe on their separate spheres of influence, and in which he might in turn be contacted by such persons without suspicion that they were giving way before pressure from a "foreign" agency.[16] Although Campbell often protested his desire to turn the leadership of the conference over to another lest his own influence become, or be seen as becoming too great, his special position among southern mountain workers and his special abilities made him a logical choice for the position, and he was regularly reelected chairman until his death. He himself acknowledged the crucial role he played in the success of the conference as early as 1914, moreover. "It is claimed by some that the conference has been successful so far largely because a representative of a nondenominational and disinterested organization . . . had guided affairs. Whether it will live when put into denominational hands remains to be seen."[17]

Throughout the period of Campbell's chairmanship, the meetings of the Conference of Southern Mountain Workers provided opportunities for persons active in mountain benevolence to share their experiences and to develop those personal relationships upon which interagency cooperation might be built. The second meeting of the conference, at Knoxville (the site of subsequent meetings) on 22 and 23 April, 1914, was attended by 102 delegates and guests, representing eleven denominations and sixty-four agencies or institutions. By 1917, the registered delegates numbered 150 and represented thirteen denominations and more than two hundred agencies or institutions.[18] Merely as a place for meeting and talking, the conference thus served an important need which Payne and Campbell had identified in 1908, and which persons active in the field must have felt most keenly, for prior to 1913 benevolent workers in Appalachia had been as isolated from each other as were the mountain people whom they sought to serve. In addition, however, the conference served as a major vehicle for the transformation of mountain benevolence from its earlier emphasis on missionary teaching and preaching to the new concerns with the creation of a viable Appalachian community which became dominant during the middle teens.

The inevitable observation by persons attending the conference and participating in its discussions, of the chaos which prevailed both in the theory and in the practice of mountain benevolence, must be credited with preparing the way for such transformations. As early as the third meeting, in 1915, the members were willing to acknowledge the existence of such confusion and to begin using the conference as a vehicle for the creation of order. After discussion of the "needed adaptations of education to environment," of "the relation of the church and independent schools of the mountains to the public schools of the mountains," and of the newly recognized need for sanitary education in the mountains, the delegates voted to "issue some publication setting forth the needs of the mountain country, and the qualifications desired in persons doing work in the mountains."[19]

As a first public effort to rationalize the state of mountain benevolence by the benevolent community itself, the preparation of this "publication" has considerable importance, but only as a gesture. The "publication" itself—*The Southern Highlands: Extracts from Letters Received from [Persons] . . . Conducting Work in the Southern Mountains* (1915)—pointed to the persisting obstacles to any such rationalization created by the widely differing notions of mountain needs and of remedies for mountain needs that prevailed among those active in mountain work. Indeed, John Campbell, who as chairman of the conference served also as editor of the volume, could do little more than compile a collection of the various views expressed by his ninety-four informants. Although his introductory remarks represent this course as appropriate to the reality of diversity within Appalachia itself, Campbell's own sense of despair is apparent. It had been the desire of the conference, "if possible, to set forth a composite view" of mountain needs, Campbell wrote, but "in the endeavor to reduce the many views to a composite, so much of the keen insight of the various contributors was obscured, and so much of the force of expression and suggestion through juxtaposition of ideas was lost, that it seemed wise . . . to publish extracts."[20]

That the conference as an entity could not reach consensus would have been no surprise to Campbell and his colleagues on the executive committee, although this fact may well have served their individual needs by convincing the agencies which sponsored their work of the importance of efforts to rationalize, professionalize, and especially to modernize mountain benevolence. After 1915 in any case, Campbell, Harlan Paul Douglass of the American Missionary Association, Frost of Berea, May Stone of the Hindman Settlement School, and others affiliated with the inner circle of the conference appear to have increased their personal efforts to use the conference as a vehicle for propagating modern ideas of social service: the need for rural-life education in Appalachia, the appropriateness of crafts rather than industrial training for children in the nonindustrialized mountain region, and the availability of the Danish folk school as a model on which to build social service and educational centers in the mountains. In the context of the debate over child labor in southern cotton mills, moreover, as Campbell and others searched for an alternative vision of Appalachia which would suggest not only the legitimacy of Appalachian otherness as a historical fact, but the viability of Appalachia's existence as a discrete region of the nation in the present, a new theme appeared. Beginning in 1915, the conference began to hear the mountaineers described as a separate people, a "folk," and mountain life described as a "folk culture."

In 1917, for example, the Campbells brought the great British folk-song collector, Cecil J. Sharp, to Knoxville, where he sang traditional songs and argued for the legitimacy of the folk culture of Appalachia and "the supreme cultural value of an inherited tradition, even when unenforced by any formal school education."[21] Sharp's words must have seemed quite outrageous to the hundred or more workers in attendance at this meeting, whose very livelihood depended on a vision of mountain life as an undesirable departure from the patterns of culture which prevailed elsewhere in the nation, and whose mission to the mountains assumed the desirability of making Appalachia more like America. His assertions of the essential Englishness of the peculiar culture of Appalachia must also have been enticing, however, as additional justification for their work among the allegedly "degenerate" mountain people. "I saw at once that the audience were thoroughly interested in hearing an outsider's view of the people amongst whom they lived and that there was no need therefore to be any more reticent than usual. And it was clear I think that they liked it," Sharp reported.[22]

The establishment of the Southern Highland Division of the Russell Sage Foundation and the Knoxville Conference of Southern Mountain Workers in order to foster communication among workers in the mountain field, encourage cooperation, and facilitate the coordination of benevolent work in Appalachia, had parallels in the establishment of analogous divisions within the several protestant churches active in the region. Designed to coordinate efforts previously carried on by a variety of denominational boards and societies and to eliminate competing efforts at the state level or in synods or other subdivisions of states, such organizations must also be seen as acknowledgments of the regional character of Appalachia and the special needs of the mountaineers. In almost all of these Campbell's presence was felt.

In 1912, for example, Campbell was called upon to advise the Committee on Mountain Work of the Southern Presbyterian Board of Home Missions concerning the reorganization of its educational work in Appalachia. At his suggestion, a plan for centralized administration of all that denomination's mountain schools, plus the thirteen schools of the Soul Winners Society, an independent organization led by a Southern Presbyterian layman, Edward O. Guerrant of Wilmore, Kentucky, was developed. Despite considerable resistance from the more conservative spokesmen for synodical independence, by 1913 a superintendent for mountain schools had been appointed and given nominal control over Southern Presbyterian school work.[23]

Out of this 1912 consultation came three other regionally based patterns of organization. At Campbell's immediate suggestion, the Southern Presbyterian Board of Home Missions took the lead in calling for an interdenominational conference of southern mountain workers, which became the annual Knoxville conference already discussed. Second, the centralization of Southern Presbyterian school work in the mountains led inevitably to a plan for the consolidation of that denomination's collegiate work in the region. Third, the experience of successful intersynodical cooperation in school work within the denomination, and the legitimation of regional thinking provided by the establishment of the Conference of Southern Mountain Workers, provided the impetus to the establishment of a Synod of Appalachia within the Southern Presbyterian church in 1914—the first formal acknowledgment that Appalachia formed a natural unit of organization comparable to the traditional if artificial units of the states by which synodical organization had previously taken place.[24]

In some ways, Campbell's support and encouragement of such denominationally-based organizations ran counter to his growing conviction of the need for federation in southern mountain work through the establishment of interdenominational agencies, and indeed to his personal predilection for federation in church work more generally. As he well knew, however, the successful conduct of mountain benevolence depended on the establishment of Appalachia as a separate field of work through the creation of appropriate denominational institutions as a first step, while the political realities of denominational (and nondenominational interagency) conflict stood in the way of any gesture on his part in support of federalism. In 1914, for example, he wrote to John Glenn explaining that he had refused an invitation from Gifford Pinchot to serve on the Committee on Church and Country Life of the Federal Council of Churches in order to avoid alienating Baptist and Southern Presbyterian workers in Appalachia. "In order to bring the Baptists and some of the Southern Presbyterians in [to the Conference of Southern Mountain Workers]," he explained, "the leaders in organizing the . . . Conference gave assurance that the Conference was for purposes of conference only, and that there were no plans contemplated for federation, union, or anything of the sort. . . . My feeling is that I would be more serviceable in the mountain field to the Federal Council by maintaining my present attitude, and that I might risk success in my field by official connection with the Committee [on Church and Country Life]."[25]

At the same time, however, where he could, Campbell worked to break down tendencies toward denominational separatism. At his instance, for example, persons connected with the so-called "independent" schools and with several of the state departments of agriculture were invited to attend the annual Maryville Conference of Southern Mountain Workers connected with the Women's Board of Home Missions of the northern Presbyterian church, beginning in 1914.[26] Also in that year, Campbell worked with a Reverend McMillan, secretary of field work, literature and publication of the Southern Presbyterian Executive Committee of Home Missions, on plans for the establishment of the Ellen Axson Wilson Memorial Fund to honor the late wife of President Wilson. This was to be administered by the women of the Southern Presbyterian church but used to support educational work in Appalachia without reference to denominational affiliation.[27] In October 1914, Campbell attended the annual meetings of the northern Presbyterian Synod of Tennessee, at Lebanon, Tennessee, and of the Southern Presbyterian Synod of West Virginia, at Lewisburg, West Virginia, where he urged interdenominational cooperation in mountain work, and hinted at the possibility of union between these two mountain synods. "One of the most promising things I noticed at both Synod meetings," Campbell reported to Glenn, "was a very evident desire on the part of these two branches of Presbyterianism to get together."[28]

As an information-gathering agency the Southern Highland Division was perhaps less effective than in other areas of activity, but there were good reasons for this. After 1912 at least, Campbell was kept continually busy with his efforts at fostering communication and cooperation among agencies working in the mountains. This involved considerable travel on his part, he explained, and required him to spend much of his office time in Asheville meeting with visitors, attending to correspondence, and answering the numerous requests for assistance or information addressed to him personally, to the Southern Highland Division, or through him to the Russell Sage Foundation. With a staff of one secretary, much of the routine work of the division necessarily rested on his shoulders even had his personal predeliction for handling things himself not impelled him to continue caring for details.[29] After 1913, moreover, as we have seen, he became increasingly involved in the campaign for child labor legislation, and after 1917 in war work. These new but not unrelated concerns drew his attention away from the more mundane tasks of collecting data about the mountains and the mountaineers of Appalachia. In addition, the state of knowledge about the real conditions in the mountain country presented a major obstacle to his efficacy in information gathering, while the diversity of those conditions created problems for the organization of such information once gathered.[30]

Prior to the inauguration of Campbell's personal survey of mountain conditions and mountain needs, begun in 1908, only one systematic study of Appalachia had been attempted, by Charles W. Dabney for the Southern Education Board. Published in 1902 as the first number of the new *Southern Education Board Bulletin*, "Educational Conditions in the Southern Appalachians" identified two problems to be solved: "how shall this beautiful country be opened up and made accessible to the modern civilization?" and how could adult illiteracy, estimated at close to 50 percent, be reduced?[31] Schools and roads were Dabney's answer. Schools were to teach practical subjects of use to the mountain people in their rural life. Roads were to make possible school consolidation and hence a broader economic base for the public schools, now organized on a county and district basis. Answers were easy, however. Dabney's purpose was to demonstrate need, and this he sought to do through an examination of educational conditions in seven "representative" counties, Claiborne, Sevier, Hawkins, and Greene in Tennessee, and Yancey, Madison, and Buncombe in North Carolina.

In 1902 and in the context of the emergent school campaign sponsored by the Southern Education Board and later the General

Education Board, demonstration of need was a first priority. By 1908, the existence of need was well enough known so that an assessment of its real extent, and of the agencies available for meeting it, seemed desirable. By 1908, however, there was no agency in a position to engage in such an assessment and no agency interested in doing this work. The Southern Education Board and the General Education Board had come to utilize the states as the basic units to be studied, just as they had come to direct their efforts at convincing the voters and legislators in the several states of the need for compulsory school laws and state support for education in "pauper" counties. The United States Bureau of Education used the states as units for its annual survey of educational conditions in the United States also, but while statistics concerning denominational as well as public schools were published in the reports of its secretary, information concerning the work of the "independent" schools was not provided. It was never Campbell's intention to remedy this situation single-handedly. His survey was to make a beginning, however, as it in fact did, and the work of the Southern Highland Division after 1912 looked increasingly to the collection of such statistical data as was available, to the preparation of lists of educational and social service agencies at work in Appalachia, and to an assessment of the nature and extent of the work being done.

It is not clear whether Campbell or the Russell Sage Foundation's trustees recognized at the outset the degree to which Campbell's survey of mountain conditions would involve him directly in the reorganization of mountain benevolence, or anticipated the role which he, and through him the foundation, would eventually come to play in the development of the mountain field. What is certain is that neither Campbell nor the trustees viewed the Appalachian survey as meeting the standards of precision and comprehensiveness currently being set by Margaret Byington and her coworkers on the Pittsburgh Survey, another 1908 project of the foundation.[32] Indeed, the Campbell survey was to be purposefully unscientific and impressionistic, and it was for this reason that Campbell stressed the choice of investigator as a critical decision. It should be someone who was impartial, that is not connected with any agency currently at work in the mountains, but it had to be someone with an "appreciative sympathy for the mountaineer and his environment," Campbell explained: "A sympathy deep enough to view the mountaineer as a man . . . and not simply as a picturesque type for journalistic exploitation. . . . A sympathy wide enough to comprehend what is fundamental in the religious and educational efforts put forth by the various boards. . . . A sympathy thoughtful enough to understand the necessity of allying all educational effort with the efforts furthered by the state."[33]

In his formal proposal to the Russell Sage Foundation, Campbell expressed the same feelings. He did plan "to interview the various county school commissioners of the mountain section . . . to learn from the teachers themselves what they are doing . . . to visit the superintendents of secondary education in the mountain states." But he wished "to avoid appearing in the light of [an] investigator" as he journeyed through the mountain country. To this end, he planned to carry a stereopticon and give lectures, to do some preaching, and to take photographs, lest the sensitive mountaineers exclude him from their homes and from their religious meetings.[34] Given the paucity of reliable information about conditions in the southern mountain region when Campbell began,[35] a "scientific" social survey could have been inappropriate in any case. Campbell's immediate task was to do the kind of preliminary work in the social taxonomy of Appalachia without which no proper social survey could be made. He had to identify the field, define the units in terms of which it might most effectively be examined, and articulate the questions which needed to be answered. In practical terms, what this meant was that Campbell spent the time between the summer of 1908 and the autumn of 1912 familiarizing himself with the mountain region, with the state of benevolent work in Appalachia, and with the personnel associated with the agencies doing this work, so that when the Southern Highland Division was finally established as a formal entity he was in a position to collect and analyze more conventional forms of statistical data concerning the region and its people.

In the end, however, Campbell's informal surveying of 1908–12 yielded only a more intense and personal sense of what he already knew when he began: that an unfortunate situation of interagency competition existed in Appalachia, that mountain workers were isolated from each other, that little coordination between the work of state and of the denominational or private agencies had been attempted, that contemporary views of the mountaineer as a picturesque subject for exploitation in fiction or as a feudist desperado in journalism stood in the way of the design of constructive programs of benevolent work. After a first year of travel in the mountains, he also knew that the whole thrust of mountain benevolence was faced in the wrong direction. Instead of seeking to prepare mountaineers for life in an urbanized, industrialized "modern" civilization, the efforts of benevolent agencies in Appalachia should be directed at improving the conditions of mountain life on its own terms.

The life that the mountaineer must live is a rural life, and his education should be adapted to meet the needs of that rural life. A number will always seek the larger centers, but our rural schools in the mountains and elsewhere must teach the youth to develop the resources of their own environment, and to find within that environment the proper responses to legitimate needs and desires.[36]

Until a beginning was made in dealing with the problems which everyone could identify—problems within the benevolence establishment but which stood in the way of effective work in the mountains—additional hard information was gratuitous. Though it might be of use to publicists in their efforts to promote the need for mountain work, it could be of little use to practitioners in, or theorists about the field itself. Nonetheless Campbell, who was himself just such a publicist in practice, began in 1912 to collect the hard data—population statistics from the thirteenth census of 1910, statistics of denominational affiliation from the United States Religious Census of 1906 and later of 1916, statistics of public education from the state superintendents of education, and statistics of private school education from schedules sent out by the Southern Highland Division to the church and independent schools in 1914.[37] These he arranged by county and by state, and also by the regional belts within the mountain region which he identified as the critical social and cultural units of Appalachia: the Blue Ridge Belt, the Greater Appalachian Valley, and the Allegheny-Cumberland Belt.[38]

After 1912–13, Campbell made this statistical data available to workers in the field and indeed, seems to have been under some pressure both from the benevolent community and from the foundation to make the Southern Highland Division into a resource center providing "hard" data concerning Appalachia. This may well have created some tension for Campbell, who preferred to be himself the impartial but intensely involved source of information and advice both. At best, he said, statistics could tell only "partial truths," but he was especially wary of statistics concerning the mountains. Not only did geography and politics combine to create obstacles for the collection of accurate data by state or federal officials, not only was the data provided by the denominational and private agencies concerning the special fields in which they worked by its nature unreliable, but also "conditions have changed so rapidly in certain sections of the mountains as to make it impossible to keep any data properly checked."[39] Campbell refused to be "merely an investigator," moreover, but insisted on being, and on being regarded as a coworker in the mountain field. As an active worker for the improvement of conditions in the mountains, however, he had little time and less patience for information gathering for its own sake, while his keen political sense told him that his role as investigator would be as unacceptable to his coworkers in mountain benevolence as it would be to the mountain people themselves. In addition, the publication of data unflattering to any agency, public or private, would be counterproductive of the ends he sought to achieve.

Although at least from 1914 Campbell had statistical information concerning social, economic, and educational conditions in Appalachia worked up in tabular form for his own use, and although he was often urged to make this data available in published form, in fact none of it appeared during his lifetime.[40] While Campbell was regularly willing to provide information concerning the southern mountains to officials of agencies working in the region, moreover, he sought to preserve a lower profile for himself. In 1917, for example, he rejected a proposal from Commissioner of Education P. P. Claxton that Campbell assume responsibility for the collection of data concerning public education in Appalachia, and he countered a proposal from James Watt Raine that Campbell write an essay on the mountains for a mission-study text to be issued by the Young Men's Christian Association with the suggestion that a symposium of the views of others would be more appropriate.[41] Although by this date he was hard at work on his own study of the southern mountains, posthumously published as *The Southern Highlander and His Homeland* (1921),[42] the priority he must have accorded his own effort does not explain this hesitance to participate in the projects of others or to publish his data. Both personally, and as the representative of the Russell Sage Foundation, Campbell preferred not to stand up in public as that single authority on mountain life whose views were, by the very fact of his status, the ones to be challenged. He believed that his views were correct, that his prescription for the ills of Appalachia was the only one which would cure, and he did not wish to jeopardize the future of his patient by involving himself in personal and political controversy.[43]

As a result of Campbell's reluctance to publish his statistical data on mountain conditions, the first "objective" study of Appalachia to appear was Norman Frost's "A Statistical Study of the Public Schools of the Southern Appalachian Mountains," in the preparation of which Campbell participated, however. Issued as a *Bulletin* of the U.S. Bureau of Education in 1915, Frost's study followed the scheme of the Southern Education Board survey of 1902, in its exclusive focus on education and in its utilization of school statistics provided by the state superintendents of education and population statistics derived from the most recent federal census (1910), supplemented by personal observation of the educational and social conditions in six "representative" counties.

Begun in 1912, as much at his own instance or on the suggestion of his father, the president of Berea College, as at the urging of Claxton and the Bureau of Education, it appears, Frost's study seems to stand as a manifestation of the desire of Berea to maintain its credibility in the new age of professionalized and scientific mountain benevolence. Its real origins are uncertain, and it connects well both with the contemporary vogue for survey research and with the more immediate encouragement to systematic study of mountain conditions provided by the presence of the Russell Sage Foundation in Appalachia after 1912. The fact that no one at Berea sought to develop existing statistical data on Appalachia or even on mountain education prior to the institutionalization of the Campbell survey as the Southern Highland Division in 1912 suggests a political motive to the preparation of this Berea-based survey. Hints of strained relations between Frost and Campbell in the Campbell correspondence support this interpretation.

That conflict between Frost and Campbell should have developed by 1912 was almost inevitable. Frost, according to Campbell, ran Berea as his own province, and must have viewed Appalachia—which he had virtually invented and the interests of which he had served with distinction and success since 1893—in a similarly protective manner. Campbell, on the other hand, was his Johnny-come-lately competitor as public spokesman for the interest of the mountaineers, the failed president of an unpretentious denominational school pretending to be a college, who continued to serve in the mountain field at all only through the grace of a "foreign" foundation. Quite apart from any personal antipathy between the two men, but necessarily reinforcing it, was the fact that the agencies with which they were connected were in direct competition, both as institutional mechanisms for the conduct of mountain work and as representatives of alternative and contradictory views of the techniques of benevolence best suited to serve the needs of the mountain people.[44] After Campbell had organized the Conference of Southern Mountain Workers in 1913, conflict between the two men became more overt, although still expressed subtly within the context of the new organization, in the activities of which they both participated. It is surely no accident, however, that it was only at the time of Frost's resignation as president of Berea College in 1921, and not immediately after Campbell's death in 1919, that headquarters of the Knoxville Conference was moved to the place it perhaps had belonged at the outset, to Berea, Kentucky.

Whether or not Campbell saw the preparation of Norman Frost's survey of educational conditions in Appalachia as an infringement upon his own and exclusive area of activity, the occasion of its preparation appears to have been the origin of some of the difficulty between Campbell and the elder Frost. Norman Frost's study was carried out late in 1912, and was apparently submitted to the Bureau of Education for publication immediately upon its completion. In 1913 and again in 1914, Commissioner of Education Claxton asked Campbell to provide additional data concerning the state of public education in Appalachia supplementary to or corrective of the information provided by Frost. This, and Claxton's insistence that Frost submit his tables to the state superintendents of education for verification, may account for the long delay in publication of the study, although Campbell may have played a more direct role in the postponement of its appearance immediately in 1913. So far as Campbell was concerned, Frost's entire study was flawed, since it exempted from any consideration the valley counties which were characterized as much as the mountain counties by that isolation with the consequences of which Frost was directly concerned.[45] It is in this context, indeed, of Campbell's stated objections to the Frost study, that Claxton's prefatory defense of its publication makes sense. "Mr. Frost did not attempt to make this study exhaustive," Claxton admitted, but as "the most exhaustive study of education in this section yet undertaken" it was deserving of publication nonetheless.[46]

The significance of the Frost study lies not in its conclusions, which were identical with those of the Southern Education Board survey of 1902 and consistent with the observations of all who had experience with education in Appalachia—that more money, more schools, more and better-trained teachers were needed—but in its status as first attempt at coherent treatment of the southern mountain region as a region, in the statistical mode of "scientific" and "objective" social survey work. It was also the first of a series of such studies sponsored by the Bureau of Education. In 1915 and 1916, Claxton employed C. G. Burkitt, formerly field secretary of the Southern Industrial Education Association, to conduct a survey of educational conditions in the mountain counties of Virginia, West Virginia, North Carolina, Tennessee, South Carolina, Georgia, and Alabama—excepting Kentucky perhaps out of deference to Berea's claim to dominate that field—which was finally completed (but not published) in

1917.[47] At that point Claxton turned to Campbell with a request that he take charge of a continuing survey of educational conditions in Appalachia for the bureau.

Campbell respectfully declined, for reasons already noted. Information gathering for its own sake never interested him, and by 1917 he had conceived of a project which would use social and educational surveying for explicitly political purposes. "I should be very glad to do what I can to help out in the work of his Bureau," Campbell wrote to John Glenn concerning this request, "if I can do so at such a time as not to conflict with other and more important things." But this was not the time. "I do not know whether [Claxton] suspects the Conference [of Southern Mountain Workers] has voted to make its own survey of the field and wants to get it under his department. . . . I should not want to risk losing the salutary effect upon all denominational boards of their working together in a survey of the mountain field."[48] As things turned out, however, Campbell might just as well have worked with the Bureau of Education, for the conference's survey, authorized at its fourth meeting in 1916, appears never to have been begun and the "salutary effects upon all denominational boards of their working together" were never achieved—perhaps because the denominations were still unwilling to collaborate when any risk to their independence, however small, was implied.[49]

By the end of 1917 in any case, a change had come over Campbell as it had come over America. From this time his own efforts, like those of many of his colleagues in mountain work, turned increasingly toward the search for a personal role of usefulness in the great war which America had joined. In December, Campbell's secretary and assistant for many years, the incomparable Miss Dickey, went to Washington to serve the cause as a stenographer,[50] but Campbell himself lacked skills of equal value to the war effort. He tried to do his part by attempting to explain the war to the mountain people, whose proud heritage of independence now seemed not only a disability (in the context of the highly socialized life of modern America), but an unforgivable rejection of the nation's plea for assistance in its hour of need and a sign of ingratitude for the efforts made on their behalf by the agencies of national philanthropy. At the same time, Campbell continued to advocate cooperation among benevolent agencies working in the mountains, and to express the hope that the spirit of cooperation engendered by the experience of war-work would carry over into peace time and be translated into practical interagency collaboration.[51] After 1918, however, all he could do was write letters, outlining his plans. In growing personal uneasiness concerning his place in mountain work, and of mountain work in the larger scheme of things which the war represented, Campbell finally turned the Asheville offices he had used for the Southern Highland Division over to Rutherford B. Hayes, Jr., fuel administrator for western North Carolina, and himself retreated from the mountains to the emotional safety of Nantucket.[52] By the end of 1919 he was dead. So was the first phase in the history of America's discovery of Appalachia. After the war, a new period would begin, built largely upon the base which Campbell had helped to erect.

9. Creating Community and Culture in Appalachia: Folk Schools and the Crafts Revival

It was not a new idea in 1915 to talk about the mountaineers as a people or to identify Appalachia as a discrete region of the nation. During the middle teens, however, a subtle shift occurred in the focus of mountain benevolence which gave these conventional generalizations new meanings. As less emphasis came to be placed on the establishment of community among the mountaineers in their local neighborhoods and more emphasis came to be placed on the establishment of community among the mountaineers as a group, in *their* neighborhood, the southern mountain region, Appalachia came increasingly to be seen as a thing in itself and the mountain people as a distinct group in the American population.

To this shift a number of tendencies contributed. The practical experience of benevolent workers with the real consequences of the mountaineers' isolation from each other, for example, when combined with those new questions about the habitabilty of Appalachia itself, suggested that the achievement of local community in the mountains might be less easy than in the more densely populated cities of the nation. At the same time, practical discouragement with the results of ad hoc programs of education and uplift, when combined with the need to defend the legitimacy of mountain work against the challenges of the cotton-mill propagandists, suggested the appropriateness of a shift in emphasis away from discussion of specific programs which might not, or could not work. A more general stance was needed, which would preserve mountain work against charges that it did not bear results but yet could offer an alternative to removal of the mountaineers to the mill towns of the New South. As the isolation of school and settlement workers from

[213]

their own colleagues was broken down by the emergence of new institutions of regional cooperation, moreover, the rhetoric of mountain benevolence itself necessarily changed. The traditional emphasis of the previous decade, on the need to establish community among the mountaineers in their several neighborhoods, was the rhetoric of interagency competition. The new emphasis of the middle teens, on the importance of serving the region as a whole by establishing a viable Appalachian culture, was phrased in the rhetoric of interagency collaboration.

The very existence of the new agencies of regional cooperation, by institutionalizing the mountain field as a unified field of benevolence, thus reinforced existing tendencies to view Appalachia as a whole. This in itself suggested that the unit of benevolent work ought to be the region rather than local areas within the region, and that the focus of the work ought to be on the creation of a viable mountain life rather than on the melioration of particular conditions or the solution of particular problems. Particular problems were to be confronted, of course, but only in the larger context of improving the conditions of mountain life more generally. The new agencies of regional cooperation provided the institutional mechanisms by which such efforts might be coordinated, even as by the fact of their existence they suggested that work on this larger, regional scale should be attempted. In the process, that fleeting possibility which the professionalization of benevolent work in Appalachia had offered, that a more realistic view of the mountains might be taken and the myth of a coherent culture among an homogeneous population might be corrected, was eliminated. Appalachia remained a strange land inhabited by a peculiar people.

From the very beginning of mountain work in the 1880s, even those agencies with the most local or restricted clientele had claimed to be serving the needs of "the mountaineers" as a group. The changes which occurred in the middle teens lay not in what was said, but in what was meant. By the middle teens, even many of the denominational agencies at work in Appalachia had begun to think of the mountain region as a region, with needs peculiar to itself, and to consider their work in the context of a larger effort at social reconstruction throughout the mountains. As a result, assertions of the legitimacy of Appalachian otherness, which had functioned exclusively as a means of resolving the intellectual dilemma posed by the existence of the strange land and peculiar people and as a defense of mountain white work, now began to function as the basis for action in benevolence. To the degree that mountain life was seen as a legitimately distinct pattern of life rather than a deviation or degeneration from the patterns of normal American life, the work of the benevolent agencies now became the melioration of conditions in Appalachia in such a way as to preserve the essence of mountain life. What this meant was unclear, however, and how this was to be done remained a problem. The needs of the mountaineers had to be defined from the point of view of mountain life, rather than in terms of the desiderata and expectations of urban sophisticates. Even more important, a set of institutional goals and an institutional mechanism alternative to the mission or the traditional public school had to be developed, so that the improvement of mountain life might take place without doing violence to the character of Appalachian culture or the personality of the mountaineers.

Perhaps the easiest way to achieve these ends was the way advocated by the settlement movement since the early 1890s, to "help them to help themselves." The possibility of offering the aid of the friendly visitor and able neighbor depended on the existence of an Appalachian community which might receive such assistance, however, while it was the absence of community in Appalachia which had long been noted as among the most significant indices of Appalachian otherness. This dilemma, that the success of efforts to create a viable mountain community turned on the existence of community in Appalachia, was solved easily, and by the same means employed by settlement workers in the contemporary city. It was simply asserted that a "natural" community existed among their clientele, whether defined ethnically as a people or geographically as a neighborhood. It was this "natural" community which established their clients as a group and which explained the distance that separated them from their would-be benefactors. And it was this "natural" community which could benefit from the friendly advice of the agents of benevolence.

In this view, Appalachia was characterized not so much by the absence of community as by the absence of *realized* community. The work of benevolence then became one of bringing this preexistent community to the level of consciousness and hence of operation. In practical terms, this was to be achieved by establishing among the mountain people a sense of their own Appalachianness and of their participation in the distinct if not unique patterns of mountain culture. In its most prevalent form, it involved the special definition of the Appalachian community as a folk community, and the inauguration by the agents of benevolence of programs designed to instruct the mountain people in the usages of their own culture. Crafts, folksong, and folkdance, symptoms of the folk culture of Appalachia, when taught in the settlement schools, thus became means of creating community in the southern mountains.

At the heart of the concept of community lay the concept of culture—a set of habits, traditions, technologies, patterns of speech, customs, a mythology, a sense of shared experience, a history. Culture was the common possession of members of the community, by which they defined themselves to themselves as different from outsiders, and by which they might in turn themselves be defined by outsiders, including social scientists and settlement workers. The complaint of benevolent workers for more than a decade had been that the mountaineers lacked a sense of community because in their isolation from each other they did not share a common culture, or else that the culture of Appalachia was culture of anarchy, and hence not culture at all. The establishment of a viable mountain community thus turned on the possibility of discovering a common culture which the mountaineers had forgotten, or of identifying common elements which might serve as the basis for the creation of a culture for Appalachia. Then it would be a simple enough task to teach the mountain people their own (or merely some) culture appropriate to the conditions of mountain life. Upon this basis might community be created.

The search to discover this essential mountain culture of Appalachia, or the elements upon which an appropriate mountain culture might be created, was implicit rather than explicit in the literature on Appalachia during the early twentieth century. The very concept of culture was itself "new," of course, as was of necessity the relationship between culture—or folkways, mores, customs, habits—and community. During the early years of the century, moreover, those who might have begun their work in or on Appalachia with an attempt to define mountain culture as a way of discovering the essence of mountain life were involved in more practical tasks. Their first job had been to justify their interest in the southern mountain region as an object of study or the mountaineers as an object of benevolence.

Within even these practical concerns we may see developing the search for an Appalachian culture, which would manifest itself more clearly during the middle teens and achieve a kind of maturity during the 1920s. It was in these years, from about 1900 until America's involvement in World War I, that new interest developed in mountain speech, in mountain folklore and folksong, and in handicrafts as an element in mountain culture as well as a mode of economic activity. It was in this period that the collection of vital statistics, as an aspect of a new interest in the health of the mountaineers, and of educational statistics, laid the basis for the physiological and mental testing which would flourish in the 1920s and 1930s. This in turn would reinforce conceptions of the existence of an Appalachian community with the "scientific" evidence of an Appalachian physical type and an Appalachian personality type. And it was in this period that the adaptation of the Danish folk school to mountain conditions, designed originally as a solution to the problem of inadequate institutional models in rural education, came to be advocated as a way of training the mountain people in the usages of their own culture, and hence as a vehicle for the creation of a viable mountain community.

In this process, the outbreak of war in the summer of 1914, and America's participation in the war after 1917, played a crucial role. By drawing the energies of the benevolent community away from Appalachia, the war created a hiatus in the history of mountain work. But in so doing, it performed a sifting function, so that those agencies which resumed full activity in Appalachia after 1918 were those which characteristically accepted the legitimacy of Appalachian otherness and which had as their goal the improvement of mountain life and the creation of a viable Appalachian community. By providing the benevolent community with the experience of serving the practical needs of a people in time of crisis, moreover, the war experience made possible the escalation of services to the mountaineers during the nineteen twenties and thirties. The organization of the frontier nursing service, for example, or the establishment of that variety of cooperative economic activities, like the Southern Mountain Handicrafts Guild or the Brasstown Poultry Cooperative, which culminated in the rural electrification campaign of the 1930s, were products of the war experience. In Appalachia, as elsewhere in America after 1918, the cry was to build upon the practice of cooperation and the spirit of service characteristic of the war years.

Even more important, however, was the manner in which the very fact of the war altered the meaning of Appalachia for America, especially after 1917 when the mountaineers came to be seen as a crucial link between the United States and our British ally. Long defined as "our contemporary ancestors" for their backwardness, during the late teens and afterward the mountain people of Appalachia became instead the conservators of our common Anglo-Saxon heritage, preservers of the folk culture of Merrie Olde England and the individualism of the days of the pioneers. It was to safeguard this heritage that the war was being fought. In practice, it seemed, there were few better equipped to stand up for these native American values than the mountaineers themselves, who sent their sons to war, "acrost the big sea." And if they did not always quite know whether Paris was near Louisville or London, their sons did them proud. The apotheosis of Alvin York, the hero of the Argonne Forest, marked the final transformation of Appalachia into a symbol of America.

Among the most specific manifestations of the otherness of Appalachia noted in the work of the local-color writers was the "persistence" of customs, superstitions, and patterns of economic organization that stood in marked contrast to the more rational and more sophisticated patterns which prevailed elsewhere in the nation.

By the end of the nineteenth century, such evidence of the "folk" character of mountain civilization ceased having merely exemplary use in assertions of Appalachian otherness or as bits of local color in descriptions of mountain life, however, and came to seem interesting for their own sake. Although again a pattern of "discovery" seems to have taken place, what was discovered was not a new, hitherto unknown "reality," but the usefulness of particular aspects of reality when seen in a new context and from a new point of view.

Interest in mountain lore and in mountain crafts, and subsequently in mountain folksong, had its origin in the turn of the century recognition of aesthetic merit in "naif" work, and of the usefulness of the "material culture" of primitive or folk societies in understanding social process generally and social evolution in particular. These patterns originated separately, out of a philological tradition searching for the origin of modern literature in the oral tales and narrative song of the Anglo-Saxons at an earlier stage in their development, led particularly by George Lyman Kittridge of Harvard, and out of the attempt to use ethnographic and ethnologic data in the development of an evolutionary social science, led particularly by William I. Thomas of the University of Chicago.[1] By 1910, however, these two patterns of interest had come together as a result of the intermingling of the philological and the social-evolutionary modes, in the context especially of a search for new ways of defining American culture. By this date also, a practical market had emerged for the tangible products of folk and primitive cultures, as quaint objects possessing inherent aesthetic merit and sometimes, as in the case of coverlets and baskets, practical utility as well. To a considerable degree, this new market derived from the efforts of benevolent agencies working among primitive peoples in the United States to develop sources of income for their clientele by retailing items of material culture, and to demonstrate the inherent nobility of the apparently ignoble peoples whose needs they sought to serve. The impact on contemporary taste of the discovery of "the primitive" more generally, as fostered by the St. Louis Exposition of 1901, for example, or by the variety of local fairs and expositions in which benevolent agencies participated more directly, must not be overlooked, however.

The new interest in the folk culture of Appalachia thus had its origin in shifts within formal academic disciplines, which created a taste for the primitive as exotic and hence a practical market for the products of Appalachian culture. The exploitation of the folk character of the southern mountain region took place within the attempts of the benevolent community to serve the needs of the mountaineers as they conceived them, however. In the context of trends in early twentieth-century philanthropy, the discovery of patterns of folk culture in Appalachia was rapidly seen to have specific utility in the work of philanthropy. Crafts products were salable items, and hence sources of much-needed cash income for the mountain people, and especially the mountain women, who might thereby obtain funds sufficient to send their children to day school or boarding school. That was helping them to help themselves with a vengeance. In addition, however, instruction in "traditional" mountain crafts—and later in folksong and folkdance—appeared to have potential as a basis for the erection of a school curriculum "appropriate" to the realities of mountain life as required by the educational tenets of the pseudo-Dewean progressive philosophy and of the rural life movement before 1915. While crafts education and folk education in the southern mountains thus began as elements in the practical work of benevolence, as part of a more general effort to facilitate the transition of the mountaineers into modern life, between 1910 and 1915 both crafts education and folk education assumed new importance, as means by which the mountaineers might be taught their own culture, and the viability of Appalachian regionalism be assured.

The crafts "revival" began in Appalachia during the mid-1890s, as a new generation of persons, trained in the first settlements and influenced by the concept of the institutional church as the central vehicle for the propagation of the social gospel, took over the educational work of the home missionary and the school teacher in the southern mountains. At this point, the crafts revival involved nothing more than a transfer to this rural region of techniques already utilized successfully in urban settlement houses. In cities and in the country, crafts work seemed particularly appropriate as a kind of activity around which to organize clubs for bringing neighbors together. This was the goal of all settlement work, of course, but in Appalachia the need for practical experience in cooperation seemed particularly pressing. It soon appeared that crafts activities had the additional advantage of producing salable items. Especially after 1900, as a consequence, benevolent agencies working in the mountains began to function not only as social centers but also as production and distribution units, the latter in their capacity as the nexus between the neighborhood and its members on the one hand, and the outside world on the other.[2]

Ironically, in fostering crafts activities by designating particular items as salable, by providing crafts instruction, and by establishing standards of workmanship and materials, the mission schools and mountain settlements characteristically utilized non-crafts models of economic activity. Often on the advice of professional engineers, business persons, or vocational education instructors called in for consultation—who were often appalled by the "primitive" manner in which the coverlets or baskets or rugs in question were manufactured—the crafts centers in Appalachia tended to emphasize product standardization and the division of labor rather than individual design and individual labor, in order to maximize production and take advantage of current trends in the "market" for crafts items. And while most tended to utilize a "putting-out" system, especially in the production of fabric items, by 1910 Asheville, North Carolina, was the site of at least one "factory" for the manufacture of handloomed coverlets, while the output of the woodworking shops at Berea and at the Mount Berry School looked toward the mass production of the native handicrafts of Appalachia.[3] For the settlement workers, however, preservation of a crafts mode of production seemed ultimately less important than the economic and social gains to be derived from the development of such native industries, and the persistence of "primitive" techniques of manufacture appeared more quaint than critical.[4]

If credit is due, the credit for bringing the crafts revival to Appalachia probably belongs to Frances Louisa Goodrich, who introduced the handloomed coverlet into the northern market for indigenous American handicrafts at the end of the 19th century, and whose successful exploitation of that market pointed up to others the economic and social returns that might follow from an encouragement of such "fireside" industries. Goodrich was a worker for the Women's Board of Home Missions of the northern Presbyterian church, and was assigned to the mission station at Brittain's Cove, in Buncombe County outside Asheville, North Carolina, in the fall of 1890.[5] Her own version of the story, often told and retold in later years, begins only in 1895, however, and hence casts her in the role of visionary— newly come to the mountains but recognizing at once that the existence of an indigenous crafts tradition offered the opportunity to bring "healthful excitement into the lives of her neighbor women" along with "the joy of making useful and beautiful things," where all others could see only hopeless poverty and irremediable ignorance.[6] Those first five years at Brittain's Cove and the terms under which she found herself in the mountains must be acknowledged, however, for it was as home missionary cum settlement worker that Goodrich transformed a forty-year-old coverlet "brought to her as a gift out of pure good will and affection" into evidence for a lost culture of Appalachia, and expanded her personal search for information concerning this culture into an occasion for neighborliness and cooperative endeavor. The coverlet itself was sent north.[7]

It was the drama of Goodrich's discovery which interested contemporaries, of course, and which came to interest Goodrich herself as she tried in later years to account for her own participation in a movement of such obvious historical importance. It was as drama, moreover, that the first reports of a revival of weaving at Brittain's Cove and then at Allanstand, North Carolina, were cast. In Max West's version of the story for his study of "The Revival of Handicrafts in America" (1904), for example, Goodrich embarked upon a systematic program to recover the details of coverlet weaving by searching out older women of the neighborhood who could contribute one essential bit or another—"the secrets of the indigo pot" or the technique of double-draft weaving or some piece of needed equipment. Then, largely by trial and error, Goodrich was able to reconstruct and then replicate the traditional process of home-manufacture beginning with the purchase of appropriate kinds of wool from local farmers, through carding, spinning, dyeing, warping, choice and design of pattern, weaving, to finishing.[8] One almost wishes it were true. Goodrich did proceed by trial and error, but her goal was not the "revival" of weaving using traditional methods so much as it was to create a reason for local women to come to the mission station, and to find an activity which would engage and retain their interest once they had come for their visit.

At the outset, indeed, what Goodrich had discovered was nothing more than a "tradition" of weaving among the women of rural Buncombe County, but this suggested weaving as a "natural" activity around which to organize social intercourse. What must have given her considerable pleasure, however, was that weaving was such a "natural" activity, for in an age before the corn-clubs and canning-clubs had been invented there seemed to be few occasions on which workers in rural missions or settlement houses and their rural neighbors could collaborate on projects of mutual benefit and interest, and through which the workers could help their clients to help themselves. (Education and religion, although areas of potential mutual interest, were no exception, of course, for both involved help rather than self-help. At the Brittain's Cove mission, moreover, education was someone else's responsibility, and religion did not attract the local women, few of whom "could come to Sunday School or preaching services after getting the children 'fixed to go' and with the dinner to prepare."[9]) Weaving must have had an additional advantage in Goodrich's eyes, moreover, for it was an activity around which women's clubs were conventionally organized in city settlements. Indeed, in 1895 Goodrich proceeded in the conventional settlement house manner, and proposed weaving as a project to the women who were already meeting "one afternoon a week at the cottage for sewing and chatting and for a short religious service." She proposed, moreover, that they "begin by making a curtain of silk pieces after the manner of a rag rug"—silk wall hangings and rag rugs were among the staples of settlement-house crafts production—using a store of silk sent them from the North, presumably at Goodrich's request.[10]

It was only during the winter of 1895–96 that Goodrich properly began to attempt the "revival" of coverlet weaving, and not at Brittain's Cove at all, but by "putting out" work to the Angel family on the Paint Fork of Ivy, sixteen miles away. Three weeks later three handloomed coverlets were delivered to the mission station, sent north for sale, and Goodrich was in business. Brittain's Cove functioned as the center of the manufactory, taking orders, putting out work, standardizing inventory by selecting patterns, sizes, items— "table-runners, pillow tops, trunk covers and the like"—and, we may assume, disbursing substantial amounts of cash.[11] In 1897, Goodrich was transferred to Allanstand, North Carolina, in Madison County, where she developed an even more extensive cloth manufactory, again on a piecework basis, by setting some to spinning, some to dyeing, some to warping, some to weaving.[12] Here also she sought to adapt the production of these "crafts" items more closely to market demand through selection of pattern and through the innovation of all-cotton woven coverlets using factory-spun yarn, to meet requests for mothproof rugs, blankets and throws.

In these years also she sought to expand the variety of crafts items produced locally, by teaching fabric design and techniques for the manufacture of embroidered bedspreads, knotted fringe, hangings made of silk scraps, and rag rugs as well as women's cornhusk hats and oak-splint baskets.[13] In 1902, Goodrich organized the Cottage Industries Guild of Allanstand, a kind of primitive crafts cooperative which served as the official purchasing and distribution agent for local handicrafts, and which functioned as a social club as well. In 1908 the focus of her operations moved to Asheville, where workshops and a sales room were established. Although the old name of Allanstand was retained, the mountain mothers in the countryside were now required to come in to town to sell the products of their spinning wheels and their looms, and to obtain the social experiences which the mission station had previously provided in situ.[14]

Shortly after Goodrich became interested in the promotion of weaving in the neighborhood of Brittain's Cove, and perhaps with knowledge of the work being done there, Susan Chester Lyman determined to initiate a weaving program at the Log Cabin Social Settlement which she had established, also outside Asheville, in March, 1895.[15] At first Lyman functioned as a broker, filling orders received from "numerous friends in the North" by passing them on to mountain women weavers, but by the end of the century an arrangement had been made with the Asheville Exchange for Women's Work to sell handwoven goods on a commission basis at their shop in Asheville, where the availability of mountain handicrafts became one of the attractions of that resort town to summer visitors. During the early years of the twentieth century, Lyman also sought to encourage the production of a more diversified line of crafts items for sale both by mail and at the Women's Exchange, including rag carpets, woolen blankets, palmetto hats, and willow and splint baskets. At about this time, a number of persons who had sold handcrafted items through the Log Cabin Settlement began to set themselves up as independent producers, selling directly through the Women's Exchange, and to develop small factories, either in the country or in Asheville. Among these was Emma A. Duckett, a skilled weaver, who moved to Asheville with her loom and subsequently hired spinning and carding done on a piecework basis, but employed women in her home to twist cotton yarn for warpings and in other ways to assist with the weaving process.[16]

William Goodell Frost appears to have seen his first homewoven coverlet about 1894, when a student from the mountains brought one to Berea to trade for his tuition at the college. Frost routinely carried coverlets with him during his fund-raising trips to Louisville, Cincinnati, New York, and New England, beginning in 1895–6, as evidence of the antique rather than the degenerate character of mountain culture—an assertion reinforced by the discovery that some of the patterns woven in mountain homes were identical with those of coverlets made "long ago in New England."[17] Frost soon found that they had the additional advantage of being salable items.

At first, Berea College received coverlets in trade for tuition and resold them to friends of the college in the North. Beginning in 1896, "Homespun Fairs" were held at the annual summer commencement to encourage the revival of weaving and innovation in design and manufacture through the principle of emulation, and to show off the handiwork of the mountain people to the philanthropist-visitors who came south for the occasion. In 1899, Miss Josephine Robinson of the Berea faculty was placed in charge of the encouragement of mountain weaving and the marketing of mountain handicrafts, and began to offer instruction in weaving to the girls at the college. Upon the organization of the Fireside Industries in 1902 as an adjunct to Berea's own industrial education curriculum, Hettie Wright Graham was brought to Berea to coordinate handicrafts activities. She was succeeded in 1904 by Jennie Lester Hill. While the college itself thereby became an important producer of handicrafts items, it also continued to operate according to the two other patterns which had originated in the settlement movement, by hiring work done on a piecework basis, and by functioning as an exchange, purchasing handicrafts directly for resale.[18]

In 1902-3, Katherine R. Pettit and May Stone of the Log Cabin Social Settlement at Hindman, Knott County, Kentucky (the "W.C. T.U. Settlement") also sought to encourage weaving by buying handmade coverlets directly or by acting as an agent for their sale in the North. In 1903 an old loom was acquired and set up in the Settlement house, and instruction in weaving was begun.[19] Encouragement of weaving and instruction in weaving and other handicrafts was begun at the Church Mission Settlement sponsored by the Protestant Episcopal church at Proctor, Lee County, Kentucky, about 1900.[20] About 1901, Eleanor P. Vance and Charlotte L. Yale initiated crafts classes in their capacity as settlement workers on the Biltmore Estate in North Carolina. By 1915, when Vance and Yale left for Tryon, North Carolina (where they later organized the Tryon Toy Makers and Wood Carvers), the Biltmore Estate Industries had developed into a full-scale program of woodworking, weaving, basketry, and other handicrafts.[21]

The same pattern was repeated, with minor variations, throughout the mountain region. About 1903 the Committee on Arts and Crafts of the Georgia Federation of Women's Clubs sought to encourage the manufacture of native crafts in that state through the purchase of handmade items and through advocacy of handicrafts instruction in the public schools, the mountain day schools, and the state normal schools.[22] With the committee's encouragement, in 1910

Martha Berry hired a crafts teacher from the Rochester Mechanics' Institute to instruct the mountain boys of the Mount Berry School at Rome, Georgia, in carpentry so that they could construct looms, and then sought a second crafts teacher to teach the mountain girls to weave on the looms their brothers had built.[23] As early as 1904, a spokesman for the Home Industrial School at Asheville reported with some embarrassment that weaving instruction had not yet been begun at the school, but that a start would be made as soon as a qualified instructor could be found.[24]

The utility of crafts instruction and the production of handicrafts items for sale were well established in settlement work by the beginning of the twentieth century. As a way of providing a source of income to the mothers of the neighborhood, as a way of training children, and especially boys, in manual skills and in the aesthetic sense which was developed by working with the hands, as a way of bringing neighbors together for parallel play activities when the cooperative spirit was not yet fully developed, and simply as a way of bringing the neighbors in to the settlement, the crafts revival admirably served the needs and the goals of settlement work. It was thus only natural that as settlement work of one kind or another was begun in Appalachia, a crafts component should emerge as one aspect of this work, and also that settlement-trained or -influenced workers in the mountain field should seek to encourage the development of a crafts program at the institutions with which they were affiliated. Because of the traditionally thin line between industrial (crafts) and vocational education, moreover—both providing an alternative to "book education" and both requiring work with the hands and a commitment to the "dignity of labor"—it was almost inevitable that weaving and rugmaking, for example, should be represented as an appropriate focus for *vocational* education for girls, instead or in addition to training in domestic science, seamstressing, or hatmaking, or that woodworking should be represented as an appropriate focus for *vocational* education for boys, instead of carpentry, agriculture, or metalworking.[25]

That crafts modes of production were almost by definition non-vocational in an economy dominated by factory modes of production tended to be overlooked in the early twentieth century, or acknowledged with the explanation that settlement work was not designed to take the place of apprenticeship programs. In rural settlement work, including that carried on in the southern mountains, however, crafts education was generally viewed as more appropriate than traditional vocational education for the mountaineers, in that it did not train children away from the farm. Indeed, crafts education seemed to hold out the promise of an improved rural life by teaching skills needed to supplement income, to occupy leisure time during the winter, and to fill farm-life with the joy that agricultural labor alone could not provide. Such a connection between crafts education and the needs of rural people involved a transformation of the settlement workers' sense of the utility of crafts instruction in the immediate context of the settlement as institution and its goals, however, which occurred only in the context of a movement for "real-life" education and the general public indictment of the traditional rural school after 1907.

The movement for "real-life" education and the indictment of the rural school had in common the assumption that traditional "book" education was inappropriate for the working classes of America, for whom instead a more practical form of education, which would equip them to make the best of the "real" possibilities of their lives, was needed. One may easily discover an implicit pattern of racism in such a conviction, since the "working classes" both North and South during the early twentieth century were readily identifiable as members of ethnic and racial minorities. There is considerable evidence also that middle-class Americans were willing to view even native-born workers as culturally, and hence perhaps genetically distinct from the "dominant" population of the United States during this period. The indictment of traditional education in the United States did not develop from this pattern of racial or ethnic distinction however, so much as from the practical difficulties which teachers had in teaching the old curriculum, and from the truancy problem which, by 1904 at least, had become sufficiently familiar as a problem to be used by opponents of child-labor legislation as justification for the employment of children.

In the contexts of the movement to restrict child labor and of the several campaigns for reform of state public school systems, the problems of curriculum and truancy yielded a set of related questions. First, how could school be made interesting enough so that children would attend of their own volition. Second, how could the school experience be made useful enough so that parents would sacrifice the immediate gain in income from a child's labor in return for the future and greater gain in the child's personal development and increased earning potential, and insist that their children remain in school at least through the established mandatory attendance age. Third, how could the economic, social, and cultural benefits of education be explained to the public so that the practical support of votes would be available for legislation requiring mandatory school attendance and prohibiting the employment of school-age children.[26] To these needs of children, the members of President Roosevelt's Country Life Commission added one additional theme by their complaint that traditional "book" education made America's farming population so dissatified with farming that they left their farms abandoned (and hence diminished the revenues available to state and local taxing districts) in their flight to the cities; and that either on the farm or in the cities, their dissatisfaction manifested itself in political activity which threatened the stability of the social order.[27]

The attack on the rural school did not begin with the investigations of the Country Life Commission in 1908–9. A more thorough investigation of conditions in rural schools, and a more thorough indictment of rural education as failing to meet the needs of America's rural population, had been made earlier by the Committee of Twelve of the National Education Association. Appointed at the annual meeting of that organization in July 1895, along with the more famous Committee of Ten on Secondary Education, the Committee of Twelve was empowered to investigate the current state of rural education and was charged to make recommendations for its improvement.[28] In a two-hundred-page report published in 1897, the committee announced that rural education in the United States did not measure up to the standards then expected in urban institutions, and identified the inadequate preparation of teachers and the inadequate

financial base provided by the system of local school-district organization as the principal obstacles to the viability of the rural schools.
Consistent with the interests of the National Education Association's
membership in school administration and the problems of superintendency, which followed from their professional commitments as
school administrators, the Committee of Twelve proceeded to suggest that school consolidation on a county or multicounty basis
would solve the problems of rural education as they had observed
them.

The Committee of Twelve in the 1890s looked at rural education
as a phenomenon independent of rural life, and found it inadequate
because it was not capable of providing students with the same sort
of "high-quality" education offered in America's city schools. The
Country Life Commission in 1908–9 looked at rural education in the
context of rural life, however, and found it inadequate precisely because it attempted to provide country people with an education more
appropriate for city than for country life. By teaching the values of
urban life, indeed, the rural school was a precipitating factor in the
current rural exodus, according to the commission, and the result
was that only the old and the incompetent were left on the farm. Who
then would feed the city, and where would the city's moral resources
come from? An educational program appropriate to rural life was
needed. This was the theme of the commission's report and of the
dozens of papers and addresses which reiterated its arguments during the next several years. Real-life education would train young
people in the skills necessary for an economically and culturally productive life in the country and would inculcate a vision of rural life as
a viable alternative to urban life. It would provide a sense of self and a
sense of pride in the separate but legitimate culture of the open country.[29]
How this could be done, however, remained a problem. Better
training of rural schoolteachers in vocational education and rural
sociology, for example, as well as in history and literature, was an
often-proposed solution, after 1909 as after 1897. School consolidation was also often suggested, although in the South some feared that

this would lead to a merging of schools for blacks and schools for whites, and hence viewed consolidation with no little suspicion.[30] Most of the literature on improving rural schools which appeared immediately following the Country Life Commission's report stressed the "need," or the need to identify the "need" through rural social surveys, however, and tended to sidestep the issue of establishing an institutional format in which rural education appropriate to rural life might be offered.[31] It was in this context that the rural-life schools of Scandinavia, which combined technical agricultural education with education in the culture of rural life, and offered handicrafts instruction in order to unite the skills of hand, head, and heart, came to have special meaning in America.[32]

The Scandinavian system of rural education for rural needs was not unknown in the United States prior to the beginning of the twentieth century, but it had been of greater interest to proponents of industrial or vocational education than to those concerned with schooling in the countryside. As early as 1871, the newly established United States Bureau of Education had distributed a circular describing the folk schools of Sweden and Norway, but in subsequent years it was the Sloyd or handicrafts schools, established as an adjunct to the rural life schools, which attracted the attention of Americans. These, like the urban-based industrial schools of Russia and Germany which sought to train boys and girls in the technical skills needed by an industrializing economy, seemed to offer an alternative to what educational reformers perceived as a failing apprenticeship system and a nearly defunct system of privately operated industrial education.[33]

In the United States, as a consequence, interest in Scandinavian education went hand-in-hand with the growth of public programs for vocational and industrial education in Boston, Milwaukee, St. Louis, and Cincinnati. Even in the 1890s, in the context of the first attack on the American system of rural education, no one seems to have looked to the Scandinavian experience for help. What American children needed, it was felt, was more book-learning, not less, and it was alternatives to book-learning which the folk schools tried to provide. By 1910, however, the situation had changed. A new interest in the handicrafts programs of the settlement houses and schools combined with the new view of the nation's rural schools as providing an education inappropriate to rural life to create an audience for the preachings of the Scandinavian educational reformers.

There was a substantial literature in English on the Scandinavian folk schools available to Americans by 1910, the product of a growing British interest in agricultural reform at the turn of the century. Much of this was neoromantic and antipositivist in tone, however, and tended to treat the folk schools rhapsodically as the source of that "essential culture" which seemed to characterize the Scandinavian farmer. It was this, the English writers explained, which set him off so markedly from his more brutish counterparts among the English, and especially the Irish and Scottish peasantry—a sense of the folk culture which rural life preserved but which could only be learned in school.[34] In England and America, however, a more technical literature on the folk schools also began to appear, prepared by and published in the journals of the education professionals.[35]

Among those newly interested in the Scandinavian system of rural-life education at the turn of the century was young Philander P. Claxton, who toured Sweden and Denmark in the 1890s to observe the folk schools at first hand. In his capacity as the Professor of Secondary Education at the University of Tennessee during the first decade of the new century, Claxton found that his experience abroad helped him to understand that America's problems with rural education were not unique, and led him to a growing conviction that the public school system ought to take on the work of adult education as well as child education, both in vocational and in traditional school subjects.[36] After 1911, as United States Commissioner of Education, Claxton's personal knowledge of the Scandinavian folk schools stood him in good stead.

Among the first problems which confronted Claxton as commissioner of education, was the need to prepare a federal response to the crisis in rural education precipitated by the 1909 publication of the Country Life Commission's report, which accused the education professionals of seeking to train rural children for urban life and thereby contributing to the"rural exodus," and which also suggested that rural education in America simply did not work. Because the rural schools did not meet the real needs of their rural clientele, country people kept their children home from school and the result was that generations of rural Americans had missed the opportunities which education offered, for literacy, self-culture, personal improvement, and economic advancement. The inconsistencies of the report, which used the "failure" of rural education to explain both the disparity between rural and urban life when country people acted like country people, and the disappearance of rural America when country people acted like city people—by engaging in collective political action or by seeking the main chance as individuals—were overlooked. The "crisis" of rural education emerged as a safe focus of political concern, and a new industry, devoted to talking about the need for reform in rural education but not about reform itself, was born.

On the heels of the Country Life Commission's report came the revelation of massive adult illiteracy in the United States, especially in the more rural sections of the nation and in those states which were predominantly agricultural, through publication of data from the thirteenth census of 1910. Here was a hard issue upon which concern might focus, the apparent consequence of a failure in the education of children. Adult illiteracy was also a problem which might be solved, however. In the face of a proposed congressional investigation of the American system of education, Claxton announced that he had directed his staff at the Bureau of Education to examine the origins and extent of adult illiteracy in the United States, and to inquire into the availability of resources and programs to remedy this problem . Reports of their findings would be made public through the *Bulletin of Education* .[37]

The first of these reports, *Illiteracy in the United States, and an Experiment for Its Elimination*, appeared during the early spring of 1913. As an acknowledgment of the problem, and by the fact of its publication an assertion of the Bureau of Education's competence to deal with it, this may be viewed as no more than a preliminary report, a gesture designed to meet political necessity. It sought to present in popular format a full discussion of the census data concerning adult illiteracy in the United States, and to provide tables, charts, and maps so that the precise dimensions of the problem might be known. Then, almost as an afterthought, it described the "moonlight schools" program inaugurated in 1910 by Cora Wilson Stewart, the superintendent of public schools for Rowan County, Kentucky, which had enrolled several thousands of illiterate or semiliterate adults in informal evening classes at schools throughout the county.

In the long run, this section of the report was to prove the most important, although in its immediate context it appears as little more than an anecdote, not incidentally from that essentially anecdotal land of Appalachia. Stewart's experiment merely proved that the situation was not hopeless. "The success of the men and women [enrolled in the moonlight schools] proves that it is not so difficult for illiterate grown-ups to learn to read and write as is generally supposed." Even more important, from the author's point of view, was "the significant fact brought out by this experiment . . . that adults of limited education have taken advantage of the opportunity to return to school and increase their knowledge."[38] From Claxton's own point of view, moreover, this brief report of Stewart's work was to be regarded as no more than a promise of what was to come. "This Bureau expects to have ready for publication soon some account of other efforts in this country to teach illiterates to read and write," he explained in his introduction, "and also some account of the efforts which some foreign countries have made to eliminate illiteracy."[39] Claxton had decided that it was time to begin explaining the Scandinavian system of rural education to Americans.

By the time *Illiteracy in the United States* was published, Claxton had already sent agents of the bureau abroad to study the Scandinavian rural schools. Harold W. Foght, one of the bureau's specialists in rural education, was head of the team. His colleagues were Lloyd L. Friend, supervisor of high schools for West Virginia, and William H. Smith of Mississippi, employed as "cooperative consultants." The reports they prepared, beginning in the summer of 1913, constitute the most important body of information concerning the folk schools published before the 1920s and served as the standard literature available to educational reformers interested in redirecting the curricula of rural schools or the public function of those schools. That indeed is what Claxton had hoped. "In adapting the work of its rural schools to the needs of its rural population," Claxton noted in his introduction to Foght's preliminary report of 1 August 1913, the educators of Denmark had provided "valuable lessons for the people of the United States, where the improvement and redirection of the rural schools constitute just now the most important problem of statesmanship."[40] In practice, however, when Claxton, Foght, or Friend (Smith seems to have prepared no report of his observations in Scandinavia) talked of the "valuable lessons" which could be learned from observation of the Danish folk schools, what they meant was that the folk school model might be of use in meeting the educational needs of Appalachia.

In transmitting Friend's *The Folk High Schools of Denmark* for publication in October 1913, Claxton noted that his own observations in Scandinavia in 1896 had "convinced me that, with minor changes necessary to adapt them to local conditions, schools of this kind might be very valuable in our own country and especially in the mountain and hill country of the South."[41] Foght and Friend followed Claxton's lead. "The most natural section of the United States in which to begin the organization of schools for grown-ups, modeled after the Danish schools, is the great broken upland region that usually goes by the name of the South Atlantic Highland."[42]

We may or may not believe Claxton's assertion that he had long been convinced of the utility of the folk-school model in Appalachia, for there is evidence on both sides. On the one hand, his work as professor of secondary education at the University of Tennessee and his practical apprenticeship to the extraordinary president of that university, Charles W. Dabney, must have made him aware of the need for alternatives to the traditional public schools in the southern mountains. On the other hand, there was nothing in either the old or this new literature on the folk schools which suggested that they would be ill-adapted to the conditions of rural life in New York or Massachusetts or Ohio or Kansas, or indeed in Mississippi or eastern Virginia. The focus of the Country Life Commission's indictment of rural education had not taken the southern mountains as a "bad example" of conditions which prevailed elsewhere in the nation, but rather had spoken of education in New York and Kansas, where everyone assumed that the country schools were doing their job. And at least in one part of Appalachia, an alternative program of education—at least to deal with adult illiteracy—had already been established. In 1913–14 there was no indication that Stewart's work would *not* be copied by county superintendents throughout the region. Why then pick on Appalachia?

It was Harold Foght's view, that folk schools would be most appropriate where American conditions replicated those for which the schools had originally been designed. Like Denmark in the 1870s, Appalachia in 1913 was an area of depressed agricultural conditions. So however were other sections of the nation, especially northern New York and western Massachusetts, those other appalachias. Given the political realities of the middle-teens, however, to say that the southern mountain region was an area of depressed agricultural conditions could have offended no one (except perhaps the mountaineers, whom everyone always ignored anyway). There were no vocal political spokesmen for Appalachia at this time, and no state boards of education in the South which would have disagreed.[43] While Appalachia was thus "safe," other sections of the nation were not so safe. To have advocated folk schools in New York or Massachusetts because of the "neediness" of their rural regions would surely have seemed like another attempt to defend the South by downgrading the Northeast, at least when Claxton or Lloyd were saying it, and might well have seemed like treading on the toes and into the spheres of influence of those most prominent and powerful figures in agricultural education, Liberty Hyde Bailey and Kenyon L. Butterfield, of the New York and Massachusetts state colleges of agriculture, respectively.

It seems not impossible that Claxton, Foght and Lloyd came to stress the utility of folk-schools in Appalachia in part by accident. In *The Educational System of Rural Denmark* (1913), Foght cited the bureau's earlier bulletin, *Illiteracy in the United States*, as evidence of the need for a program of adult education such as the folk schools provided, and pointed to Stewart's experiences as proof of the market for adult education in the nation.[44] In reworking this preliminary report, Foght merely expanded his remarks on "applications in the United States" by adding statistics on the southern mountain region as a whole obtained from John Campbell of the Southern Highland Division, in order to make his assertions of need more precise.[45]

By whatever steps Foght came to conclude that Appalachia was the place in which the establishment of folk schools might most effectively be attempted, between the publication of *The Educational System of Rural Denmark* and completion of *The Danish Folk High Schools* (1914), two critical events had taken place. First, Foght had transformed the Stewart experiment from an example of the validity of the census data of 1910 to proof of the real need for alternative educational programs in Appalachia. Second, Foght had called upon John Campbell for information about the extent of illiteracy in the mountains and about the social and economic conditions of the region. In the process, he appears to have been the means by which Campbell first learned of the Scandinavian system of rural schools. By thus engaging Campbell's attention, Foght did more to insure the establishment of folk schools in Appalachia than he could possibly have done by publication of description and analysis alone.

Prior to Foght's contact with him during the late summer or early autumn of 1913, John Campbell seems to have been aware only of the attempts of Scandinavian educators to meet the needs of rural populations for programs of adult education. He seems not to have considered the Danish folk school as a model in the design of alternative educational institutions for Appalachia.[46] By 1913, however, Campbell's own examination of mountain conditions and especially of the state of school work in Appalachia had brought him into full sympathy with those who accused the traditional rural school of teaching country people a curriculum better adapted to urban life and thereby unfitting them for life in the country. This had indeed brought him to the midst of a serious dilemma. On the one hand, the conventional rural schools in Appalachia, both public and private, seemed inadequate to the needs of the mountain people. On the other hand, the only viable alternative to the inadequacies of rural education seemed to be removal of the mountaineers to urban areas, like the new mill towns, where social needs were more adequately served by the traditional curriculum and where economic viability made professionally staffed educational institutions possible to begin with.

Before 1914, as a consequence, Campbell could only note, as he did before the National Child Labor Committee, that "removal," the apparent solution to the mountain problem, was not a real solution, and complain of the need to educate country people for country life in a country setting. When he sought a model of how such work might be done, however, the best he could find was the example of the Rockefeller Sanitary Commission and the state boards of health "who think it eminently worth while to send their physicians and place their dispensaries far back in remote mountain areas in order that the people may be cured of their ailments speedily in their own environment."[47]

To speak in this way did not mean that the primary need of the mountaineers was for improved health care, of course, although there were many during the middle teens who sought to identify the otherness of Appalachia with the prevalence of hookworm disease and trachoma, just as they sought to explain the otherness of the South generally as resulting from the prevalence of physical disease. Like others of his generation, when Campbell spoke of health he meant not only physical health but also social and economic health, the health of the body politic, of the community conceived as an organism. It was in this context that the work of the rural public health officers became exemplary for the redesign of mountain work. What Appalachia needed was dispensaries where the experience of cooperative activity might be provided along with education in needed skills and treatment for hookworm disease.[48] From this point of view, the Danish folk school or some modification of it seemed available as just such a dispensary of cooperative experience as the mountaineers needed.

Campbell's conversion to the folk-school idea was immediate and characteristically enthusiastic. Indeed, after 1914 he and his wife, Olive Dame Campbell, emerged as among the principal advocates of the Danish folk school in the United States. They saw it not only as an alternative to the traditional rural school and as a solution to the problems of rural isolation, but also as an alternative to the newer rural schools, whose emphasis on industrial and agricultural education seemed to be more of the same stress upon individual achievement instead of cooperative endeavor. "Individualism is the great American fault, and in the mountaineer, the surviving original American, individualism is raised to the highest power," Campbell insisted. "What we need more than ornamental cornices—useful as cornices are—are foundation stones. . . . Cooperation . . . beginning by stressing only the essential and minimizing the nonessential, is what we so much need."[49]

During the spring and early summer of 1914, at the Knoxville conference of southern mountain workers and perhaps also at the Maryville conference of workers connected with the Women's Board of Missions of the Presbyterian Church, as well as in private conversation and correspondence, Campbell urged the adaptation of the Danish folk school to mountain work, especially by those denominational agencies which found their traditional monopoly of school work in Appalachia challenged by the growth of the state school systems. In May he was instrumental in convincing the Women's Board of Missions of the Presbyterian church to transfer some of its workers to Warren H. Wilson's Department of Church and Country Life, and to permit other workers to accept appointment as county demonstration agents to work on the development of girls' canning clubs. In the early summer he worked on a plan for the establishment of a folk school near Tate, Pickens County, Georgia.[50] Although his projected personal visit to Denmark to study the folk schools at first hand was blocked by the outbreak of War in Europe,[51] his commitment to the folk-school idea went unabated. The folk school, he reminded the trustees of the Russell Sage Foundation in a "Confidential Report" in September 1914, "combines the cultural—the mountaineers' want—with the cooperative spirit—the mountaineers' need." At the same time "it gives training, largely developed through the cooperative spirit engendered, for bettering economic conditions. . . . The mountain field will forever remain a 'mission field' unless its people are trained to manage their own institutions and to have money enough to maintain them. The adaptation of the Danish folk-school for the mountains would, in our judgment, stimulate the many things in the mountains which wait upon native initiative, community spirit and local financial support."[52]

Ultimately, little of substance came from Campbell's advocacy of the folk-school idea during his own lifetime. Although he was able to persuade missionary schools to consider some aspect of rural-life education as an appropriate part of their curriculum, the times were not right. American involvement in World War I, Campbell's own busyness with the politics of benevolent work, and then his final illness drew energy away from the plans he projected for the development of a series of folk schools in Appalachia to meet the needs of the mountaineers. It was not until the 1920s that folk schools patterned after the Danish model were developed in Appalachia, at Berea in 1920 and at Brasstown, North Carolina—The John C. Campbell Folk School—in 1926. The more famous Highlander Folk School was established at Monteagle, Tennessee, only in 1933.[53] The importance of the folk-school idea during the middle teens lay less in what was accomplished, however, than in the new direction it suggested for rural-life education on the one hand, and for conceptions of rural life generally and mountain life in particular, on the other hand. For John Campbell himself, moreover, it provided a conduit into a new and radically different notion of the nature and meaning of Appalachian otherness.

As an advocate of the folk-school idea, rather than simply of rural education appropriate to rural life, Campbell came increasingly to be drawn away from his earlier commitment to "normal" American culture as the standard against which cultural deviance was to be measured, and from its corollary as it operated in the country life movement, that rural life and rural people were lower on the scale of civilization than urban life and urban people. Through his advocacy of the folk school and his search for institutions which would make possible the establishment of a viable mountain life, that is, he came to accept the notion that there was a culture of rural life, and of mountain life in particular, which existed independent of rather than as a lesser form of urban culture. It was this culture of rural life that the folk schools were to teach. In the southern mountains, the culture of rural life meant the culture of mountain life.

Campbell's commitment to the folk school as a solution to the problem of mountain education thus brought him to a conviction that there was a distinctive culture of Appalachia, and that it should be preserved. At the same time, perhaps because of the misunderstanding engendered by the common translation of "volksschule" as folk school rather than people's school or people's college, and in the context of a contemporary interest in the "folk" origins of art, literature, and song, Campbell's advocacy of the folk-school idea led him increasingly to see the mountaineer clients of such institutions as "folk"—a notion which his wife's discovery of an apparently vital folksong tradition in the mountains reinforced with the proof that cultural artifacts alone could provide. If only a distinct people possessing a distinct culture could produce distinct cultural artifacts, then the discovery of distinct cultural artifacts of necessity suggested the existence of a distinct people possessing a distinct culture. As Mrs. Campbell herself noted in 1915, "ballads and especially their survivals . . . have a sociological as well as a political, historical, and cultural value, for they will reflect the life, not only of those who sang them, but also, to a certain extent, of the descendants of these people."[54]

During the middle teens, in the midst of the debate over the habitability of Appalachia, the appeal of the folk-school idea lay primarily in its utility as an instrument for creating a viable rural culture in the southern mountains. Through technical and agricultural education, as well as through education in basic reading and arithmetic, the folk school might improve the economic status of the region's agricultural class. Through lectures on history and literature, including Appalachian history and the indigenous literature of the oral traditions of Appalachia as found in folktales and folksongs, the folk school might also advance the general level of "culture" among the mountaineers, thereby increasing the spiritual element in the people's lives. Through handicrafts instruction and the encouragement of native crafts, through instruction in native folksong and folkdance, through drama and pageants, moreover, the folk schools might restore to the mountain people a sense of the legitimacy of their own culture, even while creating occasions for social intercourse and cooperative activity.[55]

The utility of the Danish folk school as a mechanism for teaching rural people their own culture was well established by the Scandinavian experience. In Scandinavia as in Appalachia, however, the problem had been to discover the crafts, the songs, the dramatic incidents, the historical anecdotes which were essential parts of rural life and which, as reflections of rural culture, reinforced rather than altered that culture. It was in this context that the already established interest in mountain handicrafts came to seem so important.

Handicrafts, and especially weaving, had first appealed as ways to bring cash into the money-scarce economy of Appalachia and then as proof of the native intelligence and technical skills of the mountain people, a counter to the observations of travelers and benevolent workers who routinely remarked upon the degradation or degeneracy of mountain life. By the middle teens, crafts, and especially weaving, had come to be seen also as elements of an indigenous mountain culture which the mountaineers had forgotten just as they had forgotten the crafts techniques themselves. In the context of this new interest in weaving as a cultural phenomenon, the discovery of an apparently indigenous folksong tradition in the mountains provided critical evidence of the apparent existence of a lost or submerged folk culture of Appalachian America. At the same time, it created a new pattern of explanation for the existence of Appalachian otherness. As a folk-society manqué, the mountaineers appeared as a legitimately distinct population in a legitimately discrete region, separate from America not only as a result of physiography and historical accident, but also as a result of the ethnic distinctness of the mountain "folk" inhabiting the region.

Engendered by a misunderstanding of Francis B. Gummere's concept of the communal origins of folk literature, the definition of Appalachia as a folk-society manqué depended on the notion that economic and cultural specialization, the dominant characteristics of urban-industrial society, was absent in folk-societies. If folk culture was the creation of the folk, then all mountain people must be song-singers and tale-tellers, shingle-makers and weavers, dyers and basket-makers, in potential if not in practice. One consequence of this notion, during the teens and twenties, was a series of attempts to collect songs and tales, and information about the old crafts technologies, from "the" mountaineers, especially through the public schools where teachers might ask the pupils to set down the folk knowledge they had gained at their mothers' knees before the sophistication learned at school caused them to forget what the modernized mountaineer might find embarrassing.[56] Another consequence, again during the teens and twenties, was the transformation of the work of private and denominational schools into "folk schools," which meant in practice agencies that sought to teach the mountain folk their own culture.[57]

As members of the Appalachian ethnic group (contemporary usage preferred "race," which lacked the connotations of genetic determinism ascribed to it by more recent historians of the term, but suggested "cultural" differences), all mountaineers were assumed to have the cultural and psychological capacity to participate in the usages of their culture. All therefore ought to be taught the usages of their culture, if only because it was their own, the basis of their heritage and their personae. It was only by thus participating actively in their own culture, thought the outsiders, that the mountain people might become themselves. If they thereby became permanently alienated from the rest of America, at least their alienation would be to some purpose. Few worried about the mountaineers' alienation, however. In a pluralist society, it was generally believed, ethnic and cultural diversity could yield equilibrium and harmony only to the degree that each group began from a position of strength based on a keen sense of the uniqueness of its particular ethnic heritage. From there to patterns of accommodation, based on the common values of western civilization, would be the next and easy step. Thus once more were the mountain people placed in a niche convenient to those who defined American civilization from a point of view which found diversity disturbing and the potential for conflict that diversity implied, troubling.

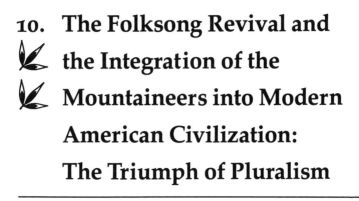

10. The Folksong Revival and the Integration of the Mountaineers into Modern American Civilization: The Triumph of Pluralism

The discovery of an indigenous folk tradition in Appalachia, like the discovery of an indigenous crafts tradition in the region, occurred by accident. Noted as early as the 1870s by local-color writers, during the 1890s it appeared as additional proof of the otherness of Appalachia, and of the primitiveness which followed from the region's historical isolation from the transforming forces that made modern America. By the turn of the century, a new fascination with folksong and folklore as the literary artifacts of a naif culture and with the simplicity of expression which seemed to characterize these forms, and a scholarly interest in such materials in their relation to the literature of more sophisticated societies, created markets for mountain folksong just as it created markets for mountain crafts in the same period. At the same time, mountain folksong like mountain crafts, became an element in the attempt to define Appalachia as a thing in itself, with positive and definite attributes.

As early as 1889, James Mooney had called attention to the southern mountain region as a resource for the collection of folksong and folklore, materials of increasing interest to Americans as the processes of civilization altered the cultural patterns which had typified earlier American life. Writing in the *Journal of American Folk Lore*, Mooney dutifully introduced his essay by noting the otherness of Appalachia and, in justification of his treatment of materials collected among white, Anglo-Saxon, native-born Americans as *folk* lore, explained that "the mountaineer of western North Carolina belongs to a peculiar type which has been developed by environment and isolation into something distinctly American, and yet unlike anything to be found outside of the Southern Alleghenies."[1] Mooney thus appears to anticipate later regionalist conceptions of the Americanness of mountain life, but his comments on the nature of Appalachian otherness were ancillary to the publication of "folk lore notes picked up incidentally while engaged in other work." The thrust of his essay was on the opportunities for collection of traditional materials among a "primitive people as yet unchanged by immigration and uncontaminated by modern civilization," and hence on the availability of Appalachia for literary exploitation of a new kind. Indeed, Mooney's essay neatly combines the twin themes of contemporary ethnology and folklore: the obligation of students in these disciplines to record the characteristics of traditional civilizations before they are altered by the processes of modernization; and the practical opportunities available to the "industrious collector" in the field.[2]

The limitations of Mooney's essay were the limitations of his own time, and his point of view was shared by his contemporaries. Thus his suggestion of Appalachia's availability as a field for folklore study and of the appropriateness of publishing tales and lore collected among the mountaineers led to the preparation of a series of similar collections, many of which appeared in the *Journal of American Folk Lore*.[3] None of these rose much above the level of simple exploitation, analogous to the local colorists' earlier use of mountain materials, and few attempted even so simple an analysis of the nature of Appalachian otherness as Mooney offered. Taken as a body, however, they tended to reinforce, and apparently with the hard facts of "scientific" study, contemporary notions that Appalachian otherness was the result of a preservation by isolation of the civilization of an earlier age. More important, despite the obvious distaste of their authors for the primitive and superstitious quality of the folklore materials collected in the mountains, by providing apparently hard information about mountain culture these articles laid the basis for the construction of an alternative vision of Appalachia, as a thing in itself rather than as an incomplete version of America.

The discovery of an indigenous folk tradition in the southern mountains could not in and of itself alter anyone's notion of the relationship of Appalachia and America. So long as Appalachia was viewed as an incomplete version of America because it retained characteristics of American life which had been transformed by the forces of modernization elsewhere in the nation, or because it lacked institutions found elsewhere in the nation, folktales, superstitions, curious agricultural practices, peculiarities of speech, and the persistence of a "ballad" tradition appeared as further evidence of Appalachia's incompleteness. As soon as Appalachia came to be viewed as a legitimately discrete region of the nation, however, those same folk elements in mountain culture became available as evidence for the existence of an indigenous mountain culture—a mountain culture which was not so much inferior to as different than the patterns of culture which prevailed in the nation at large. Because the legitimation of Appalachian otherness and the attribution of aesthetic merit to the artifacts of "primitive" civilizations occurred as simultaneous and parallel, if formally independent events, during the early twentieth century a new vision emerged, of Appalachia as both primitive and legitimately discrete. As a folk-society manqué, Appalachia could be both primitive (incomplete) and legitimately discrete, distinct from American culture and quintessentially American, a symptom and a symbol.

Just as a market for the handicrafts products of the southern mountains appeared around the turn of the century, the creation and the creator of the crafts education movement in Appalachia, so also a market for the literary products of the southern mountains developed at about the same time, the creation and the creator of what we might call the "Appalachian culture" movement in the region. Both involved the willingness of nonmountain Americans to purchase the naif products of this "primitive" culture for their intrinsic aesthetic merit or as curiosities with which to decorate their homes and lives.[4] Both generated a search, conducted largely by "outsiders," for marketable items, and led to the encouragement of increased production of such items by the mountaineers themselves. In addition, both functioned as elements in the contemporary campaign of benevolent workers to legitimize their efforts on behalf of the mountain people, by demonstrating with the proof of the handwoven coverlet or the persisting English ballad the antique, rather than the incomplete or degenerate character of mountain life. Here the similarities end, however, and a critical difference appears. For where handloomed fabrics have an intrinsic use both in nonmountain culture and in mountain culture—as bedspreads, rugs, throws, hangings, or as material from which garments can be made—the usefulness of folktales, folkdances, or folksongs in nonmountain America was minimal. Indeed, the usefulness of such literary products of a folk culture even in Appalachia itself seemed questionable.

It was the symbolic character of Appalachian folk literature, as a nexus with quintessential American culture and the traditional culture of Merrie Olde England, rather than its practical utility, which lay at the heart of its marketability after 1900. Because the ascription of usefulness to the symbolic involves the creation of an artificial market, composed of "taste" or "fashion" as well as of the recognition of the problem which the symbolic summarizes or solves, twentieth-century interest in the literary products of Appalachian folk culture was the product of time and place and of historical accident. Although one cannot say that the crafts movement in Appalachia derived from the universal human need for bedspreads and baskets, neither did it require the emergence of the special market which created a consumer's demand for Appalachian folklore, folkdance, and folksong after 1915.

In this process, the outbreak of world war and America's growing involvement in it played a crucial role, as we shall see. But it must be noted at the outset that, without the "discovery" of old English ballads in the southern mountains and of the existence of a persisting folksong tradition in Appalachia, a market for the literary products of the Appalachian folk might never have developed. At the least, it would have been restricted to the utilization of folktales in literature, and especially in children's literature, for in an age of reason, folklore and superstition were synonymous with myth and hence with falsehood. While the prettied-up versions of eighteenth-century German tales collected by the Grimms or of nineteenth-century American tales collected by Joel Chandler Harris or the "professionals" of the American Folk Lore Society might be appropriate fare for such contemporary primitives as middle-class children were acknowledged to be, it was widely assumed that no adult in modern America could derive much pleasure from reading folktales or much status from telling folktales, least of all those of a culture not his own.

Folksong and folkdance did not suffer this disability. Though "primitive" by definition, they bore close relationship to nonfunctional art-song and dance. Once a market for them was created by someone's observation that they were quintessentially American and hence "interesting," they could be viewed purely in terms of their aesthetic value, as objects of consumption in concert halls and public performances, or as forming the foundation for an "American" music and an "American" dance. They were also available for consumption by participation. Urban Americans with a sense of the aesthetic merit of mountain folksong or mountain folkdance could and did sing the songs and dance the dances, at least after 1915. But folksongs and folkdances were not merely "primitive" versions of later forms in any case. As one author noted in 1910, "like the wild strawberry, they have a flavor all their own."[5]

The first published collection of folksongs from the southern mountains appeared as early as 1893,[6] and periodic publication of song texts occurred through the first decade of the twentieth century. It was not properly until the middle teens that serious interest developed in the existence of a folksong tradition in Appalachia, however, or that the first hesitant attempts were made to utilize the existence of this folksong tradition as an indicator of the character of mountain life. In no small part, this lag may be seen to have been the result of general tendencies in professional folk-life study in the United States, which was more concerned with folklore than with folksong, and which was more interested in finding "survivals" of the British ballads canonized by Francis James Child's mammoth collecting efforts than with folksong as the product of a "living" folk.[7]

It was only when publication and debate had established the legitimacy of folksong collecting among the professionals, and when the possibility of exploiting folksong in the same ways that folklore had earlier been exploited—as "contributions" to scientific philology on the one hand, or as materials upon which to base the productions of "art" song on the other—that the collection of mountain song began in earnest. And it was only after considerable collection had taken place that persons as interested in the definition of mountain life as Olive Dame Campbell were able to suggest that the study of folksong might have "sociological" as well as purely literary interest, that the mountaineers were best understood as a "folk" misplaced in modern America.[8]

The publication of mountain folksong before the middle teens, then, tended to replicate the modes already established for the publication of folklore materials. Some collections, like Emma Bell Miles's "Some Real American Music" (1904), looked to mountain music as a potential source of a "native" American art music, more reflective of the national spirit than "the Negro themes and the aboriginal Indian music" used in the compositions of such contemporaries as "Dvorak and a few other composers."[9] Other collections, like Louise Rand Bascom's "Ballads and Songs of Western North Carolina" (1909), were mere "collectanea," a hodge-podge of curious concretions discovered by the observant traveler. Sometimes these were accompanied by notes concerning the primitive conditions which permitted traditional folksong to persist in the mountains, or the relationship of the texts presented to the ballads in the Child canon.[10] Even Hubert Gibson Shearin's seminal article of 1911, "British Ballads in the Cumberland Mountains" in *The Sewanee Review*, and his more formal presentations of texts interesting to scholars, in *Modern Language Notes* and *Modern Language Review*—which together with his *Syllabus of Kentucky Folk Songs* announced the persistence of Child ballads among the repertoire of mountain singers—did not attempt more than a simple exploitation of the collections he had made.[11]

The persistence of Child ballads in Appalachia should have come as no surprise to readers of the *Journal of American Folk Lore*, at least, but even nonprofessionals apparently knew a Child ballad when they saw one in print or heard one sung. In her *Harper's* essay of 1904, for example, Emma Miles had pointed out that "the mountaineers sing many ballads of old England and Scotland" and displayed her own sophistication concerning ballad transmission and variation by noting that "so prone are they to cling to tradition that it is often difficult to distinguish these [traditional ballads] from their own modern compositions, especially as many have been recast, words, names of localities, and obsolete or unfamiliar phrases having been changed to fit their comprehension."[12]

What made Shearin's work of 1911 important was not his announcement of the traditional character of mountain folksong, to which he could do no more than point, but the proof he offered of its extent, as a stratum of hidden ore lying just beneath the surface over which hundreds had walked blindly before. Coming so soon after the "discovery" of a similar vein of folksong in Missouri by H. M. Belden,[13] Shearin's "discovery" of more than three hundred folksongs current in the mountains, and the fact that, like Belden before him, he had used the students in his college English classes as collaborators in the work of collecting, was of great significance. Most immediately, it directed considerable public attention to the existence of the "Appalachian song pocket," and thereby contributed to a popular redefinition of Appalachia as a folk-society manqué. It also served to legitimize the sporadic collecting efforts of such amateurs in the southern mountains as E. C. Perrow of the University of Louisville and Olive Dame Campbell, however, with the result that additional collections of even greater interest soon appeared in print, most notably Perrow's "Songs and Rhymes from the South," published periodically in the *Journal of American Folk Lore* between 1912 and 1915, and *English Folk Songs from The Southern Appalachians* by Campbell and the English collector, Cecil J. Sharp, published in 1917.[14]

Shearin's work also suggested the availability of Appalachia as the focus for a systematic, collaborative effort to collect all the surviving ballads and indigenous songs of a particular region, which Belden had proposed as a needed experiment as early as 1905.[15] Between 1911 and 1915, state folklore societies were organized in North Carolina and Kentucky (1912), Virginia (1913), and West Virginia

(1915), in order to stimulate and coordinate the collecting efforts of local amateurs, while in other mountain states particular individuals, like Reed Smith in South Carolina, emerged as leaders of more informal groups of collectors. Centered around the universities, these state societies often grew out of the college English classes of individual faculty members, and they routinely enlisted the support of university graduates, especially the public school teachers of the state. Although these new collecting agencies were organized on a state basis—a pattern which was not only conventional but suggestive of cultural politics and of ties with state boards of education—their work ultimately looked to the explication of a regional culture. Like their contemporaries, the members of these state folklore societies characteristically assumed that southern mountain life was coherent and consistent across state boundaries. Indeed, what better proof of the homogeneity of mountain life could be found than the persistence of traditional song among all the mountain people?

In 1913, C. Alphonso Smith, the Edgar Allan Poe Professor of English at the University of Virginia and the founder and long-time president of the Virginia Folk-Lore Society, was instrumental in escalating the nascent folksong campaign to the national level. In an essay prepared for the U.S. Bureau of Education, titled "A Great Movement in Which Everyone Can Help," Smith noted the persistence of the Child ballads in America and outlined a plan for a survey of the "ballad resources" of the nation. Distributed by the bureau in November 1913, Smith's piece was accompanied by a return envelope addressed to the Commissioner of Education; a long endorsement of the project by Claxton; an alphabetical list of the Child ballads; and an assertion of the aesthetic and cultural value of the traditional ballads to American life. "If our American versions [of the Child ballads] are not collected quickly they can never be collected at all," Smith wrote. "It is now or never."

Many influences are tending to obliterate them. Catchy, but empty, songs not worthy of comparison with them, the decadence of communal singing, the growing diversity of interests, the appeal to what is divisive and separative in our national life, the presence of the artificial and self-conscious in modern writing are depriving our homes and school rooms of a kind of literature which, for community of feeling, for vigor of narrative, for vividness of portraiture, and for utter simplicity of style and content is not surpassed in the whole history of English or American song.[16]

Whatever the value of folksong for American culture as a whole, it was the success of these coordinated efforts at folksong collection in Appalachia—by the Virginia Folk-Lore Society under Smith, the West Virginia Folklore Society under John Harrington Cox, the North Carolina Folklore Society under Frank C. Brown, and by such private collectors as Josephine McGill of Louisville, who was invited to collect and notate folksongs at the Hindman Settlement School in 1914—which struck the public imagination during the middle teens.[17] Since the mountaineers were well acknowledged as "our contemporary ancestors," the conservators of both pioneer virtue and pioneer vice, moreover, Appalachian folksong was by definition American folksong. In addition, the existence of a persisting folk culture in Appalachia and the apparent English origins of this folk culture, offered an obvious solution to the problem of Appalachian otherness as it had emerged out of the debate on child labor during the earlier twentieth century in the legitimation it provided for the peculiarities of mountain life. With the outbreak of war in the summer of 1914, the apparent persistence of "Saxon song and speech" in the southern mountains assumed additional meaning as evidence of the essential Englishness of the "old" American civilization.[18] Indeed, the coming of the World War made Appalachia more than itself, a symbol of American civilization rather than merely a symptom of American progress, which had left the mountains behind.

The principal agent in this work of transformation, as it turned out, was not Campbell or Frost, the public spokesmen for the mountain region, but Cecil J. Sharp, the English collector of folksong and folkdance, whose accidental presence in the United States during the war years functioned to put the discovery of the folk culture of Appalachia into the broader context of Anglo-American civilization. Sharp had come to America late in December 1914, to assist in the New York production of "A Midsummer Night's Dream," for an earlier London production of which he had arranged the dances and some of the music.[19] Because of the rush of young men to the colors following the outbreak of war in the summer of 1914 had effectively eliminated the English market for instruction in folkdance, Sharp had found himself at liberty. New York City offered temporary employment and the possibility of lectures and classes to supplement a meager fee as production assistant on the play. Sharp could not have anticipated his own emergence as a symbol of Merrie Olde England to Americans by 1916.

At first, indeed, there was no hint that this might happen. No flourish of trumpets announced his arrival in New York, no audience of specialists stood waiting to be instructed in the intricacies of the Morris Dance, no crowds gathered eagerly to hear the traditional ballads of Old England sung in concert by Sharp or his protégé, Mattie Kay. A lecture on English folksong at the Colony Club in January failed to attract the interest of New York's upper-crust, and his two public lectures at the Plaza Hotel on the English country dances later that month were poorly attended. So far as New Yorkers knew, folkdancing was for school children—a form of gymnastics possessing neither aesthetic nor historical interest, or a way of organizing playground activities in the ethnic communities of lower Manhattan.[20] "There is really an enormous lot of work to be done here in popularizing the subject," Sharp complained in a letter to Maud Karpeles, "but it would take ages to do it—in fact it would be doing all over again all that I have done in England."[21]

The music and dance numbers Sharp had arranged for "A Midsummer Night's Dream" did much of the work of popularization for him, however.[22] During the early months of 1915, Sharp also made contact with the American proponents of folkdancing as recreation, whose own connections with the New York and Boston philanthropic communities put Sharp in touch with persons eminently interested in having a folk tradition of their own and entirely prepared to accept the inherent aesthetic value of the naif art forms of rural England. Beginning in March, Sharp was able to arrange a series of successful (and profitable) lectures and classes on English folkdancing in New York, Boston, Chicago, Pittsburgh, and Pittsfield, Massachusetts. By the end of the month, he had organized a "U.S.A. Branch" of his

English Folk-Dance Society, with "centres" in New York, Boston, Chicago, and Pittsburgh, and mused in his letters to England about the money which could be made if he should "get up a really swagger studio and make a bid for social people and charge enormous fees."[23] When he left for home in April 1915, indeed, the process of his lionization had already begun. In June he was scheduled to direct a pageant in Wellesley, Massachusetts, and in July to conduct a summer school of dance at a resort community in Eliot, Maine.

During the time of preparation for the Wellesley pageant, Sharp stayed at the Lincoln, Massachusetts, home of his new friend and enthusiastic supporter, Mrs. James Storrow. It was there that he received a visit one day from Olive Dame Campbell of Medford, Massachusetts, Demorest, Georgia, and Asheville, North Carolina. Mrs. Campbell brought with her the texts and tunes of some seventy folksongs she had collected from the mountain people of Appalachia beginning in 1907. Sharp looked through her material and spoke with her about the work she had done and how she came to do it. He was impressed, if not with the sophistication of Mrs. Campbell's notation of the tunes or the intrinsic merit of her material, then at least with the availability of the southern mountain region as a field for collecting. Was he perhaps also intrigued with the possibility that her husband's connection with the Russell Sage Foundation might yield support for his campaign to popularize English folk dancing in America?

After his return to England in July, 1915, Sharp initiated correspondence with Mrs. Campbell concerning the possibility of a collecting trip of his own into the southern mountains. He was "anxious not to do anything discourteous to her nor to queer her pitch in any way," he told Maude Karpeles in his delicious vernacular style, and hence proposed a kind of loose partnership. He would gain entry to Mrs. Campbell's mountains (by this time substantial claims had already been laid to both Virginia and Kentucky as collecting fields, which made her holdings in North Carolina and Georgia of considerable value), and she would receive coauthorship credit in a volume to be published out of his work in the field. She owned the mine, and he would do the digging. To this Mrs. Campbell agreed. "I want the collecting done and done by the person most competent to do it," she wrote to him in August, "and if I could have wished for a definite result from my work it would have been to attract to this region just such a person as yourself."[24]

Sharp returned to the United States in February 1916 and again began a round of lectures and dance classes, a week at a time in New York, Asheville (where he met with the Campbells and made final plans for his collecting trip), St. Louis, Cincinnati, and Kalamazoo, Michigan, and a month in Pittsburgh. In the spring, he worked with the New York Centre of the Folk-Dance Society in preparing an "English Interlude" to be performed at the Lewissohn Stadium of the City College of New York as part of Percy MacKaye's pageant in honor of the Shakespeare Tercentenary, "Caliban on the Yellow Sand," and later returned to Cincinnati to direct University of Cincinnati students in a performance of the "English Interlude" at their own Shakespeare Tercentenary pageant.[25] In mid-June, he again conducted the summer dance school, now established on a slightly more formal basis at the Massachusetts Agricultural College in Amherst. In July, Sharp and his companion, Maude Karpeles, returned to Asheville and thence, under the general guidance of the Campbells, began their first collecting tour of the southern mountains.[26]

Sharp's subsequent time in America followed much the same pattern. He scheduled lectures and dance classes in the autumn, a return to England from December to February, more lectures and classes in the United States in early spring, and collecting in the mountains during the summer, broken periodically by lecture dates and by the June sessions of the summer school at Amherst. While these later years were of the greater importance for his own career, and perhaps for the popularization of interest in American folksong as well, by the spring of 1917 his great work for the mountains had been completed, for by that time *English Folk Songs from the Southern Appalachians* was already in production. If Sharp by his remarks and singing in April of that year was unable to convince the mountain workers at their Knoxville conference of the inherent value of the naïf culture of Appalachia which they were so busily engaged in changing, within months his book would convince everyone.[27]

Published in New York by Putnam's on 23 November 1917, the appearance of the book was celebrated on that day by a party at the Russell Sage Foundation building. Sharp interrupted his fall lecture schedule to attend, of course, and prepared for the occasion not only a talk on the importance of the work already done and the work which could be done, but also a demonstration of the "Running Set" of Kentucky, which he argued was the first indigenous American folkdance ever collected.[28]

There was cause for celebration indeed. Richard Aldrich, the music critic of the New York *Times*, hailed the book as "the most valuable contribution that has yet been made to this special phase of folksong" in a four-column review which described Sharp as "the chief authority on English folksong."[29] H. M. Belden, by 1917 already the grand old man of American folksong scholarship, refrained from such excessive praise of Sharp himself, perhaps out of respect for his mentor, George Lyman Kittridge, but otherwise seconded Aldrich's judgment in a long review for *Modern Language Notes*. It was "the most noteworthy publication dealing with folksong in America that has yet appeared."[30] In the *Journal of American Folk Lore*, Charles Peabody stressed the importance of Sharp's interest in American folksong as a factor in its popularization, and noted that the discovery of the "Running Set" held out the hope that the development of an American folkdance movement would have consequences both for the future of dance in America and for conceptions of American culture more generally.[31] And in *The Dial*, William Aspenwall Bradley, that bellwether of current opinion about the southern mountains, wrote a long essay on the implications of Sharp's work, that connected the discovery of "the folk culture of the Cumberlands" with the discovery of the essence of American civilization itself.[32] Although Sharp remained one more year in America, during which he returned again to the mountains for more collecting, the great work was over. Only its impact was yet to be felt.

Sharp's demonstration of the "folk" character of Appalachian culture functioned not only to establish the peculiarities of mountain life as legitimate patterns in the present, rather than merely as patterns carried over from the past, but also to define the mountaineers themselves as a legitimately distinct people in the American present. A native-born, white, Anglo-Saxon, Protestant, American folk, their very status as "folk" defined their relationship to the rest of the American population even as the status of Italian-Americans or Afro-Americans as "hyphenates" or "immigrants" defined the relationship of these groups to, and in, America. As a distinct people, the mountaineers now appeared as one group among the many which made up the American population, just as Appalachia itself had come to seem one region among the many which made up the American nation. After 1917 the mountaineers lost their special status as one of the "exceptional populations" of the nation, whose deviance from more normal patterns of American life created a "need" for systematic benevolence and a threat to American unity and homogeneity, just as earlier Appalachia had lost its special status as an unknown land worthy of description for that reason. The publication of *English Folk Songs from the Southern Appalachians* thus involved the completion of that process of legitimation through explanation and definition which began in the 1880s, even as it effected the redefinition of Appalachian otherness as a reality to be accepted rather than as a problem to be solved.

Cecil Sharp's "discoveries" in the southern mountain region differed significantly, both in their nature and in their import, from those of earlier travelers in the region. The viability and public acceptance of his vision of the mountaineers as an American "folk," however, like the viability and public acceptance of the different visions of Appalachian otherness promulgated by local-color writers, home missionaries, advocates of southern industrial development, social scientists, social workers, or reformers of the Progressive period, depended on two factors only marginally connected with the merits of his argument or the accuracy of his vision: first, his reputation as an "expert," and second, the appropriateness of his vision to contemporary conceptions of the nature of American civilization.

Sharp's reputation as an expert followed from his status as a leading authority on English folksong and folkdance, from the publicity which attended his theatrical ventures of 1915 and 1916 and his lecture tours, and from his connection with persons and institutions "prominent" in contemporary cultural affairs, including the Russell Sage Foundation. In addition he was an outsider, hence presumably objective and free from self-interest, and he was an Englishman. During the war years especially, this fact alone gave his comments about the presistence of English folk culture in the United States special weight.

The work of earlier commentators on the mountain region had pointed to the distance which separated Appalachia and America, sought to explain this distance and its meaning and to design techniques for integrating Appalachia into American life, and thereby to resolve the dilemma posed by the fact of Appalachian otherness. All began with the assumption that America was, or ought to be, or was in the process of becoming a unified and homogeneous national entity, and that the process of modern history itself inevitably yielded nationalism, political centralization, and social complexity. In this context, all saw that the existence of the strange land and peculiar people of Appalachia posed a problem, and directed their efforts at understanding the dimensions of the problem and at solving it, both abstractly and practically.

Sharp may or may not have known that the existence of Appalachia posed a problem for Americans when he came to the United States in 1914, and he may or may not have known that certain aspects of the dilemma of Appalachian otherness had been resolved in America by the designation of Appalachia as a discrete region of the nation. As an Englishman, and as a student of folksong and folkdance, however, he stood outside this tradition. As an Englishman, he accepted the normality of regional cultural differences. As a student of folksong and folkdance, he not only accepted the normality of cultural differences between urban and rural areas, but viewed such differences in terms which saw primitivism as simplicity and simplicity as a virtue, and which identified the historical primitivism of the past as a reduction to essentials of the civilization of the present. The otherness of Appalachia thus could not bother him either abstractly or practically. It was simply a fact, like Scottish otherness, and like Scottish otherness it was to be exploited for the consequences of that otherness, the persistence of a folk tradition which had died out elsewhere, or which perhaps had never existed in more traditionally urban areas of the western world.

By accepting the otherness of Appalachia, and by providing Americans with a set of terms through which to understand both Appalachian otherness and the relationship of the mountaineers to the rest of the American population, Sharp not only established the peculiarities of mountain life as legitimate patterns in the present but also identified the mountaineers at once as a distinct people and as the conservators of the essential culture of America. And it was this, ultimately, which made his vision appropriate to contemporary conceptions of the nature of American civilization.

As a "folk" the mountaineers were for that reason a "people," with distinct cultural characteristics and perhaps with distinct genetic traits as well. Sharp was not the first to suggest that the mountaineers were a "people," but he was the first to suggest what kind of people they were: the American folk. Even so, in the nation of peoples which America seemed to be during and after World War I, the status of the mountaineers was not entirely clear. Were they simply one of the "ethnic" or "racial" groups of which the American population was composed, Appalachian-American hyphenates in a pluralist nation? Or did the traditional quality of mountain life and the identification of the mountaineers as American "folk" place them at the very center of American civilization and give them symbolic function in a culture fragmented by European adventures and the technological revolutions of modern life?[33]

The normalization of diversity which was the legacy of the war years made definition of the mountaineers as a people in a nation of people possible. They were "a subrace of the whites occupying the southern Allegheny mountains" according to the eugenicist Charles Davenport, for example, who found little else to say about them in his monumental survey of the American population classified by racial type, published in 1920. It is significant simply that the mountaineers are here included, however, as they were in other studies attempting to assess the strengths and weaknesses of the American population during the 1920s and 1930s, when examination of American society and the American economy, and of American civilization itself, seemed so compelling a task. As a people in a nation of peoples, moreover, it was only appropriate that their "racial" characteristics should be studied. In this effort Davenport himself made the first important beginning, although his conclusions appear as little more than transpositions of the conventional wisdom of the nineteenth century, unflattering replications of Will Wallace Harney's remarks a half-century earlier. "They are characterized by an exceptionally high proportion of mental defect and mental disease, by varicose veins, by numerous deformities of the extremities, and by underweight," Davenport said.[34] Later commentators would expand on these observations and debate the accuracy of some of them—especially concerning the mental abilities of the mountain people—but no one would challenge the fundamental assumption upon which they were made, that the mountaineers did form a "subrace" of the American population with measurably distinct characteristics.[35]

If the mountaineers were thus a people, they were also a special kind of people. Unlike the other "folk" whose peculiar culture and oral traditions engaged the attention not only of professional folklorists but also of American writers and American readers during the 1920s, the mountaineers were defined by ethnicity and history as an "American" folk. Unlike the lumberjacks and riverboatmen and cowboys, unlike the banjo-picking-spiritual-singing-tap-dancing blacks of the southern plantations and the northern ghettoes, unlike the Polish or Italian or Jewish children playing counting games on the sidewalks of New York or Chicago or Philadelphia, the mountaineers now appeared to be both in and of America. Their ethnic and historical characteristics connected them with the dominant white, Anglo-Saxon, native-born, Protestant civilization of the nation. As "our contemporary ancestors" in Frost's view or as the folksong-singing rural types of Sharp's vision, they now appeared as the conservators of the essential culture of America, the ur-culture from which all else, literature and life both, seemed to spring.

The story of the transformation by which Appalachia became a symbol of America, and of attempts during the 1920s and 1930s to reassess the meaning of mountain life as part of the search for an American folk tradition, cannot be fully told here. Its occurrence must at least be noted however, for in the twenties especially, the availability of that strange land and peculiar people of Appalachia as a source of information about the "real" America seemed to provide a necessary imaginative alternative to the necessities of contemporary reality. In a nation confused about the relationship of past and present, uncertain about its future, and desperately in search of a sense of self-identity, Appalachia seemed to provide a benchmark against which to measure how far the nation had come from its essential self. The persistence of Appalachia into the present seemed to hold out the possibility of returning to the nation's roots, of starting over, not in the past but in a simpler present, of refreshing the national spirit worn out by war and the peace, the possibility of going home. Although in the 1920s as at other times, going home was something one liked better to think about than to do, the possibility of "going home" which the existence of Appalachia seemed to offer had considerable attraction. The dramatist Percy MacKaye, in his characteristic 1920s distress at modern industrial civilization, said it as well as anyone.

Over there in the mountains are men who do not live in cages; a million Americans, who do not chase the dollar, who do not time-serve machines, who do not learn their manners from the movies or their culture from the beauty parlors. Shall we not then, hasten to civilize them—convert their dirty log-cabins into clean cement cages? Or first shall we inquire whether they may have something to contribute to our own brand-new civilization— something which of old we cherished but now perhaps have forgotten?[36]

As an American "folk," and thus as a legitimately distinct people in a nation of peoples, the Americanness of the mountaineers was established. No longer could they be viewed as deviants from a monolithic American civilization. In the American postwar present, they were only deviants from a dominant *modern* civilization, and some said that was more a matter of choice than of necessity. No longer either could the alleged peculiarities of mountain life be viewed as a temporary condition, consequent to the isolation of the region or to the impact of a primitive social environment on social institutions. And if the mountaineers lacked an adequate sense of themselves as mountaineers, mountaineers they were nonetheless, Appalachian-Americans, or later simply Appalachians. Benevolent workers in the folk schools which sprang up during the 1920s and 1930s in the mountains, or workers in the settlement houses in cities to which the mountain people migrated during and after the world war, could easily provide the needed sense of self. So could they provide the survival skills essential to the construction of a viable rural life in Appalachia or to individual success in the life of urbanized, industrialized America.

The emergence around 1920 of the notion that the mountaineers composed a distinct element in the American population had one other important consequence which must be noted: it made possible, for the first time, the imaginative separation of the strange land and its peculiar people. For the local-color writers of the 1870s and 1880s, as we noted, the nexus between place and persona had been central. Mountaineers who left the mountains ceased being mountaineers. In the new pluralism of the 1920s, however, one was defined in terms of where one had come from.

It was in the apotheosis of Sergeant Alvin York as American hero around 1920 that the nexus between place and persona was first broken. York was a Tennessee mountain boy who entered the American Expeditionary Forces only with reluctance, it will be remembered. Once having accepted the draft, however, he "did his duty" as contemporary mythologizers put it, and his duty included capturing single-handed a German machine-gun battalion after picking off eighteen men with his rifle and seven more with his pistol. Including stragglers whom York added to his group of prisoners on the way back to base headquarters, he captured a total of 132 German soldiers. For this derring-do, York received the Congressional Medal of Honor and the status of a folk-hero.

York took his Congressional Medal of Honor and returned with it to the Valley of Three Forks o' the Wolf, there to live out his life in relative solitude. It was as a mountaineer in France that he had made his fame, however, and this is significant, for unlike other American folk heroes of the postwar years—Lucky Lindy, Babe Ruth, or Superman himself—York was never simply an American hero. He was first and last a mountaineer, and no less a mountaineer because his virtues were the virtues of the native American folk. Tall and lanky, stolid, loyal, simple, choosing duty over his Christian convictions and his pacifism, his sinewy muscles developed splitting logs on the hillside farm, his marksman's eye trained in squirrel hunting, Alvin York was the mythic mountaineer come to life, even before there was such a thing. He carried his skills and his persona as a mountaineer with him wherever he went, across the big ocean and back again.[37]

The separation of the mountaineers from the mountains made possible the emergence of a mythology about them, at the heart of which lay the notion that the mountaineers did in fact compose a distinct element in the American population. Thus they came to take their place alongside the shrewd Yankees, the sharp-dealing Jews, and the rhythmic blacks in the pantheon of American types. As feudists like the cartoon Hatfields and McCoys in "Song of the South," Walt Disney's feature-length attempt to create a viable American folk tradition, as moonshiners and chicken thieves like Snuffy Smith in the funny papers, as representatives of an indigenous American folk tradition like the nameless country people in Doris Ullman's powerful photographs of the 1920s or like the weavers and dulcimer makers whose pictures appear in the crafts books of the 1930s and more recently in the *Foxfire Books*, or as real-life American heroes like Daniel Boone, Corporal Fess Whitaker, or Sergeant Alvin York, the mythic mountaineer has represented a people. It was a circular process, for the emergence of a folklore about the mountaineers depended upon a vision of Appalachia as a legitimately discrete region and of the mountaineers as a legitimately distinct people, while the mythic representations of mountaineers in literature, art, and folklore have reinforced the view of reality from which they sprang; but it was a process of enormous significance, and it began in the twenties.

Since the 1920s, as a result, no one has been able to ask whether the mountaineers do in fact compose a distinct group in the American population with distinct cultural and genetic traits, any more than anyone has been able to ask whether Appalachia—originally the mountainous portions of eight southern states—does in fact compose a discrete region of the nation. Indeed, those assumptions lie at the heart of the myth of Appalachia. More precise statement about the region or the people has been peripheral to this central fact. Even the debunkers, within and without the universities, who have risen to the occasion and challenged the accuracy of particular generalizations about the mountaineers in order to paint them in a more "realistic" light, have refused to ask the central question of their craft, about the reality of the phenomenon they seek to explicate. Instead, they have begun with the assumption that the mountaineers do in fact compose a distinct people with distinct and describable characteristics. They have argued from within a mythic system about the accuracy of mythology, and attacked the generalizations of folklore which are at once so vague and so potent as to defy examination or correction.

During the teens, John Campbell had room to make nice distinctions concerning the nature of Appalachia and the characteristics of the mountain population, and he divided the region into sections and subsections, the people into social, economic, and ethnic groups. When he talked about Appalachia or the mountaineers, it was only for convenience, to set them off from the rest of the South, and as an aid in organizing systematic benevolence. About the region as a discrete unit with a coherent and uniform culture, about the mountaineers as a homogeneous population, he could not generalize. Like his immediate contemporaries (and like our own), he was at his best when he dealt with the mountain people and the mountain problem historically. After that, in the present, his discussion of mountain life was necessarily anecdotal.

Thus, while Campbell labored long and diligently on his study of "the southern highlander and his homeland," he found the production of a coherent volume impossible. Preparation of a manuscript for publication demanded that the complexity of reality be reduced to simplicity, and this Campbell could not or would not do. He was well aware, Mrs. Campbell explained in her introduction to the posthumously published volume, of "the difficulties in the way of writing of a people who, while forming a definite geographical and racial group"—Mrs. Campbell was writing in 1920, remember— "were by no means socially homogeneous."[38] Thus it was that *The Southern Highlander and His Homeland* appeared only after Campbell's death. Thus it was that the volume itself replicates to a striking degree Campbell's own keen sense of the variousness of mountain life and scenery. And thus it is, that as a study of Appalachia, Campbell's book has been regarded as the best that is available, but not entirely adequate.

This we have always blamed on him, however, never on his subject, nor on the special circumstances under which it was written. Yet the volume itself was designed as a defense of mountain benevolence, and a call for its transformation from programs of Americanization to programs which would work for the establishment of a viable mountain culture. It was written in the midst of an attack on Appalachia as unsuited to human habitation, and in the midst also of a period when mountain boys and mountain girls were going off to war and to the industrial cities of the South and the North. If Campbell was uncertain about the future of the mountains, must he not have been uncertain also about the present? If he had difficulty generalizing about mountain life, might it not be that generalization was impossible, that mountain life was in fact too varied, too complex, too much like "normal" American life to permit of generalization? Might it not be that the "strange land and peculiar people" of the southern mountains were neither strange nor peculiar when seen up close, and that Appalachia was not in fact a coherent region with a uniform culture and a homogeneous population?

When we read Campbell's *Southern Highlander* as we would a home-mission text, as a work of polemics and special pleading, it makes sense. When we read it as an attempt to come to grips with an elusive reality, it also makes sense. But when we read it as a definitive study of mountain life, of the causes and consequences of Appalachian otherness, an "objective" examination of reality, we find it confused, unsatisfactory. But whose fault is this, after all? Is it that "more research" is needed, or a "more sophisticated" perspective? Or do we seek to net a reality which is not quite there, which all the effort and all the sophistication which even *we* can muster can never quite enclose? Might it not be that Appalachia did not in fact form a coherent region with a uniform culture and a homogeneous population, and does not?

We may judge the validity of the idea of Appalachia only by assessing its consequences in action. But this we can do only if we attempt first to understand its history and its function by asking what problem it solves and whose interests—intellectual as well as practical—it thereby serves.

Notes

For ease of reference, citations of items listed in the chronological section of the bibliography—on the southern mountains and mountaineers—always include date of publication. Not all citations that include date of publication refer to items listed in the chronological section of the bibliography, however.

Preface

1. Manifestations of early interest in the botany and geology of Appalachia include Thomas Jefferson, *Notes on the State of Virginia*, pp. 20ff., 31ff.; Francis William Gilmer, "On the Geological Formation of the Natural Bridge of Virginia"; Elisha Mitchell, "Notice of the Height of Mountains in North Carolina." The mixing together of scientific and social observation characteristic of this period appears, for example, in Charles Lanman, *Letters from the Allegheny Mountains*, or Elisha Mitchell's delicious *Diary of a Geological Tour*, as the entry for July 1828 (p. 34): "In the neighborhood is a hunter who has two women living with him; to one of them he owes and to the other he gratuitously discharges the duties of a husband; one has three children, and the other one and another near at hand. 'Tis a terrible region for these irregularities. The leather stocking of these regions . . . has a wife living on Sandy R. in Kentucky and the children of that wife and another woman living with him here on the Watauga. Another hunter has a wife living in N. Ca. and supports or keeps the only daughter of a man who lives in Tennessee. In a rude hunter's state of society, the women become schquaws, very pretty ones, but schquaws notwithstanding."

2. The first home-mission study text on Appalachia was Samuel Tyndale Wilson, *The Southern Mountaineers* (1906), but during the next decade most denominations active in the mountains commissioned mission-study texts of their own. These tended to retain a view of the mountaineers as quaint and picturesque in their neediness, however, which led John C. Campbell to begin work on a study text of his own, posthumously published as *The Southern Highlander and His Homeland* (1921). On Campbell, see Henry D. Shapiro, "Introduction," in Campbell, *Southern Highlander* (reprint, 1969), and chapter 7, below. The first call for a systematic study of mountain conditions was Bruce R. Payne, "Waste in Mountain Settlement Work" (1908).

3. The model which follows is derived from my ratiocinations about the consequences of dissonance in American intellectual history generally, although it bears resemblance to the model offered in Leon Festinger, *A Theory of Cognitive Dissonance*.

Chapter 1

1. Will Wallace Harney, "A Strange Land and Peculiar People" (1873), pp. 430–31.

2. Or so it appears from internal evidence. Harney (1831–1912) was one of those writers whose sketches and short stories of postwar southern life contributed to the northern discovery of the South and to the development of the "southern school" of literature during the 1870s and 1880s. He was a regular contributor to *Harper's* and the *Atlantic Monthly* during the mid-1870s; a collection of stories, sketches and poems from this period was published in 1909 as *The Spirit of the South*. He is mentioned but not dis-

cussed in Mildred L. Rutherford, *The South in History and Literature*, and his works are cited in Rayburn S. Moore, "Southern Writers and Northern Literary Magazines, 1865–1890," especially in connection with the literary discovery of Florida.

3. Cf. William M. Smallwood and Mable C. Smallwood, *Natural History and the American Mind*; Henry D. Shapiro, "Daniel Drake: The Scientist as Citizen."

4. Louise Coffin Jones, "In the Highlands of North Carolina" (1883), p. 378.

5. J. Henry Harper, *The House of Harper*, p. 87. On the rise of the monthlies, see Frank Luther Mott, *History of American Magazines, 1850–1865*, and *History of American Magazines, 1865–1885*.

6. A suggestion of this may be found in Mott, *History of American Magazines, 1850–1865*, esp. pp. 30–31, 173, 391ff.

7. On local color as a precedent for realism in American fiction, see especially Hamlin Garland, *Crumbling Idols*; Fred Lewis Pattee, *A History of American Literature since 1870* and *The Development of the American Short Story*. More recent studies in American literature, especially during the 1950s, have carried on the myth: Henry Nash Smith, "Origins of a Native American Literary Tradition"; Robert P. Falk, "The Rise of Realism"; Everett Carter, *Howells and the Rise of Realism*; Claude Simpson, ed., *The Local Colorists*.

8. A surprising number of studies of the local-color movement are derivative in this sense, either from Garland, *Crumbling Idols*, esp. pp. 57–68, who asserted that "veritism" was nothing more than local-color writing by another name, or from Pattee, *A History of American Literature since 1870*, who argued that the local color movement involved the discovery of America as an appropriate subject for literary treatment and provided the preliminary examination of American themes from which a genuine American literature might emerge.

9. Cf. Carter, *Howells*, and, for example, [unsigned], "Current Literature: *The Circuit Rider*," *Atlantic Monthly* (June 1874).

10. Hamlin Garland, "The Limitations of Authorship in America," p. 257. In this connection see also Mott, *History of American Magazines, 1850–1865*, and, for example, Alice French to Richard Watson Gilder, 3 Nov. 1887: "If you have had too much Arkansas already, I can give you a western sketch," *Century* Collection. Also of interest is the short-lived series "American Backgrounds for Fiction" in *The Bookman* (Oct. 1913–Aug. 1914) which may be said to have signaled the death of local color.

11. Harper, *House of Harper*, pp. 224–25.

12. Early examples are Benjamin Smith Barton, *A Discourse on Some of the Principal Desiderata in Natural History*; Alexander Wilson, "The Naturalist. Number III"; Daniel Drake, *Natural and Statistical View, or Picture of Cincinnati and the Miami Country*. Cf. in this connection George P. Merrill, *The First One-Hundred Years of American Geology*; Smallwood and Smallwood, *Natural History and the American Mind*; Ethel McAllister, *Amos Eaton*; William H. Goetzmann, *Army Exploration in the American West*; Joseph Ewan, "The Scientist on the Frontier."

13. Horace Greeley, *Glances at Europe*, p. iv. Also Nathaniel Parker Willis, *Hurry-Graphs; or, Sketches . . . Taken from Life*.

14. When James Lane Allen asked Henry Mills Alden in 1884 how to begin his career as a writer, he was told to find "a definite field" and mine it for literary materials, James Lane Allen, "H. M. Alden," p. 332. Allen's efforts to become Kentucky's writer are detailed in Grant Knight, *James Lane Allen and the Genteel Tradition*, and John Wilson Townsend, *James Lane Allen, A Personal Note*. See also James Lane Allen, *The Blue-Grass Region of Kentucky*, p. [iii]. On Alden's encouragement of Owen Wister, see Fanny Kemble Wister, ed., *Owen Wister Out West*, esp. pp. 165ff., and Harper, *House of Harper*, pp. 606–7. On Aldrich and the *Atlantic*, see Ferris Greenslet, *T. B. Aldrich*. Aldrich sent

Mary Noailles Murfree on a journey in search of local color during the autumn of 1885, to refresh faded memories of girlhood summers spent in the Tennessee mountains, according to Marian C. Sherman, "The Local Color Motif in the Writings of Mary Noailles Murfree," pp. 42–43. Murfree was a valuable property at this time—most authors had to pay their own way; see Harry Stillwell Edwards correspondence and Charles Dudley Warner correspondence, *Century* Collection. Garland's journeys in search of literary material for his "middle border" stories are discussed in Jean Holloway, *Hamlin Garland*.

15. John Dwight Kern, *Constance Fenimore Woolson, Literary Pioneer*, pp. 7–8. This is the definitive literary biography of Woolson, but see also Rayburn S. Moore, *Constance Fenimore Woolson*; Clare Benedict, *Voices Out of the Past* and *Constance Fenimore Woolson*; Ethel B. Colbrunn, "Regionalism in the Works of Constance Fenimore Woolson"; Henry James, Jr., "Miss Constance Fenimore Woolson."

16. See Woolson's note to a bibliography of her work in Benedict, *Constance Fenimore Woolson*, p. 550.

17. "The Happy Valley," p. 282.

18. Ibid., p. 285. It was this aesthetic distance functioning as social distance which led later critics to deny the importance of local-color writing in the emergence of a realistic tradition in American letters, and to damn it instead as a typical product of the "genteel tradition"; see William Allen White, "Fiction of the Eighties and Nineties."

19. Kern, *Constance Fenimore Woolson*, chapter 2.

20. Ibid., chapter 4 and bibliography. Woolson moved to St. Augustine, Florida, during the early months of 1873. Her first southern sketch was published in *Appleton's Journal* for 16 May 1874, as "A Voyage to an Unknown River." Her second southern summer was spent at Asheville and yielded her first Carolina sketch, "The French Broad," in *Harper's Magazine* for April 1875. A collection of stories from this period was published as *Rodman the Keeper: Southern Sketches*.

21. Caroline S. Kirkland, "The Young Man Who Went West: A Californian Epipoeia," p. 90; also Pattee, *Development of the American Short Story*, p. 268 *et passim*.

22. Arnold Hauser, *The Social History of Art*, 2: 714ff.; W. P. James, "On the Theory and Practice of Local Color"; H. A. Needham, *Le développement de l'esthetique sociologique en France et an Angleterre au XIXᵉ siècle*.

23. See Frank Luther Mott, "The Magazine Revolution and Popular Ideas in the Nineties"; Benjamin T. Spencer, *The Quest for Nationality*, pp. 257–58; Edd Winfield Parks, *Charles Egbert Craddock*, pp. 87–88.

24. Horace Spencer Fiske, *Provincial Types in American Prose Fiction*, p. 1. "Little corners" is from W. P. James, "On the Theory and Practice of Local Color."

25. Harriet Beecher Stowe, *Oldtown Folks*, p. iii.

26. Bret Harte, *The Luck of Roaring Camp, and Other Sketches* (1869); Ernest Ingersoll, "Mountain Harry: A Character Sketch" (1877); Theodore Roosevelt, *Hunting Trips of a Ranchman* (1885) and "Frontier Types" (1888); Julian Ralph, "Wyoming—Another Pennsylvania" (1893); Owen Wister, "Em'ly" (1893). On Garland's western sketches, see Holloway, *Hamlin Garland*.

27. For example, Rebecca Harding Davis, "A Night in the Mountains" (1877); James Lane Allen, "Realism and Romance" and "Mountain Passes of the Cumberlands" (1890); Charles Dudley Warner, "The South Revisited."

28. For example, William D. Kelley, *The Old South and the New* (1887). Edward A. Pollard, in "The Virginia Tourist" series for *Lippincott's* (May, June, Aug. 1870), first offered the politically neutral formula of description with no social commentary and emphasis on scenery rather than on political life. Sketches which utilized this formula include: [unsigned], "The North Carolina Mountains" (Oct. 1870); George W. Nichols,

"Six Weeks in Florida" (Oct. 1870) and "Down the Mississippi" (Nov. 1870); Edward A. Pollard, "The Real Condition of the South" (Dec. 1870); Henry E. Coulton, "Picturesque America" (Jan. 1871); John Esten Cooke, "The Natural Bridge" (Feb. 1871); T. L. Clingman, "Western North Carolina" (May 1871); F. G. de Fontaine, "Cumberland Gap" (March 1872); "Porte Crayon" [David Hunter Strother], "The Mountains" (April 1872–Sept. 1875); Edward King, "The Great South" (July 1873–Dec. 1874); Albert Webster, Jr., "A Jaunt in The South" (Aug.–Sept. 1873); and Edward de Leon, "The New South" (Jan., Feb., Sept. 1874). By mid-1874, as Paul H. Buck noted in *The Road to Reunion*, the groundwork had been laid for a more serious treatment of the problems of reunion in the magazines, beginning with the publication in June of that year of George Cary Eggleston's "A Rebel's Recollections." A most helpful study of the developing interest in the South among writers and editors is Moore, "Southern Writers and Northern Literary Magazines." Also of interest is Rutherford, *The South in History and Literature*. On the rejection of sectionalism and regionalism by the monthly magazines, see e.g. [George William Curtis], "Editor's Easy Chair," *Harper's Magazine* (Oct. 1866) and [J. G. Holland], "Our Monthly Gossip," *Lippincott's Magazine* (Jan. 1868).

29. This judgment is Henry Nash Smith's, in "Origins of a Native American Literary Tradition," pp. 69–70.

30. See White, "Fiction of the Eighties and Nineties," p. 392.

31. John Esten Cooke, "Owlet" (1878), p. 201. Also Elizabeth Haven Appleton, "A Half-Life and Half a Life" (1864); Louise Coffin Jones, "In the Highlands of North Carolina" (1883).

32. By her contemporaries as well as by later critics and literary historians, and by observers of Appalachia itself; see Charles W. Coleman, Jr., "The Recent Movement in Southern Literature" (1887), pp. 850–51; Milton T. Adkins, "The Mountains and Mountaineers of Craddock's Fiction" (1890), p. 306; E. F. Harkins, "Charles Egbert Craddock" (1901); Horace Kephart, *Our Southern Highlanders* (1913), p. 11; Edwin E. White, *Highland Heritage: The Southern Mountains and the Nation* (1937), p. 16. Murfree published extensively in the late 1870s and early 1880s; the best of her stories were collected as *In the Tennessee Mountains* (Boston, Houghton, Mifflin and Co., 1884), which went through eighteen editions by 1887. The standard biography remains Parks, *Charles Egbert Craddock*, although Richard Cary, *Mary N. Murfree*, deals more fully with her later work. On the mountaineer in American fiction generally, see Carvel Emerson Collins, "The Literary Tradition of the Southern Mountaineer, 1824–1900," and "Nineteenth Century Fiction of the Southern Appalachians"; Isabella D. Harris, "The Southern Mountaineer in American Fiction, 1824–1910." Collins and Harris both emphasize the intimate relationship between the strange land and the peculiar people in Appalachian fiction, which has meant that the mountaineer does not function as a "literary type" or stock character, a view which Parks reinforces. Lorise C. Boger, *The Southern Mountaineer in Literature*, revives the notion that the mountaineer as a "literary type" received consistent treatment in American fiction, following the analogue of Shields McIlwaine, *The Southern Poor White*.

33. My estimates are approximate, based on Collins, "Nineteenth Century Fiction of the Southern Appalachians," and Everett Eugene Edwards, *References on the Mountaineers of the Southern Appalachians*, supplemented by my own bibliographical excursions.

34. Mary Noailles Murfree to Houghton, Mifflin and Co., 24 June 1882, quoted in Parks, *Charles Egbert Craddock*, p. 103.

35. Murfree, *In the Tennessee Mountains*, p. 90.

36. Houghton, Mifflin and Co. to Mary Noailles Murfree, 11 Nov. 1883, quoted in Parks, p. 107n. Fred Lewis Pattee, *The Development of the American Short Story*, pp. 273–274, for example, explains Murfree's popularity as an extension of the contemporary

vogue of Hardy, which Parks explores in some detail, pp. 187, 207ff. See also [unsigned], "In the Tennessee Mountains [Review]," *Atlantic Monthly* (July 1884).

37. Murfree, *In the Tennessee Mountains*, pp. 154, 197 et passim, and below, chapter 3.

38. See Robert Rhode, "The Function of Setting in the American Short Story of Local Color, 1865–1900."

39. Collins, "Nineteenth Century Fiction of the Southern Appalachians," notes 46 of 320 stories and novels published between 1875 and 1900 dealing with love affairs between mountaineers and "outsiders."

40. Parks, *Charles Egbert Craddock*, p. 97 and n., states that this was the third of her stories to be accepted by the *Atlantic*, by letter of 4 May 1878.

41. "The Star in the Valley" (1878), p. 536.

42. Reginald Chevis becomes John Cleaver in "The Romance of Sunrise Rock" (1880). See also "The Despot of Broomsedge Cove" (1888) and "The Juggler" (1896).

43. James Lane Allen, *The Blue-Grass Region of Kentucky*, p. [iii]; Knight, *James Lane Allen*; Townsend, *James Lane Allen*.

44. "Through Cumberland Gap on Horseback" (1886), p. 50.

45. Charles Dudley Warner, "On Horseback" (1885), p. 194.

46. Descriptions of scenery were insufficient excuse for publication of a local color sketch according to Allen, "Local Color" and "Realism and Romance."

47. "Through Cumberland Gap on Horseback," p. 50. Allen published a second Kentucky mountain sketch, "Mountain Passes of the Cumberland" (1890), which avoids analysis and contents itself with description of the rapid economic development of Appalachia by British and American entrepreneurs. Economic development, or advocacy of economic development, appears as a legitimate mode of dealing with the dissonance generated by the fact of Appalachian otherness, however; see below, chapter 6. Allen's "Mountain Passes of the Cumberland" appears also to have been modeled after an essay by Charles Dudley Warner, in this case his "Comments on Kentucky" (1889), which also provided the inspiration for John Gilmer Speed, "The Kentuckians" (1900).

Chapter 2

1. Oliver Saxon Heckman, "Northern Church Penetration of the South, 1860–1880," remains the most comprehensive study of this phenomenon, although more recent works have dealt with freedmen's aid work in greater detail, especially Henry Lee Swint, *The Northern Teacher in the South, 1862–1871*; Willie Lee Rose, *Rehearsal for Reconstruction*; David M. Reimers, *White Protestantism and The Negro*. On the churches themselves, see Williston Walker, *A History of the Congregational Churches in the United States*; Charles J. Ryder, *Fifty Years of the American Missionary Association*; J. M. Buckley, *A History of the Methodists in the United States*; Robert Ellis Thompson, *A History of the Presbyterian Churches in the United States*.

2. *New York Times*, 29 Dec. 1863, p. 4. On confiscation generally, see James G. Randall, *Constitutional Problems under Lincoln*; Henry D. Shapiro, *Confiscation of Confederate Property in the North*.

3. Swint, *Northern Teacher in the South*, pp. 36, 58ff; [American Union Committee], *The American Union Committee: Its Origin, Operations and Purposes*.

4. Heckman, "Northern Church Penetration of the South."

5. These were the reasons for the establishment of Berea College in the postwar period; see Elisabeth S. Peck, *Berea's First Century, 1855–1955*, and such contemporary documents as John G. Fee, "Kentucky" (1855); John A. R. Rogers, "Letters from Kentucky" (1858); [unsigned], "Berea, Kentucky. Acclimating Northern Principles" (1873);

E. Henry Fairchild, "Extract from a Private Letter of President Fairchild" (1873) and *Berea College, Kentucky: An Interesting History* (1875). An anecdotal history of Berea in this early period is Charles T. Morgan, *The Fruit of This Tree*.

6. Heckman, "Northern Church Penetration of the South," p. 140.

7. Quoted ibid., pp. 226–27.

8. Ibid., pp. 269ff.; Thompson, *History of the Presbyterian Churches*, pp. 180ff.

9. Buckley, *History of the Methodists*, pp. 516–17; Wade Crawford Barclay, *The Methodist Episcopal Church: Widening Horizons, 1845–1895*, pp. 226–27, 302ff.; Heckman, "Northern Church Penetration of the South," pp. 75, 197 and notes. Also of interest is William Warren Sweet, "Methodist Unification."

10. Quoted in Heckman, "Northern Church Penetration of the South," pp. 200–204; see also Richard B. Drake, "Freedmen's Aid Societies and Sectional Compromise."

11. Augustus Field Beard, *Crusade of Brotherhood: The History of the American Missionary Association*, p. 148; also Harlan Paul Douglass, *The New Home Missions: An Account of Their Social Redirection*.

12. The Presbyterian Board of Home Missions, for example, insisted in 1871 that it was "organized for the relief of feeble churches" rather than "for the support of missionaries," but in 1874 the General Assembly divided its work into missions and sustentation, *Minutes of the General Assembly of the Presbyterian Church in the United States of America*, 1871, p. 647; 1874, p. 24; subsequently cited as *Minutes*. In 1878, the board announced that it had become "the arm of the Church for the great work of evangelizing the land," *Minutes*, 1878, pp. 107–8. Cf. in this connection Henry King Carroll's condemnation of sectarianism in home-missionary work, in *The Religious Forces of the United States, Enumerated, Classified, and Described on the Basis of the Government Census of 1890: With an Introduction on the Condition and Character of American Christianity*, pp. xvi, lxii; and such manifestations of the spirit of sect as appear passim in the proceedings of the several denominations, as in this selection from the Presbyterian Home Mission Board Report for 1872 (*Minutes*, 1872, p. 135): "It is in vain that we boast of our polity and the scriptural character of our preaching; the other denominations will carry the people with them, if their efficient ministerial force is superior to ours. God has determined to subdue the world to Himself by the preaching of the Gospel; and that branch of the Church that has the most preachers—other things being equal—will achieve the greatest successes and show the greatest growth." A helpful institutional study of this process is Earl R. MacCormac, "The Transition from Voluntary Missionary Society to the Church as a Missionary Organization."

13. Carroll, *Religious Forces of the United States*, p. lxii; Joseph B. Clark, *The Historic Policy and the New Work of the American Home Missionary Society* and *Leavening the Nation: The Story of American Home Missions*; Ryder, *Fifty Years of the American Missionary Association*; Sherman H. Doyle, *Presbyterian Home Missions*; Samuel L. Morris, *At Our Own Door: A Study of Home Missions with Special Reference to the South and West* (1904).

14. On centralization and rationalization in denominational structure, see Carroll, *Religious Forces of the United States*, p. lxiii; Frank S. Mead, *Handbook of Denominations*; Leonard Woolsey Bacon, *A History of American Christianity*; William Warren Sweet, *The Story of Religion in America*, pp. 348ff.; Presbyterian Church, "Report of the Special Committee on Voluntary Societies," *Minutes*, 1874, pp. 164–67, and "Report of the Standing Committee on Home Missions," ibid., 1879, p. 579.

15. Walker, *History of the Congregational Churches*, pp. 403ff.

16. The issue was fought out between the Home Mission Board and the Committee of Missions for Freedmen, on the one hand, and the Home Mission Board and the Foreign Mission Board, on the other. In the first case, the Committee of Missions for Freedmen was to have been absorbed by the Home Mission Board in 1879, as a result of

a report by the Special Committee on the Consolidation of the Boards, promulgated in 1874, *Minutes*, 1874, pp. 18ff. In 1878, the committee's life was extended indefinitely, and eighty black churches previously transferred to the Home Mission Board returned to its jurisdiction, ibid., 1878, pp. 74–81. In the second case, the Home Mission Board was able to establish its claim to a monopoly over missionary work within the United States, even among the "exceptional populations" to whom the Foreign Board had previously ministered, the Chinese in California and the American Indians on the plains. "The genius of the foreign work is to teach and preach in a foreign tongue, and to build up the Church under a foreign government; while that of the home work is to teach and preach in the English language, to naturalize all foreign elements, and build up our own Church in our own land," the Home Board argued; "it is not only church work, but American church work," ibid., 1878, p. 109. In the process, the Home Board initiated educational work to complement its missionary efforts. "The Department of Schools is altogether new in the work of Home Missions. Hitherto we have not established or supported them or done anything towards the employment or payment of teachers. But now we have reached a point where something of the kind must be done. We must begin work among the Indians, the Mexicans, and the Mormons, very much as we would in Persia or India; very much as foreign missionaries begin their work in foreign lands," ibid., 1877, p. 633. To fund this additional work, it was determined "to enlarge the sphere of the old Home Missionary Societies, which had been engaged for years in making up missionary boxes, by adding this more important work of sending teachers to train the youth . . . in the principles of patriotism and Christianity" by organizing the Woman's Executive Committee of Home Missions, ibid. Established in 1878, the Woman's Executive Committee remained an adjunct of the Home Mission Board even after 1883, when it assumed the status of an independent agency within the Presbyterian church, ibid., 1883, p. 754.

17. Barclay, *Methodist Episcopal Church*, pp. 226–27. The classification scheme was revised in 1880 following the establishment of Annual Conferences (the agencies of regional church governance among the Methodists) in all the "Domestic Foreign Mission" fields, although a special relationship between the Missionary Society and the missions among "exceptional populations" continued.

18. Elizabeth R. Hooker, *Religion in the Highlands*, p. 199. Hooker argues that the ladies of the Presbyterian Woman's Executive Committee, having "started a school for colored girls . . . in 1879 . . . at once discovered that white girls of the vicinity needed education as much as the colored girls; and in the same year Whitehall Seminary was opened for them three miles away." Whitehall Seminary, later Laura Sunderland School, was indeed opened in 1879 at Concord, North Carolina, but Scotia Seminary, the colored school in question, began operations in 1872 under the direction of the Presbyterian Committee of Missions for Freedmen. Its supervision was transferred to the Woman's Executive Committee under the Home Mission Board as part of the readjustment of duties in missionary work in 1878 discussed in n. 16, above, Presbyterian Committee of Missions for Freedmen, "Annual Reports," 1872–, in *Minutes*, passim.

19. Barclay, *Methodist Episcopal Church*, pp. 316ff. The process is discussed more generally in Reimers, *White Protestantism and the Negro*, pp. 51–72.

20. Charles G. Fairchild, "Address of Professor C. G. Fairchild" (1883), p. 391.

21. Ibid., p. 393; also E. H. Fairchild, *Berea College, Kentucky. An Interesting History* (1875), pp. 85ff.; (1883), pp. 67ff.

22. On Fee's antebellum ministry in Kentucky, in addition to Peck, *Berea's First Century*, see John G. Fee, "Kentucky" (1855); "Kentucky. Return of Kentucky Exiles" (1862); "Kentucky. No Compromise with Slavery" (1862); "Home Missions" (1864);

also William G. Frost, "Berea College" (1905), pp. 54ff. On Fee's break with the American Missionary Association over the issue of interdenominationalism at the time of its absorption by the Congregational church, see E. Henry Fairchild, *Berea College, Kentucky. An Interesting History* (1883), p. 8. The persuasiveness of Charles Fairchild's argument appears in the readoption of Berea as a precedent for A.M.A. work in the southern mountains, as in [unsigned], "Early Anti-Slavery Missions and Their Outcome" (1891), p. 440.

23. Charles G. Fairchild, "Address of Professor C. G. Fairchild," p. 393. The Presbyterian Board of Home Missions used virtually the same argument in its report to the General Assembly in 1886, *Minutes*, 1886, pp. 43, 184–85.

24. Washington Gladden, "Christian Education at the South," p. 390.

25. *Journal of the General Conference of the Methodist Episcopal Church*, 1880, pp. 41, 293, 345; 1884, pp. 365–66; 1888, pp. 451, 702; subsequently cited as *General Conference Journal*.

26. *Minutes*, 1884, p. 37.

27. *Minutes*, 1877, p. 633.

28. *Minutes*, 1878, p. 167. On interagency competition see also Buckley, *History of the Methodists in the United States*, pp. 653ff. By 1883, for example, Berea College had not only broken with the American Missionary Association but had emerged as an independent competitor for financial support within Congregationalism, E. H. Fairchild, *Berea College, Kentucky. An Interesting History* (1883), p. 8; Peck, *Berea's First Century*, p. 143.

29. Gladden, "Christian Education at the South," p. 385; *General Conference Journal*, 1884, p. 7; 1888, pp. 689–700; 1892, p. 687.

30. Doyle, *Presbyterian Home Missions*, pp. 188–94; *Minutes*, 1888, p. 225; John E. Calfee, "Training for Leadership" (1919) and "The Mountain Problem."

31. Doyle, *Presbyterian Home Missions*, pp. 191–92; [unsigned], "Monthly Topic: Mountain Work" (1891); also Kate W. Hamilton, "Cindy's Chance" (1891).

32. Doyle, *Presbyterian Home Missions*, pp. 191–92.

33. *Minutes*, 1885, pp. 758, 763; 1886, pp. 183–84; 1887, p. 210; 1888, p. 225. The home missions board supported on the average some fifty missionaries annually in the states of Virginia, West Virginia, North Carolina, Tennessee, and Kentucky, exclusive of ministers on sustentation, Board of Home Missions, "Annual Reports," 1870——, in *Minutes*, passim. Some of these may be presumed to have ventured into the uplands.

34. *Minutes*, 1886, pp. 183–84.

35. Hooker, *Religion in the Highlands*, pp. 194ff.; Ryder, *Fifty Years of the American Missionary Association* and "Our American Highlanders" (1897); S. L. Morris, *At Our Own Door* (1904); Walter Hughson, comp., *The Church's Mission to the Mountaineers of the South* (1908); Walter C. Whitaker, *A Round Robin: The Southern Highlands and Highlanders* (1916). By 1910, an examination of published denominational reports indicated that there were 135 denominational schools in Appalachia, exclusive of those supported by the Episcopal and Congregational churches: 11 Methodist, 35 Southern Methodist, 35 Baptist, 54 Presbyterian, according to Samuel Hunter Thompson, *The Highlanders of the South* (1910), pp. 66ff. By 1914, John C. Campbell estimated that there were some 220 denominational schools in Appalachia, on the basis of survey schedules returned to the Southern Highland Division office in Asheville, Campbell to John M. Glenn, 25 April 1914, Southern Highland Division Papers. In that year, 15 denominational agencies working in Appalachia, exclusive of those connected with the Episcopal church, spent $319,271.06 in support of evangelical and benevolent work in the region, Home Missions Council, *Annual Report*, 1915, appendix.

36. Alexander Johnson's distinction between "ameliorative, preventive, and con-

structive" benevolence, in his "Introduction," National Conference of Charities and Correction, *Proceedings*, 1909, p. iii, based in part on Joseph Lee, *Constructive and Preventive Philanthropy*, provides a useful scheme for describing the transformation of benevolent work in the United States between about 1880 and 1910, which I have loosely followed here.

Chapter 3

1. Carvel Emerson Collins, "Nineteenth Century Fiction of the Southern Appalachians," p. 186, points to one dimension of this phenomenon in noting the emergence of a new view of mountain life as "squalid and degenerate" in literary works dealing with the region published after 1890. In the same period, the degenerate–unregenerate character of the mountaineers was hotly debated, especially in the home missionary magazines, as by Mrs. S. M. Davis, "The 'Mountain Whites' of America" (1895), versus J. T. Wilds, "The Mountain Whites of the South" (1895).

2. [Unsigned], "Poor White Trash," *Cornhill Magazine* (May 1882), p. 584; reprinted in *The Living Age* (17 June 1882) and *The Eclectic* (July 1882).

3. William Goodell Frost, "Our Contemporary Ancestors in the Southern Mountains" (1899), p. 311. As early as 1864, Superintendent of the Census Joseph C. G. Kennedy referred to "the Allegheny Region, from Pennsylvania, through Virginia, Eastern Tennessee, &c., to Northern Alabama" as one of the natural divisions of the country, according to Fulmer Mood, "The Origin, Evolution, and Application of the Sectional Concept, 1750–1900," p. 74. Nonetheless, Frost's coinage seems to have been the first to suggest that the southern mountains composed a region in the modern sense of a territory defined by its characteristics and its civilization as well as by its location. Although *Appalachia* was the title of the journal published by the Appalachian Mountain Club of Boston, an "outing" organization, from 1876, "Appalachia" was first used to designate the southern mountain region by Horace Kephart in *Our Southern Highlanders* (1913), which first appeared in *Outing Magazine* (Dec. 1912–May 1913). J. Russell Smith wrote about "Farming Appalachia" (1916), but the word did not "catch on" until the 1920s, when Kephart's volume was reissued (1921, 1922, 1929) and attracted widespread attention. James Watt Raine first used the word in a book title, *The Land of Saddle-Bags: A Study of the Mountain People of Appalachia*, in 1924.

4. Charles J. Ryder, "Our American Highlanders" (1897), pp. 67, 69. Ryder claimed to have coined the phrase in an 1892 address to the American Missionary Association, published as *The Debt of Our Country to the American Highlanders during the War* (1896?), although Louise Coffin Jones, "In the Highlands of North Carolina" (1883), earlier wrote of the Highlands as high-lands. The Scotch-Irish origins of the mountaineers appears to derive from James G. Craighead, *Scotch and Irish Seeds in American Soil*, and appears for example in J. M. Davies, "Scotch-Irish Stock in the Central South" (1887). On "American Highlanders" as explanation, see also below, chapter 4.

5. "Mountain whites," to distinguish the mountaineers from the so-called "poor whites" of the South, flourished so long as traditional home-missionary work dominated mountain benevolence, and tended to disappear from use in the early twentieth century; citations include Mrs. A. A. Myers, *Mountain White Work in Kentucky* (1883); Frank E. Jenkins, "The Mountain Whites of the South" (1890); "A Scotch-Irishman," *The Mountain Whites of the South* (1893); J. Hampden Porter, "Notes on the Folk-Lore of the Mountain Whites of the Alleghenies" (1894); Mrs. S. M. Davis, "The 'Mountain Whites' of America" (1895); Robert F. Campbell, "Classification of Mountain Whites" (1901). "Mountaineer(s)" was used by Murfree and other local colorists to designate persons who lived in the mountains, but it began to appear as the "name" of the mountain dwellers of Appalachia during the late 1880s, for example in Thomas Wilson

Humes, *The Loyal Mountaineers of Tennessee* (1888); Martha Colyer Roseboro, "The Mountaineers about Montegle" (1888); Adelin Moffatt, "Mountaineers of Middle Tennessee" (1891).

6. Murfree, "The Star in the Valley" (1878), p. 536. Those who spoke of the "social class" of the mountain population generally did so in an attempt to distinguish between "shiftless and degenerate" and "hardworking but unregenerate" elements among the mountaineers, in defense of benevolent work among the latter; e.g. Robert F. Campbell, "Classification of Mountain Whites" (1901); Samuel Tyndale Wilson, *The Southern Mountaineers* (1906 and subsequent eds.); John C. Campbell, *The Southern Highlander and His Homeland* (1921).

7. James Lane Allen, "Through Cumberland Gap on Horseback" (1866), p. 60. Allen also provided Fox with his subplot concerning the impact of industrial development on mountain life, in "Mountain Passes of the Cumberland" (1890), which was published after Fox had begun but before he had completed his own story. "A Mountain Europa" first appeared in the *Century* (1892), and was published as a separate (*A Mountain Europa* [N.Y., HarpeJONES & Bros., 1899]), dedicated to James Lane Allen, only following the success of Fox's second mountain novel, *The Kentuckians* (N.Y., Harper & Bros., 1897). On Fox's relationship with Allen, see John Wilson Townsend, *James Lane Allen*, p. 20. On Fox generally, see Harold Everett Green, *Towering Pines*; Warren I. Titus, *John Fox, Jr*.

8. "A Mountain Europa," pp. 762–63.

9. Allen, "Through Cumberland Gap on Horseback," p. 60.

10. *The Kentuckians*, pp. 55–57.

11. [Unsigned], "Poor White Trash," p. 584.

12. "A Peculiar People" (1888), p. 508.

13. C. Willard Hayes, "The Southern Appalachians" (1895), pp. 33435, and "Eastern Kentucky: Its Physiography and Its People" (1895). Hayes's most important technical monograph on Appalachia, prepared for the U.S. Geological Survey, was published in *National Geographic*, then the vehicle of a professionalizing earth science, as "Geomorphology of the Southern Appalachians" (1894), with Marius R. Campbell.

14. Grace F. Ryan, "The Highlands of Kentucky" (1898), p. 363; George E. Vincent, "A Retarded Frontier" (1898), p. 1; William Goodell Frost, "Our Contemporary Ancestors in the Southern Mountains" (1899), p. 311. Also Joseph E. Roy, *Americans of the Midland Mountains* (1891); J. Stoddard Johnston, "Romance and Tragedy of Kentucky Feuds" (1899); William Goodell Frost, "The Southern Mountaineer: Our Kindred of the Boone and Lincoln Type" (1900).

15. John Fox, Jr., "The Southern Mountaineer" (1901), pp. 387–88.

16. Ellen Churchill Semple, "The Anglo-Saxons of the Kentucky Mountains: A Study in Anthropogeography" (1901), p. 588.

17. Below, chapter 5. William Goodell Frost, for whom the argument from "neglect" implied the inadequacies of Berea's work in Appalachia, dealt with this theme only following his retirement, in "God's Plan for the Southern Mountains" (1921).

18. On Appalachian otherness as an index of the impact of geography on historical process, see Hayes, "The Southern Appalachians"; Vincent, "A Retarded Frontier"; Semple, "The Anglo-Saxons of the Kentucky Mountains"; S. S. MacClintock, "The Kentucky Mountains and Their Feuds" (1901); Mary E. Verhoeff, *The Kentucky Mountains. Transportation and Commerce, 1750–1911* (1911). On Appalachian otherness as an index of the tendency of a people to "progress" or "degenerate" following lines of least resistance established by the characteristics of their environment, see James Mooney, "Folk-Lore of the Carolina Mountains" (1889); Robert F. Campbell, *Mission Work among the Mountain Whites of Asheville Presbytery* (1899) and "Classification of Mountain

Whites" (1901); Walter Claiborne Whitaker, *A Round Robin: The Southern Highlands and Highlanders* (1916). The "line of least resistance" theory derives from Spencer via Richard L. Dugdale, *"The Jukes": A Study in Crime, Pauperism, Disease and Heredity* (1874 and 1877), pp. 63ff., and in the twentieth century yielded a new concern with the role of social environment in the development of civilization; see below, chapters 8–9. As early as 1898 George E. Vincent, "A Retarded Frontier," p. 20, argued that "a series of monographs on the chief aspects of this curious social survival ought to be written before the life, now being modified so rapidly, has lost its comparatively primitive character. Let students of sociology leave their books and at first hand in the Cumberlands deal with the phenomenon of a social order arrested at a relatively early stage of development."

Chapter 4

1. Humes, *Loyal Mountaineers* (1888), pp. 7, 10. William Eleazar Barton, "The Cumberland Mountains and the Struggle for Freedom" (1897), perhaps with Humes's work in mind, argued that the mountaineers were "discovered" as a result of their loyalty to the Union during the war.

2. Humes, *Loyal Mountaineers*, pp. 8–9.

3. Joseph E. Roy, *Americans of the Midland Mountains* (1891), pp. 2–3.

4. Ryder, *The Debt of Our Country* (1892), p. 12. The Humes-Ryder argument is repeated by "A Scotch-Irishman," *The Mountain Whites of the South* (1893); Swan M. Burnett, "The 'Over-Mountain' Men" (1894); William E. Barton, "The Cumberland Mountains and the Struggle for Freedom" (1897); General J. D. Cox, "The Mountain People in the Struggle for the Union" (1897); and in Ryder's own "Our American Highlanders" (1897). Burnett's essay is essentially a piece of local-color writing by a former resident of east Tennessee; the rest were products of denominational interest in mountain work, and must be evaluated as promotional literature.

5. Ryder, *The Debt of Our Country*, p. 11. The backwoodsman-mountaineer as agent of American civilization appears during the 1880s in Nathaniel Southgate Shaler, *Kentucky: A Pioneer Commonwealth*; James R. Gilmore, *Rear Guard of the Revolution* and *Advance Guard of Western Civilization*; James Phelan, *History of Tennessee: The Making of A State*; Theodore Roosevelt, *The Winning of the West*. The backwoodsman as Scotch-Irishman appears in James G. Craighead, *Scotch and Irish Seeds in American Soil*; Roosevelt, *Winning of the West*; Charles A. Hanna, *The Scotch-Irish, or the Scot in North Britain, North Ireland, and North America* and *The Wilderness Trail, or the Ventures and Adventures of the Pennsylvania Traders on the Allegheny Path*.

6. On the "unity of the English race," see, for example, Roosevelt, *Winning of the West*, 1:19ff, 254ff., which however depends heavily on the work of E. A. Freeman, especially "The English People in Its Three Homes."

7. Roosevelt, *Winning of the West*, 1:154; Lodge, *A Short History of the English Colonies in America*, pp. 70–72, 154–55.

8. John Fiske, *Old Virginia and Her Neighbors* (1897). Portions of this appeared earlier in *Harper's Magazine* for Nov. 1882 and Feb. 1883. The best guide to Fiske's revision of the *Harper's* essays is Milton Berman, *John Fiske*, esp. pp. 241ff.

9. Fiske, *Old Virginia*, 2: 188–89, 319–21.

10. John Fiske, *Outlines of Cosmic Philosophy*, 2: 196.

11. Lodge, *Short History*, pp. 70–72, 154–55.

12. Ibid., p. 521.

13. Mrs. S. M. Davis, "The 'Mountain Whites' of America" (1895), p. 423.

14. Ibid., p. 426. The theme of the mountaineers as a leaven for the nation appears throughout the denominational literature on Appalachia after about 1890. Their poten-

tial utility to the nation as a bulwark against creeping socialism was added to this tradition after World War I, as in the epigraph printed in William J. Hutchins, *Inauguration of William James Hutchins, President of Berea College* (1920), p. 32: "At a time when restlessness and the spirit of Bolshevism pervade the industrial centers of our Nation, it is reassuring to know that the Southern Mountains contain a population of three and a half million pure-blooded Americans, growing to manhood and womanhood, and needing only the advantages of a Christian education to become a source of strength to our national life."

15. Fiske, *Old Virginia*, 2: 321–22; this note is not in the *Harper's* version.

16. William Goodell Frost, "Our Contemporary Ancestors in the Southern Mountains" (1899), p. 311.

17. For example, John C. Campbell, "Ancestry [of the Mountaineers]," in *The Southern Highlander and His Homeland* (1921), pp. 50–71, including a statement from Cecil J. Sharp concerning this matter, pp. 70–71. Campbell explored the matter more fully in "The Ancestry of the Mountaineers" [1917?], Minnesota Historical Society. See also below, chapter 8 n. 41 and chapter 10 n. 34.

18. Samuel Tyndale Wilson, *The Southern Mountaineers* (1906), p. 171.

19. William Goodell Frost, "The Southern Mountaineer: Our Kindred of the Boone and Lincoln Type" (1900), p. 307. He sounded this theme first in "University Extension in Kentucky" (1898), p. 78; reprinted as "University Extension in the Southern Mountains" (1899).

20. On the Kentucky feuds, see John R. Spears, "The Story of a Mountain Feud" (1901); S. S. MacClintock, "The Kentucky Mountains and Their Feuds" (1901); Hartley Davis and Clifford Smyth, "The Land of Feuds" (1903); R. L. McClure, "The Mazes of a Kentucky Feud" (1903); O. O. Howard, "The Feuds in the Cumberland Mountains" (1904); Charles G. Mutzenberg, *Kentucky's Famous Feuds and Tragedies: Authentic Histories of the World Renowned Vendettas of the Dark and Bloody Ground* (1917). Their "world renown" derived in part from the extensive coverage provided by the *New York Times*, between 1901 and 1905, which see, passim. Political events in Kentucky at the turn of the century are neatly summarized in C. Vann Woodward, *Origins of the New South*, pp. 377ff. While Kentucky was not all of Appalachia, in the years since Murfree's popularity it had emerged as the center of Appalachian interest, as a result of Fox's novels and especially the publicity ventures of Frost and his staff at Berea.

21. Frost, "The Southern Mountaineer" (1900), p. 308.

22. [Unsigned], "Novel Notes" (1896). "A Cumberland Vendetta" was first published in the *Century* (June–Aug. 1894) and was reprinted as *A Cumberland Vendetta and Other Stories* (N.Y., Harper & Bros., 1895). Fox dealt with moonshiners and revenue officers in "Manhunting in the Pound" (1900) and "Christmas for Big Ame" (1910). Fox's fascination with mountain lawlessness is discussed in Warren I. Titus, *John Fox, Jr.*

23. On mountain violence in literature, see the doctoral dissertations of Collins and Harris, cited above, chapter 1 n. 17. Early interest in moonshining appears in A. H. Guernsey, "Illicit Distilling of Liquors" (1867) and "Hunting for Stills" (1867); [unsigned], "The Moonshine Man: A Peep into His Haunts and Hiding Places" (1877); Young E. Allison, "Moonshine Men" (1887); Francis Lynde, "The Moonshiners of Fact" (1896). The inevitable connection of moonshining and feuding was regularly made, as by Leonidas Hubbard, Jr., "The Moonshiner at Home" (1902), although Frost particularly sought to separate them by identifying moonshining as a "quaint" survival of the economy of pioneer days, as in "University Extension in Kentucky" (1898), p. 78.

24. After about 1905, the relationship of "individualism" as an historical trait of the southern mountaineers, or indeed of all mountaineers, and "lawlessness," manifested

not only in the feuds but also in the easy sexual relations believed to prevail in Appalachia, became as regular a theme in mountain fiction as in the complaints of benevolent workers; for example Marie Van Vorst, *Amanda of the Mill. A Novel* (1905), pp. 289–90: "[Amanda] had been born of a lawless people, of primitive creatures who would scoff at the metaphysician who desired to prove them not free. Whether or not her mother had conformed to the rites of Church and State Amanda could not have said; who her father was she did not know. Witness and participant of an illicit trade [moonshining], she had been nurtured in a law-breaking midst, and raised with neither ethics nor creed. In these free-born, primitive conditions her life's flower had its spring. . . . [Now] Amanda of the Mill returned to claim her birthright of lawlessness and free love." The contrast between Amanda and the "genuine" primitives of Edgar Rice Burrough's contemporary tales of Tarzan, for example, is striking.

25. Ryder, "Our American Highlanders" (1897), pp. 67, 69. Within a year, W. G. Frost was presenting Ryder's Highlander comparison as his own observation, as reported in [unsigned], "In Kentucky's Mountains: W. G. Frost Speaks at Broadway Tabernacle to the Class on Present-Day Problems," *New York Times*, 12 Dec. 1898, p. 5.

26. Semple, "The Anglo-Saxons of the Kentucky Mountains" (1901), p. 616; also George E. Vincent, "A Retarded Frontier" (1898); S. S. MacClintock, "The Kentucky Mountains and their Feuds"; R. L. McClure, "Mazes of a Kentucky Feud"; O. O. Howard, "The Feuds in the Cumberland Mountains." Frost added this environmentalist defense of the mountaineers to all the others in "Our Southern Highlanders" (1912), p. 709.

27. Frost, "The Southern Mountaineer" (1900), pp. 303, 306.

28. John M. Moore, *The South To-Day* (1916), pp. 127–28, 132–33.

29. For example, [unsigned], ["Editorial Note"], *Berea Quarterly* (Nov. 1900), p. 4: "In previous numbers, we have discussed the reputable British origin of these people and the surprising survivals of Saxon words and Saxon traits among them."

30. Frost, "The Southern Mountaineer" (1900), p. 309, and n. 19 above. In "Our Contemporary Ancestors in the Southern Mountains" (1899), p. 319, Frost wished to keep the mountaineers from the "competition" of cities.

Chapter 5

1. The standard discussions of the idea of "region" remain Fulmer Mood, "The Origin, Evolution, and Application of the Sectional Concept, 1750–1900," and Vernon Carstensen, "The Development and Application of Regional-Sectional Concepts, 1900–1950." On regionalism as a cultural posture after 1920, see esp. Howard W. Odum, *Folk, Region, and Society*; Donald Davidson, ed., *I'll Take My Stand*; William T. Couch, ed., *Culture in the South*; John K. Wright, ed., *New England's Prospect*. Southern regionalism is ably discussed in George B. Tindall, *The Emergence of the New South*, pp. 575–606.

2. *OED* (1910), vol. 8, pt. 1, p. 371; *Webster's Third New International Dictionary of the English Language* (1961), p. 1912. The definition of region as location appears in the following: *Webster's Revised Unabridged Dictionary of the English Language* (1913); *Webster's New International Dictionary of the English Language*, 2d ed. (1940); *The Century Dictionary and Encyclopaedia* (1889); *The Century Dictionary: An Encyclopaedic Lexicon* (1914); and *Funk & Wagnalls' New Standard Dictionary* (1928).

3. The southern location of the territory later defined as Appalachia is emphasized e.g. in J. M. Davies, "Scotch-Irish Stock in the Central South" (1887); Frank E. Jenkins, "The Mountain Whites of the South" (1890); and in the explanatory arguments of the late 1880s and early 1890s. The separation of Appalachia from the South, which precipitated the search for a new designation for the region, was the product of home-

missionary efforts to distinguish the "mountain whites" from the allegedly unredeemable "poor whites" and a logical corollary to their insistence that the mountain people had sided with the Union during the Civil War; see, for example, Joseph E. Roy, *Americans of the Midland Mountains* (1891).

4. William Goodell Frost, "The Last Log School-House" (1895). The explanation for naming, that Appalachia as a separate land deserved a name of its own, is implicit in this piece, although only articulated in his later essay, "Appalachian America" (Sept. 1896), and most clearly in "Our Contemporary Ancestors in the Southern Mountains" (1899). On Frost's career at Berea see William G. Frost, *For the Mountains: An Autobiography* and especially Elisabeth S. Peck, *Berea's First Century*. John Barnard, *From Evangelicalism to Progressivism at Oberlin College* helps put Frost's Berea career in context.

5. "The Last Log School-House." A year later, on 30 November 1896, Frost made similar remarks in an address entitled "Appalachian America" at a meeting on behalf of Berea College at Trinity Church, Boston, at which Theodore Roosevelt also spoke. Roosevelt argued that "the need of education in every part of the country" was demonstrated "by the recent political campaign" which saw "an appeal being made to the basest passions of the community, to overthrow all that has made the name America a name to conjure with in the past. There is only one way we can meet that appeal: that is by education. Berea College reaches the largest section of our white native Americans to be seen in our country. . . . If we fail to help them we may rest assured that our failure will be visited upon our own heads," *Boston Evening Journal*, 1 Dec. 1896. Frost was always more temperate in his discussions of the contemporary "crisis" and of Berea's ability to aid in resolving it, avoiding the rhetoric of political confrontation and of popular millenialism both, although he repeated the "unjaded nerves" theme in "Our Contemporary Ancestors in the Southern Mountains" (1899), p. 318; "The Southern Mountaineer: Our Kindred of the Boone and Lincoln Type" (1900), p. 308; and "Educational Pioneering in the Southern Mountains" (1901), p. 558. As early as his "Inaugural Address, June 21, 1893," pp. 34–35, Frost had noted that "our cities must be purified by air from these Cumberland mountains" in his defense of the usefulness of a rural college in an urban nation; a later statement appears in "Christian Patriotism" (1913).

6. The phrase "psychologically uncomfortable" is from Leon Festinger, *A Theory of Cognitive Dissonance*.

7. Frost, "Inaugural Address," p. 36; also "Berea Ideas" (1893) and especially *Synopsis of President's Report* (1894), pp. 14–15. See also W. G. Frost, "To The Brethren at Berea" (16 July 1892); to John G. Fee, 25 July 1892; to L. V. Dodge, 25 July 1892, all in W. G. Frost Papers.

8. Enrollment figures will be found in E. H. Fairchild, *Berea College, Kentucky* (1875 & 1883), and in Peck, *Berea's First Century*. Important statements of Berea's commitment to co-education are contained in Fairchild, op. cit., and *Inauguration of Rev. E. H. Fairchild, President of Berea College, Kentucky, Wednesday, July 7, 1869* (1870); William G. Frost, *Sectional Lines: A Toast* (1895) and "Berea College" (1905). See also [unsigned], "Berea College and Its President," *Alexander's Magazine* (1907).

9. William Goodell Frost, "Berea College Problems: President's Quarterly Report to the Faculty, Feb. 3, 1894," W. G. Frost Papers.

10. William Goodell Frost, "The Call of Providence" (1894).

11. W. G. Frost to [?] Taylor, 19 March 1933, W. G. Frost Papers.

12. Cf. the difference between his comment in "The Southern Mountaineer" (1900), p. 303: "For convenience, we are giving this inland mountain realm the name of 'Appalachian America' " and the analogous remarks in "Educational Pioneering in the Southern Mountains" (1901), p. 556: "Here is one of the grand divisions of our continent, which we are beginning to name Appalachian America" and the completely re-

written "Educational Pioneering in the Southern Mountains" (1913), p. 247: "The mountain region of the South, 'Appalachian America' as the Berea people have named it, is one of the grand divisions . . ."

13. W. G. Frost Papers, passim. Cf. also the emphasis on mountain white work in J. Cleveland Cady, "A Summer Outing in Kentucky" (1896), the report of a visit to Berea College at commencement time, 1895, as Frost was beginning his campaign of publicity.

14. Peck, *Berea's First Century*; William Goodell Frost, "Berea College" (1905); [unsigned], "Berea College and Its President," *Alexander's Magazine* (1907); William E. Barton, "A New Berea," *Boston Evening Transcript* (1908).

15. For example, William Goodell Frost, "Report of President Frost to the Trustees, 1900–1901" (1901).

16. W. G. Frost to Mrs. Maria G. Frost, 29 Aug. 1893, W. G. Frost Papers.

17. William Goodell Frost, "Our Contemporary Ancestors" (1899), p. 319.

18. William Goodell Frost, "The Southern Mountaineer" (1900), p. 307, and "Report of President Frost to the Trustees, 1900–1901." On industrial education at Berea, see chapter 9, below.

19. On crafts at Berea, see chapter 9, below.

20. See chapter 10, below.

Chapter 6

1. On the rise of "cultural relativism" among social workers during this period, see Clarke A. Chambers, *Paul U. Kellogg and The Survey*. My argument here is that the legitimation of Appalachian otherness antedated and hence generated—rather than followed from—the transformation of benevolent work in the southern mountains. In other client areas, it appears that the attempt to create community among the "poor" in their neighborhoods began as technique and only later generated an appreciation of the legitimacy of the distinct cultures of immigrants, for example. Both processes, however, yield the new pluralism of the teens and 1920s. As are we all, I am indebted to the work of Robert Bremner, especially *From the Depths*, and of John Higham, especially *Strangers in the Land*, for seminal insights into this process.

2. On Semple, see John K. Wright, "Miss Semple's 'Influences of Geographic Environment' " as well as her own work, especially *American History and Its Geographic Conditions* of 1903, to which should be compared for example, Albert Perry Bingham, *Geographic Influences in American History*, published in the same year.

3. J. Stoddard Johnston, "Romance and Tragedy of Kentucky Feuds" (1899), p. 551. This article was often quoted and sometimes cited in the literature on Appalachia, for example William Henry Haney, *The Mountain People of Kentucky* (1906), pp. 47–48.

4. Johnston, "Romance and Tragedy," p. 552.

5. Robert F. Campbell, *Mission Work among the Mountain Whites of Asheville Presbytery* (1899), p. 6. Campbell repeats this argument to explain the characteristics of the "lowest class" of mountaineers in "Classification of Mountain Whites" (1901). See also chapter 3 n. 21, above.

6. Campbell, *Mission Work*, p. 7. The same argument is carried on in Walter Claiborne Whitaker, *A Round Robin: The Southern Highlands and Highlanders* (1916), p. 19. The eugenicist Arthur H. Estabrook later sought to reverse the relationship, as in "Blood Seeks Environment" and "The Real Mountain Problem of South Carolina."

7. Ellen Churchill Semple, "The Anglo-Saxons of the Kentucky Mountains" (1901), p. 588; the same argument is carried on in William Goodell Frost, "Our Southern Highlanders" (1912), p. 709. Earlier commentators had conventionally identified "frontier" as a stage of development rather than as a characterization of the state

of social and economic organization prevailing in the mountains, for example A. D. Mayo, "The Third Estate of the South" (1890); George E. Vincent, "A Retarded Frontier" (1898).

8. Henderson Daingerfield, "Social Settlement and Educational Work in the Kentucky Mountains" (1901), p. 186.

9. Mary E. Walsh, "The Social Settlement at Narrow Gap" (1903). On the donation of land as a requirement for the establishment of a social service institution, manifesting the "desire" of the community for outside assistance and its willingness to "help itself" by making available its own resources, thereby preventing "pauperization" of the client population, see [Charles W. Dabney, comp.], *Educational Conditions in the Southern Appalachians* (1902), pp. 8, 10, 11, 30 et passim; Ethel de Long, "The [Rural] School as a Community Center" (1916) and "The Pine Mountain Settlement School" (1917); Florence Elton Singer, "The Shepherd of Red Bird." In addition to the organization of the Narrow Gap Settlement, Berea sponsored at least one "people's institute," concentrating on Bible instruction, and perhaps several teachers' institutes during the summer of 1900, conducted by Eloise J. Partridge, an Oberlin graduate, and Viola Schumaker, a graduate of one of the Pennsylvania normal schools, Eloise J. Partridge, "Extension Work in Perry County" (1902). Berea faculty had done a kind of extension work from the mid-1890s in the form of periodic lecturing and preaching, William G. Frost, "University Extension in Kentucky" (1898) and "Our Southern Highlanders" (1914), p. 266, but in 1901 its actual and projected work in agricultural and home economics education, Bible instruction, and its traveling libraries program were organized under an Extension Department, [unsigned], ["Editorial Note"], *Berea Quarterly* 6 nos. 2–3: 53–54 (1901), and C. Rexford Raymond, "An Artificial Seaboard: The Work of the Extension Department" (1901). In 1908, James P. Faulkner, formerly president of Union College, Barbourville, Kentucky, after completing a postgraduate course at Harvard, was appointed head of the Extension Department at Berea; half his salary was to be paid by "a group of men in Boston who have come to know Prof. Faulkner," according to William E. Barton, "A New Berea" (1908). See also in this connection, [unsigned], "College Work Out of Doors" (1910). Traveling libraries were among the educational innovations designated as "especially applicable to conditions in the South" by the participants in the second Capon Springs Conference for Education in the South, in 1899, Edgar Gardner Murphy, *Problems of the Present South*, p. 211, and Charles W. Dabney, Jr., *Universal Education in the South*, vol. 2, chapter 1.

10. William Goodell Frost's efforts to abort the proselytizing activities of the Mormons in Appalachia appear in W. G. Frost to G. P. Combs, Supt. of Schools for Hazard, Ky., 22 Sept. 1900, and L. W. Burns, Supt. of Schools for Greenbrier Cty., Ky., to W. G. Frost, 27 Oct. 1900, W. G. Frost Papers. The apparent success of his campaign was announced in [unsigned], ["Editorial Note"], *Berea Quarterly* 6 nos. 2–3: viii (1901): "We have practically driven the mormons out of a wide region, and we are giving the friendly aid which will kindle the ambition of young Americans." The persistence of Mormonism as a threat to other Protestant denominations in Appalachia appears however in Samuel Hunter Thompson, *The Highlanders of the South* (1910). The transformation of Mormonism which underlay its missionary efforts in the South is explored in Klaus J. Hansen, *Quest for Empire*, pp. 18off.

11. [Unsigned], "The Religious World: A Log Cabin Social Settlement" (1895).

12. For example, Jane Addams, "A New Impulse to an Old Gospel"; Mary K. Simkhovitch, "The Settlement's Relation to Religion" and *Neighborhood: My Story of Greenwich House*, pp. 56–62, 89ff. I have enjoyed and profited from Allen F. Davis, *American Heroine: The Life and Legend of Jane Addams*.

13. Ellen Churchill Semple, "A New Departure in Social Settlements" (1900), p.

303. On the establishment of the Hindman Settlement, see Daingerfield, "Social Settlement and Educational Work in the Kentucky Mountains" (1901); William Aspenwall Bradley, "The Women on Troublesome" (1918); [unsigned], "The Dream of a Shirt-tail Boy Come True" (1920). Also of interest is Katherine Pettit, "Progress in the Hills" (1923), although Pettit by this date had moved to the Pine Mountain Settlement.

14. Daingerfield, "Social Settlement and Educational Work in the Kentucky Mountains," p. 182.

15. Semple, "A New Departure in Social Settlements," p. 304. On the "ideal" of settlement work generally, see esp. Allen F. Davis, *Spearheads for Reform*. On the usefulness of the settlement experience in the development of a literary career, by providing material for sketches and short stories, see Nettie Gray Daingerfield, "Mrs. Clayton's Cooking School" (1902); Henderson Daingerfield, "The Little People of Donegal and Lee" (1903); and especially the "Mothering on Perilous" stories by Lucy Furman (1910–11).

16. Caroline Williamson Montgomery, "Settlements," pp. 1106–9, and *Bibliography of College, Social, University and Church Settlements*, 5th ed. (1905). The only important settlement in Appalachia founded between this early period and World War I was the Pine Mountain Settlement School, Inc., established in 1914 by Katherine Pettit of Hindman. It had as its goal the preparation of mountain children for life in the mountains, in part by aiding them to resist the changes which economic modernization of the region would bring, especially "chewing gum, slang, the sophisticated notion that people who work with their hands are not so fine as those who keep their hands clean and are always dressed up, [and] the degradation of young girls in their contact with different standards of virtue," Ethel de Long, "The Far Side of Pine Mountain" (1917), p. 628. See also de Long, "The Pine Mountain Settlement School: A Sketch from the Kentucky Mountains" (1917); Katherine Pettit, "Progress in the Hills" (1923). A very different description of the work at Pine Mountain appeared in de Long's "The [Rural] School as a Community Center" (1916), prepared for the National Conference of Charities and Correction. Before accepting the directorship of the "Opportunity School" at Berea, Helen Dingman, long-time editor of *Mountain Life and Work*, served a phase of her apprenticeship as a worker at Pine Mountain, Ethel de Long Zande to John C. Campbell, 27 Aug. 1918, Southern Highland Division Papers.

17. Williamson lists three in Alabama, one in Georgia, three in Kentucky, one in North Carolina, one in Texas, two in Virginia. In 1906, a second Georgia settlement was established by the Free Kindergarten Association and the Federated Jewish Philanthropies of Atlanta, which *Charities and The Commons* described as worthy of notice as a development in "the far South," [unsigned], "The Common Welfare: Southern Kindergarten and Settlement," (1906).

18. I am indebted to Peter Harsham for calling my attention to the widespread use of the principle of emulation in popular (as well as political) reform efforts of the early twentieth century. The function of rural schools as community centers is discussed in Harold W. Foght, "The Country School" (1912); A. C. Monahan and Adam Phillips, *The Farragut School: A Tennessee Country-Life High School* (1913); Elwood P. Cubberly, *Rural Life and Education* (1913); John F. Smith, "Some Impressions of a Social Surveyor" (1913), condensed in [unsigned], "How to Help the Mountain Whites" (1913); Ethel de Long, "The [Rural] School as a Community Center" (1916). Rural schools as centers for community health and community sanitation education are discussed in Thomas D. Wood, "Report of the Committee on Health Problems in Education: The Sanitation of Rural Schools" (1913); Ernest Bryant Hoag, *Organized Health Work in Schools* (1913); W. Carson Ryan, Jr., ed., *School Hygeine* (1913); Fletcher B. Dressler, *Rural School Houses and Grounds* (1914); John A. Ferrell, *The Rural School and Hookworm Disease* (1914); Thomas

D. Wood, "Health Problems in the American Public Schools" (1914); George MacAdam, "The National Menace of Rural Bad Health" (1917). See also in this connection Elisabeth S. Peck, *Berea's First Century*; Harnett T. Kane and Inez Henry, *Miracle in the Mountains*; Charles W. Dabney, Jr., *Universal Education in the South*, esp. vol. 1; Henry S. Enck, "The Burden Borne: Northern White Philanthropy and Southern Black Industrial Education," pp. 439–51.

19. Sherman H. Doyle, *Presbyterian Home Missions* (1902), p. 186; also Thomas S. Evans, "The Christian Settlement" (1907); Herbert Welch, "The Relation of the Church to the Social Worker" (1908); Frederick W. Neve, "Social Settlements in the South" (1909).

20. Contemporary sources include Samuel McCune Lindsay, "The Study and Teaching of Sociology" and "The Unit of Investigation or of Consideration in Sociology"; Frederick H. Wines, "Sociology and Philanthropy"; and the essays collected in Robert A. Woods, *The Neighborhood in Nation-Building*. The critical shift towards "presentist" models in social science thinking is outlined in Louis C. Wirth, "The Social Sciences" and more recently in R. Jackson Wilson, *In Quest of Community*.

21. The relationship of attempts to create community in rural and urban areas of the nation respectively remain to be examined, although contemporary sources are readily available, including G. T. Nesmith, "The Problem of Rural Community with Special Reference to the Rural Church" and Nesmith, ed., "Country Life"; Elwood P. Cubberly, *Rural Life and Education*; Paul L. Vogt, *The Church and Country Life*. A helpful discussion of the origins of the country-life movement appears in Betty Carol Clutts, "Country Life Aspects of the Progressive Movement." See also chapter 8, below. An index of the reflexive quality of benevolence in this period is Nathan Peyser, "The School as the Community Center," which argues that the city school can be made to serve as an agent of community in the way that the rural school does.

22. John C. Campbell, "Social Betterment in the Southern Mountains" (1909), p. 137. The potency of this argument, in the context of changing perceptions of the proper function of institutional benevolence, appears most clearly by its adoption by the publicists for Berea College, as in William E. Barton, "The Church Militant in the Feud Belt" (1903), or John F. Smith, "Some Impressions of a Social Surveyor" (1913), in which not more missionaries and more churches but education in community life and cooperation are held to be the needs of the mountaineers; and Marshall Everett Vaughan, "Community Education at Berea" (1922), which represents Berea's program in agricultural education as an index of its active work for "community" education.

23. John C. Campbell, "Mountain and Rural Fields in the South" (1916) and *The Future of the Church and Independent Schools in Our Southern Highlands* (1917). Warren H. Wilson's career deserves full biographical treatment. His "country-life" work is discussed in George Frederick Wells, "Is an Organized Country Life Movement Possible?" and his own writings are both extensive and revealing, especially *The Evolution of the Country Community: A Study in Religious Sociology*. William Goodell Frost was among those who "explained" mountain conditions as "the country condition intensified" as early as "Educational Pioneering in the Southern Mountains" (1901), p. 558. In later years he adapted Campbell's description of Appalachia as "hyper-rural" for a sermon at the Battle Creek Sanitarium, published as "Our Southern Highlanders" (1914), and for his address to the 1915 Conference of Southern Mountain Workers, published as *For the Mountains: Our Aims, Strategic Principles* (1915), in which he explained Appalachian otherness as the result of "supra-rural" and "super-rural" conditions respectively.

24. Campbell, *The Future of the Church and Independent Schools*, pp. 18–19. A hint of this theme appeared in Frost, "University Extension in Kentucky" (1898), p. 78, and was more fully developed in "Our Contemporary Ancestors in the Southern Moun-

tains" (1899), p. 319, but it was not until the teens that it became an actionable proposition; see below, chapters 9–10.

25. William G. Frost, "The Southern Mountaineer" (1900) and, for example, "University Extension in Kentucky" (1898), p. 78: "Two principles have been kept steadily in mind: In the first place, our aim has been to give the essential rather than the accidental elements of civilization—to make the people sharers in the best things, but to leave them unsophisticated. We will not teach them to despise the log cabin but to adorn it. And in the second place, we respect their sturdy independence and endeavor only to help them to help themselves. . . . Instruction in the arts of life—hygiene, forestry, thrift, etc., is provided to give them at once new motives and new resources."

26. On the movement for "real-life" education in the United States, see Arthur MacArthur, *Education in Its Relation to Manual Industry*; Paul U. Kellogg, "The National Society for the Promotion of Industrial Education." The appeal of industrial education was particularly strong among those who joined in the "southern school campaign" after 1898, as a way of guaranteeing the utility of educational development to a rural clientele of voters mistrustful of the traditional curriculum, and perhaps also as a way of assuring urban elites that their own monopoly on "classical" education would not be broken by the establishment of schools among the masses. On southern mistrust of the Southern Education Board and its chairman, Robert C. Ogden, as a new generation of carpetbagging levelers, see Enck, "The Burden Borne," pp. 361–86, and cf. this defense of industrial education for whites by Edgar Gardner Murphy, *Problems of the Present South*, p. 90: "The racial heritage of the white man must be clearly accepted and recognized in the form of his educational system; and yet a white population so largely dependent on its agricultural resources and its productive industry [as the South's] must bring its public education into more articulate relations with the soil and with its work." Grace Cole, state superintendent for public instruction of Arkansas, told a story of local cooperation with the Southern Education Board, however, in "The State Superintendent and the General and Southern Education Boards."

27. C. S. Whittier, Knoxville, Tenn., quoted in [Dabney, comp.], *Educational Conditions in the Southern Appalachians* (1902), p. 29; also, G. D. Langston, "The Child and the Farm"; Junius M. Horner, "Educational Work in the Mountains of North Carolina" (1910); [unsigned], ["Editorial Note: On the Valle Crucis School"], *Outlook* (1910).

28. Murphy, *Problems of the Present South*, pp. 48–49. Among the resolutions passed at the first Capon Springs Conference on Education in the South in 1898, was that "industrial education is to be encouraged in all schools, and at least the elements of it in the public schools," quoted ibid., p. 209. On the conferences and their work, see Dabney, *Universal Education in the South*, vol 2, chapter 1. The usefulness of industrial education in the creation of a citizenry supportive of the social order appears as a regular element in the fund-raising appeals of southern institutions during this period, e.g. Booker T. Washington, *Working with the Hands*; [unsigned], "[Theodore] Roosevelt Appeals for a Georgia School" (1911); "Cosmopolitan" [pseud.], "Miss Berry's School. Takes Ignorant Mountain Boys and Makes Them Capable Men" (1912); Walter A. Dyer, "Training New Leaders for the Industrial South" (1914).

29. Martha Berry, "A School in the Woods" (1904) and "The Evolution of a Sunday School" (1906). On nature study and domestic beautification as elements in the Berry School curriculum, see Martha Berry, "Social Life of the Appalachian Region" (1909), p. 42; but compare [unsigned], "Making Good Farmers and Helping Poor Farms: A Southern School that Gives Practical Education in Agriculture" (1914) or [unsigned], "The School at Rabun Gap" (1919).

30. Mary E. Verhoeff, *The Kentucky Mountains. Transportation and Commerce* (1911), pp. 183–84.

31. William L. Hall, "To Remake the Appalachians: A New Order that is Founded on Forestry" (1914), p. 323.

32. Ibid., p. 336.

Chapter 7

1. James Lane Allen, "Mountain Passes of the Cumberland" (1890), p. 576. Almost the same words are used by later observers of the continuing phenomenon, for example B. H. Schockle, "Changing Conditions in the Kentucky Mountains" (1916); [unsigned], "Industrial Invasion of the Kentucky Mountains" (1917). Allen himself made the same observations about the impact of industrial development on the bluegrass region of Kentucky, in "Homesteads of the Blue-Grass."

2. Allen, "Mountain Passes of the Cumberland," p. 561. It is of course no accident that Allen thus defines his intentions in a manner which advertises the novels to come, and which might also serve as a paradigm for the work of his better-known literary colleague, Frank Norris, whose trilogy of "the wheat" bears comparison to Allen's earlier trilogy of "the hemp."

3. Ibid., pp. 564, 568.

4. Samuel Tyndale Wilson, *The Southern Mountaineers* (1906), pp. 19, 60, 96ff.

5. Sherman H. Doyle, *Presbyterian Home Missions*, p. 186.

6. J. Stoddard Johnston, "Romance and Tragedy of Kentucky Feuds" (1899), p. 553, and "Foreword," in Mary E. Verhoeff, *The Kentucky Mountains* (1911), pp. v–vi.

7. Broadus Mitchell, *The Rise of the Cotton Mills in the South*, pp. 160–201. On the persistence into the twentieth century of work patterns associated with agricultural production, see Mrs. John [Bessie] Van Vorst, *The Cry of the Children*, pp. 123–24; Charles Wardell Stiles, *Hookworm Disease Among Cotton Mill Operatives*, pp. 22–23. Defenders of the cotton mills often argued that this situation meant that industrialization would not mean a break with the southern past, for example Mitchell, *Rise of the Cotton Mills*; Thomas R. Dawley, *The Child That Toileth Not* (1912), pp. 72ff.

8. Leonora Beck Ellis, "A Model Factory Town [Pelzer, South Carolina]" and "A Study of Southern Cotton Mill Communities." This last was intended as a two-part article, of which only the first part appears to have been published. The classic defense of the cotton mills as philanthropy, upon which others were modeled, was David A. Tompkins, "The Sociological Work of the Cotton Mill Owners." A detailed description of "welfare work" in the South Carolina mills may be found in August Kohn, *The Cotton Mills of South Carolina, 1907*, pp. 124–76. The "necessity" for "welfare work" in the unincorporated mill towns is discussed in more objective fashion in [Charles H. Verrill], *Cotton Textile Industry* (1910), pp. 593–98 et passim. Mitchell, *Rise of the Cotton Mills*, remains a most satisfactory study of the cotton-mill campaign, its ideological assertions, and its relation to southern economic development after 1880, to be supplemented by the more general study, Melvin Thomas Copeland, *The Cotton Manufacturing Industry of the United States*, and by the monumental survey conducted by Walter B. Palmer et al. for the U.S. Bureau of Labor in 1907–8, summarized in [Verrill], *Cotton Textile Industry*.

9. Between 1890 and 1907, at the height of the cotton-mill campaign, southern trackage increased from 27,830 to 50,533 miles; a contemporary observer, president of the Southern Railway Company, noted that "the interdependence of the railway and of the communities served by them has been fully recognized . . . and each system operating in that section is endeavoring to build up its particular territory," W. W. Swift, "Southern Railroads and Industrial Development," p. 104. See also in this connection, Joseph Hyde Pratt, "The Good Roads Movement in the South."

10. On the number of cotton mills in the South, I have followed Edgar Gardner Murphy, *Problems of the Present South*, pp. 102–3. Copeland, *Cotton Manufacturing Industry*, pp. 32, 35, gives the 1880 figure as 164, the 1900 as 550, the 1910 as 731. [Verrill], *Cotton Textile Industry*, citing the U.S. Census of Manufactures for 1905 and 1908, numbers the mills in Virginia, North and South Carolina, Georgia, Alabama, and Mississippi at 726 in 1908, and estimates the number of mills in these states plus Kentucky, Tennessee, Arkansas, Texas, and Louisiana at 161 in 1880, 239 in 1890, 400 in 1900, 550 in 1905. Contemporary observers routinely noted that the number of spindles rather than the number of mills was a better index to economic activity, but number of mills is the more important index of social change.

11. Walter I. Trattner, *Crusade for Children*, p. 51. A detailed examination of the movement for child labor legislation and its relationship to other programs for social improvement in North and South Carolina, Georgia, and Alabama will be found in Elizabeth Lewis Otley, *The Beginnings of Child Labor Legislation in Certain States*, pp. 131–204. A brief summary of the movement in its southern context appears in C. Vann Woodward, *Origins of the New South*, pp. 416ff. The standard history remains Elizabeth H. Davidson, *Child Labor Legislation in the Southern Textile States*.

12. Trattner, *Crusade for Children*, pp. 50–52, and esp. Davidson, *Child Labor Legislation*, pp. 24–29; Murphy, *Problems of the Present South*, pp. 310ff. According to Copeland, *Cotton Manufacturing Industry*, p. 43, between 1880 and 1900, 25 percent of southern cotton mill operatives were under the age of sixteen, as compared with 21.4 and 14.1 percent in the Middle Atlantic and New England states in 1880, and 12.4 and 6.7 percent respectively in 1900. In 1905, 22.9 percent of southern mill operatives were under the age of sixteen as compared with 8.7 and 6.0 percent in the Middle Atlantic and New England states in that year.

13. Edgar Gardner Murphy, "Child Labor as a National Problem; With Especial Reference to the Southern States"; also "Child Labor in Alabama: A Discussion of New England's Part in the Common Responsibility for the Child-Labor Conditions of the South."

14. Trattner, *Crusade for Children*, p. 55. In 1904 only West Virginia and Tennessee had established minimum ages for factory employment, at twelve and fourteen respectively; only West Virginia and Kentucky had compulsory school attendance laws, May Wood Simons, "Education in the South," p. 401.

15. Owen R. Lovejoy, "Child Labor," p. 176.

16. My discussion of the state laws is based primarily upon the tabular comparison prepared by the National Child Labor Committee and published as an appendix to Lovejoy, "Child Labor."

17. Legislation enacted outside the South during this period characteristically placed responsibility for enforcement of child labor laws in the hands of school officials, whose professional interest in maintaining high rates of school attendance might be counted upon to insure that serious attempts at enforcement of the labor laws would be made. In compulsory attendance states, moreover, the relationship of truancy and employment as an alternative to school attendance made school officials logical supervisors of children's daytime activities.

18. Improved technology in the West Virginia glass industry during the first decade of the century yielded a significant decrease in the use of child labor in what had been that state's principal industrial employer of young children, Trattner, *Crusade for Children*, pp. 75–77.

19. Ibid., pp. 87ff. Murphy insisted that federal political action involving interference in state prerogatives was not what he meant by defining child labor as a "national" problem in his 1903 address before the National Conference of Charities and Correc-

tion, "Child Labor as a National Problem," p. 121. At that same session, however, Frederick L. Hoffman had issued a strong call for just such a survey of the extent and conditions of child labor as Congress now authorized, in "The Social and Medical Aspects of Child Labor." Bureau of Labor sponsored surveys before 1907 characteristically concerned themselves with the status of legislation, mechanisms for enforcement, and the extent to which existing laws were violated, rather than with the extent and conditions of child labor per se: see Hannah R. Sewell, "Child Labor in the United States." A hostile and anecdotal history of the survey is Thomas R. Dawley, *The Child That Toileth Not: The Story of A Government Investigation* (1912), esp. pp. 3–5, 278–93. As late as 1914, Samuel McCune Lindsay complained that while the results of the survey had "made a deep impression" on congressional supporters of national child labor legislation, "a digest of its voluminous contents has not been published and the public is not yet aroused as to its revelations," "National Child Labor Standards," p. 28.

20. Trattner, *Crusade for Children*, pp. 123ff.; Lindsay, "National Child Labor Standards."

21. Although Page's importance in Progressive Era reform warrants full and modern examination, the standard biography remains Burton J. Hendrick, *The Life and Letters of Walter H. Page* and *The Training of an American: The Earlier Life and Letters of Walter Hines Page*. Page's influence was largely behind the scenes, as appears for example in his correspondence with William Goodell Frost, Gifford Pinchot, Sir Horace Plunkett, and John M. Glenn, W. H. Page Papers. Charles Wardell Stiles also deserves full biographical study; until that complex task shall have been done, his own work must be examined along with the histories of the several institutions with which he was affiliated; in this immediate context, see esp. Charles Wardell Stiles, "The Industrial Conditions of the Tenant Class (White and Black) as Influenced by the Medical Conditions"; *Hookworm Disease Among Cotton Mill Operatives*; and n. 24, below.

22. Murphy, *Problems of the Present South*, pp. 104–5. Also Holland Thompson, *From the Cotton Field to the Cotton Mill*, pp. 112–13; August Kohn, *The Cotton Mills of South Carolina, 1907*; Lawton B. Evans, "A Message of Achievement from the Southland: The Glory of Its Children," pp. 175–78. Evans sounded a different note prior to the organization of the National Child Labor Committee's campaign, however, as in "The Child of the Operative." Agents of the Bureau of Labor were generally less enthusiastic about the social condition of the class from which the mill operatives were drawn: the rate of illiteracy was an index of "past conditions . . . on the farms or in the mountain districts where the opportunities of attending school and acquiring an education were much less than in the larger towns and cities"; company organization of public services followed from the fact that many of the operatives were from a class which has "always been more or less dependent upon others for guidance," and from this also followed the unsightliness of the mill towns, since "before coming to the mill the operatives have, in general, belonged to an improvident class of laborers or were unsuccessful small farmers. Their aesthetic tastes have not been developed, and when left to themselves they seldom do anything in the way of improving their surroundings," [Verrill], *Cotton Textile Industry* (1910), pp. 247–48, 522, 530; but a more sympathetic view is presented ibid., pp. 585–87.

23. Kohn, *Cotton Mills of South Carolina, 1907*, pp. 22–25, 199–206; Thompson, *From the Cotton Field to the Cotton Mill*, p. 24, however, insists that the mountaineers "need not be considered as an industrial factor." The agents of the Bureau of Labor were unable to establish exactly the number of mountaineers in the mills: "The exact proportion of those coming from the mountains was not secured, and the proportion varies greatly in different sections. Taking the mill population as a whole, for the mills visited during this investigation the percentage . . . was very much smaller than the percentage of

those who come from the lowland farms surrounding the cotton-mill villages. . . . Attempts to import mountaineers in large numbers have usually proved unsatisfactory," [Verrill], *Cotton Textile Industry*, pp. 120–21. From the report, however, it is clear that the issue was acknowledged as an important one.

The ethnogeographic origins of the southern mill operatives is an issue only if defense of the mills is based on the inhabitability of the rural regions from which their labor supply is drawn; proponents of child labor restriction argued that employment of children in factories was undesirable irrespective of who they were or where they came from, as in John C. Campbell, "From Mountain Cabin to Cotton Mill" (1913). A thoughtful summary of the contemporary confusion concerning the ethnogeographic origins of southern mill operatives, combined with a serious attempt to establish the truth of the matter, appears in Mitchell, *Rise of the Cotton Mills*, pp. 162ff., 182ff. More recent studies do not attempt to deal with the issue, for example Herbert J. Lahne, *The Cotton Mill Worker*.

24. Charles Wardell Stiles was perhaps the most vociferous in defense of the mill towns on sanitary grounds, as in *Hookworm Disease Among Cotton Mill Operatives*, p. 22, where he argues that "cotton mill anaemia" is not to be classed as an occupational disease consequent to inhalation of cotton fibers but resulted from untreated hookworm disease, and that "the cotton mill not only plays an important role in bettering the sanitary conditions of at least 12.6 hookworm cases in every 100 hands it employs, but in addition it betters the sanitary conditions for 16.8 other sick people as well." A contemporary study, Arthur R. Perry, *Causes of Death among Women and Child Cotton-Mill Operatives*, pointed to the high incidence of tuberculosis among cotton-mill operatives in Massachusetts, where hookworm disease was extremely rare, however. Kohn, *Cotton Mills of South Carolina, 1907*, pp. 75–85, cited Stiles's early work in defense of the healthiness of mill-town life as compared with rural life in the South generally, and gratuitously insisted that high humidity levels within the mills, necessary to maintain the flexibility of the cotton thread, was beneficial to the health of the operatives and made the factories comfortable places to work.

25. Alexander J. McKelway, "The Physical Evils of Child Labor" (1906), pp. 24, 25.

26. Julia Macgruder, "The Child Labor Problem: Fact *versus* Sentimentality" (1907), p. 250. The Van Vorsts' work on social problems consisted primarily of Mrs. John [Bessie] Van Vorst and Marie Van Vorst, *The Woman Who Toils* (1903), with an introduction by Theodore Roosevelt on "race suicide"; Marie Van Vorst, *Amanda of the Mill. A Novel* (1905); Mrs. John [Bessie] Van Vorst, *The Cry of the Children* (1908), with an introduction by Albert J. Beveridge, reprinted from *Saturday Evening Post* (1906), where it appeared as "The Cry of the Children: Human Documents in the Case of the New Slavery." Beveridge was himself a regular contributor to the *Saturday Evening Post* during this period.

27. Kohn, *Cotton Mills of South Carolina, 1907*, pp. 102–4. His 1903 letters were published as *The Cotton Mills of South Carolina*. On the designation of underage children as "helpers" to avoid violation of state child labor laws, however, see [Verrill], *Cotton Textile Industry*, pp. 189–91.

28. Kohn, *Cotton Mills of South Carolina, 1907*, pp. 22–25, 117, 199ff. Availability of foreign labor for the southern textile industry was also curtailed by passage of the immigration act of 1907, [Verrill], *Cotton Textile Industry*, pp. 125–26.

29. Kohn, *Cotton Mills of South Carolina, 1907*, p. 117.

30. August Kohn, "Child Labor in the South," p. 586. Contrast between the vigorous mill workers and the "vegetable like" existence of southern poor whites before industrialization is made in Peter H. Goldsmith, "The Cotton Mill South," *Boston Evening Transcript*, esp. 10 May 1908. The analogous assertion, that mountain life was "un-

civilized," in order to justify the work of benevolent agencies among them, continued to be made through the middle teens, as in a publicity piece for Berea College by Bruce Barton, "The Children of the Feudists" (1913), to which a "former mountaineer" responded that the mountaineers were no more uncivilized than any other group in the American population, including "the 'mill people' of Massachusetts, Alabama, Georgia, and the Carolinas," J. W. Carlin, "The Kentucky Mountaineer" (1913), p. 26.

31. Dawley, *The Child That Toileth Not*, pp. 11–12, 489–90, and on his removal from office as a Bureau of Labor investigator, pp. 485–87. His name is not listed in the acknowledgments printed in the first volume of the published report, [Verrill], *Cotton Textile Industry*, p. 10.

32. Walter Hines Page, ["Editorial Note"] (1910), p. 12704. On Page's "genius at rewriting titles," see Burton J. Hendrick, *The Life and Letters of Walter H. Page*, 1:60. I am indebted to Louis R. Harlan for calling this passage to my attention. On relations between Frost and Page, see correspondence in W. H. Page Papers.

33. Thomas R. Dawley, *Our Mountain Problem and Its Solution* (1910), p. 4. By his own account, Dawley was invited to speak as an acknowledged opponent of child labor restriction, *The Child That Toileth Not*, pp. 489–90. A less extreme version of this statement appears in "The Southern Mountaineer: Removal the Remedy" (1910), p. 12707.

34. Dawley, *Our Mountain Problem and Its Solution*, p. 5. The inhabitability of Appalachia also appears in Kohn, "Child Labor in the South," p. 54, and David A. Tompkins, "The Mountain Whites as an Industrial Labor Factor in the South" (1909), pp. 59 ff., who later noted, however, that "the bulk of this element [mountaineers employed in cotton mills] never lived high up in the mountains, but generally upon the foot-hills," ibid., p. 61.

35. Walter B. Palmer, "Economic and Legal Aspects of the Labor of Women and Children in the South," p. 54.

36. [Verrill], *Cotton Textile Industry*, p. 120.

37. Ibid., p. 123. The same argument was made by Mrs. J. Borden Harriman at the 1910 meeting of the National Child Labor Committee, published as "The Cotton Mill as a Factor in the Development of the South," to which A. J. McKelway replied that from her remarks he would venture to guess which mill agents she had interviewed during her southern tour and where she had been told to go to see rural poverty at its worst. The debate continues in C. E. Weltner, "Social Welfare and Child Labor in South Carolina Mill Communities"; Walter A. Dyer, "Training New Leaders for the Industrial South" (1914) and "Whole-hearted Half-Time School" (1914); William L. Hall, "To Remake the Appalachians: A New Order in the Mountains That is Founded on Forestry" (1914); J. Russell Smith, "Farming Appalachia" (1916).

38. Alexander J. McKelway, "The Mill or the Farm" (1910), p. 56.

39. Murphy, *Problems of the Present South*, p. 140. He used the same words in "Child Labor as a National Problem," p. 129.

40. John C. Campbell, "From Mountain Cabin to Cotton Mill" (1913), p. 82. See also W. H. Swift, "The Campaign in North Carolina. The Mountain Whites—By One of Them" (1913); A. J. McKelway, "Child Wages in the Cotton Mills: Our Modern Feudalism." Explicit replies to Dawley were William Leavitt Stoddard, " 'The Child That Toileth Not'," *Survey* (Feb. 1913) and [unsigned; McKelway?], "'The Child That Toileth Not': A Reply to Mr. Dawley," *Child Labor Bulletin* (Feb. 1913).

41. Campbell, "From Mountain Cabin to Cotton Mill," pp. 82–83.

42. W. H. Swift, "The Last Stand of the One Business Which Opposes Child Labor Legislation in the South" (1914).

43. Attempts to define a more manageable and more appropriate unit for social investigation and social work practice than the "region" of Appalachia absorbed

the attention of the Council of Southern Mountain Workers in the late 1920s, for example Mary Camp Sprinkle, "Unit of Organization for Rural Social Work"; William Carl Hunt, "Social Case Work Principles Modified to Meet Rural Conditions." In the early 1930s, however, focus on the region as a whole was renewed; see below, chapter 8 n. 50.

Chapter 8

1. On Campbell, Claxton, et al., see below; the "rediscovery" of Hayes appears for example in John C. Campbell to John Glenn, 23 April 1917, Southern Highland Division Papers.

2. Samuel Tyndale Wilson, *The Southern Mountaineers* (N.Y., Literature Department, Presbyterian Home Missions, 1906). The 1915 printing is marked 5th ed.; later editions appeared in 1916, 1921, 1922.

3. Walter Hughson, *The Church's Mission to the Mountaineers of the South* (1908); Samuel Hunter Thompson, *The Highlanders of the South* (1910); also Sherman H. Doyle, *Presbyterian Home Missions* (1902); Samuel L. Morris, *At Our Own Door: A Study of Home Missions with Special Reference to the South and West* (1904); S. B. Groves, *The Strength of the Hills Is His Also* (1906); William Henry Haney, *The Mountain People of Kentucky: An Account of Present Conditions with the Attitude of the People Toward Improvement* (1906); Harlan Paul Douglass, *Christian Reconstruction in the South* (1909); John M. Moore, *The South To-Day* (1916); Walter C. Whitaker, *A Round Robin: The Southern Highlands and Highlanders* (1916); James Watt Raine, *The Land of Saddle-Bags: A Study of the Mountain People of Appalachia* (1924).

4. John M. Glenn et al., *Russell Sage Foundation, 1907–1946*, 1:62; Francis H. McLean, "The Mountain Folk" (1908). On the emergence of the South as a field for northern benevolent work in the twentieth century, and on the relationship of northern agencies and southern workers generally, see Glenn, *Russell Sage Foundation*, vol. 1; Charles W. Dabney, Jr., *Universal Education in the South*, vol. 2; Raymond B. Fosdick, *Adventure in Giving: The Story of the General Education Board*; [General Education Board], *The General Education Board: An Account of Its Activities, 1902–1914*; and for example Mrs. John [Mary] Glenn, "The Working Force of Societies for Organizing Charity." C. Vann Woodward provides a general survey of this movement in *Origins of the New South*.

5. Glenn, *Russell Sage Foundation*, 1:62. On Campbell's career before 1908 see Henry D. Shapiro, "Introduction," in John C. Campbell, *The Southern Highlander and His Homeland* (reprint, 1969); Isaac Messler, "Our Co-Worker," *Mountain Life and Work* (April 1928). This number of *Mountain Life and Work* was a Campbell memorial issue.

6. Francis H. McLean, "The Mountain Folk," *Charities and The Commons* (23 May 1908); Bruce R. Payne, "Waste in Mountain Settlement Work," National Conference of Charities and Correction, *Proceedings* (1908). The discussion appears ibid., pp. 95–99.

7. Payne, "Waste in Mountain Settlement Work," p. 95.

8. John C. Campbell to Mrs. Glenn, 16 May 1908, Southern Highland Division Papers.

9. The only source of information about this conversation is John M. Glenn's personal recollection of the occasion set down in *Russell Sage Foundation*, 1:62, and Campbell's letter to Mrs. Glenn on 16 May 1908, in Southern Highland Division Papers. That Campbell and the Glenns were not personally acquainted previous to their meeting in Richmond is apparent from this letter also, in which he provides biographical information about himself and Mrs. Campbell and names several persons as references. Campbell was not a member of the National Conference of Charities and Correction prior to his attendance at the 1908 meeting and may indeed have joined only after his association with the Russell Sage Foundation in the summer of that year; his

name first appears in the printed list of members as of 1 Nov. 1908, National Conference of Charities and Correction, *Proceedings* 35: 480. Mrs. Campbell did not become a member until the 1909 meeting, at which her husband presented a paper, ibid., 36: 556 (1909).

10. John C. Campbell, "Statement for a Proposed Study Plan of the Southern Highland Section," 15 May 1908, typescript, enclosed in Campbell to Mrs. Glenn, 16 May 1908, Southern Highland Division Papers.

11. Glenn, *Russell Sage Foundation*, 1:62. The Campbells continued to list Demorest, Georgia, as their home at least through 1913, in the membership rosters of the National Conference of Charities and Correction.

12. Glenn, *Russell Sage Foundation*, 1:47, 69 et passim, indicates that full responsibility for the activities of the foundation's several divisions was regularly accorded the respective directors or "secretaries."

13. On the work of the division, see Glenn, *Russell Sage Foundation*, 1:115–24, and below.

14. Olive Dame Campbell, "Editorial," *Mountain Life and Work* (July 1928). On the organization of the conference, see also Glenn, *Russell Sage Foundation*, 1: 122; Isaac Messler, "Our Co-Worker"; John C. Campbell, "Confidential Report of the Activities of the Southern Highland Division of the Russell Sage Foundation, Sept. 30, 1913–Sept. 30, 1914," typescript, Southern Highland Division Papers, pp. 38–39; Conference of Southern Mountain Workers, *The Southern Highlands: Extracts of Letters Received from . . . [Persons] Conducting Work in the Southern Mountains*, comp. John C. Campbell (1915), p. 66.

15. Administrative expenses of the conference were paid through the budget of the Southern Highland Division until that unit's dissolution in 1919 following Campbell's death. Beginning in 1920, the Russell Sage Foundation provided a direct grant for administrative expenses averaging $1,000 per annum and, after 1924, an additional subsidy for publication of *Mountain Life and Work*. The total dollar amount granted for these purposes, 1920–46, was $30,505, Glenn, *Russell Sage Foundation*, 2: 479, 657, 691.

16. Campbell's sensitivity to the need for delicacy in establishing relationships with mountain work agencies is best expressed in his "Confidential Report," pp. i–ii, 49–52, and Campbell to Glenn, 20 June 1914, Southern Highland Division Papers.

17. Campbell, "Confidential Report," pp. 39–40; Messler, "Our Co-Worker"; Helen H. Dingman, "Our Common Task."

18. Attendance information for the 1914 meeting is drawn from "List of Persons Registering at the Conference of Southern Mountain Workers, Knoxville, Tennessee, April 22 & 23, 1914," typescript, enclosed in Campbell to Glenn, 4 May 1914, Southern Highland Division Papers; for the 1917 meeting from Glenn, *Russell Sage Foundation*, 1: 122.

19. Conference of Southern Mountain Workers, *The Southern Highlands: Extracts of Letters*, pp. 3, 66–67. The document thus issued, edited by Campbell as chairman of the conference, was further evidence of the state of chaos which prevailed in mountain work, ibid., p. 3 et passim.

20. Ibid., p. 3; the list of contributors appears ibid., pp. 4–7.

21. There is no transcript of Sharp's comments at the 1917 conference, but this was his "line," e.g. Cecil J. Sharp, "Introduction," in Olive Dame Campbell and Cecil J. Sharp, *English Folk Songs from the Southern Appalachians* (1917), p. xxi.

22. Cecil J. Sharp to Glenn, 15 April 1917, enclosed in Campbell to Glenn, 15 April 1917, which also see, Southern Highland Division Papers. On Sharp in America, see below, chapter 10.

23. Campbell, "Confidential Report," pp. 20–21, 38–39.

24. Ibid. A brief history of the movement to establish a Synod of Appalachia will be found in Robert F. Campbell, "Proposal for the Synod of Appalachia," 1 Nov. 1914, stenographic transcript, typescript, Southern Highland Division Papers; cf. also Glenn to John C. Campbell, 12 Dec. 1917, and Campbell to Glenn, 17 Dec. 1917, Southern Highland Division Papers.

25. Campbell to Glenn, 20 June 1914, Southern Highland Division Papers; that the work of the federal council's Committee on Church and Country Life was to focus on the condition of the rural church in Ohio as its initial project made membership on the committee seem even less appropriate to Campbell. On the Ohio survey see Charles O. Gill, "Secretarial Preface," in *The Church and Country Life*, ed. Paul L. Vogt.

26. Campbell, "Confidential Report," p. 38.

27. Campbell to Glenn, 31 Oct. 1914; also Campbell to Glenn, 9 Dec. 1914, and Glenn to Campbell, 14 Dec. 1914, Southern Highland Division Papers. On the Ellen Axson Wilson Memorial Fund, see also Mrs. W. S. Elkin to Walter Hines Page, n.d. [June 1915], and Mrs. T. H. Latham to Walter Hines Page, 27 Sept. 1915, enclosing *The Ellen Wilson Memorial* [pamphlet], W. H. Page Papers.

28. Campbell to Glenn, 31 Oct. 1914; also Campbell to Glenn, 29 Sept. 1914; Glenn to Campbell, 1 Oct. 1914, Southern Highland Division Papers.

29. Glenn, *Russell Sage Foundation*, 1: 115; the "one secretary" was the incomparable Miss Dickey, Campbell to Glenn, 11 May 1918; Glenn to Campbell, 13 May 1918, Southern Highland Division Papers.

30. The diversity of mountain conditions and the heterogeneity of the mountain population was indeed a continuing theme in Campbell's attempts to educate his co-workers and the public at large. In his "Introduction" to Conference of Southern Mountain Workers, *The Southern Highlands: Extracts of Letters*, p. 3, he noted that a single, coherent statement of the "needs" of the mountain country could not be made "without the risk of furthering the spread of an erroneous impression—which is too general—namely, that the mountain country is the same throughout, and that its people are socially homogeneous." See also *The Southern Highlander and His Homeland* (1921), and chapter 10 n. 37, below.

31. Op. cit., pp. 5, 11 et passim. The campaign of fact-finding and publicity conducted by the Southern Education Board focused on the states more normally, however, as the essential units of legislative action, or upon the southern section as a whole.

32. The foundation's original expectation was that the Campbell study would focus on institutional resources and programs in Appalachia, in order "to standardize work in the mountains and lead to more intelligent giving," Glenn to Campbell, 20 June 1908, John C. and Olive D. Campbell Papers. The Campbells found that there was more to do, and it is a warrant of the Russell Sage Foundation's flexibility during this period that, although it had assumed financial responsibility for the "Pittsburgh Survey" begun by the staff of *Charities and The Commons*, and stood as a most vocal advocate of the type of systematic and scientific venture which the "Pittsburgh Survey" represented, it was also willing to support the necessarily impressionistic survey work of the Campbells. On the foundation's early work, in addition to Glenn, *Russell Sage Foundation*, vol. 1, see also Robert W. de Forest, "The Initial Activities of the Russell Sage Foundation," and Clarke A. Chambers, *Paul U. Kellogg and The Survey*. On the development of the social survey as technique, see Carl C. Taylor, *The Social Survey: Its History and Methods*, and Shelby M. Harrison, "Introduction," in *A Bibliography of Social Surveys: Reports of Fact Finding Studies Made as a Basis for Social Action*, comp. Allen Eaton and Shelby M. Harrison. More recent studies offer additional information but do not alter our knowledge of the general phenomenon.

33. John C. Campbell to Mrs. Glenn, 16 May 1908, Southern Highland Division Papers.

34. John C. Campbell, "Statement for a Proposed Study Plan of the Southern Highland Section," 15 May 1908, Southern Highland Division Papers.

35. As late as 1917, for example, not all the mountain states were included in the U.S. Registration Area for births and deaths, Campbell, *The Southern Highlander and His Homeland*, pp. 207–8.

36. John C. Campbell, "Social Betterment in the Southern Mountains," National Conference of Charities and Correction, *Proceedings* (1909), p. 133; summarized in *Survey* (26 June 1909).

37. Campbell to Glenn, 6 April, 20 May 1914, Southern Highland Division Papers.

38. Campbell, *The Southern Highlander and His Homeland*, appendix E. His choice of such regional or cultural units, rather than the more conventional units of social class, denominational affiliation, or "ethnicity" as the critical units in a discussion of Appalachia, relates to his commitment to "community" as the goal of mountain benevolence, and his recognition of the relationship between the taxonomy of reality—the way one thinks about the world—and the way one acts in it. So far as I know, these "belts" are his own invention, although they are dependent upon the insights of the new "science" of anthropogeography, expressed in the work of Ellen Churchill Semple discussed above, and more immediately upon the physiographical analysis of Appalachia provided in C. Willard Hayes, "The Southern Appalachians" (1895). On Campbell's knowledge of Hayes, see Campbell to Glenn, 23 Aug. 1917, Southern Highland Division Papers.

39. Campbell, *The Southern Highlander and His Homeland*, pp. xvii, xix, and Olive Dame Campbell, "Preface"; Campbell to Mrs. Glenn, 16 May 1908, and "Statement for a Proposed Study Plan of the Southern Highland Section," 15 May 1908, Southern Highland Division Papers.

40. John C. Campbell, *The Future of the Church and Independent Schools in Our Southern Highlands*, Southern Highland Division Pamphlets no. 1 (1917). On plans to distribute this pamphlet, which called for redirection of mountain education in the face of a developing public school system in the mountains and pointed to the need for folk schools to fill a gap left by the public school programs, see Campbell to Glenn, 12 Jan. 1917, Southern Highland Division Papers. The content of this pamphlet was based on talks delivered during January 1916: "The Future of the Church-School in the Southern Highlands: An Address Delivered before the Council of Women for Home Missions, Atlanta, Georgia, Jan. 6, 1916," and "Mountain and Rural Fields in the South: An Address Delivered before the Home Missions Council, New York City, Jan. 13, 1916," both in Southern Highland Division Papers; a version of the latter was published in Home Missions Council, *Annual Report*, 1916: 171–80.

Following Campbell's death, Olive Dame Campbell published a list of mountain schools, *Southern Highland Schools Maintained by Denominational and Independent Agencies*, Southern Highland Division Pamphlets no. 2 (1921).

41. Campbell to Glenn, 23 Aug. 1917, Southern Highland Division Papers. Campbell's suggestion was not accepted by Raine, who prepared a mission-study text of his own, *The Land of Saddle-Bags: A Study of the Mountain People of Appalachia* (N.Y., Council of Women for Home Missions & Missionary Education Movement of the U. S. & Canada, 1924) to capitalize on the new interest in Appalachia which followed the reissue of Kephart's *Our Southern Highlanders* in 1921 and its revision in 1922, and publication of Campbell's *The Southern Highlander and His Homeland* in 1921.

42. Beginning with Campbell to Glenn, 27 Dec. 1917, the Campbell correspondence in Southern Highland Division Papers contains periodic references to his work on "the book," although which book was meant is not clear: about this time Campbell was also working on a monograph, "The Ancestry of the Mountaineers," typescript,

Minnesota Historical Society, parts of which appear in the first chapters of *The Southern Highlander*. The typescript of this monograph was originally deposited with the Carnegie Institution of Washington, perhaps at John Glenn's suggestion with the idea that they might underwrite its publication; Cecil J. Sharp, whose involvement with the Campbells and Mr. Glenn is discussed in chapter 10, below, was advised to make application to the Carnegie Institution for financial aid in support of his folksong collecting during the winter of 1917–18, about the time "The Ancestry of the Mountaineers" must have been written, Maud Karpeles, *Cecil J. Sharp*, p. 137. Literary style, format, and typewriter face suggest this MS. to be of the 1917–19 period, although it was surely based upon an earlier MS. on "The Ancestry of the Mountaineers" prepared by Campbell with the assistance of his sister-in-law, Ruth Coolidge, in 1910 (Olive Dame Campbell, ["Memoir of John C. Campbell"], p. 217, John C. and Olive D. Campbell Papers), and submitted to the Russell Sage Foundation later that year, John Campbell to John M. Glenn, 20 Dec. 1910, Campbell Papers.

43. The "good physician" image is Campbell's, from "Confidential Report," pp. i–ii.

44. John C. Campbell's comments on W. G. Frost and his role at Berea appear in Campbell to Glenn, 30, 31 Oct. 1914, Southern Highland Division Papers. The apotheosis of Frost appears about this time, for example in Bruce Barton, "The Children of the Feudists" (1913), and in Frost's own emphasis on his priority in the "discovery" of the mountaineers, as in "Christian Patriotism" (1913), "Educational Pioneering in the Southern Mountains" (1913), and "Our Southern Highlanders" (1914).

45. Campbell to Glenn, 20 May 1914, Southern Highland Division Papers.

46. P. P. Claxton, "Letter of Transmittal," in Frost, *Statistical Study* (1915), p. 5.

47. U.S. Commissioner of Education, *Report of the Commissioner of Education* 1916, 1: xix; 1917, 1:19. C. G. Burkett was field secretary of the Southern Industrial Education Association, with offices in Washington, D.C., and attended the 1914 Knoxville Conference, "List of Persons Registering at the Conference of Southern Mountain Workers . . . 1914," Southern Highland Division Papers. On this occasion or some other in 1914, Burkett visited Campbell in Asheville and was taken on a tour of the highlands and introduced to the "leading workers in the field," Campbell, "Confidential Report," p. 19.

48. Campbell to Glenn, 17 April 1917, Southern Highland Division Papers. As U.S. commissioner of education, Claxton naturally sought to bring school work in Appalachia under his bureau, at least in the sense of defining public school work as central to the improvement of mountain conditions. "The great factor in the solution of the problem is the public school," he told the Conference of Southern Mountain Workers in 1915, for example; "all other agencies should co-operate with the public school as the central agency. It is only through the public school that the people help themselves," Conference of Southern Mountain Workers, *The Southern Highlands: Extracts of Letters*, p. 9. The threat of that posture to denominational workers must have been considerable. On Claxton's apprenticeship under Dabney at the University of Tennessee, see Charles W. Dabney, Jr., *Universal Education in the South*, vol. 2.

49. The intention of the conference to conduct a survey was announced in a brief note, [unsigned], "Better Living for Southern Mountaineers" (1916). Of interest in this connection is John C. Campbell to William Goodell Frost, 18 Oct. 1917, W. G. Frost Papers: "My dear Dr. Frost, You will doubtless recall that the 1916 Conference of Southern Mountain Workers appointed a committee to make an educational survey of the mountain field. This committee, composed of Rev. Franklin J. Clark, Mr. Marshall C. Allaben, Dr. A. E. Brown, Dr. Samuel T. Wilson and yourself, was continued by vote

of the last Conference. Recently, by action of the committee, my name has been added, and I have been asked to serve as chairman. I am therefore submitting the enclosed list of questions for your suggestion and criticism." It is not clear whether Frost replied to this letter, and the "enclosed list of questions" are attached to Campbell's letter with no sign of emendation by Frost. The idea of an educational survey conducted under interagency auspices did not disappear, however. In 1929, at the instance of Helen H. Dingman, secretary of the Conference of Southern Mountain Workers, a meeting was called in New York under the aegis of the Russell Sage Foundation, to plan for a survey of mountain conditions, [Helen H. Dingman], "A Cooperative Survey of the Mountains: Report of a Conference" (Jan. 1930). Periodic reports of progress were Thomas Cooper, "An Economic and Social Study of the Southern Appalachians" (July 1930); L. C. Gray, "Objectives and Progress of the Economic and Social Survey of the Southern Appalachians" (July 1931) and "Economic Conditions and Tendencies in the Southern Appalachians as Indicated by the Cooperative Survey" (July 1933); Helen H. Dingman, "Our Common Task" (July 1933). The Institute for Social and Religious Research, which received its funding from the Russell Sage Foundation, organized a religious survey to coordinate with the social and economic survey, M[argaret] T[rotter], "Dr. Morse Outlines the Religious Survey" (July 1931); this yielded Elizabeth R. Hooker, *Religion in the Highlands: Native Churches and Missionary Enterprises in the Southern Appalachian Area* (N.Y., Home Missions Council, 1933). Additional information on the early survey should be available in the papers of the conference, recently deposited in the Berea College Archives, which I have not yet had opportunity to examine.

50. Campbell to Glenn, 11 May 1918; Glenn to Campbell, 13 May 1918, Southern Highland Division Papers.

51. Campbell especially hoped to establish cooperative support for rural nursing by the American Red Cross and the Department of Church and Country Life of the Presbyterian church, Campbell to Glenn, 9 Dec. 1914, 9 Dec. 1918; Campbell to George E. Scott, General Manager of the Red Cross, 31 Dec. 1918; and to bring the ecumenical spirit of the YMCA and YWCA into mountain work, Campbell to Glenn, 16 Dec. 1918, Southern Highland Division Papers. Both desires were ultimately fulfilled, but only after Campbell's death.

52. Campbell to Glenn, 11 Feb., 11 May, 12 May, 4 June 1918; Glenn to Campbell, 21 May, 21 June 1918; Rutherford P. Hayes, Jr., to Campbell, 18 July 1918, Southern Highland Division Papers.

Chapter 9

1. On the origins of "folk" study in the United States, the role of Kittridge, and the dominance of the philological tradition in scholarship, see the splendid study by Donald K. Wilgus, *Anglo-American Folksong Scholarship since 1898*, esp. pp. 143–88. On Thomas's role in the history of social science see Morris Janowitz, "Introduction," *W. I. Thomas on Social Organization and Social Personality*, ed. Morris Janowitz, and esp. William I. Thomas, *Source Book for Social Origins*.

2. The standard "histories" are also the most important works of advocacy: Max West, "The Revival of Handicrafts in America," U. S. Bureau of Labor *Bulletin* 9: 1573–1622 (1904 no. 55); Allen Eaton, *Handicrafts of the Southern Highlands, with an Account of the Rural Handicraft Movement in the United States and Suggestions for the Wider Use of Handicrafts in Adult Education and in Recreation* (N.Y., Russell Sage Foundation, 1937). On the role of crafts in settlement work, see Allen F. Davis, *Spearheads for Reform*, pp. 47ff.; Jane Addams, *Twenty Years at Hull House*; Mary K. Simkhovich, *Neighborhood: My Story of Greenwich House*, and especially "Handicrafts in the City"; [unsigned], "Hingham Village Industries." Crafts for their own sake are emphasized in Frances L. Good-

rich, "Old Ways and New in the Carolina Mountains" (1900); Ralph Erskine, "The Handicraftsmen of the Blue Ridge" (1907); and Eliza Calvert Obenchain, *A Book of Hand-Woven Coverlets* (1912).

3. West, "Revival of Handicrafts"; also Caroline Williamson Montgomery, comp., *Bibliography of College, Social, University and Church Settlements* (1905). Eaton, *Handicrafts of the Southern Highlands*, tends toward the polemical and the rhapsodic; it is most useful for the period of his own involvement in the crafts movement via the Russell Sage Foundation's Department of Surveys and Exhibits, after 1915.

4. Frances Louisa Goodrich, *Mountain Homespun*, p. 25, and cf. this remark by Allen Eaton, whose part in the handicrafts movement of the 1920s was central: "The first and most obvious measure of the value of the handicrafts is their economic return, the money which they bring to those who practice them," Allen Eaton, "The Mountain Handicrafts: Their Importance to the Country and to the People in the Mountain Homes," p. 26. An early suggestion of this appears in Jennie Lester Hill, "Fireside Industries in the Kentucky Mountains" (1903), and in West, "Revival of Handicrafts." See also Goodrich, *Mountain Homespun*, pp. 21ff., and below.

5. West, "Revival of Handicrafts," p. 1577, and Goodrich's statement, quoted in Eaton, "The Mountain Handicrafts," p. 27. On Goodrich's role in the establishment of the Laurel Hospital, White Rock, North Carolina, by the Presbyterian Board of Home Missions, see Margaret Miller, "The Great Physician's Work."

6. Goodrich, *Mountain Homespun*, p. 21.

7. Ibid., pp. 21–22.

8. West, "Revival of Handicrafts," pp. 1577–78.

9. Goodrich, *Mountain Homespun*, p. 22.

10. Ibid. See also, for example, Louisa Walker, *Varied Occupations in String Work*, and similar hand-head-heart-handicrafts manuals.

11. Goodrich, *Mountain Homespun*, p. 23.

12. Ibid., p. 24; West, "Revival of Handicrafts," p. 1578; Marguerite Butler, "A Dream Come True," p. 2.

13. West, "Revival of Handicrafts," pp. 1578–79.

14. The Allanstand Cottage Industries was incorporated in 1917; in 1931 its Asheville sales shop and its entire capital were turned over to the Southern Mountain Handicrafts Guild, a distributing cooperative of eighteen crafts cooperatives or manufactories in Appalachia. A brief history of Allanstand will be found in Marguerite Butler, "A Dream Come True," to be supplemented by West, "Revival of Handicrafts," p. 1579, and Goodrich, *Mountain Homespun*, pp. 29 et passim. See also John M. Glenn et al., *Russell Sage Foundation*, 2:374–75.

15. Montgomery, *Bibliography of Settlements*, p. 90; West, "Revival of Handicrafts," p. 1577.

16. West, "Revival of Handicrafts," pp. 1576–77.

17. On Berea's crafts activities and the emergence of Frost's interest in mountain handicrafts as a manifestation of the indigenous culture of the southern mountains, see West, "Revival of Handicrafts," pp. 1579–82; Elisabeth S. Peck, *Berea's First Century*, pp. 116ff. In preparing his essay of 1898, "University Extension in Kentucky," for republication in *Berea Quarterly* as "University Extension in the Southern Mountains" (1899), Frost added to the original illustrations a photograph of handloomed coverlets as "typical" products of mountain homes. The *Berea Quarterly* was sent to the friends and supporters of the college. See also Josephine G. Robinson, "Mountain Homespun," *Berea Quarterly* (1900) and "Homespun 'Bed Kivers'," ibid. (1902); the latter is an advertisement of items available for purchase by mail, with prices.

18. On the Fireside Industries at Berea, see West, "Revival of Handicrafts," pp. 1579–82; Jennie Lester Hill, "Fireside Industries in the Kentucky Mountains" (1903).

19. West, "Revival of Handicrafts," p. 1585.

20. Ibid., pp. 1584–85.

21. Goodrich, *Mountain Homespun*, pp. 30–35; Lida Rose McCabe, "Regenerating Handicrafts in the Carolinas" (1917).

22. West, "Revival of Handicrafts," pp. 1585–86. Even a decade later, crafts as distinct from vocational education in the public schools of the South was sufficiently unusual to warrant public notice, as for example, [unsigned], "Craft Work in a Southern High School [John Marshall High School, Richmond]," *Craftsman* (1912).

23. Harnett T. Kane and Inez Henry, *Miracle in the Mountains*, p. 121, and above, chapter 6 n. 29.

24. West, "Revival of Handicrafts," p. 1596.

25. It is worthy of note that the great contemporary study by C. M. Woodward, "The Rise and Progress of Manual Training" (1894), written in the midst of the vocational education movement, identifies the impetus for manual training in America as coming from the Russian exhibit at the U.S. Centennial Exposition of 1876 of schoolboy hand work emphasizing technical excellence, as does Arthur U. Craig, "The Rise and Progress of Manual Training" (1902); while Charles Alpheus Bennett, *History of Manual and Industrial Education*, 2 vols. (1926 & 1937), written in the midst of the handicrafts movement of the postwar period, sees the impetus as coming from the exhibit of the work of the Scandinavian "sloyd" schools, which emphasized the use of manual training to "reunite" hand, head, and heart and to stimulate the native aesthetic sense of the lower classes. A middle position is taken by an earlier commentator, Charles H. Ham, "Manual Training" (1886).

26. Charles L. Coon, *Facts About Southern Educational Progress*; Edgar W. Knight, *Public School Education in North Carolina*; also Edgar Gardner Murphy, *Problems of the Present South*; Charles W. Dabney, Jr., *Universal Education in the South*. Lawrence Cremin, *The Transformation of the School*, attempts to put the whole in context.

27. [Commission on Country Life], *Report of the Commission on Country Life* (1910).

28. Henry Sabin, et al., "Report of the Committee of Twelve on Rural Schools"; also E. T. Fairchild, "Preliminary Report of the Committee on Rural School Education." On the Committee of Ten report and its impact, see Theodore R. Sizer, *Secondary Schools at the Turn of the Century*.

29. Frederick W. Neve, "Virginia Mountain Folk" (1909); John W. Zeller, "Education in the Country for the Country" (1910); W. H. Whitfield, *An Indictment of the Rural School* (1913), esp. pp. 43–44; Walter A. Dyer, "Working for Play: The Country School Developed into A Social Center" (1914).

30. Samuel E. Weber, "Southern Education Problems" and comment by Thomas P. Bailey, in National Education Association, *Addresses and Proceedings 1910*, pp. 234–41; also Louis Harlan, *Separate and Unequal: Public School Campaigns and Racism in the Southern Seaboard States, 1901–1915*.

31. Articulation of the problem and avoidance of the solution appears in Elwood P. Cubberley, *Rural Life and Education* (1913); A. C. Monahan, *The Status of Rural Education in the United States* (1913); W. H. Whitfield, "An Indictment of the Rural School" (1913); Walter A. Dyer, "Our Country Public Schools: What We Are Doing and Where We Fail" (1914). Also of interest is American Academy of Political and Social Science, *Country Life* (1912); George Frederick Wells, "Is an Organized Country Life Movement Possible?" (1913).

32. So far as I know, there is no history of the folk-school movement in the United States, although a substantial beginning has been made through the publication of Roland G. Paulston's bibliography, *Folk Schools in Social Change*. Of special interest concerning the adaptation of the folk-school idea in America, in addition to items cited

below, is Joseph K. Hart, *Light from the North: The Danish Folk Highschools. Their Meaning for America*.

33. [Unsigned], "Annual Statement of the Progress of Education in Foreign Countries: Denmark" (1871); [unsigned], "Statistics of Schools of Manual and Industrial Training" (1897); James C. Boykin, "Typical Institutions Offering Manual or Industrial Training" (1898). William G. Frost, "Educational Pioneering in the Southern Mountains" (1913), p. 248, notes the introduction of sloyd in the foundation department at Berea.

34. For example, Horace Plunkett, *Ireland in the New Century* (1904). So vital was this tradition that a reviewer of H. Ryder Haggard, *Rural Denmark and Its Lessons* (1911), thought it worth noting that the book was "free from that indiscriminate laudation of the Danish farmer and his methods, which has been preached somewhat 'ad nauseam' to the English agricultural community," *Nature* 86: 509 (15 June 1911); my own reading of Haggard suggests that such a judgment derived from the advertisements for the book, not the book itself. See also in this connection Frederic C. Howe, "A Commonwealth Ruled by Farmers" (1910); Booker T. Washington, "How Denmark Has Taught Itself Prosperity and Happiness: The Rural High Schools which Have Made Over a Nation" (1911); Jacob Riis, "Cooperation in Denmark: Educating the Farmers to Rule the Nation" (1913).

35. Frances Graham French, "Education in Denmark" (1897), esp. pp. 83–86; "Education in Norway" (1897); "Education in Sweden and Iceland" (1898), esp. pp. 983–86; Oscar Gundersen, "Report of the Committee of Twelve on Rural Schools. Appendix N: School Systems, Norway" (1897); [unsigned], "Education in Central Europe: Rural High Schools in Denmark" (1909); [unsigned], "Education in the Kingdoms of Northern Europe: Scandinavia" (1912).

36. Claxton indicates the origin of his interest in the folk schools as dating from a tour of Sweden and Denmark in 1896, "Letter of Transmittal," in L. L. Friend, *The Folk High Schools of Denmark*.

37. P. P. Claxton, "Letter of Transmittal," in [unsigned], *Illiteracy in the United States* (1913), p. 5. On the Congressional investigation and the Bureau of Education's role in it, see A. C. Monahan, "Rural Education" (1912), p. 180; an early report is Anna Tolman Smith, "Rural Uplift in Foreign Countries" (1911).

38. [Unsigned], *Illiteracy in the United States*, p. 29; also Cora Wilson Stewart, "The Moonlight Schools of Kentucky" (1914); "Moonlight Schools" (1916), condensed in [unsigned], "Kentucky's Moonlight Schools" (1916); "Elimination of Illiteracy" (1916). A first report of Stewart's program was [unsigned], "'Moonlight Schools' in the Kentucky Mountains" (1912), based on a report in the *New York Christian Herald*. The interest in Appalachian illiteracy which made Stewart's work of interest to a general philanthropic, rather than the narrower education public exclusively, followed from publication of Norman Frost, *A Statistical Study of the Public Schools of the Southern Appalachian Mountains* (1915); see for example McFall Kerby, "Illiteracy in the Appalachians" (1915). On the moonlight schools see also Raymond B. Fosdick, *Adventure in Giving: The Story of the General Education Board*, pp. 74–76, and the titles in Everett E. Edwards, *References on the Mountaineers of the Southern Appalachians*.

39. P. P. Claxton, "Letter of Transmittal," in [unsigned], *Illiteracy in the United States*, p. 5.

40. Claxton, "Letter of Transmittal," in Harold W. Foght, *The Educational System of Rural Denmark*, p. 5. The series consisted of: Harold W. Foght, *The Educational System of Rural Denmark*, U. S. Bureau of Education *Bulletin*, 1913 no. 58; L. L. Friend, *The Folk High Schools of Denmark*, ibid. 1914 no. 5; Harold W. Foght, *The Danish Folk High Schools*, ibid. 1914 no. 22; Harold W. Foght, *Danish Elementary Rural Schools, With Some Reference*

to *Seminaries for the Training of Rural Teachers*, ibid. 1914 no. 24. See also Martin Hegland, *The Danish People's High School, Including a General Account of the Educational System of Denmark*, ibid. 1915 no. 45. Claxton's introductory remarks suggest that he had shifted away from his earlier concern with adult illiteracy and returned to a yet-earlier interest in rural-life schools and education appropriate to country life through agricultural education, the integration of nature study and gardening into the primary school curriculum, and so forth; in this connection see also Mrs. Hetty S. Browne, *An Experimental Rural School at Winthrop College, Rock Hill, South Carolina*, U. S. Bureau of Education *Bulletin*, 1913 no. 42; Eugene C. Brooks, *Agriculture and Rural Life Day: Material for Its Observance*, ibid. 1913 no. 43; A. C. Monahan and Adam Phillips, *The Farragut School: A Tennessee Country-Life High School*, ibid. 1913 no. 49; W. S. Jesien, *Secondary Agricultural Schools in Russia*, ibid. 1917 no. 4. Advocacy of state systems of secondary education because the high schools served as "the people's colleges" appears for example in William A. Hand, "Secondary Education in the South" (1909), p. 280. Contemporary confusion resulting from the designation of private secondary schools as "colleges" is discussed in [General Education Board], *The General Education Board*, pp. 109ff., and earlier in Charles Foster Smith, "Southern Colleges and Schools."

41. Claxton, "Letter of Transmittal," in Friend, *The Folk High Schools of Denmark*, p. 5.

42. Foght, *The Danish Folk High Schools*, p. 89; Friend, *The Folk High Schools of Denmark*, pp. 18ff.

43. Friend, as a West Virginian, as Claxton noted, had special qualifications for understanding the needs of mountain people, Claxton, "Letter of Transmittal," in Friend, *The Folk High Schools of Denmark*, p. 5.

44. Foght, *The Educational System of Rural Denmark*, p. 42.

45. Foght, *The Danish Folk High Schools*, pp. 88–89.

46. Campbell, "From Mountain Cabin to Cotton Mill" (1913), p. 78. Before 1910, even the sense of alternatives was lacking, and it was conventional merely to note the need for "adaptation of traditional school programs" to meet the "unusual conditions" in the mountains; see for example [unsigned], "A Program for Two Million People," *Berea Quarterly* (1900).

47. John C. Campbell, ["Preliminary Report to the Russell Sage Foundation, Oct. 1, 1909"], p. 32: "Some interesting suggestions have come regarding the Folk schools of Sweden and Denmark, where illiterate adults are instructed, through inspirational teaching, in the many ways that pertain to better living. . . . The mountaineer is ever ready to attend lectures and meetings. It would seem that the Folk schools might be studied profitably as a very promising means to promote a community spirit, of which the State could later avail itself."

48. On the rural school as dispensary, see Charles Wardell Stiles, *Soil Pollution as a Cause of Ground Itch, Hookworm Disease (Ground Itch Anaemia) and Dirt Eating: A Circular for Use in Schools* (1910); Ernest Bryant Hoag, *Organized Health Work in Schools* (1913); John A. Ferrell, *The Rural School and Hookworm Disease* (1914). On the urban school as dispensary, cf. John Spargo, "The Nurse and Doctor in the Public School" (1907). The function of the settlement-influenced school as dispensary of social information and experience has already been discussed, but see also Lee F. Hanmer, "The Schoolhouse Evening Center: What It Is, What It Costs, What It Pays" (1913). Hanmer was at this time director of the Department of Recreation of the Russell Sage Foundation.

49. John C. Campbell, "The Future of the Church-School in the Southern Highlands: An Address Delivered before the Council of Women for Home Missions, Atlanta, Georgia, Jan. 6, 1916," pp. 15–16, 40.

50. John C. Campbell, "Confidential Report of the Activities of the Southern High-

land Division of the Russell Sage Foundation, Sept. 30, 1913–Sept. 30, 1914," pp. 12–17, 23–25; also of interest in this connection is later correspondence concerning the possibility of making Lincoln Memorial University into a folk school, Campbell to John Glenn, 17, 20 April 1917; Glenn to Campbell, 19 April 1917, Southern Highland Division Papers; also John C. Campbell, *The Future of the Church and Independent Schools in Our Southern Highlands* (1917).

51. Campbell, "Confidential Report," p. 16; Campbell to Glenn, 18 June, 4 Aug. 1914; Glenn to Campbell, 5 Aug. 1914, Southern Highland Division Papers. Olive Dame Campbell eventually did visit Denmark, in 1923, in connection with her plans for the John C. Campbell Folk School at Brasstown, North Carolina, which was to serve as a living memorial to her husband's work and ideas, John M. Glenn, *Russell Sage Foundation*, 1: 282; Olive Dame Campbell, *The Danish Folk School* (1928). For the date of her trip, ibid., p. 23n.

52. Campbell, "Confidential Report," pp. 14–15.

53. References to materials relating to the folk schools established in Appalachia after 1920 will be found in Edwards, *References on the Mountaineers of the Southern Appalachians*, and Paulston, comp., *Folk Schools in Social Change*. On the John C. Campbell Folk School, see also Glenn, *Russell Sage Foundation*, 1: 282, and the volumes of *Mountain Life and Work* after 1926.

54. Olive Dame Campbell, "Songs and Ballads of the Southern Mountains" (1915), p. 371; also below, chapter 10. On the contemporary assumption that "racial" identity and cultural participation (including the "communal" production of cultural artifacts) were continuous, see Daniel Kilham Dodge, "Scandinavian Character and Scandinavian Music" (1911); on the less radical, Gummerean assumption that cultural artifacts presuppose the existence of a culture, see Hamilton Wright Mabie, "Four English Songs by Shakespeare, Lovelace, and Herrick" (1909) and "Two Famous Ballads: Barbara Allen's Cruelty and Robin Hood and Allen-a-Dale" (1909). The seminal work in this discussion was Francis B. Gummere, "Primitive Poetry and the Ballad," published in *Modern Philology* (June, Oct. 1903, Jan. 1904), but see also Gummere, *The Popular Ballad* (1907), and George Lyman Kittridge, "The Popular Ballad [Review]" (1908). On the communalist controversy generally, see Donald K. Wilgus, *Anglo-American Folksong Scholarship*, and MacEdward Leach and Tristram P. Coffin, eds., *The Critics and the Ballad*.

55. Campbell, "Confidential Report," pp. 46–47. On the pageant movement more generally see Hazel MacKaye, "Outdoor Plays and Pageants: A Sketch of The Movement in America" (1910); Mary Master Needham, *Folk Festivals: Their Growth and How to Give Them* (1912); Percy MacKaye, *The Civic Theatre in Relation to the Redemption of Leisure* (1912) and *Community Drama: Its Motive and Method of Neighborliness* (1917); Katherine Lord, Alice Minnie Herts Heniger, and Howard Bradstreet, eds., *A Guide and Index to Plays, Festivals and Masques for Use in Schools, Clubs, and Neighborhood Centers* (1913); Arthur Farwell, "Community Music-Drama" (1914). On pageants and settlements, see Allen Davis, *Spearheads for Reform*, pp. 49ff.

56. Cecil J. Sharp, whose work collecting folksongs in Appalachia is discussed below, was a "communalist" when he began (cf. "The English Folksong" [Feb. 1917], reprinted from *One Hundred English Folksongs* [1916]) but experience eventually forced him to acknowledge diversity, if not cultural specialization, as a characteristic of folk societies, at least in Appalachia: "This trip is causing me to modify the opinion that I first formed that the singing of folk-songs was universal in the mountains. . . . Primitiveness in custom and outlook is not, I am finding, so much the result of remoteness as bad economic conditions. Where there is coal and good wages [or] where the land is rich and the valleys broad . . . the families soon drop their old fashioned ways," Sharp

to John Glenn, 2 Sept. 1917, quoted in Maud Karpeles, *Cecil Sharp*, p. 159. Sharp's work nonetheless functioned to "demonstrate" the folk character of the totality of mountain life and thus to contradict the actual observations of workers in the field. The normalization of the view of Appalachia as a "folk" society is apparent for example in James A. Robinson, "Artistic Weaving in the Mountains of North Carolina" (1917), where emphasis is on artistry rather than on the peculiarity of a persisting handicrafts tradition.

57. By September 1917, ballads were sung after meals at the Pine Mountain Settlement, in the same way that grace was sung before meals, Sharp to Olive Dame Campbell, 2 Sept. 1917, quoted in Karpeles, *Cecil Sharp*, p. 161; by May 1931, May Day was celebrated in the mountains with sword and morris dancing, ibid., p. 162. As early as 1902, however, public events at Berea included performances of "Saxon ballads" by the student glee club (William Goodell Frost to Walter Hines Page, Oct. 1902, W. H. Page Papers), although this was merely the analogue to the "plantation songs" presented by Berea's black students. Isabelle Rawn, herself an active collector of folksong, prepared and directed what appears to have been the first "Appalachian pageant" at the Berry School in 1914, according to John C. Campbell, "Confidential Report," pp. 46–47, although this may in fact have been the dramatization of Longfellow's poem, "The Courtship of Miles Standish," a photograph of which appears in *Outlook* 107: 853 (8 Aug. 1914); that would only qualify as a first "pageant" in the southern mountains. The possibility of developing a proper folk drama of and for Appalachia followed only from the intitial production in 1918 of "The Return of Buck Gavin" written by the young Asheville author, Thomas C. Wolfe, for the Carolina Playmakers at Chapel Hill, Frederick H. Koch, ed., *Carolina Folk Plays* (1922), p. xviii. More modest claims for the role of music in creating community in Appalachia—or in New York—appear in Max Schoen, "Music and Rural Life" (1917).

Chapter 10

1. James Mooney, "Folk-Lore of the Carolina Mountains" (1889), p. 95.
2. Ibid., p. 95. On the "catch 'em while you still can" motif among social scientists, see Nathaniel Southgate Shaler, "Peculiarities of the South" (1890); Adeline Moffatt, "Mountaineers of Middle Tennessee" (1890); George E. Vincent, "A Retarded Frontier" (1898). Prior to the publication of John A. Lomax, *Cow-boy Songs and Other Frontier Ballads* in 1910, few imagined the possibility of discovering an indigenous American folksong tradition, and even afterwards, the principal focus of folksong scholarship remained on the apparently more fruitful problem of the transmission of the Child ballads to America; cf. Haywood Parker, "Folk-lore of the North Carolina Mountains" (1907).
3. Adeline Moffatt, "Mountaineers of Middle Tennessee" (1890); N. C. Hoke, "Folk Custom and Folk Belief in North Carolina" (1892); J. Hampden Porter, "Notes on the Folk-lore of the Mountain Whites of the Alleghenies" (1894); H. M. Wiltse, "Some Mountain Superstitions of the South" (1899); Sadie F. Price, "Kentucky Folk-Lore" (1901); Mrs. R. F. Herrick, "The Black Dog of the Blue Ridge" (1907); Haywood Parker, "Folk-lore of the North Carolina Mountains" (1907).
4. On the aesthetic appeal of the naif products of folk cultures, see, for example [unsigned], "Editorial: Uncle Remus" (1908) and Mrs. L. H. Harris, "The Passing of Uncle Remus" (1908); K. MacGowan, "The New Life of Folk-Songs: Their Use to Modern People (1913). A dissenting note however is Montrose J. Moses, "The Children's Christmas Book Shelf: Folk Lore and Its Antidote" (1908).
5. "Genoel" [pseud.], "Mountain Song" (1910), p. 29.
6. Lila W. Edmands, "Songs from the Mountains of North Carolina" (1893).
7. On the dominance of folklore over folksong, see Donald K. Wilgus, *Anglo*

American Folksong Scholarship since 1898, pp. 143ff. Of interest in connection with the emergence of the sociological study of primitive society as an aspect of the Darwinian revolution, in place of the philological, see William I. Thomas, *Source Book for Social Origins*, and chapter 9 n. 1, above.

8. Olive Dame Campbell, "Songs and Ballads of the Southern Mountains," *Survey* (Jan. 1915); William Aspenwall Bradley, "Song Ballets and Devil's Ditties," *Harper's Magazine* (May 1915), "In Shakespeare's America," ibid. (Aug. 1915), and "The Folk Culture of the Cumberlands," *Dial* (Jan. 1918); Winifred Kirkland, "Mountain Music," *Outlook* (Dec. 1919). Bradley was among the most effective exploiters of Appalachian folksong materials of his generation, as in *Old Christmas, and Other Kentucky Tales in Verse* (1917) and *Singing Carr, and Other Song-Ballads of the Cumberlands* (1918); other attempts to use such materials during this period include Louise Rand Bascom, "The Better Man" (1916); Emma Bell Miles, *Strains from a Dulcimore*, ed. Abby Crawford Milton (1930).

9. Emma Bell Miles, "Some Real American Music" (1904), p. 118; on the use of folksong in "art" music more generally, see John Tasker Howard, *Our American Music*, pp. 437ff.

10. Louise Rand Bascom, "Ballads and Songs of Western North Carolina," *Journal of American Folk Lore* (June 1909); also C. Rexford Raymond, "British Ballads in Our Southern Highlands," *Berea Quarterly* (Nov. 1899) and "An Artificial Seaboard: The Work of the Extension Department," ibid. (May 1901), condensed in [unsigned], "Old Kentucky Ballads," *Independent* (20 June 1901); [unsigned], "Mountain Minstrelsy," *Berea Quarterly* (April 1905); George Lyman Kittridge, ed., "Ballads and Rhymes from Kentucky [collected by Katherine Pettit of the Hindman Settlement School]," *Journal of American Folk Lore* (Dec. 1907); Arthur Beatty, "Some Ballad Variants and Songs," ibid. (March 1909); Josiah H. Combs, "A Traditional Ballad from the Kentucky Mountains," ibid. (Sept. 1910); George Lyman Kittridge, ed., "Various Ballads," ibid. (June 1913).

11. Hubert Gibson Shearin, "British Ballads in the Cumberland Mountains," *Sewanee Review* (July 1911), condensed in [unsigned], "Oversea Ballads in Kentucky Valleys," *American Review of Reviews* (Oct. 1911); "*The Glove* and *The Lions* in Folk-Song," *Modern Language Notes* (April 1911); "Kentucky Folk-Songs," *Modern Language Review* (Oct. 1911); *A Syllabus of Kentucky Folk-Songs*, with Josiah H. Combs (1911). George Lyman Kittridge sought to explain the importance of Shearin's discoveries in "The Ballad of *The Den of Lions*," *Modern Language Notes* (June 1911). Josiah H. Combs was one of Shearin's students at Transylvania after 1905 and may well have been the stimulus to his interest in Appalachian folksong. As a student at the Hindman Settlement School after 1902, Combs had himself been one of Katherine Pettit's informants at the beginning of her collecting activities, and after graduation from Transylvania in 1911, he appears to have been one of the first to lecture on mountain folksong and folklore, Donald K. Wilgus, "Foreword," in Josiah H. Combs, *Folk Songs of the Southern United States*. Combs was also Shearin's informant for "Some Superstitions in the Cumberland Mountains," *Journal of American Folk Lore* (Sept. 1911), and perhaps also for "An Eastern Kentucky Word List," *Dialect Notes* (1911). Combs's own publications during this period include "A Traditional Ballad from the Kentucky Mountains," *Journal of American Folk Lore* (Sept. 1910); "Sympathetic Magic in the Kentucky Mountains," ibid. (July 1914); "Dialect of the Folk-Song," *Dialect Notes* (1916); and "Old, Early and Elizabethan English in the Southern Mountains," ibid. (1916).

12. Emma Bell Miles, "Some Real American Music," p. 121. Even William Goodell Frost, "Our Contemporary Ancestors in the Southern Mountains" (1899), p. 314, noted that "not a few old English ballads, familiar in Percy's *Reliques*, have been handed down . . . with interesting variants like those of the Homeric lays."

13. Henry Melvin Belden, "The Study of Folk-Song in America," *Modern Philology* (April 1905). On Belden's role, see Wilgus, *Anglo-American Folksong Scholarship*.

14. Also George Lyman Kittredge, ed., "Various Ballads," *Journal of American Folk Lore* (June 1913); Olive Dame Campbell, "Songs and Ballads of the Southern Mountains," *Survey* (Jan. 1915); Isabel Newton Rawn and Charles Peabody, "More Songs and Ballads from the Southern Appalachians," *Journal of American Folk Lore* (June 1916); Josephine McGill, "The Cherry-Tree Carol," ibid. (June 1916); Loraine Wyman and Howard Brockway, *Lonesome Tunes: Folksongs of the Kentucky Mountains* ([Dec.] 1916); Josephine McGill, *Folksongs of the Kentucky Mountains* (1917); George Lyman Kittredge, ed., "Ballads and Songs [collected by Loraine Wyman]," *Journal of American Folk Lore* (Sept. 1917); Loraine Wyman and Howard Brockway, *Twenty Kentucky Mountain Songs* (1920). Wyman and Brockway became interested in Appalachian folksong from reading Bradley, "Song Ballets and Devil's Ditties," according to [unsigned], "Hunting the Lonesome Tune in the Wilds of Kentucky," *Current Opinion* (Feb. 1917), but see also Howard Brockway, "The Quest of the Lonesome Tunes," *Art World* (June 1917). McGill discusses her collecting experiences in "'Following Music' in a Mountain Land," *Musical Quarterly* (July 1917), and less formally in "The Kentucky Mountain Dulcimer," *Musician* (Jan. 1917) and "Old Ballad Burthens," *Musical Quarterly* (April 1918). Important manifestations of popular interest in Appalachia as a source for the collection of folksongs, in addition to items cited above, include Natalie Curtis, "Folk-Music of America," *Craftsman* (Jan. 1912); W. A. Bradley, "Song Ballets and Devil's Ditties," *Harper's Magazine* (May 1915); [unsigned], "The Revival of Interest in Folk Song," *American Review of Reviews* (March 1916); [unsigned], "Rescuing the Folk Songs," *Literary Digest* (Feb. 1917); [unsigned], "Hunting the Lonesome Tune in the Wilds of Kentucky," *Current Opinion* (Feb. 1917). Important professional assessment of the discovery of Appalachian folksong appears in Reed Smith, "The Traditional Ballad in the South," *Journal of American Folk Lore* (March 1914); George Lyman Kittredge, "Ballads and Songs," ibid. (Sept. 1917); Henry Melvin Belden, "Folk-Song in America—Some Recent Publications," *Modern Language Notes* (March 1919).

15. Belden's plan is outlined in "The Study of Folk-Song in America." On collaborative collecting in Appalachia and the emergence of the state societies more generally, see Wilgus, *Anglo-American Folksong Scholarship*, pp. 79, 156, 175, and such published collections as John Harrington Cox, *Folk Songs of the South* (Cambridge, Harvard University Press, 1925); Arthur Kyle Davis, ed., *Traditional Ballads of Virginia: Collected under the Auspices of the Virginia Folk-Lore Society* (Cambridge, Harvard University Press, 1929) and *Folksongs of Virginia: A Descriptive Index and Syllabus* (Durham, Duke University Press, 1949).

16. C. Alphonso Smith, "A Great Movement in Which Everyone Can Help," in U.S. Bureau of Education, *An Opportunity to Help in An Important Work* [circular], (1913), p. 3; in a revised version under the same title, this also appeared in [State of Virginia, Dept. of Public Instruction], *Virginia Folk-Lore Society. A Great Movement to Collect and Save to the State and Nation the English and Scottish Ballads Surviving in this Commonwealth: Teachers, Pupils and School Patrons Asked to Help* (1914). Also of interest in this connection is Natalie Curtis, "Folk-Music of America" (1912); [unsigned], "The Revival of Interest in Folk-Song" (1916), based in part on C. Alphonso Smith, "Ballads Surviving in the United States" (1916). The use of circulars to aid in collecting folksong materials was not new with Smith, although he may have been unaware of the precedent, Francis James Child, *Invitation to Unite in an Effort to Collect Popular Ballads from Oral Tradition: Addressed Particularly to Students in Colleges* (n.p. [Cambridge, Mass.?], Jan. 29, 1881).

17. Wilgus, *Anglo-American Folksong Scholarship*, pp. 167ff, and n. 14, above.

18. It was during this period that John Campbell prepared his monograph on "The

Ancestry of the Mountaineers" ([1917?]), to "prove" that the highlanders of Appalachia were not Scotch-Irish, as had traditionally been claimed, but were of good old English stock—a theme which informed also the work of Josiah Henry Combs during this period, as in "Old, Early and Elizabethan English in the Southern Mountains" (1916) and "Early English Slang Survivals in the Mountains of Kentucky" (1921).

19. For the details of Sharp's visit to America, I have depended on Maud Karpeles, *Cecil Sharp: His Life and Work*.

20. See Luther Halsey Gulick, *The Healthful Art of Dancing*; [unsigned], "Teaching American Children to Play: Significance of the Revival of Folk Dances, Games, and Festivals by the Playground Association." I am indebted to Patricia Mooney Melvin for calling my attention to the role of folkdance in the playground movement.

21. Cecil J. Sharp to Maud Karpeles, 18 Jan. 1915, quoted in Karpeles, *Cecil Sharp*, pp. 124–25.

22. Richard Aldrich, "Folk Music for Shakespearean Drama—Mr. Cecil Sharp's Interesting Experiment in the 'Midsummer Night's Dream' Production," *New York Times*, 7 Feb. 1915, and "Mr. Barker Gives Some Shakespeare: Many Beauties and Some Curiosities in His Production . . . With Gilded Immortals Dancing to Old English Music Before Backgrounds of Fantastic Decoration," ibid., 17 Feb. 1915; also Charles Peabody, "The English Folk-Dance Society and Its Work"; Grace Hodson Boutelle, "A Leader of the Folk Dance"; Henry Wysham Lanier, "The Morris Dance Comes to America." By the end of 1915, Sharp had contracted with the Oliver Ditson Co., music publishers, for *One Hundred English Folk Songs*.

23. Karpeles, *Cecil Sharp*, p. 127.

24. Ibid., p. 142. During his first collecting trip in the mountains in 1916, after eight weeks in the North Carolina and Tennessee territory "controlled" by O. D. Campbell, Sharp thought to spend some time collecting from Alphonso Smith's students at Charlottesville, Virginia, "but I should not wish to do this without your approval, or unless I felt assured of your cooperation," he wrote Smith, quoted ibid., p. 155.

25. In addition to Karpeles, *Cecil Sharp*, p. 133, see [Richard Aldrich], "MacKaye Masque a Rare Spectacle: 'Caliban' The Biggest Dramatic Entertainment in History of New York," *New York Times*, 25 May 1916, and "'Caliban' Is Closed in a Feast of Fun," ibid., 6 June 1916; Ernest Hamlin Abbott, "A Masque of Masques," *Outlook* (7 June 1916); [unsigned], "A Week of Pageantry", *Independent* (12 June 1916). On Sharp in Cincinnati, see *University [of Cincinnati] News* (29 March 1916); [unsigned], "The Cincinnati Shakespeare Tercentenary Given by the University of Cincinnati," *Outlook* (5 July 1916). By 1918, Shakespeare Day in the American public schools had become a regular element in allied propaganda; see P. P. Claxton to Walter Hines Page, 1918, passim., W. H. Page Papers.

26. Karpeles, *Cecil Sharp*, pp. 133–35; John Campbell to John Glenn, 17 April, 8 Sept. 1917, 27 April 1918, Southern Highland Division Papers.

27. In the fall of 1916, for example, Sharp noted that "some of the women [missionaries] I have met are very nice and broadminded. But I don't think many of them realize that the people they are here to improve are in many respects far more cultivated than their would-be instructors . . . Something might be done in teaching them better methods of farming . . . Beyond that I should not go," Sharp to Mrs. James Storrow, 13 Sept. 1916, quoted in Karpeles, *Cecil Sharp*, p. 153. On Sharp at the Knoxville Conference of Southern Mountain Workers, see above, pp. 199–200.

28. Olive Dame Campbell and Cecil Sharp, *English Folk Songs from the Southern Appalachians* (N.Y., G. P. Putnam's Sons, 1917); the party is described in Karpeles, *Cecil Sharp*, pp. 136–37. See also Putnams' advertisement, *New York Times*, 25 Nov. 1917, IV, p. 498.

29. Richard Aldrich, "English and Scottish Folk Songs in America—Cecil Sharp Publishes His Finds in the South," *New York Times*, 2 Dec. 1917.

30. Henry Melvin Belden, "Folk-Song in America—Some Recent Publications" (1919); see also [unsigned], "The Appalachian Treasure 'Pocket' of American Folk-Song and Dance: Cecil Sharp Amazes London by Discovering Old English Songs Still Alive in America" (1919).

31. Charles Peabody, "Folk Dancing and jfolk Singing" (1918). Sharp saw and notated the "Running Set" at the Pine Mountain Settlement School and again at the Hindman Settlement School in late September 1917, according to Karpeles, *Cecil Sharp*, p. 163, who adds that the "Running Set" was "an unsophisticated form of the now popular American Square Dance." Its impact on American dance is well known.

32. William Aspenwall Bradley, "The Folk Culture of the Cumberlands" (1918). On Appalachia as America, see also Winifred Kirkland, "Mountain Music" (1919) and "Mountain Mothers" (1920); Percy MacKaye, "Untamed America: A Comment on a Sojourn in the Kentucky Mountains" (1924); James Watt Raine, *The Land of Saddle-Bags: A Study of the Mountain People of Appalachia* (1924); Robert Lindsay Mason, *The Lure of the Great Smokies* (1927); John Jacob Niles, "In Defense of the Backwoods" (1928); Doris Ullman, "The Mountaineers of Kentucky: A Series of Portrait Studies" (1928); R. W. Gordon, "Folk Etchings" (1928); Edwin E. White, *Highland Heritage: The Southern Mountains and the Nation* (1937).

33. In the context of the "cultural crisis" of the 1920s, the meaning of Appalachian folk culture became transformed, as in [unsigned], "Fireside Industries" (1921), p. 454: "Finally, America has some native art worth perpetuating. Weaving and basket-making as found in many of the highland homes constitute a highly developed art that is thoroughly American and well worth encouraging." Helpful guides to the "cultural crisis" of the 1920s and its consequences are Alan Trachtenberg, ed., *Critics of Culture*; Warren Susman, ed., *Culture and Commitment, 1929–1945*.

34. Albert G. Love and Charles B. Davenport, *Defects Found in Drafted Men*, pp. 290–91; also pp. 238, 255, 270, 292–93. An important index of the "peopleness" of the mountaineers in the American consciousness was their inclusion in studies which viewed literature as a source of information about social systems, as for example Harry Aubrey Toulmin, Jr., *Social Historians* (1911); Marion Clifford Harrison, "Social Types in Southern Prose Fiction" (1921).

35. Of particular interest in this connection is the long debate between hereditarians and environmentalists concerning the intelligence of "the" mountaineer, which flourished during the 1920s and 1930s; see for example N. D. M. Hirsch, "A Summary of Some of the Results from an Experimental Study of the East Kentucky Mountaineers," National Academy of Sciences, *Proceedings* (1927), and *An Experimental Study of the East Kentucky Mountaineers: A Study in Heredity and Environment*, Genetic Psychology Monographs (1928), abstracted in *Science* 67: supplement, pp. xii–xiv (1928); Mandel Sherman, "Environment and Mental Development: A Study of an Isolated Community," *Journal of the American Association of University Women* (1930); Lester R. Wheeler, "The Intelligence of East Tennessee Mountain Children," *Journal of Educational Psychology* (1932); Mandel Sherman and Cora B. Key, "The Intelligence of Isolated Mountain Children," *Child Development* (1932); Mandel Sherman and Thomas R. Henry, *Hollow Folk: A Study in the Blue Ridge* (1933); Lester R. Wheeler and Viola D. Wheeler, "The Musical Ability of Mountain Children as Measured by the Seasore Test of Musical Talent," *Journal of Genetic Psychology* (1933); E. J. Asher, "The Inadequacy of Current Intelligence Tests for Testing Kentucky Mountain Children," *Journal of Genetic Psychology* (1935); Jack Manne, "Mental Deficiency in a Closely Inbred Mountain Clan," *Mental Hygiene* (1936); Lester R. Wheeler, "A Comparative Study of the Intelligence of East Tennessee Mountain Children," *Journal of Educational Psychology* (1942).

36. Percy MacKaye, "Untamed America," p. 327. On MacKaye's love affair with the southern mountains, see his preface to *This Fine-Pretty World: A Comedy of the Kentucky Mountains* (1924) and his several ventures at using mountain materials as the basis for dramatic literature, especially *Tall Tales of the Kentucky Mountains*, first printed in the *Century* (July–Nov. 1924) as "A Mountain Munchausen," and *Kentucky Mountain Fantasies: Three Short Plays for an Appalachian Theatre* (1928).

37. Sam K. Cowan, *Sergeant York and His People* (1922); also [unsigned], "Sgt. York, War Hero, Dies," *New York Times*, 3 Sept. 1964, pp. 1, 26, and editorial note, p. 28; William Bradford Huie, "Last Humble Wish Fulfilled, Sgt. York is Buried in the Land He Loved," *New York Herald Tribune*, 6 Sept. 1964, p. 1: 8.

38. Olive Dame Campbell, "Preface," in John C. Campbell, *The Southern Highlander and His Homeland* (1921), p. xiv: "It should be added that Mr. Campbell understood thoroughly the difficulties in the way of writing of a people who, while forming a definite geographical and racial group, were by no means socially homogeneous. Many statements applicable to the remote rural folk who were the particular object of his study were not true of their urban and valley kinfolk, yet to differentiate groups in discussing phases of life common to all was not easy. Moreover it was impossible usually to secure data on a strictly group basis."

✣ Bibliography

This bibliography does not pretend to be a complete list of materials relating to the history of Appalachia any more than it pretends to be a complete list of materials relating to the history of America. It does attempt to be complete in the context of this book by providing full references to materials cited in briefer form in the notes. But because in the notes I have attempted to cite all materials relevant to a history of the "idea" of Appalachia, a compilation of such references functions also as an integral element in the argument of this book, as an indication of the "raw material" from which it is constructed.

The bibliography itself is divided into four parts: Part IV lists the locations of manuscripts collections consulted and cited in the notes. Part III lists bibliographies and all "secondary" sources cited in the notes, that is, materials read primarily for the information they contain and with the presumption that such information is correct, or as nearly correct as I needed it to be in the context of this book. Part II lists all "primary" sources cited in the notes *except* materials on the southern mountains and mountaineers published before 1923. Part I lists all "primary" sources cited in the notes which deal with the southern mountains and mountaineers, and which were published before 1923.

By "primary" sources in both cases I mean materials read not only for their content, but as historical phenomena in and of themselves, manifestations for example of an interest in the "strange land and peculiar people" of Appalachia and of the dominance of particular kinds of interest at particular times. I have cited selectively rather than extensively the local-color fiction of Appalachia, however, on the principle that adequate guides to this material are readily available elsewhere, and with the understanding that the emergence of local-color writing as an "industry" during the 1880s meant that its history after the age of Mary Noailles Murfree had more to do with the history of literature in America than with the history of Appalachia in America. And I have excluded from this bibliography items which, though they appear to be "about" the southern mountains and mountaineers, in fact are not, most notably the numerous localized studies of the geology and natural history of Appalachia (as distinct from those studies which at least claim to deal with the region as a whole).

Because the process by which the mountainous portions of several southern states came to be defined as a discrete region inhabited by a distinct people occurred across time, it has seemed most appropriate that Part I of this bibliography be arranged chronologically rather than alphabetically. For this reason also, I have integrated references to unpublished reports and addresses among the references to published material, and have, to the best of my ability, entered separate issues of a single book or article separately, on the principle that subsequent issues have the same "public impact" and "historical importance" as would an "original" publication saying the same thing written by the same or a different author. In such cases I have indicated where an item was originally published, and when. In all cases, moreover, I have physically seen and actually read each item in the bibliography. And while I cannot claim to have read everything written about the southern mountains and mountaineers between 1870 and 1920 I have certainly tried to do so, and am convinced that what I read is "representative" of the whole. Whatever the whole is like, however, the materials upon which the argument of this book is based were produced and consumed not at a glance or a gulp but over fifty years. That is how they are presented here, so that as historians we may view the process "as under a glass and in an hour"; and so that we may, if we wish, begin to understand the experience of trying to understand the nature and meaning of Appalachian otherness in 1880 or 1896 or 1908 or 1920—an experience different than our own.

I. Chronological List of References on the Southern Mountains and Mountaineers

1850s

Fee, John G. "Kentucky. For the American Missionary [Nov. 9, 1855]." *American Missionary* 10: 13–14 (December 1955).

Rogers, John A. R. "Letters from Kentucky. No. I. The 'Hill Country'; No. II. A Ride Through the Mountains; No. III. A Ride Through the Mountains—A Rural Meeting-House; No. IV. Cumberland Falls—A Post Office—A Prison." *Independent*, 23 September, 7 October, 4 November, 2 December 1858.

Fee, John G. ["Letter to the Editor. April 12, 1859"]. *American Missionary*, n.s. 3: 114 (May 1859).

[unsigned]. "Rev. John G. Fee." *American Missionary*, n.s. 3: 275–77 (December 1859).

1860s

Fee, John G. "Kentucky. Return of Kentucky Exiles. To the Editors of the Independent." *American Missionary*, n.s. 6: 186–87 (August 1862).

Fee, John G. "Kentucky. No Compromise with Slavery. To the Editors of the Independent [Oct. 24, 1862]." *American Missionary*, n.s. 6: 278–79 (December 1862).

Appleton, Elizabeth Haven. "A Half-Life and Half a Life." *Atlantic Monthly* 13: 157–82 (February 1864).

Fee, John G. "Home Missions [Feb. 15, 1864]." *American Missionary*, n.s. 8: 94–95 (April 1864).

Guernsey, A. H. "Illicit Distilling of Liquors." *Harper's Weekly* 11: 773 (7 December 1867).

Guernsey, A. H. "Hunting for Stills." *Harper's Weekly* 11: 811 (21 December 1867).

1870

Pollard, Edward A. "The Virginia Tourist." *Lippincott's Magazine* 5: 487–97, 599–609; 6: 140–49 (May, June, August 1870). Reprinted with other material as *The Virginia Tourist. Sketches of the Springs and Mountains of Virginia . . .* Philadelphia: J. B. Lippincott and Company, 1870.

Fairchild, E. Henry. *Inauguration of Rev. E. H. Fairchild, President of Berea College, Kentucky, Wednesday, July 7, 1869*. Cincinnati: Elm Street Printing Company, 1870.

Pollard, Edward A. *The Virginia Tourist. Sketches of the Springs and Mountains of Virginia. Containing an Exposition of Fields for the Tourist in Virginia; Natural Beauties and Wonders of the State; Also Accounts of Its Mineral Springs; and a Medical Guide to the Use of Its Waters*. Philadelphia: J. B. Lippincott and Company, [September] 1870. Reprinted in part from *Lippincott's Magazine* 5: 487–97, 599–609; 6: 140–49 (May, June, August 1870).

[unsigned]. "The North Carolina Mountains." *Appleton's Weekly* 4: 465 (15 October 1870).

1871

Coulton, Henry E. "Picturesque America." *Appleton's Journal* 5: 15–18 (January 1871).

Cooke, John Esten. "The Natural Bridge." *Appleton's Journal* 5: 168–70, 195–98 (February 1871).

Clingman, T. L. "Western North Carolina." *Appleton's Journal* 5: 587 (May 1871).

1872

de Fontaine, F. G. "Cumberland Gap." *Appleton's Weekly* 7: 281–82 (16 March 1872).
Strother, David Hunter [pseud.: "Porte-Crayon"]. "The Mountains." *Harper's Magazine* 44: 659–75, 801–15; 45: 21–34, 347–61, 502–16, 801–15; 46: 669–80; 47: 821–32; 49: 156–67; 51: 475–85 (April–June, August, September, November 1872; April, November 1873; July 1874; September 1875).

1873

[unsigned]. "Berea, Kentucky. Acclimating Northern Principles." *American Missionary*, n.s. 17: 58–59 (March 1873).
Fairchild, E. Henry. "Extract from a Private Letter of President Fairchild." *American Missionary*, n.s. 17: 59 (March 1873).
Strother, David Hunter [pseud.: "Porte-Crayon"]. "The Mountains." *Harper's Magazine* 46: 669–80; 47: 821–32 (April, November 1873). Continued from 1872.
Webster, Albert, Jr. "A Jaunt in The South." *Appleton's Journal* 10: 263–66, 297–99, 322–25 (30 August, 6 September, 13 September 1873).
Harney, Will Wallace. "A Strange Land and Peculiar People." *Lippincott's Magazine* 12: 429–38 (October 1873).
[unsigned]. "Berea College." *American Missionary*, n.s. 17: 253 (November 1873).

1874

King, Edward. "The Great South: Among the Mountains of North Carolina." *Scribner's Monthly* 7: 513–44 (March 1874).
King, Edward. "The Great South: Southern Mountain Rambles: In Tennessee, Georgia, and South Carolina." *Scribner's Monthly* 8: 5–33 (May 1874).
Strother, David Hunter [pseud.: "Porte-Crayon"]. "The Mountains." *Harper's Magazine* 49: 156–67 (July 1874). Continued from 1873.
Fairchild, E. Henry. "Berea College, Kentucky. Full Attendance—Interesting Exercises." *American Missionary*, n.s. 18: 195–96 (September 1874).
Davis, Rebecca Harding. "The Rose of Carolina." *Scribner's Monthly* 8: 723–26 (October 1874).

1875

Fairchild, E. Henry. *Berea College, Kentucky: An Interesting History. Approved by the Prudential Committee*. Cincinnati: Elm Street Printing Company, 1875. 2d ed., 1883.

Davis, Rebecca Harding. "The Yares of the Black Mountains." *Lippincott's Magazine* 16: 35–47 (July 1875).

Strother, David Hunter [pseud.: "Porte-Crayon"]. "The Mountains." *Harper's Magazine* 51: 475–85 (September 1875). Continued from 1874.

Davis, Rebecca Harding. "Qualla." *Lippincott's Magazine* 16: 576–86 (November 1875).

1876

Davis, Rebecca Harding. " 'Effie.' " *Peterson's Magazine* 69: 61–66 (January 1876).

1877

Burnett, Frances Hodgson. "Seth." *Lippincott's Magazine* 19: 296–307 (March 1877).

Burnett, Frances Hodgson. "Esmeralda." *Scribner's Monthly* 14: 80–91 (May 1877).

Burnett, Frances Hodgson. "Lodusky." *Scribner's Monthly* 14: 673–87 (September 1877).

[unsigned]. "The Moonshine Man: A Peep into His Haunts and Hiding Places." *Harper's Weekly* 21: 820–22 (21 October 1877).

Davis, Rebecca Harding. "A Night in the Mountains." *Appleton's Journal*, n.s. 3: 505–10 (December 1877).

1878

Cooke, John Esten. "Owlet." *Harper's Magazine* 57: 199–211 (July 1878).

Woolson, Constance Fenimore. "Up in the Blue Ridge." *Appleton's Journal*, n.s. 5: 104–25 (August 1878). Reprinted in *Rodman the Keeper: Southern Sketches*, pp. 276–339. New York: D. Appleton and Company, 1880.

Schayer, Julia. "Molly." *Scribner's Monthly* 16: 713–20 (September 1878).

Murfree, Mary Noailles [pseud.: Charles Egbert Craddock]. "The Star in the Valley." *Atlantic Monthly* 42: 532–43 (November 1878). Reprinted in *In the Tennessee Mountains*. Boston: Houghton, Mifflin Company, 1884 and subsequent editions.

1879

1880

Woolson, Constance Fenimore. "Up in the Blue Ridge." In *Rodman the Keeper: Southern Sketches*, pp. 276–339. New York: D. Appleton and Company, 1880. Reprinted from *Appleton's Journal*, n.s. 5: 104–25 (August 1878).

Woodbridge, Maria P. "Wildwood Studies." *Lippincott's Magazine* 25: 238–42 (February 1880).

Murfree, Mary Noailles [pseud.: Charles Egbert Craddock]. "The Romance of Sunrise Rock." *Atlantic Monthly* 46: 775–86 (December 1880). Reprinted in *In the Tennessee Mountains*. Boston: Houghton, Mifflin Company, 1884 and subsequent editions.

1881

1882

[unsigned]. "Poor White Trash." *Cornhill Magazine* 45: 579–84 (May 1882). Reprinted in *Living Age* 153: 688–91 (17 June 1882) and *Eclectic*, n.s. 36: 129–33 (July 1882).

[unsigned]. "Poor White Trash." *Living Age* 153: 688–91 (17 June 1882). Reprinted from *Corhnill Magazine* 45: 579–84 (May 1882).

[unsigned]. "Poor White Trash." *Eclectic*, n.s. 36: 129–33 (July 1882). Reprinted from *Cornhill Magazine* 45: 579–84 (May 1882).

1883

Fairchild, E. Henry. *Berea College, Kentucky: An Interesting History. Approved by the Prudential Committee*. 2d ed. Cincinnati: Elm Street Printing Company, 1883. First published 1875.

McDowell, Katherine Sherwood [pseud.: Sherwood Bonner]. *Dialect Tales*. New York: Harper and Brothers, 1883.

Myers, Mrs. A. A. *Mountain White Work in Kentucky*. New York: American Missionary Association, 1883.

Smith, Charles Foster. "On Southernisms." American Philological Association, *Transactions* 14: 42–56 (1883).

Jones, Louise Coffin. "In the Highlands of North Carolina." *Lippincott's Magazine* 32: 378–86 (October 1883).

Fairchild, Charles G. "Address of Professor C. G. Fairchild." *American Missionary*, n.s. 36: 391–93 (December 1883).

1884

Murfree, Mary Noailles [pseud.: Charles Egbert Craddock]. *In the Tennessee Mountains*. Boston: Houghton, Mifflin and Company, 1884 and subsequent editions.

[unsigned]. "In the Tennessee Mountains [Review]." *Atlantic Monthly* 54: 131–33 (July 1884).

1885

Murfree, Mary Noailles [pseud.: Charles Egbert Craddock]. "The Prophet of
   the Great Smoky Mountains." *Atlantic Monthly* 55: 1–12, 186–200, 289–302,
   433–43, 601–16, 744–57; 56: 31–44, 244–56 (January–August 1885). Reprinted, Boston: Houghton, Mifflin and Company, 1885.
Warner, Charles Dudley. "On Horseback." *Atlantic Monthly* 56: 88–100, 194–
   207, 388–98, 540–54 (July–October 1885). Reprinted, Boston: Houghton,
   Mifflin and Company, 1888.
Murfree, Mary Noailles [pseud.: Charles Egbert Craddock]. *The Prophet of the
   Great Smoky Mountains*. Boston: Houghton, Mifflin and Company, 1885.
   Reprinted from *Atlantic Monthly* 55: 1–12, 186–200, 289–302, 433–43, 601–
   16, 744–57; 56: 31–44, 244–56 (January–August 1885).
Fairchild, E. Henry. "[Report from] The South: Berea College." *American Mis-
   sionary*, n.s. 39: 251–52 (September 1885).
Smith, Charles Foster. "Southern Dialect in Life and Literature." *Southern
   Bivouac*, n.s. 1: 343–51 (November 1885).

1886

Allen, James Lane. "Through Cumberland Gap on Horseback." *Harper's
   Magazine* 73: 50–66 (June 1886). Reprinted in *The Blue-Grass Region of Ken-
   tucky and Other Kentucky Articles*, pp. 217–46. New York: Harper and
   Brothers, 1892, 1899.

1887

Allison, Young E. "Moonshine Men." *Southern Bivouac*, n.s. 2: 528–34 (Feb-
   ruary 1887).
Davies, J. M. "Scotch-Irish Stock in the Central South." *The Church at Home
   and Abroad* 2: 128–29 (August 1887).
Davies, J. M. "Knoxville, Tenn. Some Men Located and More Needed." *The
   Church at Home and Abroad* 2: 232–33 (September 1887).

1888

Humes, Thomas Wilson. *The Loyal Mountaineers of Tennessee*. Knoxville:
   Ogden Brothers and Company, 1888.
Warner, Charles Dudley. *On Horseback: A Tour through Virginia, North Carolina
   and Tennessee*. Boston: Houghton, Mifflin and Company, 1888. Reprinted
   from *Atlantic Monthly* 56: 88–100, 194–207, 388–98, 540–54 (July–October
   1885).

Murfree, Mary Noailles [pseud.: Charles Egbert Craddock]. "The Despot of Broomsedge Cove." *Atlantic Monthly* 61: 95–111, 194–212, 366–86, 532–56, 661–80, 813–34; 62: 68–89, 230–50, 398–419, 536–59, 674–99, 808–34 (January–December 1888). Reprinted, Boston: Houghton, Mifflin and Company, 1888.

Roseboro, Martha Colyer. "The Mountaineers about Montegle." *Century* 36: 771–79 (September 1888).

Edwards, Harry Stillwell. "An Idyl of 'Sinkin' Mount'in." *Century* 36: 895–907 (October 1888).

Brown, William Perry. "A Peculiar People." *Overland Monthly*, 2d ser., 12: 505–8 (November 1888).

Murfree, Mary Noailles [pseud.: Charles Egbert Craddock]. *The Despot of Broomsedge Cove*. Boston: Houghton, Mifflin and Company, 1888. Reprinted from *Atlantic Monthly* 61: 98–111, 194–212, 366–86, 532–56, 661–80, 813–34; 62: 68–89, 230–50, 398–419, 536–59, 674–99, 808–34 (January–December 1888).

1889

Warner, Charles Dudley. "Comments on Kentucky." *Harper's Magazine* 78: 255–71 (January 1889).

Mooney, James. "Folk-lore of the Carolina Mountains." *Journal of American Folk Lore* 2: 95–104 (June 1889).

1890

Barton, William E. *Life in the Hills of Kentucky*. Oberlin, Ohio: E. J. Goodrich, 1890.

Jenkins, Frank E. "The Mountain Whites of the South." In Evangelical Alliance, *National Needs and Remedies*, pp. 79–89. New York: Bayard and Taylor, 1890.

Allen, James Lane. "Mountain Passes of the Cumberland." *Harper's Magazine* 81: 561–76 (September 1890). Reprinted in *The Blue-Grass Region of Kentucky and Other Kentucky Articles*, pp. 249–301. New York: Harper and Brothers, 1892, 1899.

Shaler, Nathaniel Southgate. "The Peculiarities of the South." *North American Review* 151: 477–88 (October 1890).

Mayo, A. D. "The Third Estate of the South." *New England Magazine*, n.s. 3: 299–311 (November 1890).

1891

Roy, Joseph E. *Americans of the Midland Mountains*. New York: American Missionary Association, 1891.

Hamilton, Kate W. "Cindy's Chance." *Home Mission Monthly* 5: 51–54, 74–76 (January, February 1891).

Moffatt, Adeline. "Mountaineers of Middle Tennessee." *Journal of American Folk Lore* 4: 314–20 (December 1891).

Presbyterian Church in the United States of America. Woman's Executive Committee of Home Missions. *Home Mission Monthly* 6 no. 2 (pp. 25–35), December 1891. [issue devoted to mountain white work.]

[unsigned]. "Monthly Topic: Mountain Work." *Home Mission Monthly* 6: 30 (December 1891).

1892

Allen, James Lane. "Through Cumberland Gap on Horseback." In *The Blue-Grass Region of Kentucky and Other Kentucky Articles*, pp. 217–46. New York: Harper and Brothers, 1892, 1899. Reprinted from *Harper's Magazine* 73: 50–66 (June 1886).

Allen, James Lane. "Mountain Passes of the Cumberland." In *The Blue-Grass Region of Kentucky and Other Kentucky Articles*, pp. 249–301. New York: Harper and Brothers, 1892, 1899. Reprinted from *Harper's Magazine* 81: 561–76 (September 1890).

Hoke, N. C. "Folk Custom and Folk Belief in North Carolina." *Journal of American Folk Lore* 5: 113–20 (June 1892).

Frost, William Goodell. "To the Brethren at Berea," 16 July 1892. MS. in William Goodell Frost Papers, Berea College Archives.

Fox, John, Jr. "A Mountain Europa." *Century* 42: 760–65, 846–58 (September, October 1892). Reprinted, New York: Harper and Brothers, 1899.

1893

"A Scotch-Irishman." *The Mountain Whites of the South*. Pittsburgh: Presbyterian Banner Company, 1893.

Edmands, Lila W. "Songs from the Mountains of North Carolina." *Journal of American Folk Lore* 6: 131–34 (June 1893).

Frost, William Goodell. "Inaugural Address, June 21, 1893." In *Spent Arrows: Extracts from the Speeches and Writings of William Goodell Frost*, pp. 32–38. Cincinnati: no publisher, 1893.

Frost, William Goodell. "Berea Ideas." Address, autumn? 1893. Typescript in William Goodell Frost Papers, Berea College Archives.

1894

Frost, William Goodell. "Berea College Problems. President's Quarterly Report to the Faculty, Feb. 3, 1894." MS in William Goodell Frost Papers, Berea College Archives.

Hayes, C. Willard, and Campbell, Marius R. "Geomorphology of the Southern Appalachians." *National Geographic* 4: 63–126 (23 May 1894).

Fox, John, Jr. "A Cumberland Vendetta." *Century* 48: 163–78, 366–73, 496–505 (June–August 1894). Reprinted in *A Cumberland Vendetta and Other Stories*. New York: Harper and Brothers, 1895.

Porter, J. Hampden. "Notes on the Folk-Lore of the Mountain Whites of the Alleghenies." *Journal of American Folk Lore* 7: 105–17 (June 1894).

Frost, William Goodell. *Synopsis of President's Report. Berea College. Presented to Trustees and Faculty, June 28, 1894*. [Berea: Berea College, 1894].

Frost, William Goodell. "The Call of Providence." Address, Hotel Thorndike, Boston, Mass., 21 Nov. 1894. Typescript in William Goodell Frost Papers, Berea College Archives.

Burnett, Swan M. "The 'Over-Mountain' Men." *American Historical Register and Monthly Gazette of the Patriotic-Hereditary Societies of the United States of America* 1: 313–24, 421–31 (December 1894, January 1895).

1895

Fox, John, Jr. *A Cumberland Vendetta and Other Stories*. New York: Harper and Brothers, 1895.

Frost, William Goodell. *Sectional Lines: A Toast*. Berea: Students' Press, 1895.

Hayes, C. Willard. "The Southern Appalachians." *National Geographic Society Monographs* 1: 305–36 (1895). Also printed as National Geographic Society Monograph no. 10. New York: D. Appleton and Company, 1895.

Hayes, C. Willard. *The Southern Appalachians*. National Geographic Society Monographs, No. 10. New York: D. Appleton and Company, 1895. Also in *National Geographic Society Monographs* 1: 305–36 (1895).

Burnett, Swan M. "The 'Over-Mountain' Men." *American Historical Register and Monthly Gazette of the Patriotic-Hereditary Societies of the United States of America* 1: 421–31 (January 1895). Continued from 1894.

[unsigned]. "The Religious World: A Log Cabin College Settlement." *Outlook* 51: 64 (12 January 1895).

Hayes, C. Willard. "Eastern Kentucky: Its Physiography and Its People." *Berea Quarterly* 1 no. 1: 3–8 (May 1895).

Davis, Mrs. S. M. "The 'Mountain Whites' of America." *Missionary Review of the World* 8: 422–26 (June 1895).

Wilds, J. T. "The Mountain Whites of the South." *Missionary Review of the World* 8: 921–23 (December 1895).

Frost, William Goodell. "The Last Log School-House." Address before the Cincinnati Teachers' Club, 13 December 1895. *Cincinnati Commercial Gazette*, 14 December 1895. Reprinted in revised form as "An Educational Program for Appalachian America," *Berea Quarterly* 1 no. 4: 3–11 (May 1896).

1896

Ryder, Charles Jackson. *The Debt of our Country to the American Highlanders during the War*. Address before the American Missionary Association, 1892. New York: American Missionary Association, 1896?

Lynde, Francis. "The Moonshiners of Fact." *Lippincott's Magazine* 57: 66–76 (January 1896).

[unsigned]. "Novel Notes." *Bookman* 2: 434 (January 1896).

Cady, J. Cleveland. "A Summer Outing in Kentucky." *Outlook* 53: 56–59 (11 January 1896).

Frost, William Goodell. "An Educational Program for Appalachian America." Berea Quarterly 1 no. 4: 3–11 (May 1896). Revised from "The Last Log School-House," *Cincinnati Commerical Gazette*, 14 December 1895.

Frost, William Goodell. "Appalachian America." *Womans Home Companion* 23 no. 9: 3–4, 21 (September 1896).

Cable, George W. "The Unique Value of Berea." Appended to William Goodell Frost, "Appalachian America," *Womans Home Companion* 23 no. 9: 3–4, 21 (September 1896), p. 21.

Hayes, Charles Willard. "The Mountain Region of the South." Appended to William Goodell Frost, "Appalachian America," *Womans Home Companion* 23 no. 9: 3–4, 21 (September 1896), p. 21.

Mayo, A. D. "The New Crisis of the South." Appended to William Goodell Frost, "Appalachian America," *Womans Home Companion* 23 no. 9: 3–4, 21 (September 1896), p. 21.

Shaler, Nathaniel Southgate. "Needs of the Mountain People." Appended to William Goodell Frost, "Appalachian America," *Womans Home Companion* 23 no. 9: 3–4, 21 (September 1896), p. 21.

Murfree, Mary Noailles [pseud.: Charles Egbert Craddock]. "The Juggler." *Atlantic Monthly* 78: 597–609, 804–22; 79: 188–98, 386–99, 508–27, 651–64, 825–37 (November, December 1896; February–June 1897). Reprinted, Boston: Houghton, Mifflin and Company, 1897.

Frost, William Goodell. "Appalachian America." Address, Trinity Church, Boston, 30 November 1896. *Boston Evening Journal*, 1 December 1896; *Boston Evening Transcript*, 1 December 1896.

Roosevelt, Theodore. ["Address on Behalf of Berea College."] Trinity Church, Boston, November 30, 1896. *Boston Evening Journal*, 1 December 1896.

1897

Fox, John, Jr. *The Kentuckians*. New York: Harper and Brothers, 1897.

Cox, General J. D. "The Mountain People in the Struggle for the Union." *Berea Quarterly* 2 no. 2: 5–11 (February 1897).

Murfree, Mary Noailles [pseud.: Charles Egbert Craddock]. "The Juggler."
    Atlantic Monthly 79: 188–98, 386–99, 508–27, 651–64, 825–37 (February–
    June 1897). Continued from 1896.
Barton, William E. "The Cumberland Mountains and the Struggle for Free-
    dom." *New England Magazine* 22: 65–87 (March 1897). Reprinted in *Berea
    Quarterly* 2 no. 3: 3–25 (May 1897).
Barton, William E. "The Cumberland Mountains and the Struggle for Free-
    dom." Berea Quarterly 2 no. 3: 3–25 (May 1897). Reprinted from *New En-
    gland Magazine* 22: 65–87 (March 1897).
Murfree, Mary Noailles [pseud.: Charles Egbert Craddock]. *The Juggler*. Bos-
    ton: Houghton, Mifflin and Company, 1897. Reprinted from *Atlantic
    Monthly* 78: 597–609, 804–22; 79: 188–98, 386–99, 508–27, 651–64, 825–37
    (November, December 1896; February–June 1897).
Ryder, Charles Jackson. "Our American Highlanders: Problems and Prog-
    ress." *Education* 18: 67–82 (October 1897).
Pierson, Mrs. D. L. "The Mountaineers of Madison County, N.C." *Missionary
    Review of the World*, n.s. 10: 821–31 (November 1897).

1898

Elliott, Sarah Barnwell. *The Durket Sperrit: A Novel*. New York: Henry Holt and
    Company, 1898.
Ryan, Grace F. "The Highlands of Kentucky." *Outlook* 58: 363–68 (5 February
    1898).
Vincent, George E. "A Retarded Frontier." *American Journal of Sociology* 4:
    1–20 (July 1898).
Frost, William Goodell. "University Extension in Kentucky." *Outlook* 60:
    73–79 (3 September 1898). Reprinted as "University Extension in the
    Southern Mountains," *Berea Quarterly* 4 no. 2: 9–16 (May 1899), and as a
    separate (1900?).
[Frost, William Goodell]. "In Kentucky's Mountains: W. G. Frost Speaks at
    Broadway Tabernacle to the Class on Present-Day Problems." *New York
    Times*, 12 December 1898, p. 5.

1899

Allen, James Lane. "Through Cumberland Gap on Horseback." In *The Blue-
    Grass Region of Kentucky and Other Kentucky Articles*, pp. 217–46. New York:
    Harper and Brothers [1892], 1899. Reprinted from *Harper's Magazine* 73:
    50–66 (June 1886).
Allen, James Lane. "Mountain Passes of the Cumberland." In *The Blue-Grass
    Region of Kentucky and Other Kentucky Articles*, pp. 249–301. New York:

Harper and Brothers [1892], 1899. Reprinted from *Harper's Magazine* 81: 561–76 (September 1890).

Campbell, Robert F. *Mission Work among the Mountain Whites of Asheville Presbytery*. 2d. ed. Asheville: Citizen Company, 1899.

John, Jr. *A Mountain Europa*. New York: Harper and Brothers, 1899. Reprinted from *Century* 42: 760–65, 846–58 (September, October 1892).

Frost, William Goodell. "Our Contemporary Ancestors in the Southern Mountains." *Atlantic Monthly* 83: 311-19 (March 1899).

Frost, William Goodell. "University Extension in the Southern Mountains." *Berea Quarterly* 4 no. 2: 9–16 (May 1899). Originally printed as "University Extension in Kentucky," *Outlook* 60: 73–79 (3 September 1898). Reprinted as a separate (1900?).

Wiltse, H. M. "Some Mountain Superstitions in the South." *Journal of American Folk Lore* 12: 131–35 (June 1899).

Johnston, J. Stoddard. "Romance and Tragedy of Kentucky Feuds." *Cosmopolitan* 27: 551–58 (September 1899).

Raymond, C. Rexford. "British Ballads in Our Southern Highlands." *Berea Quarterly* 4 no. 3: 12–14 (November 1899).

1900

Barton, William E. *The Cumberland Mountains and the Struggle for Freedom. Reprinted from The New England Magazine, March 1897*. [Berea?: Berea College Press?, 1900?].

Barton, William E. *Pine Knot: A Story of Kentucky Life*. New York: D. Appleton and Company, 1900.

Frost, William Goodell. *University Extension in the Southern Mountains. Reprinted from The Outlook*. [New York?: 1900?]. Originally printed as "University Extension in Kentucky," *Outlook* 60: 73–79 (3 September 1898).

Frost, William Goodell. *University Extension in the Southern Mountains*. [Berea?: 1900?]. Reprinted from *Berea Quarterly* 4 no. 2: 9–16 (May 1899). Originally printed as "University Extension in Kentucky," *Outlook* 60: 73–79 (3 September 1898).

Rayner, Emma. *Visiting the Sin: A Tale of Mountain Life in Kentucky and Tennessee*. Boston: Small, Maynard and Company, 1900.

Robinson, Josephine G. "Mountain Homespun." *Berea Quarterly* 4 no. 4: 7–9 (February 1900).

Frost, William Goodell. "The Southern Mountaineer: Our Kindred of the Boone and Lincoln Type." *American Review of Reviews* 21: 303–11 (March 1900).

Semple, Ellen Churchill. "A New Departure in Social Settlements." *American Academy of Political and Social Science, Annals* 15: 301–4 (March 1900).

Speed, John Gilmer. "The Kentuckians." *Century* 68: 946–52 (April 1900).

Goodrich, Frances L. "Old Ways and New in the Carolina Mountains." *Southern Workman* 29: 207–11 (April 1900).

Fox, John, Jr., "Manhunting in the Pound: A Personal Experience in Kentucky Border Life." *Outing* 36: 344–50 (July 1900).

[unsigned]. ["Editorial Note: On the British Origin of the Mountaineers"]. *Berea Quarterly* 5 no. 3: 4 (November 1900).

[unsigned]. "A Program for Two Million People." *Berea Quarterly* 5 no. 3: 21 (November 1900).

1901

Frost, William Goodell. "Educational Pioneering in the Southern Mountains." National Education Association, *Addresses and Proceedings* 1901, pp. 555–60.

Frost, William Goodell. "Report of President Frost to the [Berea] Trustees, 1900–1901." Typescript, marked "not in printed reports." In W. G. Frost Papers, Berea College Archives.

Frost, William Goodell. "In the Land of Saddle-Bags." *Missionary Review of the World* 24: 21–31 (January 1901). Reprinted as *In the Land of Saddle-Bags: The Protestant People of Appalachian America*. New York: no publisher, 1901.

Frost, Willliam Goodell. *In the Land of Saddle-Bags: The Protestant People of Appalachian America*. New York: no publisher 1901. Reprinted from *Missionary Review of the World* 24:21–31 (January 1901).

Campbell, Robert F. "Classification of Mountain Whites." *Southern Workman* 30: 110–16 (February 1901). Reprinted as *Classification of Mountain Whites*. Hampton, Virginia: Hampton Institute Press, 1901.

Campbell, Robert F. *Classification of Mountain Whites*. Hampton, Virginia: Hampton Institute Press, 1901. Reprinted from *Southern Workman* 30: 110–16 (February 1901).

Price, Sadie F. "Kentucky Folk-Lore." *Journal of American Folk Lore* 14: 30–38 (March 1901).

Fox, John, Jr. "The Southern Mountaineer." *Scribner's Magazine* 29: 387–99, 556–70 (April, May 1901).

Raymond, C. Rexford. "An Artificial Seaboard: The Work of the Extension Department." *Berea Quarterly* 6 no. 1: 5–14 (May 1901). Condensed in [unsigned], "Old Kentucky Ballads," *Independent* 53: 1452 (20 June 1901).

Waldo, Frank. "Among the Southern Appalachians." *New England Magazine*, n.s. 24: 231–47 (May 1901).

Semple, Ellen Churchill. "The Anglo-Saxons of the Kentucky Mountains: A Study in Anthropogeography." *Geographical Journal* (London) 17: 588–623 (June 1901). Reprinted in *Bulletin of the American Geographical Society* 42: 561–94 (August 1910).

Spears, John R. "The Story of a Mountain Feud." *Munsey's Magazine* 24: 494–509 (June 1901).

[unsigned]. "Old Kentucky Ballads." *Independent* 53: 1452 (20 June 1901).

MacClintock, S. S. "The Kentucky Mountains and Their Feuds." *American Journal of Sociology* 7: 1–28, 171–87 (July, September 1901).

Cady, J. Cleveland. "In the Mountains." *Outlook* 69: 320–25 (5 October 1901).

Daingerfield, Henderson. "Social Settlement and Educational Work in the Kentucky Mountains." *Journal of Social Science* 39: 176–89 (November 1901).

[unsigned]. ["Editorial Note: On the Threat of Mormonism in the Mountains"]. *Berea Quarterly* 6 nos. 2–3: vii (August–November 1901).

[unsigned]. "[Editorial Note: On the Organization of an] Extension Department [at Berea]." *Berea Quarterly* 6 nos. 2–3: 53–54 (August–November 1901).

1902

Southern Education Board. *Educational Conditions in the Southern Appalachians.* [Compiled by Charles W. Dabney]. Southern Education Board Bulletin, 1 no. 1. Knoxville: Southern Education Board, 1902.

Partridge, Eloise J. "Extension Work in Perry County." *Berea Quarterly* 6 no. 4: 12–19 (February 1902).

Wright, Frances M. "In the Highlands of North Carolina." *Southern Workman* 31: 206–10 (April 1902).

Robinson, Josephine G. "Homespun 'Bed-Kivers'." *Berea Quarterly* 7 no. 1: 27–28 (May 1902).

Hubbard, Leonidas, Jr. "The Moonshiner at Home." *Atlantic Monthly* 90: 234–41 (August 1902).

Daingerfield, Nettie Gray. "Mrs. Clayton's Cooking School." *Southern Workman* 31: 545–53 (October 1902).

1903

Daingerfield, Henderson. "The Little People of Donegal and Lee." *Southern Workman* 32: 32–34 (January 1903).

Hill, Jennie Lester. "Fireside Industries in the Kentucky Mountains." *Southern Workman* 32: 208–13 (April 1903).

Walsh, Mary E. "The Social Settlement at Narrow Gap." *Berea Quarterly* 8 no. 4: 9–13 (May 1903).

Ralph, Julian. "Our Appalachian Americans." *Harper's Magazine* 107: 32–41 (June 1903).

McClure, R. L. "The Mazes of a Kentucky Feud." *Independent* 55: 2216–24 (17 September 1903).

Barton, William E. "The Church Militant in the Feud Belt." *Century* 75: 351–52 (10 October 1903).

Davis, Hartley, and Smyth, Clifford. "The Land of Feuds. A Region of the United States in Which Bloodshed Is a Pastime and Cruel and Cowardly Murder Goes Unpunished—The Terrible Story of the Seven Great Kentucky Feuds." *Munsey's Magazine* 30: 161–72 (November 1903).

MacGowan, Alice. "The Homecoming of Byrd Forebush: A Love Story of Little Turkey Track." *Munsey's Magazine* 30: 397–404 (December 1903).

Stone, Frank Z. "Children of the Enemy." *Munsey's Magazine* 30: 429–32 (December 1903).

1904

Morris, Samuel L. *At Our Own Door: A Study of Home Missions with Special Reference to the South and West*. New York: Fleming H. Revell Company, 1904.

West, Max. "The Revival of Handicrafts in America." U.S. Bureau of Labor *Bulletin* 9: 1573–1622 (1904 no. 55).

Williams, Lillian Walker. "In The Kentucky Mountains: Colonial Customs That Are Still Existing in That Famous Section of the Country." *New England Magazine*, n.s. 30: 37–45 (March 1904).

Howard, O. O. "The Feuds in the Cumberland Mountains." *Independent* 56: 783–88 (7 April 1904).

Miles, Emma Bell. "Some Real American Music." *Harper's Magazine* 109: 118–23 (June 1904).

Berry, Martha. "A School in the Woods." *Outlook* 77: 833–41 (6 August 1904).

Van Vorst, Marie. "Amanda of the Mill. A Novel." *Bookman* 20: 237–50, 350–60, 464–73, 569–77; 21: 81–97, 190–209, 271–85 (November 1904–May 1905). Reprinted, New York: Dodd, Mead and Company, 1905.

1905

Van Vorst, Marie. "Amanda of the Mill. A Novel." *Bookman* 20: 464–73, 569–77; 21: 81–97, 190–209, 271–85 (January–May 1905). Continued from 1904.

[unsigned]. "Mountain Minstrelsy." *Berea Quarterly* 9 no. 3: 2, 5–13 (April 1905).

Van Vorst, Marie. *Amanda of the Mill. A Novel*. New York: Dodd, Mead and Company, 1905. Reprinted from *Bookman* 20: 237–50, 350–60, 464–73, 569–77; 21: 81–97, 190–209, 271–85 (November 1904–May 1905).

Frost, William Goodell. "Berea College." In [American Unitarian Association], *From Servitude to Service. Being the Old South Lectures on the History and Work of Southern Institutions for the Education of the Negro*, pp. 49–79. Boston: American Unitarian Association, [September] 1905.

1906

Groves, S. B. *The Strength of the Hills Is His Also*. New York: American Missionary Association, 1906.

Haney, William Henry. *The Mountain People of Kentucky: An Account of Present Conditions with the Attitude of the People toward Improvement*. Cincinnati: The Robert Clarke Company, 1906.

Hubbard, Mary B. *In the Sky Country*. New York: American Missionary Association, 1906?

Knight, Edgar W. *Public School Education in North Carolina*. Boston: Houghton Mifflin Company, 1906.

McKelway, Alexander J. "The Physical Evils of Child Labor." North Carolina Board of Health, *Biennial Report* 11: 23–25 (1905–6).

Parker, Haywood. *Folklore of the North Carolina Mountaineer. A Paper Read Before the Pen and Plate Club, Asheville, N.C., 1906*. [Asheville: no publisher, 1906]. Also printed in *Journal of American Folk Lore* 20: 241–50 (December 1907).

Wilson, Samuel Tyndale. *The Southern Mountaineers*. New York: Literature Department, Presbyterian Home Missions, 1906 and subsequent editions.

Elliott, A. S. "The Kentucky Mountaineer." *Bibliotheca Sacra* 63: 487–509 (July 1906).

Berry, Martha. "The Evolution of a Sunday School." *Charities and The Commons* 17: 195–99 (3 November 1906).

1907

Revere, C. T. "Beyond the Gap. The Breeding Ground of Feuds." *Outing* 49: 609–21 (February 1907).

[unsigned]. "Berea College and Its President." *Alexander's Magazine* 3: 231–39 (15 March 1907).

Herrick, Mrs. R. F. "The Black Dog of the Blue Ridge." *Journal of American Folk Lore* 20: 151–52 (April 1907).

Frost, William Goodell. "Slanders Refuted." *Berea Quarterly* 11 no. 3: 20–27 (October 1907).

Macgruder, Julia. "The Child Labor Problem: Fact *versus* Sentimentality." *North American Review* 186: 245–56 (October 1907).

Erskine, Ralph. "The Handicraftsmen of the Blue Ridge: A Simple, Homeloving Folk Who Have Lived Their Own Lives, Heedless of the March of Events." *Craftsman* 13: 158–67 (November 1907).

Parker, Haywood. "Folk-lore of the North Carolina Mountains." *Journal of American Folk Lore* 20: 241–50 (December 1907). Previously printed as

Folklore of the North Carolina Mountaineer. . . . [Asheville: no publisher, 1906].

Kittridge, George Lyman, ed. "Ballads and Rhymes from Kentucky [collected by Katherine Pettit]." *Journal of American Folk Lore* 20: 251–77 (December 1907).

1908

Hughson, Walter, comp. *The Church's Mission to the Mountaineers of the South*. Hartford: Church Missions Publishing Company, 1908.

MacGowan, Alice. *Judith of the Cumberlands*. New York: G. P. Putnam's Sons, 1908.

MacGowan, Alice. *Judith of the Cumberlands*. New York: Grossett and Dunlap, 1908.

Payne, Bruce R. "Waste in Mountain Settlement Work." National Conference of Charities and Correction, *Proceedings* 35: 91–95 (1908).

Campbell, John C. "Statement for a Proposed Study Plan of the Southern Highland Section [15 May 1908]." Typescript in Southern Highland Division Papers, Russell Sage Foundation.

McLean, Francis H. "The Mountain Folk." *Charities and The Commons* 20: 252–53 (23 May 1908).

Mathews, John L. "Miss Berry and Her School." *Boston Evening Transcript*, 3 June 1908, p. 19.

Barton, William E. "A New Berea: Revelation at This Year's Commencement." *Boston Evening Transcipt*, 10 June 1908, p. 18.

Johnson, Samuel. "Life in the Kentucky Mountains. By A Mountaineer." *Independent* 65: 72–82 (9 July 1908).

1909

Douglass, Harlan Paul. *Christian Reconstruction in the South*. Boston: The Pilgrim Press, 1909.

Beatty, Arthur. "Some Ballad Variants and Songs." *Journal of American Folk Lore* 22: 63–71 (March 1909).

Child, Richard Washburn. "Stalking the Biggest of Big Game." *Everybody's Magazine* 20: 427–32 (March 1909).

Campbell, John C. "Social Betterment in the Southern Mountains." National Conference of Charities and Correction, *Proceedings* 36: 130–37 ([May] 1909).

Bascom, Louise Rand. "Ballads and Songs of Western North Carolina." *Journal of American Folk Lore* 22: 238–50 (June 1909).

Campbell, John C. "[Summary:] Social Betterment in the Southern Mountains." *Survey* 22: 463–64 (26 June 1909).

Campbell, John C. ["Preliminary Report to the Russell Sage Foundation, October 1, 1909."] Typescript in John C. and Olive D. Campbell Papers, Southern Historical Collection.

Neve, Frederick W. "Virginia Mountain Folk." *Outlook* 93: 825–29 (11 December 1909).

Berry, Martha. "Social Life of the Appalachian Region." In *The South in the Building of the Nation*, edited by Samuel C. Mitchell, vol. 6, pp. 38–43. Richmond: Southern Historical Publication Society, 1909 [–1913].

Tompkins, David A. "The Mountain Whites as an Industrial Labor Factor in the South." In *The South in the Building of the Nation*, edited by Samuel C. Mitchell, vol. 6, pp. 58–61. Richmond: Southern Historical Publication Society, 1909 [–1913].

Neve, Frederick W. "Social Settlements in the South." In *The South in the Building of the Nation*, edited by Samuel C. Mitchell, vol. 10, pp. 614–22. Richmond: Southern Historical Publication Society, 1909 [–1913].

1910

MacGowan, Alice. *The Sword in the Mountains*. New York: G. P. Putnam's Sons, 1910.

McKelway, Alexander J. "The Mill or the Farm."' National Child Labor Committee, *Proceedings* 1910, pp. 52–57. In American Academy of Political and Social Science, *Annals* 35: supplement (1910).

Thompson, Samuel Hunter. *The Highlanders of the South*. Published for the Methodist Episcopal Church, Home Missions Board. New York: Eaton and Mains; Cincinnati: Jennings and Graham, 1910.

[Verrill, Charles H.] *Cotton Textile Industry*. U.S. Congress. Report on Condition of Women and Child Wage Earners in the United States, vol. 1 (1910). 61st Congress, 2d session, Senate Document 645.

Weeks, Abigail E. "A Word List from Barbourville, Kentucky." *Dialect Notes* 3: 456–57 (1910).

Norman, Henderson Daingerfield. "The English of the Mountaineer." *Atlantic Monthly* 105: 276–78 (February 1910).

[Page, Walter Hines]. ["Editorial Note"]. *World's Work* 19: 12704 (March 1910). Prefatory to Thomas R. Dawley, "Our Southern Mountaineers: Removal the Remedy . . .," ibid. 19: 12704–14 (March 1910).

Dawley, Thomas R. "Our Southern Mountaineers: Removal The Remedy for the Evils that Isolation and Poverty Have Brought." *World's Work* 19: 12704–14 (March 1910).

Horner, Junius M. "Letters to *The Outlook*: Educational Work in the Mountains of North Carolina." *Outlook* 94: 589–90 (12 March 1910).

[unsigned]. ["Editorial Note: On the Plan of 'Industrial' (i.e. Agricultural) Education Proposed for the Valle Crucis School"]. *Outlook* 94: 590 (12 March 1910). Appended to Junius M. Horner, "Letters to *The Outlook*: Educational

Work in the Mountains of North Carolina," ibid. 94: 589–90 (12 March 1910).

Dawley, Thomas R. *Our Mountain Problem and Its Solution: An Address Delivered before the 14th Annual Convention of the American Cotton Manufacturers Association, May 17–18, 1910*. [Charlotte, North Carolina]: American Cotton Manufacturers Association, 1910.

Montague, Margaret Prescott. "Little Kaintuck." *Atlantic Monthly* 105: 609–16 (May 1910).

Fox, John, Jr. "On Horseback to Kingdom Come." *Scribner's Magazine* 48: 175–86 (August 1910).

Semple, Ellen Churchill. "The Anglo-Saxons of the Kentucky Mountains: A Study in Anthropogeography." *Bulletin of the American Geographical Society* 42: 561–94 (August 1910). Reprinted from *Geographical Journal* (London) 17: 588–623 (June 1901).

Combs, Josiah H. "A Traditional Ballad from the Kentucky Mountains." *Journal of American Folk Lore* 23 : 381–82 (September 1910).

Fox, John, Jr. "On the Road to Hell-fer-Sartain." *Scribner's Magazine* 48: 350–61 (September 1910).

Fox, John, Jr. "On the Trail of the Lonesome Pine." *Scribner's Magazine* 48: 417–29 (October 1910).

"Genoel." "Mountain Song." *Berea Quarterly* 14 no. 3: 25–29 (October 1910).

Fox, John, Jr. "Christmas for Big Ame." *Scribner's Magazine* 48: 690–95 (December 1910).

[unsigned]. "College Work Out of Doors." *Outlook* 96: 805–6 (10 December 1910).

Furman, Lucy. "Mothering on Perilous: Kentucky Mountain Sketches." *Century* 81: 296–302, 445–49, 561–65, 767–74, 853–59; 82: 57–64, 297–304, 391–96 (December 1910–July 1911). Reprinted as *Mothering on Perilous*. New York: The Macmillan Company, 1913, 1915.

Kephart, Horace. "Clapboards and Puncheons." *Outing* 87: 285–90 (December 1910).

1911

Johnston, J. Stoddard. "Foreword." In Mary E. Verhoeff, *The Kentucky Mountains. Transportation and Commerce, 1750–1911: A Study in the Economic History of a Coal Field*, pp. v–vi. Filson Club Publications no. 26. Louisville: John P. Morton and Company, 1911.

Obenchain, Eliza Calvert [pseud. Eliza Calvert Hall]. *To Love and to Cherish*. Boston: Little, Brown and Company, 1911.

Shearin, Hubert Gibson. "An Eastern Kentucky Word List." *Dialect Notes* 3: 537–40 (1911).

Shearin, Hubert Gibson, and Combs, Josiah H. *A Syllabus of Kentucky Folk-Songs*. Transylvania University Studies in English, no. 2. Lexington: Transylvania Printing Company, 1911.

Toulmin, Harry Aubrey, Jr. *Social Historians*. Boston: Richard G. Badger, The Gorham Press, 1911.

Verhoeff, Mary E. *The Kentucky Mountains. Transportation and Commerce, 1750–1911: A Study in the Economic History of a Coal Field*. Filson Club Publications no. 26. Louisville: John P. Morton and Company, 1911.

Furman, Lucy. "Mothering on Perilous: Kentucky Mountain Sketches." *Century* 81: 445–49, 561–65, 767–74, 853–59; 82: 57–64, 297–304, 391–96 (January–July 1911). Continued from 1910.

Shearin, Hubert Gibson. "*The Glove* and *The Lions* in Folk-Song." *Modern Language Notes* 26: 113–14 (April 1911).

[unsigned]. "[Theodore] Roosevelt Appeals for a Georgia School. Urges a Gathering at the Astor to Aid Miss Berry's Possom Trot Institution. Pictures of It Shown. And the Colonel Himself Is Flashed on the Screen as He Mounts the Platform." *New York Times*, 26 April 1911, p. 6: 4.

Kittridge, George Lyman. "The Ballad of *The Den of Lions*." *Modern Language Notes* 26: 167–69 (June 1911).

Shearin, Hubert Gibson. "British Ballads in the Cumberland Mountains." *Sewanee Review* 19: 313–27 (July 1911). Condensed in [unsigned], "Oversea Ballads in Kentucky Valleys," *American Review of Reviews* 44: 497–98 (October 1911).

Shearin, Hubert Gibson. "Some Superstitions in the Cumberland Mountains." *Journal of American Folk Lore* 24: 319–22 (September 1911).

[unsigned]. "An American Backwater." *Blackwood's Magazine* (Edinburgh) 190: 355–66 (September 1911).

Shearin, Hubert Gibson. "Kentucky Folk-Songs." *Modern Language Review* 6: 513–17 (October 1911).

[unsigned]. "Oversea Ballads in Kentucky Valleys." *American Review of Reviews* 44: 497–98 (October 1911).

1912

Dawley, Thomas R. *The Child That Toileth Not: The Story of a Government Investigation*. New York: Gracia Publishing Company, 1912.

Obenchain, Eliza Calvert [pseud. Eliza Calvert Hall]. *A Book of Hand-Woven Coverlets*. Boston: Little, Brown and Company, 1912.

"Cosmopolitan." "[Letter to the Editor:] Miss Berry's School. Takes Ignorant Mountain Boys and Makes Them Capable Men." *New York Times*, 1 January 1912, p. 12:6.

Curtis, Natalie. "Folk-Music of America: Four Types of Folk-Song in the U.S. Alone." *Craftsman* 31: 414–20 (January 1912).

Murfree, Mary Noailles [pseud.: Charles Egbert Craddock]. "His Unquiet Ghost." *Century* 83: 127–39 (March 1912).

Furman, Lucy. "'Hard Hearted Barbary Allen': A Kentucky Mountain Sketch." *Century* 83: 739–44 (March 1912).

Perrow, E. C. "Songs and Rhymes from the South." *Journal of American Folk Lore* 25: 137–55; 26: 123–27; 28: 120–90 (March 1912, June 1913, June 1915).

Frost, William Goodell. "Our Southern Highlanders." *Independent* 72: 708–14 (4 April 1912).

[unsigned]. "A Defense of the Mountaineer." *Literary Digest* 44: 800–801 (20 April 1912).

[unsigned]. "The College Not the Sheriff." *Outlook* 101: 381– 82 (22 June 1912).

Furman, Lucy. "Sight to the Blind: A Kentucky Mountain Story. Doings on Perilous." *Century* 84: 390–97 (July 1912). Reprinted as *Sight to the Blind: A Story*. New York: The Macmillan Company, 1914.

[unsigned]. "'Moonlight Schools' in the Kentucky Mountains." *Craftsman* 23: 118 (October 1912).

Kephart, Horace. "The Southern Highlander." *Outing* 61: 259–70, 396–406, 548–54, 703–15; 62: 89–95, 210–12 (December 1912–May 1913). Reprinted as *Our Southern Highlanders*. New York: The Outing Publishing Company, 1913 and subsequent editions.

[unsigned]. "Backwynds of the Blue Ridge." *Blackwood's Magazine* (Edinburgh) 192: 786–96 (December 1912).

1913

Furman, Lucy. *Mothering on Perilous*. New York: The Macmillan Company, 1913. Reprinted from *Century* 81: 296–302, 445–49, 561–65, 767–74, 853–59; 82: 57–64, 297–304, 391–96 (December 1910–July 1911).

Morley, Margaret W. *The Carolina Mountains*. Boston, Houghton Mifflin Company, 1913.

Kephart, Horace. "The Southern Highlander." *Outing* 61: 396–406, 548–54, 703–15; 62: 89–95, 210–12 (January–May 1913). Continued from 1912.

[unsigned: A. J. McKelway?]. "'The Child That Toileth Not': A Reply to Mr. Dawley." *Child Labor Bulletin* 1 no. 4: 88–95 (February 1913).

Stoddard, William Leavitt. "'The Child That Toileth Not.'" *Survey* 29: 705–8 (15 February 1913).

Smith, John F. "Some Impressions of a Social Surveyor." *Berea Quarterly* 17 no. 1: 5–8 (April 1913). Condensed in [unsigned], "How to Help the Mountain Whites," *Literary Digest* 46: 1065–66 (10 May 1913).

[unsigned]. *Illiteracy in the United States, and an Experiment for Its Elimination*. [April 1913]. U.S. Bureau of Education Bulletin, 1913 no. 20.

Kephart, Horace. *Our Southern Highlanders*. New York: The Outing Publishing Company, 1913 and subsequent editions. Originally printed as "The Southern Highlander," *Outing* 61: 259–70, 396–406, 548–54, 703–15; 62: 89–95, 210–12 (December 1912–May 1913).

Campbell, John C. "From Mountain Cabin to Cotton Mill." *Child Labor Bulletin* 2 no. 1: 74–84 (May 1913). Reprinted as National Child Labor Committee Pamphlet no. 195 (New York: National Child Labor Committee, 1913).

Swift, W. H. "The Campaign in North Carolina. The Mountain Whites—By One of Them." *Child Labor Bulletin* 2 no. 1: 96–104 (May 1913).

Campbell, John C. *From Mountain Cabin to Cotton Mill*. National Child Labor Committee Pamphlets, no. 195. New York: National Child Labor Committee, 1913. Reprinted from *Child Labor Bulletin* 2 no. 1: 74–84 (May 1913).

[unsigned]. "How to Help the Mountain Whites." *Literary Digest* 46: 1065–66 (10 May 1913).

Perrow, E. C. "Songs and Rhymes from the South." *Journal of American Folk Lore* 26: 123–27 (June 1913). Continued from 1912.

Kittridge, George Lyman, ed. "Various Ballads." *Journal of American Folk Lore* 26: 180–82 (June 1913).

Ashworth, John H. "The Virginia Mountaineers." *South Atlantic Quarterly* 12: 193–211 (July 1913).

Frost, William Goodell. "Christian Patriotism." Sermon, delivered in the Chapel of the Battle Creek Sanitarium, July? 1913. *Medical Missionary* 22: 231–36 (August 1913).

Barton, Bruce. "Children of the Feudists." *Collier's* 51 no. 23: 7–8, 29 (23 August 1913).

Frost, William Goodell. "Educational Pioneering in the Southern Mountains." *Chautauquan* 47: 247–49 (23 August 1913).

Carlin, J. W. "[Letter to the Editor:] The Kentucky Mountaineer." *Collier's* 52 no. 1: 26 (20 September 1913).

Harben, Will N. "American Backgrounds for Fiction: Georgia." *Bookman* 38: 186–92 (October 1913).

Smith, C. Alphonso. "A Great Movement in Which Everyone Can Help." In U.S. Bureau of Education, *An Opportunity to Help in an Important Work*. U.S. Bureau of Education Special Inquiry, November 1913.

Daviess, Maria Thompson. "American Backgrounds for Fiction: Tennessee." *Bookman* 38: 394–99 (December 1913).

1914

Furman, Lucy. *Sight to the Blind: A Story*. New York: The Macmillan Company, 1914. Originally published as "Sight to the Blind: A Kentucky Mountain

Story. Doings on Perilous," *Century* 84: 390–94 (July 1912).

Furman, Lucy. "Afterword [on the Hindman Settlement]." In *Sight to the Blind: A Story*, pp. 77–92. New York: The Macmillan Company, 1914.

Smith, C. Alphonso. "A Great Movement in Which Everyone Can Help." In [State of Virginia. Department of Public Instruction]. *Virginia Folk-Lore Society. A Great Movement to Collect and Save to the State and Nation the English and Scottish Ballads Surviving in this Commonwealth: Teachers, Pupils and School Patrons Asked to Help*. Richmond: State of Virginia, Department of Public Instruction, 1914.

Stewart, Cora Wilson. "The Moonlight Schools of Kentucky." National Education Association, *Addresses and Proceedings* 1914, pp. 193–99.

Wilson, Samuel Tyndale. *The Southern Mountaineers*. 4th ed. New York: Literature Department, Presbyterian Home Missions, 1914. First published 1906.

Dixon, Thomas. "American Backgrounds for Fiction: North Carolina." *Bookman* 38: 510–14 (January 1914).

Smith, Reed. "The Traditional Ballad in the South." *Journal of American Folk Lore* 27: 55–66 (March 1914).

Conference of Southern Mountain Workers. "List of Persons Registering at the Conference of Southern Mountain Workers, Knoxville, Tennessee, April 22 & 23, 1914." Typescript, enclosed in John C. Campbell to John Glenn, 4 May 1914, Southern Highland Division Papers, Russell Sage Foundation.

[unsigned]. "Tells of Work for Mountain Whites. Berea College, Says Mrs. Frost, Is Finding Long Lost Americans." *New York Times*, 26 April 1914, VIII, 15: 1.

Swift, W. H. "The Last Stand of the One Business Which Opposes Child Labor Legislation in the South." *Child Labor Bulletin* 3: 85–89 (May 1914).

Combs, Josiah H. "Sympathetic Magic in the Kentucky Mountains." *Journal of American Folk Lore* 27: 328–30 (July 1914).

Dyer, Walter B. "Training New Leaders for the Industrial South: What One Small School is Doing for an Aspiring Population of Half-A-Million Native Americans, Largely Illiterate, Who Are Just Beginning to Feel Their Strength." *World's Work* 28: 285–92 (July 1914).

Hall, William L. "To Remake the Appalachians: A New Order in the Mountains that is Founded on Forestry—What the Government's Appalachian Forests Mean to the People in the Mountains and to the Millions who Want Recreation." *World's Work* 28: 321–38 (July 1914).

[unsigned]. "Making Good Farmers and Helping Poor Farms: A Southern School That Gives a Boy a Chance to Earn His Living by a Practical Education in Agriculture [Patterson School, Caldwell County, North Carolina]." *Craftsman* 26: 418–24 (July 1914).

Leupp, Constance D. "'Removing the Blinding Curse of the Mountains: How Dr. McMullen, of the Public Health Service, is Organizing the War Against Trachoma in the Appalachians." *World's Work* 28: 426–30 (August 1914).

Dyer, Walter A. "Whole-Hearted Half-Time School." *Worlds' Work* 28: 452–60 (August 1914).

[unsigned]. "[Photograph:] 'Miles Standish.' Pageant of Longfellow's Poem at Berry School." *Outlook* 107: [853] (8 August 1914).

Frost, William Goodell. "Our Southern Highlanders." Sermon, delivered in the Chapel of the Battle Creek Sanitarium, 17 July 1914. *Medical Missionary* 23: 264–70 (September 1914).

Campbell, John C. "Confidential Report of the Activities of the Southern Highland Division of the Russell Sage Foundation, Sept. 30, 1913–Sept. 30, 1914." Typescript in Southern Highland Division Papers, Russell Sage Foundation.

Campbell, Robert F. "Proposal for the Synod of Appalachia." 1 November 1914. Stenographic transcript. Typescript in Southern Highland Division Papers, Russell Sage Foundation.

[unsigned]. "The Spectator." *Outlook* 108: 896–99 (16 December 1914).

1915

Campbell, John C. "Introduction." In Conference of Southern Mountain Workers, *The Southern Highlands: Extracts of Letters Received from . . . [Persons] Conducting Work in the Southern Mountains*. Compiled by John C. Campbell. Asheville: The Inland Press, 1915.

Conference of Southern Mountain Workers. *The Southern Highlands: Extracts of Letters Received from . . . [Persons] Conducting Work in the Southern Mountains*. Compiled by John C. Campbell. Asheville: The Inland Press, 1915.

Ellen Wilson Memorial, Inc. *The Ellen Wilson Memorial* [pamphlet soliciting contributions for "The Ellen Wilson Fund for the Christian Education of Mountain Youth"]. [Atlanta, 1915].

Wilson, Samuel Tyndale. *The Southern Mountaineers*. 5th ed. New York: Literature Department, Presbyterian Home Missions, 1915. First published 1906.

Furman, Lucy. *Mothering on Perilous*. New York: The Macmillan Company, 1915. First published 1913.

Campbell, Olive Dame. "Songs and Ballads of the Southern Mountains." *Survey* 33: 371–74 (2 January 1915).

Claxton, Philander P. "Letter of Transmittal [19 March 1915]." In Norman Frost, *A Statistical Study of the Public Schools of the Southern Appalachian Mountains*, p. 5. U.S. Bureau of Education Bulletin, 1915 no. 11 (April–May? 1915).

Frost, Norman. *A Statistical Study of the Public Schools of the Southern Appalachian Mountains*. U.S. Bureau of Education Bulletin, 1915 no. 11 (April–May? 1915).

Frost, William Goodell. *For the Mountains: Our Aims, Strategic Principles. Address at Knoxville Mountain Workers Conference*. [Berea: Berea College Press, 1915].

Bradley, William Aspenwall. "Song Ballets and Devil's Ditties." *Harper's Magazine* 130: 901–14 (May 1915). Reprinted in *Berea Quarterly* 18 no. 4: 5–20 (October 1915).

Perrow, E. C. "Songs and Rhymes from the South." *Journal of American Folk Lore* 28: 120–90 (June 1915). Continued from 1913.

Bradley, William Aspenwall. "In Shakespeare's America." *Harper's Magazine* 131: 436–46 (August 1915).

Kerby, McFall. "Illiteracy in the Appalachians." *Survey* 34: 418–19 (14 August 1915).

Kerr, J. W. "The Trachoma Problem." U.S. Public Health Service, *Public Health Reports* 30: 2437–42 (1915 no. 34; 20 August 1915).

Bradley, William Aspenwall. "Song Ballets and Devil's Ditties." *Berea Quarterly* 18 no. 4: 5–20 (October 1915). Reprinted from *Harper's Magazine* 130: 901–14 (May 1915).

Klingberg, Elizabeth Wysor. "Glimpses of Life in the Appalachian Highlands." *South Atlantic Quarterly* 14: 371–78 (October 1915).

Bradley, William Aspenwall. "Hobnobbing with Hillbillies." *Harper's Magazine* 132: 91–103 (December 1915).

1916

Combs, Josiah H. "Old, Early and Elizabethan English in the Southern Mountains." *Dialect Notes* 4: 283–97 (1916).

Combs, Josiah H. "Dialect of the Folk-Song." *Dialect Notes* 4: 311–18 (1916).

Moore, John M. *The South To-Day*. New York: Missionary Education Movement of the United States and Canada, 1916.

Whitaker, Walter Claiborne. *A Round Robin: The Southern Highlands and Highlanders*. Hartford: Church Missions Publishing Company, 1916.

Wilson, Samuel Tyndale. *The Southern Mountaineers*. 6th ed. New York: Literature Department, Presbyterian Home Missions, 1916. First published 1906.

Campbell, John C. "The Future of the Church-School in the Southern Highlands: An Address Delivered before the Council of Women for Home Missions, Atlanta, Georgia, January 6, 1916." Typescript in Southern Highland Division Papers, Russell Sage Foundation.

Campbell, John C. "Mountain and Rural Fields in the South: An Address Delivered before the Home Missions Council, New York City, January 13, 1916." Typescript in Southern Highland Division Papers, Russell Sage Foundation.

Campbell, John C. "Mountain and Rural Fields in the South." Home Missions Council, *Annual Report* 1916, pp. 171–80.

Smith, C. Alphonso. "Ballads Surviving in the United States." *Musical Quarterly* 2: 109–29 (January 1916). Condensed in [unsigned], "The Revival of Interest in Folk-Song," *American Review of Reviews* 53: 370–71 (March 1916).

Stewart, Cora Wilson. "Moonlight Schools." *Survey* 35: 429–31 (7 January 1916). Condensed in [unsigned], "Kentucky's 'Moonlight Schools,'" *American Review of Reviews* 53: 239–40 (February 1916).

Bascom, Louise Rand. "The Better Man." *Harper's Magazine* 132: 462–72 (February 1916).

[unsigned]. "Kentucky's 'Moonlight Schools.'" *American Review of Reviews* 53: 239–40 (February 1916).

Canby, Henry Seidel. "Top o' Smoky." *Harper's Magazine* 132: 573–83 (March 1916).

Smith, J. Russell. "Farming Appalachia." *American Review of Reviews* 53: 329–36 (March 1916).

[unsigned]. "The Revival of Interest in Folk-Song." *American Review of Reviews* 53: 370–71 (March 1916).

[unsigned]. "Better Living for Southern Mountaineers." *Survey* 36: 92–93 (22 April 1916).

de Long, Ethel. "The [Rural] School as a Community Center." National Conference of Charities and Correction, *Proceedings* 1916, pp. 608–14.

Rawn, Isabel Newton, and Peabody, Charles. "More Songs and Ballads from the Southern Appalachians." *Journal of American Folk Lore* 29: 198–202 (June 1916).

McGill, Josephine. "The Cherry-Tree Carol." *Journal of American Folk Lore* 29: 293–94 (June 1916).

Branson, E. C. *Our Carolina Highlanders*. Chapel Hill: University of North Carolina Extension Bureau, Circular no. 2 (July 1916).

Stewart, Cora Wilson. "Elimination of Illiteracy." [July 1916]. National Education Association, *Addresses and Proceedings* 1916, pp. 54–58.

Schockle, B. H. "Changing Conditions in the Kentucky Mountains." *Scientific Monthly* 3: 105–31 (August 1916). Condensed in [unsigned], "Industrial Invasion of the Kentucky Mountains," *Geographical Review* 3: 146–47 (February 1917).

Kelly, Fred C. "A Judge with Brains and Heart." *American Magazine* 82: 52–53 (December 1916).

[unsigned]. "His 'Young Uns.'" *Literary Digest* 53: 1768 (30 December 1916). Based on Ethel de Long talk before the National Geographic Society.

Wyman, Loraine, and Brockway, Howard. *Lonesome Tunes: Folksongs of the Kentucky Mountains*. New York: H. W. Gray Company, ([December] 1916).

1917

Bradley, William Aspenwall. *Old Christmas, and Other Kentucky Tales in Verse*. Boston: Houghton Mifflin Company, 1917.

Campbell, John C. "The Ancestry of the Mountaineers." No date, 1917? Typescript in Minnesota Historical Society.

Kephart, Horace. "A Word List from the North Carolina Mountains." *Dialect Notes* 4: 407–19 (1917).

McGill, Josephine. *Folk Songs of the Kentucky Mountains. Twenty Traditional Ballads and Other English Folk-Songs. Notated from the Singing of the Kentucky Mountain People*. New York: Boosey and Company, 1917.

Mutzenberg, Charles G. *Kentucky's Famous Feuds and Tragedies: Authentic Histories of the World Renowned Vendettas of the Dark and Bloody Ground*. New York: R. F. Fenno, 1917.

McGill, Josephine. "The Kentucky Mountain Dulcimer." *Musician* 22: 21 (January 1917).

[unsigned]. "Industrial Invasion of the Kentucky Mountains." *Geographical Review* 3: 146–47 (February 1917).

de Long, Ethel. "The Pine Mountain Settlement School: A Sketch from the Kentucky Mountains." *Outlook* 115: 318–20 (21 February 1917).

[unsigned]. "Hunting the Lonesome Tune in the Wilds of Kentucky." *Current Opinion* 62:100–101 (February 1917).

[unsigned]. "Rescuing the Folk Songs." *Literary Digest* 54: 403–4 (17 February 1917).

deLong, Ethel. "The Far Side of Pine Mountain." *Survey* 37: 627–30 (3 March 1917).

Campbell, John C. *The Future of the Church and Independent Schools in Our Southern Highlands*. Southern Highland Division Pamphlets no. 1 [April 1917]. New York: Russell Sage Foundation, 1917.

Schoen, Max. "Music and Rural Life." *Musician* 22: 255–56 (April 1917).

Cline, W. M. "Mountain Men of Tennessee. Photographs." *Outing* 70: 192–99 (May 1917).

Evarts, Mrs. C. S. "Modern Methods Invading the Mountains." *Missionary Review of the World* 40: 365–67 (May 1917).

Brockway, Howard. "The Quest of the Lonesome Tunes." *Art World* 2: 227–3((June 1917).

Gielow, Martha Sawyer. "The Call of the Race: Save and Lift up Our Own Neglected People!—A Woman's Eloquent Plea for a Great and Noble Patriotic Cause." *Journal of American History* 11: 215–19 (June 1917).

McGill, Josephine. " 'Following Music' in A Mountain Land." *Musical Quarterly* 3: 364–84 (July 1917).

Robinson, James A. "Artistic Weaving in the Mountains of North Carolina [by Mrs. Finley Mast, Watauga County]." *Art World* 2: 484–85 (August 1917).

Kittridge, George Lyman, ed. "Ballads and Songs [collected by Loraine Wyman]." *Journal of American Folk Lore* 30: 283–369 (September 1917).

McCabe, Lida Rose. "Regenerating Handicrafts in the Carolinas." *Art World* 3: 159–61 (November 1917).

Campbell, Olive Dame, and Sharp, Cecil J. *English Folk Songs from the Southern Appalachians. Comprising 122 Songs and Ballads and 323 Tunes.* New York: G. P. Putnam's Sons, [November] 1917.

Sharp, Cecil J. "Introduction." In Olive Dame Campbell and Cecil J. Sharp, *English Folk Songs from the Southern Appalachians.* New York: G. P. Putnam's Sons, 1917.

[G. P. Putnam's Sons]. "[Advertisement:] *English Folk Songs from the Southern Appalachians.*" *New York Times*, 25 November 1917, IV, 498.

Aldrich, Richard. "English and Scottish Folk Songs in America—Cecil Sharp Publishes His Finds in the South." *New York Times*, 2 December 1917, IX, 3: 1–4.

1918

Bradley, William Aspenwall. *Singing Carr, and Other Song-Ballads of the Cumberlands.* New York: Alfred A. Knopf, 1918.

Steadman, J. M. "A North Carolina Word List." *Dialect Notes* 5: 18–21 (1918).

Bradley, William Aspenwall. "The Folk Culture of the Cumberlands." *Dial* 64: 95–98 (31 January 1918).

Hartt, Rollin Lynde. "The Mountaineers: Our Own Lost Tribes." *Century* 95: 395–404 (January 1918).

Bradley, William Aspenwall. "The Women on Troublesome." *Scribner's Magazine* 63: 315–38 (March 1918).

Peabody, Charles. "Folk Dancing and Folk Singing." *Journal of American Folk Lore* 31: 274–75 (March 1918).

McGill, Josephine. "Old Ballad Burthens." *Musical Quarterly* 4: 293–306 (April 1918).

Maguire, Margaret T. "The Passing of the Backwoods: They Vanished Overnight, Never to Return." *Ladies Home Journal* 35 no. 12: 16, 44 (December 1918).

1919

Clopper, Edward N., ed. *Child Welfare in Kentucky. An Inquiry by the National Child Labor Committee for the Kentucky Child Labor Association and the State*

Board of Health. New York: National Child Labor Committee, 1919.

Combs, Josiah H. "A Word List from the South." *Dialect Notes* 5: 31–40 (1919).

Wilson, Samuel Tyndale. *A Century of Maryville College, 1819–1919: A Story of Altruism*. Maryville, Tennessee: Maryville College, 1919.

Belden, Henry Melvin. "Folk-Song in America—Some Recent Publications." *Modern Language Notes* 34: 139–45 (March 1919).

Winter, Nevin O. "Our Romantic Southern Highlands: Incomparable Beauties of the Little Known Appalachians—A Region Larger than the British Isles, Reminiscent of Colonial Days." *Travel* 32 no. 5: 32–35, 47–48 (March 1919).

[unsigned]. "The Appalachian Treasure 'Pocket' of American Folk-Song and Dance: Cecil Sharp Amazes London by Discovering Old English Songs Still Alive in America." *Current Opinion* 67: 32 (July 1919).

Calfee, John E. "Training for Leadership." *Home Mission Monthly* 34: 4–6 (November 1919).

Masters, Victor I. "The Mountaineers of the South." *Missionary Review of the World* 42: 845–49 (November 1919).

[unsigned]. "The School at Rabun Gap." *Outlook* 123: 319–21 (12 November 1919).

Kirkland, Winifred. "Mountain Music." *Outlook* 123: 593 (31 December 1919).

1920

Hutchins, William J. *Inauguration of William James Hutchins, President of Berea College*. Berea: Berea College Press, 1920.

Steadman, J. M. "Addenda and Corrigenda [to "A North Carolina Word List" (1918)]." *Dialect Notes* 5: 86 (1920).

Thomas, Daniel Lindsey, and Thomas, Lucy Blayney. *Kentucky Superstitions* Princeton: Princeton University Press, 1920.

Wyman, Loraine, and Brockway, Howard. *Twenty Kentucky Mountain Songs* Boston: Oliver Ditson Company, 1920.

Kephart, Horace. "Primitive Mills in Southern Mountains." *Outing* 75 220–22 (January 1920).

Breitigam, Gerald B. "Lifting Up Mountains: Bringing a Knowledge o America to Pure-Blooded Americans." *Ladies Home Journal* 37 no. 7: 45, 15 (July 1920).

[unsigned]. "The Dream of a Shirt-tail Boy Come True." *Outlook* 125: 557–5 (28 July 1920).

Kirkland, Winifred. "Mountain Mothers." *Ladies Home Journal* 37 no. 12 26–27, 193 (December 1920).

1921

Campbell, John C. *The Southern Highlander and His Homeland*. New York: Russell Sage Foundation, 1921.

Campbell, Olive Dame. "Preface." In John C. Campbell, *The Southern Highlander and His Homeland*. New York: Russell Sage Foundation, 1921.

Campbell, Olive Dame, comp. *Southern Highland Schools Maintained by Denominational and Independent Agencies*. Southern Highland Division Pamphlets no. 2. New York: Russell Sage Foundation, 1921.

Combs, Josiah H. "Early English Slang Survivals in the Mountains of Kentucky." *Dialect Notes* 5: 115–17 (1921).

Combs, Josiah H. "Kentucky Items." *Dialect Notes* 5: 118–19 (1921).

Harrison, Marion Clifford. "Social Types in Southern Prose Fiction." Ph.D. Thesis, University of Virginia, 1921. Mimeographed. Ann Arbor: Edmunds Brothers, 1921.

Kephart, Horace. *Our Southern Highlanders*. New York: The Outing Publishing Company, 1921. First published 1913.

Wilson, Samuel Tyndale. *The Southern Mountaineers*. New York: Literature Department, Presbyterian Home Missions, 1921. First published 1906.

Holton, Cecelia Cathcart. "A Funeralizing on Robber's Creek." *Outlook* 127: 588–89 (13 April 1921).

Frost, William Goodell. "God's Plan for the Southern Mountains." *Biblical Review* 6: 405–25 (July 1921).

[unsigned]. "Fireside Industries." *Survey* 47: 453–54 (24 December 1921).

1922

Cobb, Ann. *Kinfolks: Kentucky Mountain Rhymes*. Boston and New York: Houghton Mifflin Company, 1922.

Combs, Josiah H. "A Word List from Georgia." *Dialect Notes* 5: 183–84 (1922).

Combs, Josiah H., et al. "Marbles [: A Glossary of Terms]." *Dialect Notes* 5: 186–88 (1922).

Cowan, Sam K. *Sergeant York and His People*. New York: Funk and Wagnalls Company, 1922.

Kephart, Horace. *Our Southern Highlanders. A Narrative of Adventure in the Southern Appalachians and a Study of Life among the Mountaineers*. Rev. ed. New York: The Macmillan Company, 1922. First published 1913.

Koch, Frederick H., ed. *Carolina Folk Plays*. New York: Henry Holt and Company, 1922.

Wilson, Samuel Tyndale. *The Southern Mountaineers*. New York: Literature Department, Presbyterian Home Missions, 1922. First published 1906.

Wightman, Robert S. "The Southern Mountain Problem: A Study of the Efforts to Solve a Great Unfinished Task." *Missionary Review of the World* 45: 120–26 (February 1922).

Vaughan, Marshall Everett. "Community Education at Berea." *Survey* 47: 728–29 (4 February 1922).

Harlow, Alvin H. "The Frontier People of the Appalachians. The Southern Mountaineers, Our Purest Racial Stock—A Surviving Segment of the 18th Century—Real 'Made in America' Goods—Our Most Independent and Self-Reliant Citizens." *Travel* 39 no. 2: 11–14, 40 (June 1922).

Porter, Laura Spencer. "In Search of Local Color." *Harper's Magazine* 145: 281–94, 451–66 (August, September 1922).

Wenrick, Lewis A. "Teaching the Mountaineers of Tennessee." *Missionary Review of the World* 45: 811–12 (October 1922).

II. Other Primary Sources Cited

Abbott, Ernest Hamlin. "A Masque of Masques." *Outlook* 113: 308, 317–18 (7 June 1916).

Addams, Jane. "A New Impulse to an Old Gospel." *Forum* 14: 345–58 (November 1902).

———. *Twenty Years at Hull House, with Autobiographical Notes*. New York: The Macmillan Company, 1910.

Adkins, Milton T. "The Mountains and Mountaineers of Craddock's Fiction." *Magazine of American History* 24: 305–9 (October 1890).

[Aldrich, Richard]. " 'Caliban' Is Closed in a Feast of Fun." *New York Times*, June 1916, 11: 4.

———. "Folk Music for Shakespearean Drama—Mr. Cecil Sharp's Interesting Experiment in the 'Midsummer Night's Dream' Production." *New York Times*, 7 February 1915, VIII, 3: 1–3.

———. "MacKaye Masque a Rare Spectacle: 'Caliban' The Biggest Dramatic Entertainment in History of New York." *New York Times*, 25 May 1916, 11: 1–3.

———. "Mr. Barker Gives Some Shakespeare: Many Beauties and Some Curiosities in His Production . . . with Gilded Immortals Dancing to Old English Music before Backgrounds of Fantastic Decoration." *New York Times*, 17 February 1915, 11: 3.

Allen, James Lane. "The Blue-Grass Region of Kentucky." *Harper's Magazine* 72: 365–82 (February 1886). Reprinted in *The Blue-Grass Region of Kentucky and Other Kentucky Articles*, pp. 3–41. New York: Harper and Brothers, 1892.

———. *The Blue-Grass Region of Kentucky, and Other Kentucky Articles*. New York: Harper and Brothers, 1892, 1899.

———. "H. M. Alden." *Bookman* 50: 330–36 (November 1919).

_____. "Homesteads of the Blue-Grass." *Century* 44: 51–63 (May 1892). Reprinted in *The Blue-Grass Region of Kentucky and Other Kentucky Articles*, pp. 181–213. New York: Harper and Brothers, 1892.

_____. "Local Color." *The Critic*, n.s. 5: 13–14 (9 January 1886).

_____. "Realism and Romance." *New York Evening Post*, 31 July 1886, p. 4.

American Academy of Political and Social Science. *Country Life*, edited by J. P. Lichtenberger. *Annals of the American Academy of Political and Social Science* 40 (March 1912).

"American Backgrounds for Fiction [Series]." "Georgia," by Will N. Harben; "The Pennsylvania 'Dutch' Country," by Helen R. Martin; "Tennessee," by Maria Thompson Daviess; "North Carolina," by Thomas Dixon; "The North Country of New York," by Irving Bacheller; "Arkansas, Louisiana and the Gulf Country," by Ruth McEvery Stuart. *Bookman* 38: 186–92, 244–47, 394–99, 510–14, 624–28; 39: 620–30 (October 1913–February 1914; August 1914).

[American Union Committee]. *The American Union Committee: Its Origin, Operations and Purposes*. New York: Sanford Harroun and Company, 1865.

Asher, E. J. "The Inadequacy of Current Intelligence Tests for Testing Kentucky Mountain Children." *Journal of Genetic Psychology* 46: 480–86 (June 1935).

Bacon, Leonard Woolsey. *A History of American Christianity*. New York: The Christian Literature Company, 1897.

Bailey, Liberty Hyde. "Community Life in the Open Country." National Conference of Charities and Correction, *Proceedings* 36: 123–29 (1909).

_____. "Rural Development in Relation to Social Welfare." National Conference of Charities and Correction, *Proceedings* 35: 83–92 (1908).

Barton, Benjamin Smith. *A Discourse on Some of the Principal Desiderata in Natural History, and on the Best Means of Promoting the Study of this Science, in the United States*. Philadelphia: Denham and Town, 1807.

Beard, Augustus Field. *Crusade of Brotherhood: The History of the American Missionary Association*. Boston: The Pilgrim Press, 1909.

Belden, Henry Melvin. "The Study of Folk-Song in America." *Modern Philology* 2: 573–79 (April 1905).

Bennett, Charles Alpheus. *History of Manual and Industrial Education*. 2 vols. Peoria, Illinois: The Manual Arts Press, 1926 and 1937.

Beveridge, Albert J. "Introduction." In Mrs. John [Bessie] Van Vorst, *The Cry of the Children: A Study of Child Labor*. New York: Moffat, Yard and Company, 1908.

Bledsoe, Mary Lina. "The Hidden People of the Blue-Ridge. The Little-Known People of the Mountains—Moonshine and Gun Play—A Marooned Civilization—Forgotten Pioneers." *Travel* 45 no. 6: 15–18 (October 1925).

Boutelle, Grace Hodson. "A Leader of the Folk Dance." *Bellman* (Minneapolis) 20: 429–31 (15 April 1916).

Boykin, James C. "Typical Institutions Offering Manual or Industrial Training." U.S. Commissioner of Education, *Report of the Commissioner of Education 1896–1897*, pp. 1001–52.

Brigham, Albert Perry. *Geographic Influences in American History*. Boston: Ginn and Company, 1903.

Brooks, Eugene C. *Agriculture and Rural Life Day: Materials for Its Observance*. U.S. Bureau of Education Bulletin, 1913 no. 43.

Browne, Mrs. Hetty S. *An Experimental Rural School at Winthrop College, Rock Hill, South Carolina*. U.S. Bureau of Education Bulletin, 1913 no. 42.

Buckley, J. M. *A History of the Methodists in the United States*. New York: The Christian Literature Company, 1897.

Butler, Marguerite. "A Dream Come True." *Mountain Life and Work* 7 no. 3: 1–4 (October 1931).

Byers, Tracy. "The Berry Schools of Georgia: The Romance of a Sunday School That Became Famous." *Missionary Review of the World* 56: 33–36 (January 1933).

Calfee, John E. "The Mountain Problem: Blue Prints of the Blue Ridge." *Presbyterian Magazine* 35: 241–42 (May 1929).

Campbell, Olive Dame. *The Danish Folk School: Its Influence in the Life of Denmark and the North*. New York: The Macmillan Company, 1928.

_____. "Editorial." *Mountain Life and Work* 4 no. 2: 1 (July 1928).

_____. ["Memoir of John C. Campbell"]. Typescript in John C. and Olive D. Campbell Papers, Southern Historical Collection.

Carroll, Henry King. *The Religious Forces of the United States, Enumerated, Classified, and Described on the Basis of the Government Census of 1890: With an Introduction on the Condition and Character of American Christianity*. New York: The Christian Literature Company, 1893.

Child, Francis James. *Invitation to Unite in an Effort to Collect Popular Ballads from Oral Tradition: Addressed Particularly to Students in Colleges*. n.p. [Cambridge, Mass.?], 29 January 1881. In Francis James Child Papers, Harvard University Archives.

Clark, Joseph B. *The Historic Policy and the New Work of the American Home Missionary Society*. New York: American Home Missionary Society, 1885.

_____. *Leavening the Nation: The Story of American Home Missions*. New York: The Bayard and Taylor Company, 1903.

Claxton, P. P. "Letter of Transmittal." 4 April 1913. In [unsigned], *Illiteracy in the United States, and an Experiment for Its Elimination*. U.S. Bureau of Education Bulletin, 1913 no. 20.

_____. "Letter of Transmittal." 23 September 1913. In Harold W. Foght, *The*

Educational System of Rural Denmark. U.S. Bureau of Education Bulletin, 1913 no. 58 (1914).

———. "Letter of Transmittal." 16 October 1913. In L. L. Friend, *The Folk High Schools of Denmark*. U.S. Bureau of Education Bulletin, 1914 no. 5.

———. See also, U.S. Commissioner of Education.

Cole, Grace. "The State Superintendent and the General and Southern Education Boards." National Education Association, *Addresses and Proceedings* 1911, pp. 305–8.

Coleman, Charles W., Jr. "The Recent Movement in Southern Literature." *Harper's Magazine* 74: 837–55 (May 1887).

Combs, Josiah H. "Addenda from Kentucky." *Dialect Notes* 5: 242–43 (1923).

[Commission on Country Life]. *Report of the Commission on Country Life*. 1910. 60th Congress, 2d session, Senate Document 705.

———. *Report of the Commission on Country Life*. New York: Sturgis and Walton Company, 1911.

Coon, Charles L. *Facts About Southern Educational Progress: A Present Day Study in Public School Maintenance for Those Who Look Forward*. Knoxville: Southern Education Board Campaign Committee, 1905.

Cooper, Thomas. "An Economic and Social Study of the Southern Appalachians." *Mountain Life and Work* 6 no. 2: 20–22 (July 1930).

Copeland, Melvin Thomas. *The Cotton Manufacturing Industry of the United States*. Cambridge: Harvard University Press, 1912.

Cox, John Harrington. *Folk Songs of the South*. [Collected by the West Virginia Folk Lore Society.] Cambridge: Harvard University Press, 1925.

Craig, Arthur U. "The Rise and Progress of Manual Training." *Southern Workman* 31: 33–35, 161–64, 228–30, 349–51 (January, March, April, June 1902).

Craig, Edward Marshall. *Highways and Byways of Appalachia: A Study of the Work of the Synod of Appalachia of the Presbyterian Church in the United States*. Kingsport, Tennessee: Kingsport Press, 1927.

Craighead, James G. *Scotch and Irish Seeds in American Soil*. Philadelphia: Presbyterian Board of Publication, 1878.

Cubberly, Elwood P. *Rural Life and Education: A Study of the Rural School Problem as a Phase of the Rural-Life Problem*. Boston: Houghton, Mifflin Company, 1913.

[Curtis, George William]. "Editor's Easy Chair." *Harper's Magazine* 31: 398 (October 1866).

Davenport, Walter. "Just a-settin'." *Colliers*, 30 July 1927, pp. 8–9, 28.

———. "Up an' gettin'." *Colliers*, 10 September 1927, pp. 19, 42–43.

Davidson, Donald, ed. *I'll Take My Stand: The South and the Agrarian Tradition. By Twelve Southerners*. New York: Harper and Brothers, 1930.

Davis, Arthur Kyle, ed. *Traditional Ballads of Virginia. Collected under the Au-*

spices of the Virginia Folk-Lore Society. Cambridge: Harvard University Press, 1929.

Davis, D. H. "The Changing Role of the Kentucky Mountains and the Passing of the Kentucky Mountaineer." *Journal of Geography: A Magazine for Schools* 24: 41–52 (February 1925).

deForest, Robert W. "The Initial Activities of the Russell Sage Foundation." *Survey* 22: 68–75 (3 April 1909).

de Leon, Edward. "The New South." *Harper's Magazine* 48: 270–80, 406–22; 49: 555–68 (January, February, September 1874).

Dickerman, G. S., ed. *Educational Conditions in Tennessee*. Southern Education Board Bulletin, 1 no. 3. Knoxville: Southern Education Board, 1902.

––––––. ed. *Educational Progress in the South*. Knoxville: Southern Education Board, 1907.

Dingman, Helen H. "A Body's Friends." *Women and Missions* 3: 302–3, 313 (November 1926).

––––––. "A Cooperative Survey of the Mountains: Report of a Conference." *Mountain Life and Work* 5 no. 4: 12–14 (January 1930).

––––––. "New Trails in the Southern Highlands." *Missionary Review of the World* 56: 437–41 (September 1933).

––––––. "Our Common Task." *Mountain Life and Work* 9 no. 2: 1–7 (July 1933).

Dingus, L. R. "Appalachian Mountain Words." *Dialect Notes* 5: 468–71 (1927).

Dodge, Daniel Kilham. "Scandinavian Character and Scandinavian Music." *Sewanee Review* 19: 279–84 (July 1911).

Douglass, Harlan Paul. *From Survey to Service*. New York: Council of Women for Home Missions and Missionary Education Movement of the United States and Canada, 1914.

––––––. *The New Home Missions: An Account of Their Social Redirection*. New York: Missionary Education Movement of the United States and Canada, 1914.

Doyle, Sherman H. *Presbyterian Home Missions: An Account of the Home Missions of the Presbyterian Church in the United States of America*. Philadelphia: Presbyterian Board of Publication and Sabbath School Work, 1902.

Drake, Daniel. *Natural and Statistical View, or Picture of Cincinnati and the Miami Country*. Cincinnati: Looker and Wallace, 1815. Reprinted in Henry D. Shapiro and Zane L. Miller, eds., *Physician to the West: Selected Writings of Daniel Drake on Science and Society*, pp. 67–124. Lexington: University Press of Kentucky, 1970.

Dressler, Fletcher B. *Rural School Houses and Grounds*. U.S. Bureau of Education Bulletin, 1914 no. 12.

Dugdale, Richard L. *"The Jukes": A Study in Crime, Pauperism, Disease and Heredity*. New York: G. P. Putnam's Sons, 1877. Originally published 1874.

Duncan, Hannibal G. "The Southern Highlanders." *Journal of Applied Sociology* 10: 556–61 (August 1926).

Dyer, Walter A. "Our Country Public Schools: What We Are Doing and Where We Fail: The Problem for the Community." *Craftsman* 26: 599–605 (September 1914).

———. "Working for Play. The Country School Developed into a Social Center." *Craftsman* 27: 304–8, 316 (December 1914).

Eaton, Allen. *Handicrafts of the Southern Highlands, with an Account of the Rural Handicraft Movement in the United States and Suggestions for the Wider Use of Handicrafts in Adult Education and in Recreation*. New York: Russell Sage Foundation, 1937.

———. "The Mountain Handicrafts: Their Importance to the Country and to the People in the Mountain Homes." *Mountain Life and Work* 6 no. 2: 22–30 (July 1930).

Eggleston, George Cary. "A Rebel's Recollections." *Atlantic Monthly* 33: 730–36; 34: 95–101, 163–67, 333–40, 467–74, 594–602 (June–November 1874). Reprinted, New York: Hurd and Houghton, 1875.

Ellis, Leonora Beck. "A Model Factory Town [Pelzer, South Carolina]." *Forum* 32: 60–65 (September 1901).

———. "A Study of Southern Cotton Mill Communities. Child Labor. The Operatives in General." *American Journal of Sociology* 8: 623–30 (March 1903).

Estabrook, Arthur H. "[Summary:] The Population of the Southern Appalachians." *Eugenical News* 12: 120 (September 1927).

———. "Presidential Address: Blood Seeks Environment." *Eugenical News* 11: 106–14 (August 1926).

———. "The Real Mountain Problem of South Carolina." *Mountain Life and Work* 5 no. 4: 15–20 (January 1930).

Evans, Lawton B. "The Child of the Operative." *Southern Workman* 31: 427–30 (August 1902).

———. "A Message of Achievement from the Southland: The Glory of Its Children." National Education Association, *Addresses and Proceedings* 1911, pp. 175–78.

Evans, Thomas S. "The Christian Settlement." American Academy of Political and Social Science, *Annals* 30: 483–89 (November 1907).

Fairchild, E. T. "Preliminary Report of the Committee on Rural School Education." National Education Association, *Addresses and Proceedings* 1896, pp. 549–59.

Farwell, Arthur. "Community Music-Drama: Will Our Country People in Time Help Us to Develop the Real American Theater?" *Craftsman* 26: 418–24 (July 1914).

Felton, Ralph A. *Our Templed Hills*. New York: Council of Women for Home Missions and Missionary Education Movement, 1926.

Ferrell, John A. *The Rural School and Hookworm Disease*. U.S. Bureau of Education Bulletin, 1914 no. 20.

Finley, W. W. "Southern Railroads and Industrial Development." American Academy of Political and Social Science, *Annals* 35: 99–104 (January 1910).

Fiske, Horace Spencer. *Provincial Types in American Prose Fiction*. Chautauqua, New York: Chautuaqua Press, 1903.

Fiske, John. "Old Virginia, and Her Neighbors." *Harper's Magazine* 65: 895–907; 66: 414–25 (November 1882, February 1883). Reprinted with revisions as *Old Virginia and Her Neighbors*. 2 vols. Boston: Houghton, Mifflin and Company, 1897.

――――. *Outlines of Cosmic Philosophy*. 2 vols. London: The Macmillan Company, 1874.

Foght, Harold W. "The Country School." American Academy of Political and Social Science, *Annals* 40: 149–57 (March 1912).

――――. *Danish Elementary Rural Schools, with Some Reference to Seminaries for the Training of Rural Teachers*. U.S. Bureau of Education Bulletin, 1914 no. 24.

――――. *The Danish Folk High Schools*. U.S. Bureau of Education Bulletin, 1914 no. 22.

――――. *The Educational System of Rural Denmark*. U.S. Bureau of Education Bulletin, 1913 no. 58 (1914).

Freeman, E. A. "The English People in Its Three Homes." In *Lectures to American Audiences*. Philadelphia: Porter and Coates, 1882.

French, Frances Graham. "Education in Denmark." U.S. Commissioner of Education, *Report of the Commissioner of Education* 1897, pp. 71–101.

――――. "Education in Norway." U.S. Commissioner of Education, *Report of the Commissioner of Education* 1897, pp. 103–23.

――――. "Education in Sweden and Iceland." U.S. Commissioner of Education, *Report of the Commissioner of Education* 1898, pp. 967–1001.

Friend, L. L. *The Folk High Schools of Denmark*. U.S. Bureau of Education Bulletin, 1914 no. 5.

Frost, William Goodell. *For the Mountains: An Autobiography*. New York: Fleming H. Revell Company, 1937.

Garland, Hamlin. *Crumbling Idols*. Chicago and Cambridge: Stone and Kimball, 1894.

――――. "The Limitations of Authorship in America." *Bookman* 59: 257–61 (May 1924).

[General Education Board]. *The General Education Board: An Account of Its Activities, 1902–1914*. New York: General Education Board, 1915.

Gill, Charles O. "Secretarial Preface." In *The Church and Country Life*, edited by Paul L. Vogt, pp. v–xi. New York: Missionary Education Movement of the United States and Canada, 1916.

Gilmer, Francis William. "On the Geological Formation of the Natural Bridge of Virginia." *American Philosophical Society, Transactions*, n.s. 1: 187–92 (1816).

Gilmore, James R. *Advance Guard of Western Civilization*. New York: D. Appleton and Company, 1888.

———. *Rear Guard of the Revolution*. New York: D. Appleton and Company, 1886.

Gladden, Washington. "Christian Education at the South." *American Missionary*, n.s. 36: 385–91 (December 1883).

Glenn, Mrs. John [Mary]. "The Working Force of Societies for Organizing Charity." National Conference of Charities and Correction, *Proceedings* 35: 57–69 (1908).

Goldsmith, Peter H. "The Cotton Mill South." *Boston Evening Transcript*, 25, 29 April, 6, 9, 10 May 1908.

Goodrich, Frances Louisa. *Mountain Homespun*. New Haven: Yale University Press, 1931.

Gordon, R. W. "Folk Etchings." *Forum* 80: 473–75 (September 1928).

Gray, L. C. "Economic Conditions and Tendencies in the Southern Appalachians as Indicated by the Cooperative Survey." *Mountain Life and Work* 9 no. 2: 7–12 (July 1933).

———. "Objectives and Progress of the Economic and Social Survey of the Southern Appalachians." *Mountain Life and Work* 7 no. 2: 31–35 (July 1931).

Greeley, Horace. *Glances at Europe: In a Series of Letters from Great Britain, France, Italy, Switzerland, etc. during the Summer of 1851. Including Notices of the Great Exhibition or World's Fair*. New York: Dewitt and Davenport, 1851.

Greenslet, Ferris. *T. B. Aldrich*. Boston: Houghton, Mifflin Company, 1908.

Gulick, Luther Halsey. *The Healthful Art of Dancing*. New York: Doubleday, Page and Company, 1911.

Gummere, Francis B. *The Popular Ballad*. Boston: Houghton, Mifflin and Company, 1907.

———. "Primitive Poetry and the Ballad." *Modern Philology* 1: 193–202, 217–34, 373–90 (June, October 1903; January 1904).

Gundersen, Oscar. "Report of the Committee of Twelve on Rural Schools. Appendix N: School Systems, Norway." National Education Association, *Addresses and Proceedings* 1897, pp. 575–77.

Haggard, H. Ryder. *Rural Denmark and Its Lessons*. London and New York: Longmans, Green and Company, 1911.

Ham, Charles H. "Manual Training." *Harper's Magazine* 72: 404–12 (February 1886).

Hand, William A. "Secondary Education in the South." In *The South in the Building of the Nation*, edited by Samuel C. Mitchell, vol. 6, pp. 271–81. Richmond: Southern Historical Publication Society, 1909[–1913].

Hanmer, Lee F. "The Schoolhouse Evening Center: What It Is, What It Costs, What It Pays." National Education Association, *Addresses and Proceedings* 51:58–63 (1913).

Hanna, Charles A. *The Scotch-Irish, or the Scot in North Britain, North Ireland, and North America*. 2 vols. New York: G. P. Putnam's Sons, 1902.

————. *The Wilderness Trail, or the Ventures and Adventures of the Pennsylvania Traders on the Allegheny Path*. New York: G. P. Putnam's Sons, 1911.

Harbison, Emmeline E. "National Topic: The Southern Mountaineer." *Women and Missions* 3: 279 (October 1926).

Harkins, Edward F. "Charles Egbert Craddock." In *Famous Authors: Women*. Boston: L. C. Page and Company, 1901. Reprinted in E. F. Harkins and C. H. L. Johnston, *Little Pilgrimages Among the Women Who Have Written Famous Books*, pp. 75–90. Boston: L. C. Page and Company, 1902.

Harney, Will Wallace. *The Spirit of the South*. Boston: R. G. Badger, 1909.

Harper, J. Henry. *The House of Harper: A Century of Publishing in Franklin Square*. New York: Harper and Brothers, 1912.

Harriman, Mrs. J. Borden. "The Cotton Mill as a Factor in the Development of the South." National Child Labor Committee, *Proceedings* 1910, pp. 49–52. In American Academy of Social and Political Science, *Annals* 35: Supplement (1910).

Harris, Mrs. L. H. "The Passing of Uncle Remus." *Journal of American Folk Lore* 65: 190–92 (23 July 1908).

Hart, Joseph K. *Light from the North: The Danish Folk Highschools. Their Meaning for America*. New York: Henry Holt and Company, 1927. Originally published as "The Plastic Years: How Denmark Uses Them in Education for Life"; "The Secret of the Independent Farmers of Denmark"; "The Plastic Years and the Open Mind in America," *Survey* 56: 5–9, 55, 59, 312–15, 340–43, 569–71, 598–602 (1 April, 1 June, 1 September 1926).

Harte, Bret. *The Luck of Roaring Camp, and Other Sketches*. Boston: Houghton, Mifflin Company, 1869.

Hayward, Charles E., comp. *Institutional Work for the Country Church*. Burlington, Vermont: The Pilgrim Press, 1912.

Hegland, Martin. *The Danish People's High School, Including a General Account of the Educational System of Denmark*. U.S. Bureau of Education Bulletin, 1915 no. 45.

Hirsch, N. D. M. *An Experimental Study of the East Kentucky Mountaineers: A Study in Heredity and Environment*. Genetic Psychology Monographs, Vol. 3 no. 3 (March 1928).

————. "An Experimental Study of the East Kentucky Mountaineers. A

Study in Heredity and Environment." *Science* 67: supplement, pp. xii, xiv (6 April 1928).

———. "A Summary of Some of the Results from an Experimental Study of the East Kentucky Mountaineers." National Academy of Sciences, *Proceedings* 13 no. 1: 18–21 (15 January 1927).

Hoag, Ernest Bryant. *Organized Health Work in Schools, with an Account of a Campaign for School Hygiene in Minnesota*. U.S. Bureau of Education Bulletin, 1913 no. 44.

Hoffman, Frederick L. "The Social and Medical Aspects of Child Labor." National Conference of Charities and Correction, *Proceedings* 30: 138–57 (1903).

[Holland, J. G.] "Our Monthly Gossip." *Lippincott's Magazine* 1: 114 (January 1868).

Hooker, Elizabeth R. *Religion in the Highlands: Native Churches and Missionary Enterprises in the Southern Appalachian Area*. New York: Home Missions Council, 1933.

Howard, John Tasker. *Our American Music: Three Hundred Years of It*. New York: Thomas Y. Crowell, 1924.

Howe, Frederic C. "A Commonwealth Ruled by Farmers." *Outlook* 94: 441–50 (26 February 1910).

Hunt, William Carl. "Social Case Work Principles Modified to Meet Rural Conditions." *Mountain Life and Work* 5 no. 2: 20–24 (July 1929).

Hurst, Sam N. *The Mountains Redeemed: The Romance of the Mountains. A True Story of Life and Love in Southwest Virginia, Interwoven with an Exposition of Her Mountain Life. . . .* Appalachia, Virginia: Hurst and Company, 1929.

Ingersoll, Ernest. "Mountain Harry: A Character Sketch." *Appleton's Journal*, n.s. 3: 524–27 (December 1877).

Israel, Henry, ed. *The Country Church and Community Cooperation*. New York: [Young Men's Christian] Association Press, 1913.

James, W. P. "On the Theory and Practice of Local Color." *Living Age* 213: 743–48 (12 June 1897).

Jefferson, Thomas. *Notes on the State of Virginia* [1785], edited by William Peden. Chapel Hill: University of North Carolina Press, 1955.

Jesien, W. S. *Secondary Agricultural Schools in Russia*. U.S. Bureau of Education Bulletin, 1917 no. 4.

Johnson, Alexander. "Introduction." National Conference of Charities and Corrections, *Proceedings* 36: iii (1909).

Kelley, William D. *The Old South and the New: A Series of Letters*. New York: G. P. Putnam's Sons, 1887, 1888.

Kellogg, Paul U. "The National Society for the Promotion of Industrial Education." *Charities and The Commons* 17: 363–71 (1 December 1906).

Kephart, Horace. *Our Southern Highlanders. A Narrative of Adventure in the*

Southern Appalachians and a Study of Life among the Mountaineers. Rev. ed. New York: The Macmillan Company, 1922, 1926, 1929. First published 1913.

King, Edward. "The Great South." *Scribner's Monthly* 6: 257–88; 7: 1–32, 129–60, 302–30, 401–31, 513–44, 645–74; 8: 5–33, 129–60, 257–84, 385–412, 513–35, 641–69; 9: 1–31, 129–57 (July, November, December 1873; January–December 1874). Reprinted, Hartford: American Publishing Company, 1875.

Kirkland, Caroline S. "The Young Man Who Went West: A Californian Epipoeia." *Lippincott's Magazine* 19: 83–91 (January 1877).

Kittridge, George Lyman. "[Review:] The Popular Ballad." *Atlantic Monthly* 101: 276–78 (February 1908).

Kohn, August. "Child Labor in the South." In *The South in the Building of the Nation*, edited by Samuel C. Mitchell, vol. 10, pp. 582–97. Richmond: Southern Historical Publication Society, 1909 [–1913].

———. *The Cotton Mills of South Carolina: A Series of Observations and Facts, As Published in Letters Written to the [Charleston] News and Courier*. Charleston: Walker, Evan and Cogswell, 1903.

———. *The Cotton Mills of South Carolina, 1907: Letters Written to the [Charleston] News and Courier*. Charleston: Daggett Printing Company, 1907.

Langston, G. D. "The Child and the Farm." National Conference of Charities and Correction, *Proceedings* 30: 204–5 (1903).

Lanier, Henry Wysham. "The Morris Dance Comes to America." *Country Life* 33 no. 2: 45–49 (December 1917).

Lanman, Charles. *Letters from the Allegheny Mountains*. New York: G. P. Putnam's Sons, 1849.

Lee, Joseph. *Constructive and Preventive Philanthropy*. New York: The Macmillan Company, 1902, 1906.

Lindsay, Samuel McCune. "National Child Labor Standards." *Child Labor Bulletin* 3: 25–33 (May 1914).

———. "The Study and Teaching of Sociology." American Academy of Political and Social Science, *Annals* 12: 1–48 (July 1898).

———. "The Unit of Investigation or of Consideration in Sociology." American Academy of Political and Social Science, *Annals* 12: 214–28 (September 1898).

Lodge, Henry Cabot. *A Short History of the English Colonies in America*. New York: Harper and Brothers, 1881.

Lomax, John A. *Cow-boy Songs and Other Frontier Ballads*. New York: Sturgis and Walton, 1910.

Lord, Katherine; Heninger, Alice Minnie Herts; and Bradstreet, Howard, eds. *A Guide and Index to Plays, Festivals and Masques for Use in Schools, Clubs, and Neighborhood Centers*. New York: Harper and Brothers, 1913.

Love, Albert G., and Davenport, Charles B. *Defects Found in Drafted Men: Statistical Information Compiled from the Draft Records*. Washington: U.S. Government Printing Office, 1920.

Lovejoy, Owen R. "Child Labor." In *The New Encyclopaedia of Social Reform*, edited by D. W. P. Bliss. 3rd ed. New York: Funk and Wagnalls Company, 1910.

Mabie, Hamilton Wright. "Four English Songs by Shakespeare, Lovelace, and Herrick." *Outlook* 43: 221–26 (25 September 1909).

_____. "Two Famous Ballads: Barbara Allen's Cruelty and Robin Hood and Allen-a-Dale." *Outlook* 43: 463–68 (23 October 1909).

MacAdam, George. "The National Menace of Rural Bad Health: A Remedy." *Outlook* 115: 321–22, 326–27 (21 February 1917).

MacArthur, Arthur. *Education in Its Relation to Manual Industry*. New York: D. Appleton and Company, 1884, 1895.

McCord, Mary Rose. "Twenty-Five Years in the Mountains." *Women and Missions* 3: 292–95 (November 1926).

McGowan, K. "The New Life of Folk-Songs: Their Use to Modern People." *Craftsman* 24: 316–21 (June 1913).

MacKaye, Hazel. "Outdoor Plays and Pageants: A Sketch of the Movement in America." *Independent* 68: 1227–34 (2 June 1910).

MacKaye, Percy. *The Civic Theatre in Relation to the Redemption of Leisure: A Book of Suggestions*. New York: M. Kennerley, 1912.

_____. *Community Drama: Its Motive and Method of Neighborliness. An Interpretation*. Boston: Houghton Mifflin Company, 1917.

_____. *Kentucky Mountain Fantasies: Three Short Plays for an Appalachian Theatre*. New York: Longmans, Green and Company, 1928.

_____. "A Mountain Munchausen." *Century* 108: 357–63, 442–48, 657–65, 819–27 (July–November 1924). Reprinted as *Tall Tales of the Kentucky Mountains*. New York: George H. Doran Company, 1926.

_____. *This Fine-Pretty World: A Comedy of the Kentucky Mountains*. New York: The Macmillan Company, 1924.

_____. "Untamed America: A Comment on a Sojourn in the Kentucky Mountains." *Survey* 51: 326–31, 360, 362–63 (1 January 1924).

McKelway, Alexander J. "The Awakening of the South Against Child Labor." American Academy of Political and Social Science, *Annals* 29: 9–18 (January 1907).

_____. *Child Labor in Georgia*. National Child Labor Committee Publication no. 138. New York: National Child Labor Committee, 1910.

_____. "Child Labor in the Carolinas." *Charities and The Commons* 21: 743–57 (30 January 1909). Summary of A. E. Sedden, A. H. Ulm, and Lewis W. Hine, *Child Labor in the Carolinas*. New York: National Child Labor Committee, 1910.

_____. "Child Labor in the South." American Academy of Political and Social Science, *Annals* 35 no. 1: 156–64 (January 1910).

_____. *Child Labor in Virginia*. National Child Labor Committee Publication no. 171. New York: National Child Labor Committee, 1912.

_____. "Child Wages in the Cotton Mills: Our Modern Feudalism." *Child Labor Bulletin* 2 no. 1: 7–16 (May 1913).

_____. "The Fight for Child Labor Reform in the Carolinas." *Charities and The Commons* 21: 1224–26 (20 March 1909).

Manne, Jack. "Mental Deficiency in a Closely Inbred Mountain Clan." *Mental Hygiene* 20: 269–79 (April 1936).

Mason, Robert Lindsay. *The Lure of the Great Smokies*. Boston: Houghton Mifflin Company, 1927.

Messler, Isaac. "Our Co-Worker [John C. Campbell]." *Mountain Life and Work* 4 no. 1: 7–9 (April 1928).

Methodist Episcopal Church. *Journal of the General Conference of the Methodist Episcopal Church*.

Miles, Emma Bell. *Strains from a Dulcimore*. Edited by Abby Crawford Milton. Atlanta: The Bozart Press, 1930.

Miller, Margaret. "The Great Physician's Work." *Women and Missions* 3: 306–7 (November 1926).

Mitchell, Broadus. *The Rise of the Cotton Mills in the South*. Baltimore: The Johns Hopkins Press, 1921.

_____, and Mitchell, George Sinclair. *The Industrial Revolution in the South*. Baltimore: Johns Hopkins Press, 1930.

Mitchell, Elisha. *Diary of a Geological Tour by Dr. Elisha Mitchell in 1827 and 1828*, edited by Kemp P. Battle. James Sprunt Historical Monographs, no. 6. Chapel Hill: University of North Carolina Press, 1905.

_____. "Notice of the Height of Mountains in North Carolina." *American Journal of Science* 35 no. 2: 377–80 (January? 1839).

Monahan, A. C. "Rural Education." In U.S. Commissioner of Education, *Report of the Commissioner of Education* 1912, 1: 177–225.

_____. *The Status of Rural Education in the United States*. U.S. Bureau of Education Bulletin, 1913 no. 8.

_____, and Phillips, Adam. *The Farragut School: A Tennessee Country-Life High School*. U.S. Bureau of Education Bulletin, 1913 no. 47.

Montgomery, Caroline Williamson. *Bibliography of College, Social, University and Church Settlements*, 5th ed. Chicago: College Settlements Association, 1905.

_____. "Settlements." In *The New Encyclopaedia of Social Reform*, edited by William D. P. Bliss. 3d ed. New York: Funk and Wagnalls Company, 1910.

Moorehead, Warren H. "The People of the Ozarks. Natives That Are Little Known to Travellers: Husky and Intelligent Mountaineers Who Have None of the Lawless Feuds of the Appalachian Dwellers." *Boston Evening Transcript*, 3 July 1908, p. 12.

Moses, Montrose J. "The Children's Christmas Book Shelf: Folk Lore and Its Antidote." *Independent* 65: 1473–74 (17 December 1908).

Murphy, Edgar Gardner. "Child Labor as a National Problem; With Especial Reference to the Southern States." National Conference of Charities and Correction, *Proceedings* 30: 121–34 (1903).

———. "Child Labor in Alabama: A Discussion of New England's Part in the Common Responsibility for the Child-Labor Conditions of the South." 1902. Reprinted in *Problems of the Present South. A Discussion of Certain of the Educational, Industrial and Political Issues in the Southern States*, pp. 309–29. New York: The Macmillan Company, 1904.

———. *Problems of the Present South. A Discussion of Certain of the Educational, Industrial and Political Issues in the Southern States*. New York: The Macmillan Company, 1904.

Needham, Mary Master. *Folk Festivals: Their Growth and How to Give Them*. New York: B. W. Huebsch, 1912.

Nesmith, G. T. "The Problem of Rural Community with Special Reference to the Rural Church." *American Journal of Sociology* 8: 812–37 (May 1903).

———, ed. "Country Life." American Academy of Political and Social Science, *Annals* 40 (March 1912).

Nichols, George W. "Down the Mississippi." *Harper's Magazine* 41: 835–45 (November 1870).

———. "Six Weeks in Florida." *Harper's Magazine* 41: 655–67 (October 1870).

Niles, John Jacob. "In Defense of the Backwoods." *Scribner's Magazine* 83: 738–45 (June 1928).

Odum, Howard W. *Folk, Region, and Society: Selected Papers of Howard W. Odum*, edited by Katherine Jocher, Guy B. Johnson, George L. Simpson, and Rupert Vance. Chapel Hill: University of North Carolina Press, 1964.

Otley, Elizabeth Lewis. *The Beginnings of Child Labor Legislation in Certain States: A Comparative Study*. U.S. Congress. Report on the Condition of Women and Child Wage Earners in the United States, vol. 6 (1910). 61st Congress, 2d session, Senate Document 645.

Page, Walter Hines. *The Rebuilding of Old Commonwealths: Being Essays toward the Training of the Forgotten Man in the Southern States*. New York: Doubleday, Page and Company, 1902.

Palmer, Walter B. "Economic and Legal Aspects of the Labor of Women and Children in the South." In *The South in the Building of the Nation*, edited by Samuel C. Mitchell, vol. 6, pp. 53–58. Richmond: Southern Historical Publication Society, 1909[–1913].

Pattee, Fred Lewis. *The Development of the American Short Story: An Historical Survey*. New York: Harper and Brothers, 1923.

———. *A History of American Literature Since 1870*. New York: The Century Company, 1915.

Peabody, Charles. "The English Folk-Dance Society and Its Work." *Journal of American Folk Lore* 28: 316–17 (September 1915).

Perry, Arthur R. *Causes of Death among Women and Child Cotton-Mill Operatives*. U.S. Congress. Report on the Condition of Women and Child Wage Earners in the United States, vol. 14 (1912). 61st Congress, 2d session, Senate Document 645.

Pettit, Katherine. "Progress in the Hills." *Survey* 50: 211 (15 May 1923).

Peyser, Nathan. "The School as the Community Center." *Survey* 36: 621–23 (23 September 1916).

Phelan, James. *History of Tennessee: The Making of a State*. American Commonwealths Series. Boston: Houghton, Mifflin and Company, 1888.

———. *School History of Tennessee*. Philadelphia: E. H. Butler and Company, 1889.

Plunkett, Horace. *Ireland in the New Century*. New York: E. P. Dutton and Company, 1904.

———. *The Rural Life Problem of the United States: Notes of an Irish Observer*. New York: The Macmillan Company, 1911.

Pollard, Edward A. "The Real Condition of the South." *Lippincott's Magazine* 6: 612–20 (December 1870).

Pratt, Joseph Hyde. "The Good Roads Movement in the South." American Academy of Political and Social Science, *Annals* 35: 105–10 (January 1910).

Presbyterian Church in the United States of America. *Minutes of the General Assembly of the Presbyterian Church*.

———, Board of Home Missions. "Annual Report." In *Minutes of the General Assembly of the Presbyterian Church*, 1870–.

———, Committee of Missions for Freedmen. "Annual Report." In *Minutes of the General Assembly of the Presbyterian Church*, 1872–.

———, Special Committee on the Consolidation of the Boards. "Report." In *Minutes of the General Assembly of the Presbyterian Church*, 1874, pp. 18ff.; 1878, pp. 74–81.

———, Special Committee on Voluntary Societies. "Report." In *Minutes of the General Assembly of the Presbyterian Church*, 1874, pp. 164–67.

———, Standing Committee on Home Missions. "Report." In *Minutes of the General Assembly of the Presbyterian Church*, 1879, pp. 579ff.

Pridemore, Francis. "What Prohibition Has Done for the Mountaineers." *Outlook* 146: 384–85 (20 July 1927).

Raine, James Watt. *The Land of Saddle-Bags: A Study of the Mountain People of Appalachia*. New York: Council of Women for Home Missions and Missionary Education Movement of the United States and Canada, 1924.

Ralph, Julian. "Wyoming—Another Pennsylvania." *Harper's Magazine* 87: 63–77 (June 1893).

Reed, Louis E. "My Little Learning: A Fragment of Autobiography." *Atlantic Monthly* 135: 749–54 (June 1925).

Riis, Jacob. "Cooperation in Denmark: Educating the Farmers to Rule the Nation." *Craftsman* 23: 609–14 (March 1913).

Risley, Eleanor de la Vergne. *The Road to Wildcat: A Tale of Southern Mountaineering*. Boston: Little, Brown and Company, 1930.

Roosevelt, Theodore. "Frontier Types." *Century* 36: 831–43 (October 1888).

———. *Hunting Trips of a Ranchman: Sketches of Sport on the Northern Cattle Plains*. New York: G. P. Putnam's Sons, 1885.

———. "Introduction." In Mrs. John [Bessie] Van Vorst and Marie Van Vorst, *The Woman Who Toils: Being the Experiences of Two Ladies as Factory Girls*. New York: Doubleday, Page and Company, 1903.

———. "The Ranchman's Rifle on Crag and Prairie." *Century* 36: 200–12 (June 1888).

———. "Sheriff's Work on A Ranch." *Century* 36: 39–51 (May 1888).

———. *The Winning of the West*. 4 vols. New York: G. P. Putnam's Sons, 1889–96 and subsequent editions.

Ross, Edward Alsworth. "Pocketed Americans." *New Republic* 37: 170–72, 224–36 (9, 23 January 1924).

Rutherford, Mildred L. *The South in History and Literature: A Handbook of Southern Authors*. Athens, Georgia: n.p., 1906.

Ryan, W. Carson, Jr., ed. *School Hygiene: A Report of the Fourth International Congress of School Hygiene*. U.S. Bureau of Education Bulletin, 1913 no. 48.

Ryder, Charles Jackson. *Fifty Years of the American Missionary Association*. New York: American Missionary Association, 1896. Reprinted from *New England Magazine* 15: 225–44 (October 1896).

Sabin, Henry, et al. "Report of the Committee of Twelve on Rural Schools." National Education Association, *Addresses and Proceedings* 1897, pp. 385–583.

———. "Report of the Committee of Twelve on Rural Schools." U.S. Commissioner of Education, *Report of the Commissioner of Education* 1896–97, pp. 811–90.

Sedden, A. E.; Ulm, A. H.; and Hine, Lewis W. *Child Labor in the Carolinas*. National Child Labor Committee Publication no. 92. New York: National Child Labor Committee, 1910. Summarized in Alexander J. McKelway, "Child Labor in the Carolinas." *Charities and The Commons* 21: 743–57 (30 January 1909).

Seitz, Don C. "Mountain Folks. Some Glimpses of the One Hundred Per Cent Americans in the Blue Ridge Country." *Outlook* 144: 146–47 (29 September 1926).

Semple, Ellen Churchill. *American History and Its Geographic Conditions*. Boston: Houghton Mifflin Company, 1903.

Sewell, Hannah R. "Child Labor in the United States." U.S. Bureau of Labor *Bulletin* 9: 485–637 (1904 no. 52; May 1904).

Shaffer, E. T. H. "Heredity." *Atlantic Monthly* 14: 349–54 (September 1929).

Shaler, Nathaniel Southgate. *Kentucky: A Pioneer Commonwealth*. American Commonwealths Series. Boston: Houghton, Mifflin and Company, 1884.

Sharp, Cecil J. "The English Folksong." *Musician* 22: 91–92 (February 1917). Reprinted from *One Hundred English Folksongs*. Boston: Oliver Ditson Company, 1916.

————. *One Hundred English Folksongs*. Boston: Oliver Ditson Company, 1916.

Sherman, Mandel. "Environment and Mental Development: A Study of an Isolated Community." *Journal of the American Association of University Women* 23 no. 3: 137–40 (April 1930).

————, and Henry, Thomas R. *Hollow Folk: A Study in the Blue Ridge*. New York: Thomas Y. Crowell Company, 1933.

————, and Key, Cora B. "The Intelligence of Isolated Mountain Children." *Child Development* 2: 279–90 (December 1932).

Simkhovitch, Mary K. "Handicrafts in the City—What Their Commercial Significance is Under Metropolitan Conditions." *Craftsman* 11: 363–65 (December 1906).

————. *Neighborhood: My Story of Greenwich House*. New York: W. W. Norton, 1938.

————. "The Settlement's Relation to Religion." American Academy of Political and Social Science, *Annals* 30: 490–95 (November 1907).

Simons, May Wood. "Education in the South." *American Journal of Sociology*. 10: 382–407 (November 1904).

Singer, Florence Elton. "The Shepherd of Red Bird." *Mountain Life and Work* 4 no. 4: 17–19 (January 1929).

Smith, Anna Tolman. "Rural Uplift in Foreign Countries." In U.S. Commissioner of Education, *Report of the Commissioner of Education* 1911, 1: 371–88.

Smith, Charles Foster. "Southern Colleges and Schools." *Atlantic Monthly* 54: 542–57; 56: 738–50 (October, 1884; December 1885).

Somerndike, J. M. "The Southern Mountaineers, Past, Present and Future." *Missionary Review of the World* 51: 198–203 (March 1928).

Spargo, John. "The Nurse and the Doctor in the Public School Are Evidences of a Growing Regard for Child Life." *Craftsman* 11: 472–80 (January 1907).

Sprinkle, Mary Camp. "Unit of Organization for Rural Social Work." *Mountain Life and Work* 4 no. 2: 21–26 (July 1928).

Steer, Mary A. "New Roads through the Southern Mountains." *Women and Missions* 3: 286–89 (November 1926).

Stewart, Anna Belle. "Intimate Glimpses of a West Virginia School. Extracts from a Series of News Letters Sent Out . . . from the Pattie C. Stockdale Memorial School, Concord, West Virginia." *Missionary Review of the World* 50: 503–506, 591–94 (July, August 1927).

Stiles, Charles Wardell. *Hookworm Disease among Cotton Mill Operatives*. U.S. Congress. Report of the Condition of Women and Child Wage Earners in the United States, vol. 17 (1912). 61st Congress, 2d session, Senate Document 645.

———. "The Industrial Conditions of the Tenant Class (White and Black) as Influenced by the Medical Conditions." In *The South in the Building of the Nation*, edited by Samuel C. Mitchell, vol. 6, pp. 594–601. Richmond: Southern Historical Publication Society, 1909[–1913].

———. *Soil Pollution as a Cause of Ground Itch, Hookworm Disease (Ground-Itch Anaemia), and Dirt Eating: A Circular for Use in Schools*. Rockefeller Sanitary Commission Publication no. 1. Washington: Rockefeller Sanitary Commission, 1910.

Stowe, Harriet Beecher. *Oldtown Folks*. Boston: Fields, Osgood, and Company, 1859.

Swift, W. W. "Southern Railroads and Industrial Development." American Academy of Political and Social Science, *Annals* 35: 99–104 (January 1910).

Tannenbaum, Frank. "The South Buries Its Anglo-Saxons." In *Darker Phases of the South*, pp. 39–73. New York: G. P. Putnam's Sons, 1924.

Thomas, William I. *Source Book for Social Origins: Ethnological Materials, Psychological Standpoint, Classified and Annotated Bibliographies for the Interpretation of Savage Society*. Boston: Richard G. Badger: The Gorham Press, 1909 and subsequent editions.

Thompson, Holland. *From the Cotton Field to the Cotton Mill: A Study of the Industrial Transition in North Carolina*. New York: The Macmillan Company, 1906.

Thompson, Robert Ellis. *A History of the Presbyterian Churches in the United States*. New York: The Christian Literature Company, 1895.

Thornborough, Laura. "Americans the Twentieth Century Forgot: A Visit to Our Contemporary Ancestors in the Great Smokies—Customs Surviving from the Elizabethan Age—The Results of Centuries of Isolation." *Travel* 50: 25–28, 42 (April 1928).

Tompkins, David A. "The Sociological Work of the Cotton Mill Owners." National Conference of Charities and Correction, *Proceedings* 30: 157–66 (1903).

T[rotter], M[argaret]. "Dr. Morse Outlines the Religious Survey." *Mountain Life and Work* 7 no. 2: 35–36 (July 1931).

Ullman, Doris. "The Mountaineers of Kentucky: A Series of Portrait Studies." *Scribner's Magazine* 83: 658, 675–81 (June 1928).

U.S. Commission on Country Life. See: Commission on Country Life.

U.S. Commissioner of Education [P. P. Claxton]. ["Report on Southern Appalachian School Survey"]. In *Report of the Commissioner of Education* 1916, 1: xix; 1917, 1: 19.

[unsigned]. "Acclimating Northern Principles." *American Missionary*, n.s. 17: 58–59 (March 1873).

[unsigned]. "The American Problem." *American Missionary*, n.s. 17: 253–54 (November 1873).

[unsigned]. "Annual Statement of the Progress of Education in Foreign Countries: Denmark." In U.S. Commissioner of Education, *Report of the Commissioner of Education* 1871, 1: 457–58.

[unsigned]. "Cecil Sharp Tells How He Became Interested in Folk Dances." *University [of Cincinnati] News*, 12 April 1916.

[unsigned]. "The Cincinnati Shakespeare Tercentenary Given by the University of Cincinnati." *Outlook* 113: 545–46 (5 July 1916).

[unsigned]. "The Common Welfare: Southern Kindergarten and Settlement." *Charities and The Commons* 6: 329–30 (24 November 1906).

[unsigned]. "Craft Work in a Southern High School [John Marshall High School, Richmond, Virginia]." *Craftsman* 21: 692, 693 (March 1912).

[unsigned]. "Current Literature: *The Circuit Rider: A Tale of the Heroic Age*." *Atlantic Monthly* 33: 745–46 (June 1874).

[unsigned]. "Early Anti-Slavery Missions and Their Outcome." *American Missionary*, n.s. 45: 435–40 (December 1891).

[unsigned]. "Editorial: Uncle Remus [on the Death of Joel Chandler Harris]." *Independent* 65: 110 (9 July 1908).

[unsigned]. "Education in Central Europe: Rural High Schools in Denmark." In U.S. Commissioner of Education, *Report of the Commissioner of Education* 1909, pp. 491–92.

[unsigned]. "Education in the Kingdoms of Northern Europe: Scandinavia." In U.S. Commissioner of Education, *Report of the Commissioner of Education* 1912, pp. 511–16.

[unsigned: Hingham, Massachusetts, Society of Arts and Crafts]. "Hingham Village Industries." *Southern Workman* 32: 422–26 (September 1903).

[unsigned]. "Recent American Fiction: *Hunting Trips of A Ranchman* [by Theodore Roosevelt]." *Atlantic Monthly* 56: 563–65 (October 1885).

[unsigned]. "[Review:] H. Ryder Haggard, *Rural Denmark and Its Lessons*." *Nature* 86: 509 (15 June 1911).

[unsigned]. "Second Lecture Given by Cecil Sharp—Folk Dances Explained." *University [of Cincinnati] News*, 12 April 1916.

[unsigned]. "Statistics of Schools for Manual and Industrial Training." In U.S. Commissioner of Education, *Report of the Commissioner of Education* 1896–97, pp. 2279–94.

[unsigned]. "Teaching American Children to Play: Significance of the Revival

of Folk Dances, Games, and Festivals by the Playground Association."
Craftsman 15: 192–99 (November 1908).

[unsigned]. "A Week of Pageantry." *Independent* 86: 433–34 (12 June 1916).

Van Vorst, Mrs. John [Bessie]. "The Cry of the Children: Human Documents in the Case of the New Slavery." *Saturday Evening Post* 173 no. 37: 1–3, 28–29; no. 42: 3–5; no. 44: 10–11; no. 45: 11–13; no. 47: 12–13, 26–27; 174 no. 1: 12–13; no. 4: 17–18; no. 7: 17–18 (10 March, 14, 28 April, 11, 19 May, 7, 28 July, 18 August 1906). Reprinted as *The Cry of the Children: A Study of Child Labor*. New York: Moffat, Yard and Company, 1908.

———, and Van Vorst, Marie. *The Woman Who Toils: Being the Experiences of Two Ladies as Factory Girls*. New York: Doubleday, Page and Company, 1903.

Vogt, Paul L. *The Church and Country Life*. New York: Missionary Education Movement of the United States and Canada, 1916.

Walker, Louisa. *Varied Occupations in String Work: Comprising Knotting, Netting, Looping, Plaiting, and Macramé*. London: The Macmillan Company, 1896. Reissued as *Graded Lessons in Macramé, Knotting and Netting*. New York: Dover Publications, 1971.

Walker, Williston. *A History of the Congregational Churches in the United States*. New York: The Christian Literature Company, 1894.

Warner, Charles Dudley. "The South Revisited." *Harper's Magazine* 74: 634–40 (March 1887).

Washington, Booker T. "How Denmark Has Taught Itself Prosperity and Happiness: The Rural High Schools Which Have Made Over a Nation." *World's Work* 22: 14486–94 (June 1911).

———. *Working with the Hands: Being a Sequel to "Up From Slavery" Covering the Author's Experience in Industrial Training at Tuskeegee*. New York: Doubleday, Page and Company, 1904.

Weber, Samuel E. "Southern Education Problems." National Education Association, *Addresses and Proceedings* 1910, pp. 234–41.

Welch, Herbert. "The Relation of the Church to the Social Worker." National Conference of Charities and Correction, *Proceedings* 35: 69–75 (1908).

Wells, George Frederick. "Is an Organized Country Life Movement Possible?" *Survey* 29: 449–56 (4 January 1913).

Weltner, C. E. "Social Welfare and Child Labor in South Carolina Mill Communities." *Child Labor Bulletin* 2 no. 1: 85–90 (May 1913).

Wheeler, Lester R. "A Comparative Study of the Intelligence of East Tennessee Mountain Children." *Journal of Educational Psychology*, 33: 321–34 (May 1942).

———. "The Intelligence of East Tennessee Mountain Children." *Journal of Educational Psychology* 23: 351–70 (May 1932).

———, and Wheeler, Viola D. "The Musical Ability of Mountain Children as

Measured by the Seashore Test of Musical Talent." *Journal of Genetic Psychology* 43: 352–75 (December 1933).

White, Edwin E. *Highland Heritage: The Southern Mountains and the Nation*. New York: Friendship Press, 1937.

White, William Allen. "Fiction of the Eighties and Nineties." In *American Writers on American Literature*, edited by John Macy, pp. 389–98. New York: Horace Liveright Incorporated, 1931.

Whitfield, W. H. "An Indictment of the Rural School." In *Education for the South: Abstracts of Papers Read at the 16th Conference for Education in the South*, pp. 43–44. U.S. Bureau of Education Bulletin, 1913 no. 30.

———. *An Indictment of the Rural School*. U.S. Bureau of Education Bulletin, 1913 no. 40.

Willis, Nathaniel Parker. *Hurry-Graphs; or, Sketches of Scenery, Celebrities, and Society, Taken from Life*. New York: Charles Scribner, 1851.

Wilson, Alexander. "The Naturalist. Number III." *Port-Folio* (Philadelphia), 3d series 2: 119–23 (August 1809).

Wilson, Charles Morrow. "Elizabethan America." *Atlantic Monthly* 144: 238–44 (August 1929).

Wilson, Warren H. *The Evolution of the Country Community: A Study in Religious Sociology*, Boston: The Pilgrim Press, 1912.

Wines, Frederick H. "Sociology and Philanthropy." American Academy of Political and Social Science, *Annals* 12: 49–57 (July 1898).

Wister, Owen. "Em'ly." *Harper's Magazine* 87: 941–48 (November 1893).

Wood, Thomas D. "Health Problems in the American Public Schools [and] Minimum Sanitary Requirements for Rural Schools." National Education Association, *Addresses and Proceedings* 1914: 294–301.

———. "Report of the Committee on Health Problems in Education: The Sanitation of Rural Schools." National Education Association, *Addresses and Proceedings* 1913, pp. 380–84.

Woods, Robert A. *The Neighborhood in Nation-Building: The Running Comment of Thirty Years at the South End House*. Boston: Houghton Mifflin Company, 1923.

Woodward, C. M. "The Rise and Progress of Manual Training." In U.S. Commissioner of Education, *Report of the Commissioner of Education 1893–94*, pp. 877–949.

Woolson, Constance Fenimore. "American Cities: Detroit." *Appleton's Journal* 8: 85–92 (27 July, 1872).

———. "Fairy Island." *Putnam's Magazine*, n.s. 6: 62–69 (July 1870).

———. "The French Broad." *Harper's Magazine* 50: 617–36 (April 1875).

———. "The Happy Valley." *Harper's Magazine* 41: 282–85 (July 1870).

———. "Lake Shore Relics." *Lippincott's Magazine* 12: 606–11 (November 1873).

————. "Mackinac Island." *Appleton's Journal* 9: 321–23 (8 March, 1873).

————. *Rodman the Keeper: Southern Sketches*. New York: D. Appleton and Company, 1880.

————. "Round by Propeller." *Harper's Magazine* 45: 518–33 (September 1872).

————. "A Voyage to an Unknown River." *Appleton's Journal* 11: 614–16 (16 May 1874).

————. "The Wine Islands of Lake Erie." *Harper's Magazine* 47: 27–36 (June 1873).

Wright, John K., ed. *New England's Prospect: 1933*. American Geographic Society Special Publication no. 16. New York: American Geographic Society, 1933.

Young, Bertha K. "Cecil Sharp to Spend a Week in Cincinnati in Connection with Tercentenary." *University [of Cincinnati] News*, 29 March 1916.

Zeller, John W. "Education in the Country for the Country." National Education Association, *Addresses and Proceedings* 1910, pp. 245–53.

III. Secondary Sources Cited

Ballou, Ellen B. *The Building of the House: Houghton Mifflin's Formative Years*. Boston: Houghton Mifflin Company, 1970.

Barclay, Wade Crawford. *The Methodist Episcopal Church: Widening Horizons, 1845–1895*. New York: Board of Missions of the Methodist Church, 1957.

Barnard, John. *From Evangelicalism to Progressivism at Oberlin College, 1866–1917*. Columbus: Ohio State University Press, 1969.

Benedict, Clare. *Constance Fenimore Woolson*. London: Ellis, 1932.

————. *Voices Out of the Past*. 2 vols. London: Ellis, 1929.

Berman, Milton. *John Fiske: Origins of a Popularizer*. Cambridge: Harvard University Press, 1961.

Berthoff, Warner. *The Ferment of Realism: American Literature, 1884–1919*. New York: The Free Press. 1965.

Boger, Lorise C. *The Southern Mountaineer in Literature: An Annotated Bibliography*. Morgantown: West Virginia University Library, 1964.

Bremner, Robert. *From the Depths: The Discovery of Poverty in the United States*. New York: New York University Press, 1956.

Buck, Paul H. *The Road to Reunion*. Boston: Little, Brown and Company, 1937.

Carstensen, Vernon. "The Development and Application of Regional-Sectional Concepts, 1900–1950." In *Regionalism in America*, edited by Merrill Jensen, pp. 99–118. Madison: University of Wisconsin Press, 1952.

Carter, Everett. *Howells and the Rise of Realism*. Philadelphia: J. B. Lippincott Company, 1954.

Cary, Richard. *Mary N. Murfree*. New York: Twayne Publishers, 1967.

Caudill, Harry M. *Night Comes to the Cumberlands*. Boston: Atlantic, Little Brown, 1963.

Chambers, Clarke A. *Paul U. Kellogg and The Survey: Voices for Social Welfare and Social Justice*. Minneapolis: University of Minnesota Press, 1971.

Clutts, Betty Carol. "Country Life Aspects of the Progressive Movement." Ph.D. dissertation, Ohio State University, 1962.

Colbrunn, Ethel B. "Regionalism in the Works of Constance Fenimore Woolson." M.A. thesis, Ohio State University, 1941.

Collins, Carvel Emerson. "The Literary Tradition of the Southern Mountaineer, 1824–1900." Ph.D. dissertation, University of Chicago, 1944.

———. "Nineteenth Century Fiction of the Southern Appalachians." *Bulletin of Bibliography* 17: 186–90, 215–18 (December 1942, April 1943).

Couch, William T., ed. *Culture in the South*. Chapel Hill: University of North Carolina Press, 1935.

Cremin, Lawrence. *The Transformation of the School: Progressivism in American Education, 1865–1957*. New York: Alfred A. Knopf, 1961.

Dabney, Charles W., Jr. *Universal Education in the South*. 2 vols. Chapel Hill: University of North Carolina Press, 1936.

Davidson, Elizabeth H. *Child Labor Legislation in the Southern Textile States*. Chapel Hill: University of North Carolina Press, 1939.

Davis, Allen F. *American Heroine: The Life and Legend of Jane Addams*. New York: Oxford University Press, 1973.

———. *Spearheads for Reform: The Social Settlements and the Progressive Movement, 1890–1914*. New York: Oxford University Press, 1967.

Davis, Arthur Kyle, ed. *Folksongs of Virginia: A Descriptive Index and Syllabus*. Durham: Duke University Press, 1949.

Drake, Richard B. "Freedmen's Aid Societies and Sectional Compromise." *Journal of Southern History* 29: 175–86 (May 1963).

Dusenbury, Richard B. "Truth and Technique: A Study of Sociology and the Social Survey Movement, 1895–1930." Ph.D. dissertation, University of Wisconsin, 1969.

Edwards, Everett Eugene. *References on the Mountaineers of the Southern Appalachians*. U.S. Department of Agriculture Library, Bibliographical Contributions no. 28 (December 1935).

Enck, Henry S. "The Burden Borne: Northern White Philanthropy and Southern Black Industrial Education." Ph.D. dissertation, University of Cincinnati, 1970.

Ewan, Joseph. "The Scientist on the Frontier." In *Research Opportunities in American Cultural History*, edited by John Francis McDermott, pp. 81–101. Lexington: University of Kentucky Press, 1961.

Falk, Robert P. "The Rise of Realism." In *Transitions in American Literary His-*

tory, edited by Harry Hayden Clark, pp. 381–442. Durham: Duke University Press, 1953.

Festinger, Leon. *A Theory of Cognitive Dissonance*. Evanston: Row-Peterson, 1957.

Fosdick, Raymond B. *Adventure in Giving: The Story of the General Education Board. A Foundation Established by John D. Rockefeller*. New York: Harper and Row, 1961.

Glenn, John M.; Brandt, Lilian; and Andrews, F. Emerson. *Russell Sage Foundation, 1907–1946*. 2 vols. New York: Russell Sage Foundation, 1947.

Goetzmann, William H. *Army Exploration in the American West, 1803–1863*. New Haven: Yale University Press, 1959.

Green, Harold Everett. *Towering Pines: The Life of John Fox, Jr.* Boxton: Meador Publishing Company, 1943.

Hansen, Klaus J. *Quest for Empire: The Political Kingdom of God and the Council of Fifty in Mormon History*. East Lansing: Michigan State University Press, 1970.

Harlan, Louis. *Separate and Unequal: Public School Campaigns and Racism in the Southern Seaboard States, 1901–1915*. Chapel Hill: University of North Carolina Press, 1958.

Harris, Isabella D. "The Southern Mountaineer in American Fiction, 1824–1910." Ph.D. dissertation, Duke University, 1948.

Harrison, Shelby M. "Introduction." In *A Bibliography of Social Surveys: Reports of Fact Finding Studies Made as a Basis for Social Action*, compiled by Allen Eaton and Shelby M. Harrison. New York: Russell Sage Foundation, 1930.

Hauser, Arnold. *The Social History of Art*. 2 vols. New York: Alfred A. Knopf, 1956.

Heckman, Oliver Saxon. "Northern Church Penetration of the South, 1860–1880." Ph.D. dissertation, Duke University, 1939.

Hendrick, Burton J. *The Life and Letters of Walter H. Page*. 2 vols. Garden City, New York: Doubleday, Page and Company, 1924.

———. *The Training of an American: The Earlier Life and Letters of Walter Hines Page, 1855–1913*. Boston: Houghton, Mifflin Company, 1928.

Higham, John. *Strangers in the Land: Patterns of American Nativism, 1865–1925*. New Brunswick: Rutgers University Press, 1955.

Holloway, Jean. *Hamlin Garland: A Biography*. Austin: University of Texas Press, 1960.

Huie, William Bradford. "Last Humble Wish Fulfilled, Sgt. York is Buried in the Land He Loved." *New York Herald Tribune*, 6 September 1964, I, 8.

James, Henry, Jr. "Miss Constance Fenimore Woolson." *Harper's Weekly* 31: 114–15 (12 February 1887).

Janowitz, Morris. "Introduction." In *W. I. Thomas on Social Organization and*

Social Personality, edited by Morris Janowitz, pp. vii–lviii. Chicago: University of Chicago Press, 1966.

Kane, Harnett T., and Henry, Inez. *Miracle in the Mountains*. Garden City, New York: Doubleday and Company, 1956.

Karpeles, Maud. *Cecil Sharp: His Life and Work*. Chicago: University of Chicago Press, 1967.

Kern, John Dwight. *Constance Fenimore Woolson, Literary Pioneer*. Philadelphia: University of Pennsylvania Press, 1934.

Knight, Grant. *James Lane Allen and the Genteel Tradition*. Chapel Hill: University of North Carolina Press, 1935.

Lahne, Herbert J. *The Cotton Mill Worker*. New York: Farrar and Reinhart, 1944.

Leach, MacEdward, and Coffin, Tristram P., eds. *The Critics and the Ballad: Readings*. Carbondale: Southern Illinois University Press, 1961.

McAllister, Ethel. *Amos Eaton, Scientist and Educator*. Philadelphia: University of Pennsylvania Press, 1941.

MacCormac, Earl R. "The Transition from Voluntary Missionary Society to the Church as a Missionary Organization among the American Congregationalists, Presbyterians and Methodists." Ph.D. dissertation, Yale University, 1960.

McIlwaine, Shields. *The Southern Poor White from Lubberland to Tobacco Road*. Norman: University of Oklahoma Press, 1939.

Mead, Frank S. *Handbook of Denominations*. New York: Abingdon-Cokesbury Press, 1951.

Merrill, George P. *The First One-Hundred Years of American Geology*. New Haven: Yale University Press, 1924.

Mood, Fulmer. "The Origin, Evolution, and Application of the Sectional Concept, 1750–1900." In *Regionalism in America*, edited by Merrill Jensen, pp. 5–98. Madison: University of Wisconsin Press, 1952.

Moore, Rayburn S. *Constance Fenimore Woolson*. New York: Twayne Publishers, 1963.

————. "Southern Writers and Northern Literary Magazines, 1865–1890." Ph.D. dissertation, Duke University, 1956.

Moore, William Cabell. *John Fox, Jr.: 1862–1919. An Address Delivered October 21, 1957, at the Club of Colonial Dames, Washington, D.C.* Lexington: University of Kentucky Library, 1957.

Morgan, Charles T. *The Fruit of This Tree: The Story of a Great American College and Its Contributions to the Education of a Changing World*. Berea: Berea College, 1946.

Mott, Frank Luther. *History of American Magazines, 1850–1865*. Cambridge: Harvard University Press, 1938.

_____. *History of American Magazines, 1865–1885*. Cambridge: Harvard University Press, 1938.

_____. "The Magazine Revolution and Popular Ideas in the Nineties." American Antiquarian Society, *Proceedings*, n.s. 64, pt. 1: 195–214 (1954).

Munn, Robert F. *The Southern Appalachians: A Bibliography and Guide to Studies*. Morgantown: West Virginia University Library, 1961.

Needham, H. A. *Le développement de l'esthétique sociologique en France et en Angleterre au XIXe siècle*. Bibliothéque de la Revue de Littérature Comparée, vol. 28. Paris: Librairie Ancienne Honoré Champion, 1926.

Parks, Edd Winfield. *Charles Egbert Craddock (Mary Noailles Murfree)*. Chapel Hill: University of North Carolina Press, 1941.

Paulston, Roland G., comp. *Folk Schools in Social Change: A Partisan Guide to the International Literature*. Pittsburgh: University of Pittsburgh Center for International Studies, 1974.

Peck, Elisabeth S. *Berea's First Century, 1855–1955*. Lexington: University of Kentucky Press, 1955.

Randall, James G. *Constitutional Problems under Lincoln*. Urbana: University of Illinois Press, 1951.

Reimers, David M. *White Protestantism and the Negro*. New York: Oxford University Press, 1965.

Rhode, Robert. "The Function of Setting in the American Short Story of Local Color, 1865–1900." Ph.D. dissertation, University of Texas, 1940. Issued in revised form as *Setting in the American Short Story of Local Color, 1865–1900*. The Hague: Mouton, 1975.

Rose, Willie Lee. *Rehearsal for Reconstruction: The Port Royal Experiment*. Indianapolis: Bobbs-Merrill, 1964.

Shapiro, Henry D. *Confiscation of Confederate Property in the North*. Cornell Studies in American History, Literature, and Folklore, no. 7. Ithaca: Cornell University Press, 1962.

_____. "Daniel Drake: The Scientist as Citizen." In *Physician to the West: Selected Writings of Daniel Drake on Science and Society*, edited by Henry D. Shapiro and Zane L. Miller, pp. xi–xxii. Lexington: University Press of Kentucky, 1970.

_____. "Introduction." In John C. Campbell, *The Southern Highlander and His Homeland*, pp. xxii–xxxi. Lexington: University Press of Kentucky, 1969. Reprint, originally published 1921.

Sherman, Marian C. "The Local Color Motif in the Writings of Mary Noailles Murfree." M.A. thesis, Ohio State University, 1944.

Simpson, Claude, ed. *The Local Colorists: American Short Stories, 1857–1900*. New York: Harper and Brothers, 1960.

Sizer, Theodore R. *Secondary Schools at the Turn of the Century*. New Haven: Yale University Press, 1964.

Smallwood, William M., and Smallwood, Mable C. *Natural History and the American Mind*. New York: Columbia University Press, 1941.

Smith, Henry Nash. "Origins of a Native American Literary Tradition." In *The American Writer and the European Tradition*, edited by Margaret Denny and William H. Gilman, pp. 63–77. Minneapolis: University of Minnesota Press, 1950.

Spencer, Benjamin T. "The New Realism and a National Literature." *PMLA* 56: 1116–32 (December 1941).

_____. *The Quest for Nationality: An American Literary Campaign*. Syracuse: Syracuse University Press, 1957.

Susman, Warren, ed. *Culture and Commitment, 1929–1945*. New York: George Braziller, 1973.

Sweet, William Warren. "Methodist Unification." In *American Culture and Religion: Six Essays*, pp. 64–77. Dallas: Southern Methodist University Press, 1951.

_____. *The Story of Religion in America*. New York: Harper and Brothers, 1950.

Swint, Henry Lee. *The Northern Teacher in the South, 1862–1871*. Nashville: Vanderbilt University Press, 1941.

Taylor, Carl C. *The Social Survey: Its History and Methods*. University of Missouri Bulletin, Social Science Series no. 3. Columbia, Missouri: University of Missouri, 1919.

Tindall, George B. *The Emergence of the New South, 1913–1945*. Baton Rouge: Louisiana State University Press, 1967.

Titus, Warren I. *John Fox, Jr.*. New York: Twayne Publishers, 1969.

Townsend, John Wilson. *James Lane Allen, a Personal Note*. Louisville: Courier-Journal Job Printing Company, 1928.

Trachtenberg, Alan, ed. *Critics of Culture: Literature and Society in the Early Twentieth Century*. New York: John Wiley and Sons, 1976.

Trattner, Walter I. *Crusade for Children: A History of the National Child Labor Committee and Child Labor Reform in America*. Chicago: Quadrangle Books, 1970.

[unsigned]. "Sgt. York, War Hero, Dies." *New York Times*, 3 September 1964, pp. 1, 26, 28.

Wilgus, Donald K. *Anglo-American Folksong Scholarship since 1898*. New Brunswick: Rutgers University Press, 1959.

_____. "Foreword." In Josiah H. Combs, *Folk Songs of the Southern United States*, edited by Donald K. Wilgus, pp. ix–xxi. Austin: University of Texas Press, 1967.

Wilson, R. Jackson. *In Quest of Community: Social Philosophy in the United States*. New York: John Wiley and Sons, 1968.

Wirth, Louis C. "The Social Sciences." In *American Scholarship in the Twentieth*

Century, edited by Merle Curti, pp. 33–82. Cambridge: Harvard University Press, 1953.

Wister, Fanny Kemble, ed. *Owen Wister Out West: His Journals and Letters*. Chicago: University of Chicago Press, 1958.

Woodward, C. Vann. *Origins of the New South, 1877–1913*. Baton Rouge: Louisiana State University Press, 1951.

Wright, John K. "Miss Semple's 'Influences of Geographic Environment': Notes toward a Biobibliography." *Geographical Review* 52: 346–61 (July 1962).

IV. Manuscripts Collections Cited

Note: Persons wishing to quote from manuscripts collections cited in connection with this study are advised to obtain appropriate permissions directly from the repository holding such collections.

John C. Campbell and Olive D. Campbell Papers. Southern Historical Collection, University of North Carolina Library, Chapel Hill.

Century Collection. New York Public Library Manuscript Division, New York City.

Francis James Child Papers. Harvard University Archives, Cambridge, Massachusetts.

William Goodell Frost Papers. Berea College Archives, Berea, Kentucky.

Walter Hines Page Papers. Houghton Library of Harvard University, Cambridge, Massachusetts.

Southern Highland Division Papers. Russell Sage Foundation Archives, New York City.

Index

278–79 (n. 24); availability as objects of home missionary work, 35, 39–41, 46, 48, 51–53, 60, 85, 91, 102, 121, 126, 214; relationship with the South, 39, 46, 87–90, 97, 128; origins and identity of, 53, 81, 85, 87, 88, 91, 99, 107; as an exceptional population of the nation, 59–60, 83, 86–87, 118; as degenerates, 61, 75, 92–94, 97, 98, 110–11, 128, 131, 141, 159, 178, 247; as conservators of pioneer virtue (and vice), 88–90, 106–7, 108–10, 111, 118–20, 128–29, 131, 260–63, 277–78 (n. 14); as American highlanders, 89, 90–92, 107–8, 110–12; as labor force in southern textile mills, 170–71, 173–74, 175–80, 181; defined as a "folk," 249, 257–59, 261; as the real Americans, 261–63
Mountain whites: as name, 275 (n. 5)
Mount Berry School for Boys, 221, 227
Murfree, Mary Noailles, xv, 7, 15, 18, 19–20, 22, 24–26, 66–67, 69, 71–72, 116; used as a guide to Appalachian reality, xv, 57, 60, 79
Murphy, Edgar Gardner, 153–54, 164–65, 167, 169–70, 180

N

Nation, American: unity and homogeneity of the, x, xi, xiii, xiv, xvi, 14–16, 61, 65, 117–18, 258; to be achieved artificially, 32–33, 34, 41–42, 48, 59, 73–74, 262–63. *See also* Pluralism; Regionalism
National Child Labor Committee, 164–66, 176, 190. *See also* McKelway, Alexander J.
National Conference of Charities and Correction, 165, 190, 191–93
National Education Association, 229–30
Neighborhood: idea of, 103, 150, 212, 213
New York Woman's Home Missionary Society (Presbyterian), 55
Norman, Henderson Daingerfield, 143–44
Norris, Frank, 7, 286 (n. 2)

O

Otherness: of Appalachia. *See* Appalachian otherness

P

Page, Thomas Nelson, 7
Page, Walter Hines, 169, 177
Pageants, 255, 301 (n. 55), 302 (n. 57)
Palmer, Walter B., 179
Pattee, Fred Lewis, 7–8
Payne, Rev. Bruce R., 192–94
Peabody, Charles, 256
Pease, Rev. L. M., 54
Perrow, E. C., 250
Perry, Arthur R., M.D., 289 (n. 24)
Pettit, Katherine, 191, 226, 282–83 (n. 13), 283 (n. 16); as folksong collector, 303 (nn. 10, 11)
Philanthropy. *See* Benevolence, systematic, in Appalachia
Physicians: as authors, 3–4, 9; and Appalachia, 283–84 (n. 18), 287–88 (n. 19), 289 (n. 24), 300 (n. 48)
Pinchot, Gifford, 201
Pine Mountain Settlement School, Inc., 283 (n. 16)
Pluralism: emergence of the idea of, xviii, 8, 99, 103, 108–9, 110, 113, 243, 246, 258, 263, 265, 284 (n. 20); consequences for the idea of Appalachia, 257, 259–60. *See also* Regionalism
Pollard, Edward A., 6, 269–70 (n. 28)
Presbyterian Church in the United States of America (northern), 36, 41, 48, 54–56, 202; freedmen's aid work of, 36, 54–55; home missionary work of, 49–50, 54–55, 196, 222, 239; educational work of, 54–55; country life work of, 196, 239
Presbyterian Church in the United States (southern), 188, 196, 200–202; home missionary work of, 56, 196, 200–201
Primitive: fascination with the, 219, 244
Proctor, Kentucky, Church Mission Settlement, 226
Progress: as a characteristic of American life, 84, 118, 140; undesirable consequences of, 89; as the proper focus of historical study, 95
Protestant Episcopal church, 35, 56, 196, 226